THE HEBREW BOOK

An Historical Survey

THE HEBREW BOOK

An Historical Survey

Edited by
Raphael Posner and Israel Ta-Shema

Foreword by
Dr. Jacob Rothschild
Director, Graduate Library School
The Hebrew University of Jerusalem

LEON AMIEL PUBLISHER
New York–Paris

KETER PUBLISHING HOUSE JERUSALEM LTD.

Editorial assistant and illustration research — Nechama Unterman

Design and Layout — Murray Bloom
Execution — Shemuel Kaldaron

Administration and co-ordination — Hayyim Schneid

Published in the Western Hemisphere by
LEON AMIEL PUBLISHER
New York — Paris

ISBN 0-8148-0597-3
Library of Congress Catalogue Number 74-12587

Distributed in the rest of the world by
KETER PUBLISHING HOUSE JERUSALEM LTD.
P.O. Box 7145, Jerusalem, Israel

ISBN 0-7065-1389-4
Catalogue Number 25099

Set by Isratypeset Ltd., Jerusalem
Printed and bound by Keterpress Enterprises, Jerusalem
Printed in Israel

foreword

Liber librorum is the title of a magnificent book which appeared on the occasion of the International Book Year in 1972. The name *Book of Books* was not used in its original meaning, indicating the Bible, but rather as a description of a book about books – the 5000-year history of the book. And now we are given a *Liber librorum hebraicorum,* a book about Hebrew books – a book about books written by the People of the Book par excellence, the Bible. But is not a book about the history of books an anachronism today when many are convinced that the age of the book is coming to an end? Even the most optimistic cannot but occasionally doubt whether the mass media – television, radio, the cinema and even the newspapers and magazines – will not supersede the book; whether we have not, to quote the Canadian sociologist MacLuhan, reached the end of the Gutenberg Galaxy. It is not the function of a foreword to refute skepticism about the future of the book, but I do want to make one point. It is a fact that people read books for information – both for its own sake and for its application – for pleasure through identification and re-creation, and even for escapism from the dreary reality that surrounds them.

What is distinctive about the present volume is that it illuminates a unique aspect of the book which is, perhaps, largely ignored today, but which, to my mind, is crucial to the Hebrew book. I am referring to the book and to the collection of books as an index of a people's history and culture in so far as the book represents its quintessence. I do not believe that nowadays it is possible to accept Heinrich Graetz's description of the history of the Jewish people in exile as the story of "suffering and savants." Nonetheless, with all our criticism of his lack of recognition of the political and social aspects of Jewish history, it is worthwhile to quote his remarks in the introduction to the third volume of his *History*: "Open history books from the beginning of time until today. Was there ever anything like it? Was there ever a people, tribe or family who cast aside the sword and took up a book in its stead? – a people who, when it lost its homeland, turned its back on the passing acquisitions of nationalism, ceased caring about temporary matters and the pleasures of life, and devoted itself completely to the work of the heart and the brain and became a thinking nation for whom the House of Study became the House of Life?" Little wonder then that the love of study of the contents of books should with time become a love of the book as an object in its own right, both as a manuscript and as a printed book. This fondness for books found expression in many epigrams such as that of the 14th-century Castilian rabbi, Isaac Canpanton: "A man's wisdom extends only as far as his books reach."

But what can be done in the face of the common ignorance of the continuity binding the contemporary Jew with the great creative periods of his people? One is often seized by a feeling of impotence at the alienation of the modern Jew — and even Israeli — from his rich culture, even if he is committed nationalistically. This is the motif of the return which often comes too late, a motif which may be seen in Bialik's poem, *In Front of the Bookcase:*

Once again fate brought me before you, treasures of the bookcase,
Products of Lvov, Slavita, Amsterdam and Frankfort.
Once again my hand turns your pages
And my eyes seek between the lines,
Silently searching among the letters . . .
Look, you who made my youth happy,
My heart stays silent . . .
For I look, and see, but do not recognize your aged faces.
No more do your clear eyes peer from between your letters
Into the depths of my soul . . .
Your columns are like a string of black pearls whose thread has snapped.
Your pages are widowed.
Each letter stands alone, an orphan.

In view of this kind of cultural alienation, the appearance of a volume on the history of the book is a timely contribution to those who, honestly and earnestly, want to bridge the chasm to find a true return, for the gates are never closed. A volume of this nature can encourage a renewed identification with the Jewish heritage at an acceptable intellectual level. For this book does not speak to the seeker of information alone; but also to the person who is in search of a creative encounter with the Jewish treasury of values. True, it has been said: "Do not judge by the container, only by the contents." But often a beautiful container can so impress that one is led to examine the contents.

The hope and prayer that this book will contribute toward such a renewed, creative encounter, is perhaps legitimate when it comes from one such as myself, whose role in life is to educate toward the love of the book and to prepare others for that task, in respect of the book in general and the Hebrew book in particular.

Jacob Rothschild

The Hebrew University,
Jerusalem.
Kislev 5735
December 1974.

introduction

Not for nothing has the Jewish people been known as the "people of the Book." The most important object in Judaism is – albeit in scroll form – a book, the Torah. And the cultural history of the Jewish people is a story told, not in pictures, buildings, or statues, but in books. It is hardly possible to think of Judaism or the Jewish people, without books. The Bible, the Talmud, the prayer book, Rashi's Commentaries, Maimonides' *Mishneh Torah* and the *Shulḥan Arukh* are only few of the thousands of books that are signposts on the long journey of the Jewish people. The first dated Hebrew printed book, Rashi's Commentary to the Bible, was printed in 1475, and thus 1975, the 500th anniversary of that event is an excellent occasion to issue a book whose entire subject is The Hebrew Book.

This volume is primarily based on the monumental *Encyclopaedia Judaica* which was published in 1972 in Jerusalem. Throughout the 16 volumes of that immense work, the story of the Hebrew book is scattered, and its constituent parts are presented, as is fitting, in an encyclopaedic manner. For the purpose of this book, all that information was gathered, re-edited and re-organized to present this fascinating subject to the reader in a form which, to quote the biblical phrase about an early piece of Hebrew writing, is "plain upon the tables, that a man may read it swiftly." Clearly, the present editors are entirely responsible for the material as it appears in this volume.

Some sections of this book were written especially for it. It is worthwhile to note that Chapter 4, about the state of Hebrew bibliographical research, was written by Israel Ta-Shema and in fact clearly indicates why we have done this book. The amount of literature on the Hebrew book is not unsubstantial, but by and large it is in the form of articles and monographs dealing with specific aspects, such as the history of printing in a particular locality. This is true of literature in Hebrew, but how much more so for literature in the English language which is, after all, the *lingua franca* of most Jews today? This book, therefore, is intended to be a general survey of the subject for both the student and the layman who wants to know more about this most important ingredient of the Jewish cultural heritage. Although the work is obviously deficient both because of the state of research into the subject and because of the natural limitations of the Encyclopaedia (which also reflect that state of knowledge), we feel that it is still an important contribution and hope that it will serve to inspire greater interest in the subject which should lead to more activity.

A great deal of attention has been given to the matter of illustration because "hearing cannot be compared with seeing." From the fourth chapter until the end of the book, all the illustrations which are not accompanied by a credit were by courtesy of Israel Ta-Shema and are chosen out of his own extensive collection. All printers' marks were taken from Abraham Yaari's *Diglei ha-Madpisim ha-Ivriyyim* ("Hebrew Printers' Marks," Jerusalem, 1943). All the illustrations are intended to bring home to the reader visually the enormous scope of the Hebrew book. When printing was invented, the Jews took it up with gusto and were active in it throughout the world. The illustrations clearly indicate the dynamic development of the art of Hebrew writing and printing, and this fact, besides the intrinsic beauty of the pages, sufficiently warrants their inclusion.

At the end of the book we have appended a list of some of the more important books on various aspects of our subject in order to provide a guide for the reader who is interested in pursuing the subject further. An alphabetical index of the title pages that appear in the book as well as a transliteration table is also appended.

For us, the editors, it has been an intensely exciting experience to work on this book; we can only hope that the reader will enjoy it as much as we have.

contents

1. writing

The history of Hebrew bookmaking is as old as the history of the Jewish people and goes back for more than 3,000 years. It may be divided into three periods: from earliest times to the final editing of the Talmud (sixth or seventh centuries); from geonic times to the end of the 15th century and the first printed Hebrew books; and from then to the present day. To the first period belong the books of the Bible, the Apocrypha, and the non-biblical texts found among the Dead Sea Scrolls. Other books are mentioned in the Bible (cf. Ecclesiastes 12:12, "of making many books there is no end") and also in the Talmud, but it may be assumed that in the materials used, the writing techniques, and their format they were no different from books of the Bible. Toward the middle of the geonic period (ninth and tenth centuries) technical changes resulted from Arab influence and the growth of a European Diaspora and – more important still – from the common use of paper as writing material. The revolutionary impact of printing ushered in further developments.

The Gilgamesh Epic, Tablet XI, c. 2000-1800 b.c.e. which gives, in cuneiform script, the Babylonian version of the flood. London, British Museum.

IN ANCIENT TIMES

From the end of the third millennium b.c.e., the art of writing was practiced in the ancient Near East. Here, the pictographic, cuneiform, and hieroglyphic scripts were invented and developed. In particular Canaan, situated on the cultural crossroads between Egypt and Mesopotamia and beneficiary of their scribal traditions, produced new indigenous writing systems. Some, like the Byblian pseudo-hieroglyphs, the enigmatic Balua stele, or the inscribed bricks from Deir Alla, ancient Succoth, were limited to specific centers. These short-lived systems indicate a high degree of scribal experimentation and originality. It is no wonder then that the Canaanites invented the alphabet. They discovered that their language contained some 30 phonemes and that each one could be represented by an individual sign. Like many revolutionary discoveries, its implications were not immediately appreciated and the social effects of the linear alphabet were not to be felt for several generations.

Proto-Sinaitic, c. 1500 B.C.E.
Palestinian Proto-Canaanite inscriptions, 13–11th cent. B.C.E.
Phoenician c. 1000 B.C.E. (Ahiram Sarcophagus)
Modern Hebrew
א
ב
ג
ד
ה
ו
ז
ח
י
כ
ל
מ
נ
ע
צ
ר
ש
ת

Development of Proto-Canaanite script from Proto-Sinaitic script, with its main offshoot, Hebrew.

Between the 17th and 12th centuries b.c.e., the primitive, pictographic alphabet was employed in Shechem, Gezer, Tell al-Ḥāsī, Tell al-'Ajūl, Beth-Shemesh, Megiddo, Tell Rehov, Tell Beit Mirsim, and Lachish. These inscriptions are generally called Proto-Canaanite. Another larger group, the so-called Proto-Sinaitic inscriptions (1500 b.c.e.) were probably written by a colony of northwest Semitic slaves who worked the mines in Wadi Ma'ara in the Sinai Peninsula. It seems that this script generally served a religious function and may have been developed by the Canaanite priesthood. Certainly, all official government documents were written in cuneiform (e.g. the Tell el-Amarna letters) which obscured the alphabetic script.

It was during this period that a novel attempt to employ the alphabet was initiated at Ugarit (1370–1200 b.c.e.). Perhaps as a result of the desire to express the local literature in its own medium, a cuneiform alphabet, influenced by the dominant Mesopotamian system, was devised. A similar trend may be noted in other Canaanite cities as well (Beth Shemesh, Taanach, Mount Tabor). This script as well as an earlier attempt to adapt the cuneiform signs to surfaces other than clay by giving them linear form did not survive the disappearance of the Babylonian scribal centers in Canaan and Syria toward the end of the Bronze Age.

Limestone seal from Lachish, 18th century b.c.e. Jerusalem, Rockefeller Museum, Israel Department of Antiquities.

The political and cultural break with Mesopotamia, as well as the administrative needs of emerging young societies, accelerated the development of the linear alphabet. The letters were simplified, beginning the process that was to evolve into a cursive form. The first alphabetic system to emerge was the 22-letter Phoenician script, which appeared by about 1100 b.c.e. and was to be adopted by the Israelites, Ara-

Two Egyptian tablets of the XVIII dynasty bearing cuneiform inscriptions, found in Tell el-Amarna. Both are letters to the king of Egypt from the ruler of Tyre stating that he has carried out the king's orders. New York City, Metropolitan Museum of Art, Rogers Fund, 1924.

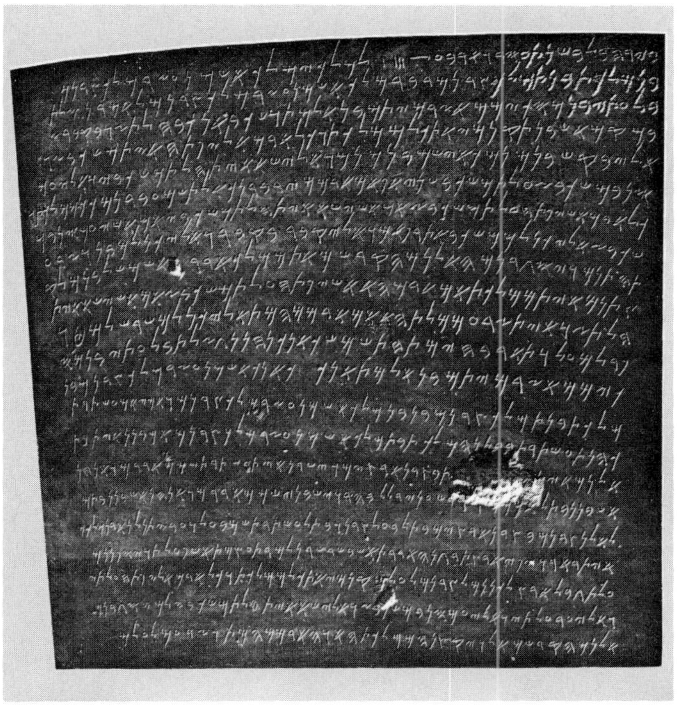

Phoenician inscription on the sarcophagus of King Eshmun-Azar of Sidon, fifth to fourth century b.c.e.

Back and front views of three seals from about 600 b.c.e. They were found in the Israelite citadel of Arad, and their inscriptions (lower row) read "to Eliashib son of Eshyahu." Y. Aharoni, Tel Aviv.

Impression of a seal ring believed to be that of Jotham, king of Judah, c. 742–735 b.c.e. The seal, from Ezion Geber, depicts a ram and the Hebrew letters *LYTM*. Washington, D.C., Smithsonian Institution.

means, and later by the Greeks. The new medium was adopted early in Israel's history and deeply affected its civilization; monotheism was grasped now in terms of a written covenant between God and Israel. The central cult object was the Decalogue cut in stone, and later became the written Torah scroll. Israelite religion thus elevated writing from a means of recording the mundane to a medium of revelation.

Perhaps it was because of the relative simplicity of the alphabet or the fact that Israel had no conservative scribal class with vested interests, that biblical society as a whole became "book-centered." Any tribesman, even a nonpriest, could emerge as a literate leader (Joshua 8:32–35; 24–26). The establishment of the monarchy and the process of urbanization resulted in a greater diffusion of writing (among members of the government service, army personnel, the mercantile class, stonemasons, ivory cutters, potters, and others). The Torah, as well, legislated for a society where both king and commoner were to be familiar with the religious literature (Deuteronomy 7:18; 6:9).

Certainly by Hezekiah's time, in the eighth century b.c.e., a great deal of literary activity was going on. Older written traditions were collected and edited (Proverbs 25:1). The classical prophets, or their disciples, wrote down their messages. Prophesies were illustrated by written texts (Isaiah 8:1; Jeremiah 17:1; Ezekiel 37:16; Habbakuk 2:2), which could only have meaning for a literate populace (cf. Isaiah 10:19). Also the wide use of inscribed personal seals bearing fewer designs and iconographic motifs again argues for a growing literate social body during the First Temple period.

WRITING SURFACES

STONE is the earliest known writing surface; it continued to be used throughout the ages, especially when permanence was desired. Three main types of stone inscriptions can be noted in the Ancient Near East: monumental inscriptions for public display; seals made of semiprecious stones; and flakes or pieces of soft stone (e.g. limestone) which constituted cheap writing material. Examples of all three types are plentiful.

PAPYRUS. The papyrus reed, cultivated from earliest times especially in the Delta, was a major natural resource of ancient Egypt; indeed the hieroglyphic sign for Lower Egypt is the papyrus plant. Papyrus was found in Ereẓ Israel in the Ḥuleh swamp, though in limited quantities, and near the Naḥal Arnon in Transjordan. During the Arab conquest it was introduced into Sicily where it can still be found.

In Egypt, it was an all-purpose plant used for making, among other things, clothing and boats; primarily, it was employed as a writing surface. The earliest written papyri date from the Fifth Dynasty (2750–2625 b.c.e.), though uninscribed rolls have been found dating to as early as the First Dynasty (c. 3000 b.c.e.). Pliny the Elder, the Roman naturalist (died 79 c.e.), gives a detailed description of the manufacture of papyrus writing material:

> The raw material taken from the tall plants – some as high as 35 feet – consisted of strips cut length-wise from the pith of the three-sided stalks. Strips of equal length and quality were then arranged on a flat surface, in the manner of lattice-work, in a horizontal and vertical layer, the former representing the recto and the latter the verso side of the sheet. Through the application of pressure and water from the Nile – perhaps with the occasional addition of glue – the layers were merged into a fairly homogeneous mass, which was then exposed to the sun. After drying, the sheets were rubbed smooth with shells or ivory and perhaps whitened with chalk. Excess moisture was forced out by additional pounding.

The manufacture and trade in papyrus was probably always a royal or state monopoly. Such was the case in the time of the Ptolemies and Caesars. The earliest reference to papyrus in Canaan is found in the Egyptian text "The Journey of Wen-Amon to Phoenicia" (c. 1090 b.c.e.). Smendes (Ne-su-Ba-neb-Ded), the founder of the 21st Dynasty and ruler of Lower Egypt, sent 500 rolls of papyrus to Zakar-Baal, king of Byblos, in partial payment for a shipment of cedars. This large quantity of writing material most likely reflects the extensive use of the alphabetic script by this time in Canaan, which is corroborated by the repeated references to written documents in the story. Byblos became an agent for the export of papyrus throughout the Mediterranean lands. So much so that it gave its name to the product: in Greek, *biblos* came to mean "book" or "papyrus," and from this the word "Bible" is derived. By Herodotus' time (the fifth century b.c.e.) papyrus had become the standard writing material for most of the ancient world surrounding the Mediterranean Sea. It was to remain in

The Nash Papyrus, the oldest biblical text known until the discovery of the Dead Sea Scrolls. From E.L. Sukenik, *Megillot Genuzot*, Jerusalem, 1948.

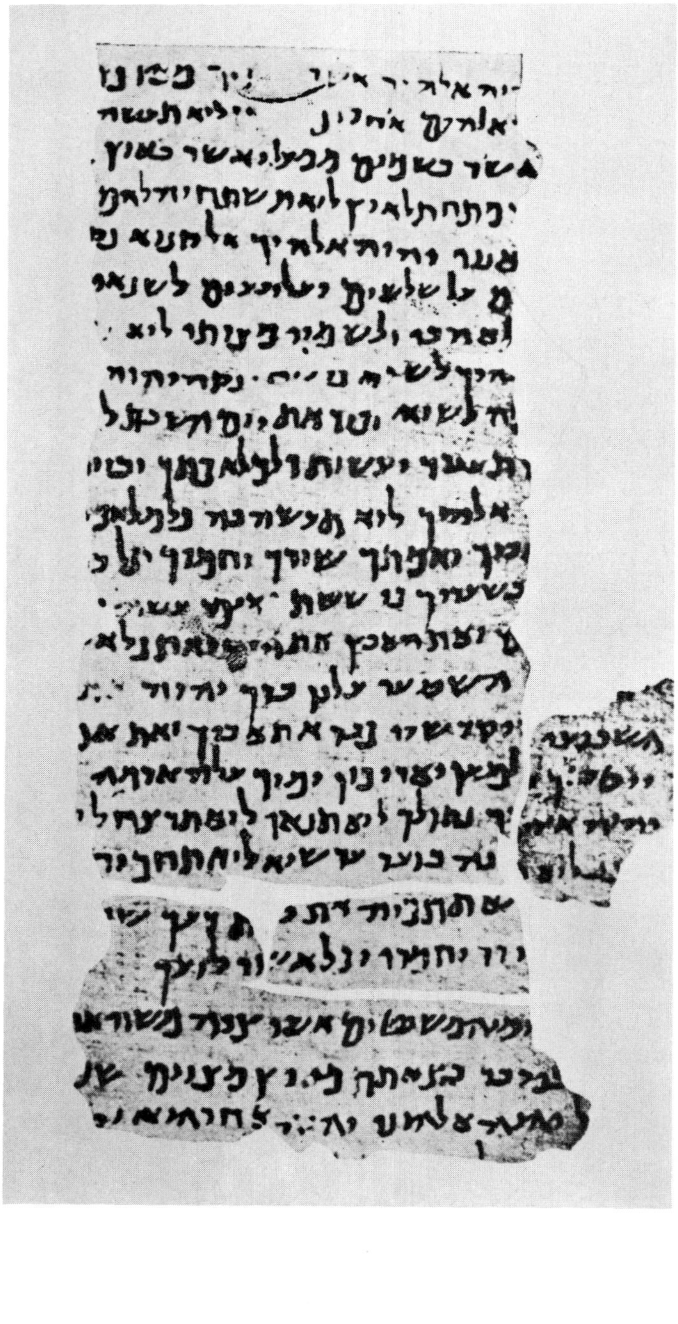

Papyrus growing today in the Ḥuleh valley nature reserve. J.N.F., Jerusalem. Photo: Hirschfeld.

use until replaced by true paper, brought from China between the seventh and tenth centuries c.e. There is no specific reference to papyrus in the Bible (but cf. Isaiah 23:3). Some scholars, though, infer from the description in Jeremiah 36:23-25 that the prophet's scroll was made of papyrus, which is more easily cut and less odorous than leather.

The earliest Hebrew papyrus dates from the late eighth or early seventh century b.c.e. and was discovered in 1951 in Wadi Murabba'at in the Judean desert. This palimpsest contains the remains of a letter and instructions for the delivery of food supplies. Several clay bullae (a type of seal) from the sixth century bear the marks of papyrus fibers upon which they had been impressed.

The oldest known Aramaic papyrus is a letter discovered in Saqqara, Egypt, from a king by the name of Adon to his Egyptian overlord. Most scholars agree that it was sent from the Philistine coast, possibly from Ashdod, just before Nebuchadnezzar's invasion in 604 or 598 b.c.e.

The second half of the first millennium b.c.e. saw the widespread use of papyrus for sundry government, religious, and personal documents. Of particular Jewish interest are the Elephantine papyri (late fifth century). They include official letters and private papers that shed much light on the internal affairs, religious life, and relations with gentile neighbors in this Jewish military colony situated near the First Cataract on the Nile. A small number of the Dead Sea Scrolls were also written on this material.

Tablet recording the reburial of the remains of King Uzziah in Jerusalem, some time between the first century b.c.e. and the first century c.e. It reads, "Hither were brought the bones of Uzziah, king of Judah. Do not open." Jerusalem, Israel Museum.

ANIMAL HIDES. Sheep, goat, and calf hides, after proper preparation, served as one of the principal types of writing surfaces in the Fertile Crescent.

The first section of the Book of Ezekiel, written on leather parchment. It dates from the 17th century c.e. London, Cecil Roth Collection.

Aramaic papyrus of the Jewish garrison at Elephantine in Egypt, fifth century b.c.e. New York, Brooklyn Museum.

There is no contemporary record of preparation of this material, which probably did not differ from the modern process. The skins were washed, limed, unhaired, scraped, washed a second time, stretched evenly on a frame, scraped a second time, inequalities being pared down, and then dusted with sifted chalk and rubbed with a pumice. In the earlier period, the skin was prepared to receive writing only on the hairy side, though in exceptional cases, such as in a long text, it was inscribed on both sides.

During the Hellenistic period the skins were treated so as to receive writing on both sides. The improved method was attributed to Eumenes II (197–158 b.c.e.) whose capital, Pergamum, gave its name to the new product — "parchment." In due time, a distinction was made between the coarser and finer types of this material. The latter was manufactured from more delicate calfskin or kidskin, especially from stillborn calves or lambs, and was called vellum. By the second century c.e., vellum began to compete with papyrus. In the next two or three centuries, with the introduction of the codex, its popularity was assured and it superseded ordinary parchment for the most valued books.

The earliest mention of a leather writing surface is found in an Egyptian text from the Fourth Dynasty (c. 2550 b.c.e.), while the oldest extant example of such a writing surface dates from the 12th Dynasty (2000–1800 b.c.e.). It continued to be used in Egypt until the Arab conquest, though to a limited extent, because of the ubiquitous papyrus.

The use of skins as a writing surface first appeared in Mesopotamia in eighth-century Assyrian reliefs. No doubt, this surface was introduced by the Aramean scribes who found clay tablets unsuitable for their alphabetic script. The fifth-century Greek historians Herodotus and Ctesias noted that the barbarians continued to use leather for writing, while on the Greek mainland this substance had been replaced by papyrus. Ctesias remarked that the Persians wrote their royal records on *diphtherai,* i.e. skins. This has been corroborated by the discovery of 12 letters belonging

Plate 1 (above). The Habakkuk Commentary, one of the Dead Sea Scrolls. Shrine of the Book, Israel Museum, Jerusalem.
Plate 2 (below). Showcases of the Dead Sea Scrolls at the Hebrew University, Jerusalem, before they were transferred to the Shrine of the Book at the Israel Museum. Photo: Werner Braun.

ואעידה ה' וסימנ' הקהילו אלי עדים נאמנים עלמי אתבה שמעה עמי שמע עמי ‧ לקחי ג' וסימנ' יערף כמטר ויאמר אליה ותאמר זך לקחי וחד ולקחי חד בת
וחד בנבי וחד בכת ‧ כשעירם ל' וספרים ל' המוסרים ל' הגזרים ל' והדברים ל' כצפרים ל' בפרורים ל' לנטרים ל' לנטורים ל' המתבררים ל' הכדברים ל' בזבורים

ואעידה בם את השמים ואת הארץ כי ידעתי
אחרי מותי כי השחת תשחתון וסרתם מן
הדרך אשר צויתי אתכם וקראת אתכם הרעה
באחרית הימים כי תעשו את הרע בעיני יהוה
להכעיסו במעשה ידיכם וידבר משה באזני כל
קהל ישראל את דברי השירה הזאת עד תמם

האזינו השמים ואדברה	ותשמע הארץ אמרי פי
יערף כמטר לקחי	תזל כטל אמרתי
כשעירם עלי דשא	וכרביבים עלי עשב
כי שם יהוה אקרא	הבו גדל לאלהינו
הצור תמים פעלו	כי כל דרכיו משפט
אל אמונה ואין עול	צדיק וישר הוא
שחת לו לא בניו מומם	דור עקש ופתלתל
הליהוה תגמלו זאת	עם נבל ולא חכם
הלוא הוא אביך קנך	הוא עשך ויכננך
זכר ימות עולם בינו שנות דר ודר	שאל אביך ויגדך זקניך ויאמרו לך
בהנחל עליון גוים	בהפרידו בני אדם
יצב גבלת עמים	למספר בני ישראל
כי חלק יהוה עמו	יעקב חבל נחלתו
ימצאהו בארץ מדבר	ובתהו ילל ישמן
יסבבנהו יבוננהו	יצרנהו כאישון עינו
כנשר יעיר קנו על גוזליו ירחף	יפרש כנפיו יקחהו ישאהו על אברתו
יהוה בדד ינחנו	ואין עמו אל נכר
ירכבהו על במותי ארץ	ויאכל תנובת שדי

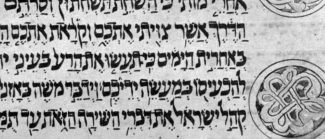

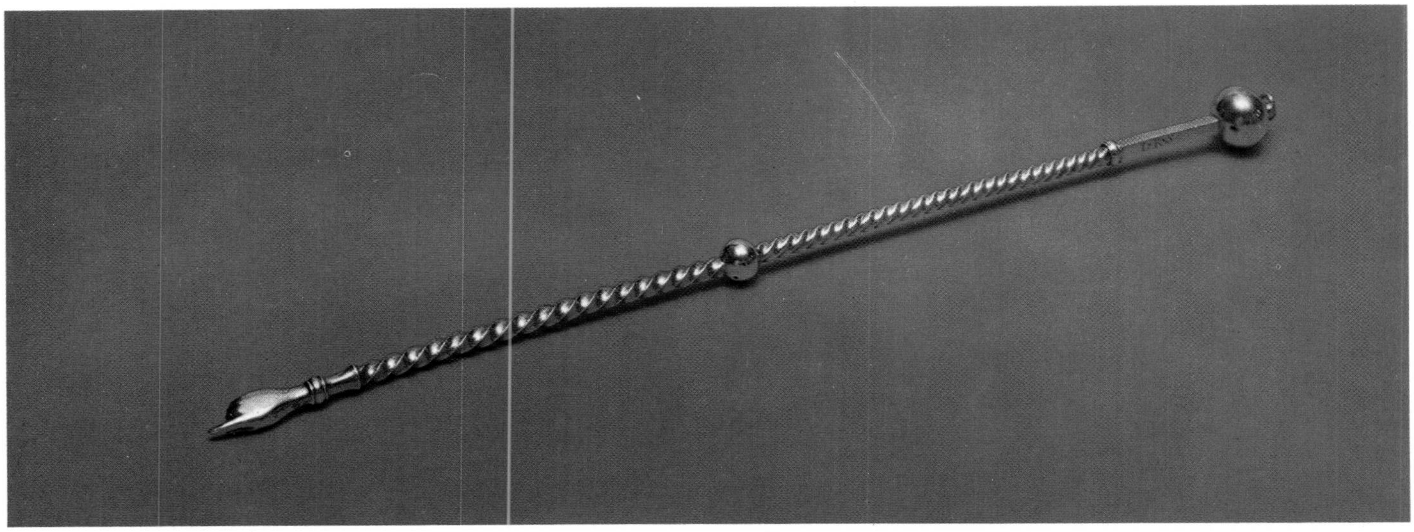

Plate 4 (above). The rabbis declared: "He who touches a naked *Sefer Torah* will be buried naked," to emphasize the sanctity of the Torah scroll. Therefore, the *yad* (pointer) is used during the reading of the Torah. Pictured is a silver Torah pointer made by Abraham d'Oliviera, c. 1730, from the Hambro Synagogue. The Jewish Museum, London.

Plate 5 (right). A scribe's inkwell in an embroidered purse from Persia, 19th century. Hechal Shlomo, Sir Isaac and Lady Wolfson Museum, Jerusalem.

Plate 3 (opposite). The Song of Moses *(Ha'azinu)*, Sana'a, Yemen, 1469. The prose section is written in a single column at the top, and below it are two ornamented columns of poetic text. The Masorah is written in the margins and between the columns in micrographic geometric shapes. London, British Museum, Or. Ms. 2348, fol. 151v.

Plate 6. Set of Ashkenazi ornaments from Germany, comprising mantle, *rimmonim,* breastplate, and pointer. Mantle: velvet with silver thread embroidery, 1749. *Rimmonim:* silver, partly gilt, early 19th century. Breastplate: silver, partly gilt, early 18th century, Pointer: silver gilt, Nuremburg, early 17th century. The ornaments are displayed against a *parokhet* from Glogau, Silesia, 1795. Jerusalem, Israel Museum.

to Arsames, the satrap of Egypt (fifth century b.c.e.) where the cache was found.

There is no explicit biblical reference to writing on leather, nor are there extant leather rolls, prior to those discovered at Qumran. In spite of this, there is general agreement that throughout the First and Second Temple periods the ancient Israelites primarily used animal hides on which to write their official documents and religious literature. Leather is a much more durable surface than papyrus. The sheepherding Israelites, like the Arameans and the Transjordanian nations, were more likely to use this local resource than to import Egyptian papyrus. During the Second Temple period the references to writing on animal hides are clearer. They no doubt reflect a continuation of the earlier period, since there was no reason to change suddenly to leather at this time.

Passage from the Book of Exodus, written on animal skin, found at Murabba'at. It is written in Jewish square script and dates from the second century c.e. Jerusalem, Israel Department of Antiquities and Museums.

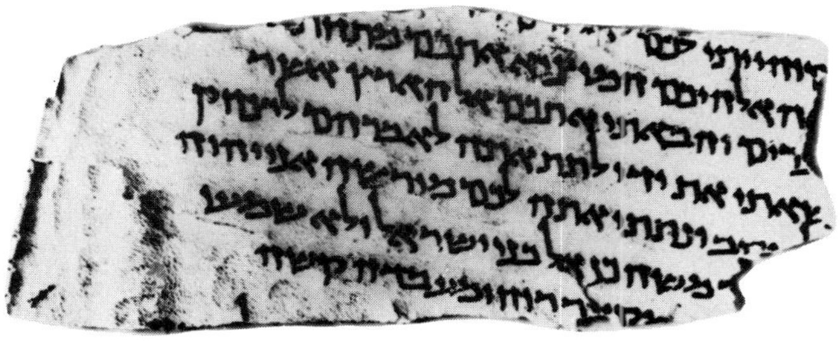

The Dead Sea Scrolls are the earliest Hebrew texts written on leather that have been discovered so far. They provide firsthand evidence of the ancient scribal technique of preparing and writing on this surface. This scribal tradition was codified by the rabbis and is still followed in the writing of Torah scrolls, *mezuzot,* and *tefillin* (see Chapter II).

POTTERY. By far the largest number of inscriptions from the biblical period were written on pottery. The material can be classified into two distinct types: 1) Whole pots that bear a short notice, inscribed either before or after firing and 2) ostraca, or broken potsherds, generally bearing longer inscriptions. While there is no biblical reference to this writing surface, this cheap and easily available material was widely used not only in Israel but throughout the ancient world. The inscriptions on pottery usually give the owner's name, the capacity of the jar, e.g. *bt lmlk* ("royal bath"), or a dedicatory notice.

From the end of the eighth century b.c.e., it became customary to indicate important data on the handles of jars. Generally, this was done by impressing a seal on the soft clay before firing. Some 80 "private" and

Section from the scroll of the Thanksgiving Psalms, one of the Dead Sea Scrolls, among the earliest Hebrew texts written on leather. It is believed to date from the first century b.c.e. Jerusalem, Israel Museum, Shrine of the Book.

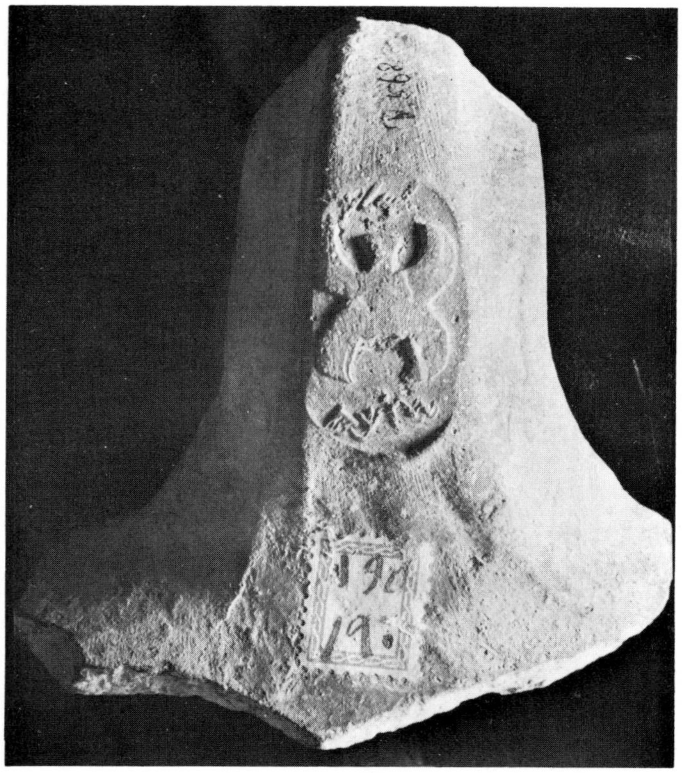

Handle of jar from the seventh century b.c.e., found at Lachish. It is impressed with a winged sun-disk, scarab seal and the royal stamp "to the king." The legend *"lmlk"* may represent weights and measures standardized by the royal administration. Jerusalem, Israel Department of Antiquities and Museums.

about 800 royal seal impressions have been counted. The latter indicate a standard capacity guaranteed by the king, as well as noting one of the four Judean cities where the contents were "bottled" (Hebron, Ziph, Socoh, and *mmst).*

Ostraca is the technical term for potsherds that were used for writing. Pottery was particularly suitable for those scripts employing pen and ink or brush and paint, though the surface might be incised as well. The earliest literary reference to ostraca is that of the fifth-century Athenian custom of voting powerful and dangerous citizens into exile. In order to do so, 10,000 ostraca had to be inscribed with the unlucky man's name. The term "ostracism" is derived from this custom. In Israel, small pieces of potsherds seem to have been used in local lotteries in biblical Arad and in Masada of the Second Temple period. A survey of the ostraca shows that this surface was used for letters, tax dockets, fiscal notices, name lists, and at least one court petition. The cheapness of the material indicates the secondary importance of most of the inscriptions or possibly the hard-pressed circumstances at the time of writing, when papyrus and leather were reserved for more important documents. Furthermore, the ostraca provide some idea of the caliber and diffusion of writing among the bureaucracy, army personnel, and local scribes in ancient Israel.

CLAY. This substance was the standard writing material in Mesopotamia from the third to the first millennia b.c.e. The alluvial soil of the Tigris-Euphrates valley made clay the most readily available and thus the cheapest form of writing material in this area. This medium spread with the cuneiform script to the Elamites, Hittites, and Canaanites.

The Ugaritic literature and the el-Amarna letters, in addition to other smaller archives (Alalakh, Taanach) and single documents from Syria and Canaan, were inscribed on clay. With the decline of Mesopotamian influence toward the end of the second millennium b.c.e., this writing surface became obsolete. Furthermore, suitable clay was not commonly found in this area, nor was it easily adaptable to the emerging linear alphabet. The only biblical reference to an incised clay tablet is one found in a Babylonian context and interestingly not an inscription but rather a "blueprint" of Jerusalem: "Son of man, take thee a tile *[levenah]* and lay it before thee and trace upon it a city, even Jerusalem" (Ezekiel 4:1).

METALS. Various inscriptions from the ancient and classical worlds have been found written on gold, silver, copper, bronze, and lead. These artifacts corroborate the many Hebrew and north Semitic literary sources which mention these writing surfaces. A small (6.7 cm. x 2.2 cm.) gold case from the north Syrian kingdom of Samal bears the dedicatory inscription:

One of the Ugaritic tablets, c. 15th–14th century b.c.e.

"This *smr* fashioned by Kilamuwa son of Ḥayya, for Rakabel. May Rakabel grant him long life" (c. 825 b.c.e.). Similarly, Yehawmilk, king of Byblos (fourth century b.c.e.) presented a gold votive inscription to his divine patroness. In ancient Israel, this precious metal was employed in Temple ornaments and priestly vestments. The high priest's diadem was made of gold and inscribed: "Consecrated to the Lord" (Exodus 28: 36–38).

Examples of ex-voto inscriptions on silver platters were found near Ismailya in north Egypt. One of them reads: "This Qinu the son of Gashmu, king of Kedar offered to Hani'ilat." These date from the fifth century b.c.e. The donor may be the son of Nehemiah's enemy Geshem the Arab (Nehemiah 6:1ff).

The famous Copper Scroll from Qumran is a unique find. This writing surface was chosen specifically to record a list of fabled treasures. Its weight and inflexibility would make it an impractical writing surface for frequently read scrolls.

Bronze seems to have been a more common writing surface. In the 1950s and 1960s, inscribed bronze arrow-heads and javelin heads as well as a spatula were discovered in Phoenicia and Israel and explained as cultic or magical texts. These inscriptions date from the 12th century to 950 b.c.e. and, therefore represent paleographically the earliest form of the Phoenician alphabet. Several inscriptions in the so-called pseudo-hieroglyphic script of Byblos were written on bronze as well.

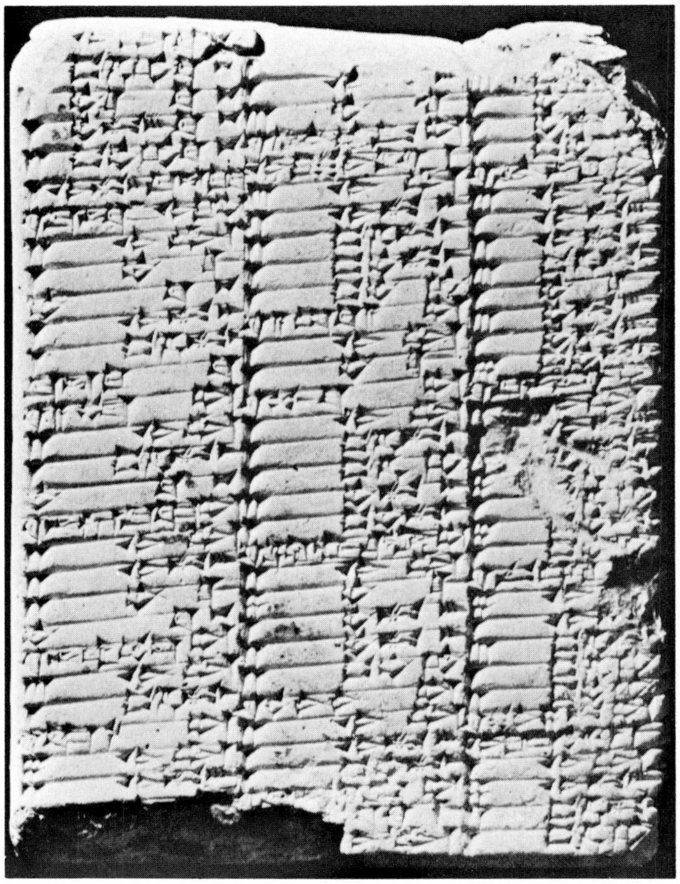

Large clay tablet on which commercial transactions were recorded during the time of Abraham. E. Chiera, *They Wrote on Clay*, University of Chicago, 1938.

Ostracon from Tel Qasila, north of Tel Aviv, eighth century b.c.e. It bears the legend, "to the king thousand (?) oil and hundred . . . (?)" Jerusalem, Israel Department of Antiquities.

There is a growing collection of bronze weights, many of which were cast in the form of animals or parts of the human body. One turtle-shaped weight found at Ashkelon reads "quarter shekel" and weighs 2.63 gm. Another of the same design from Samaria reads "a fifth" and weighs 2.499 gm.

There are many references in Greek and Roman sources to lead as a surface for magical texts and even for such literary work as that of Hesiod. Probably following this tradition, a lead scroll inscribed with Psalm 80 in Greek was found at Rhodes. No such material is known from ancient Israel, though some have understood the term *oferet,* "lead" (Job 19:24) as referring to such a writing surface. Apart from the bronze weights, inscriptions on metal were generally of a religious nature, many of which bore dedicatory formulas and were ultimately donated to a temple treasury.

IVORY. Excluding several personal seals, most, if not all, inscriptions on ivory can be classified into two

Bronze dagger from Lachish, 18th to 17th centuries b.c.e. The inscription is in Proto-Canaanite lettering. Jerusalem, Rockefeller Museum, Israel Department of Antiquities.

The letter *dalet* on a fragment of an ivory plaque from Samaria, c. 850–722 b.c.e. Jerusalem, Israel Department of Antiquities and Museums.

types: joiners' markings and dedicatory formulas. The former are single letters of the alphabet incised on the back of ivory inlays in order to facilitate the process of assembling them. The ivory inlays found in the palace at Samaria are indicative of contemporary styles of decorative art favored by the Israelite aristocracy (Amos 3:15).

As was the case with precious metals, ivory was donated to the patron deities. Of particualr interest is one of the Megiddo ivories dated between 1350–1150 b.c.e. which bears the hieroglyphic inscription:

> The Singer of Ptah, South-of-His Wall
> Lord of the Life of the Two Lands [i.e., Egypt]
> and Great Prince of Ashkelon, Kerker.

The dedication is to the Egyptian god Ptah, who is here called by three of his titles, the third of which indicates a cult seat in Ashkelon. The votaress Kerker seems to be a singer at the Canaanite temple. W.F. Albright has suggested that she be identified with Calcol, a pre-Israelite singer of renown (I Kings 5:11). Ivory gifts were presented to the king as well. An example may be found in a recently discovered ivory piece from Tell Nimrūd, ancient Calah, dating to the mid-eighth century b.c.e. The legible part of the inscription is in good Hebrew (probably from Samaria) and reads *mmlk gdl,* "from the Great King." There is a similar ivory inscription from Arslan Tash, north Syria, which reads *lmrn ḥz'l* "for our lord Hazael" (cf. I Kings 19:15). It was most likely among the spoils taken from Damascus in 796 b.c.e. by Adadnirari III, king of Assyria.

WOOD was employed throughout the ancient world as a writing surface. Egyptian inscriptions have been preserved on wooden statues and sarcophagi, as well as on wooden tablets coated with stucco which were frequently used for school exercises. The Bible seldom explicitly mentions this surface. The earliest clear reference to writing on wood is found in connection with an attempt to challenge Aaron's priestly authority and is employed in substantiating his legitimacy: "Speak to the Israelite people and take from them – from the chieftains of their ancestral houses – . . . 12 staffs in all. Inscribe each man's name on his staff. . . also inscribe Aaron's name on the staff of Levi. . . " (Numbers 17: 17–26). The inscription is the simple type indicating ownership and was probably incised *le-Aharon* – the writing surface being almond wood (verse 23).

Ezekiel employed a wood writing surface in his famous prophesy of the restoration of national unity

(37:16–23): "And thou, son of man, take thee one stick [*ez*] and write upon it: 'For Judah' [*li-Yhudah*] and for the children of Israel his companions; then take another stick, and write upon it: 'For Joseph' [*le-Yosef*], the stick of Ephraim, and all the house of Israel his companions; and join them for thee one to another into one stick, that they may become one in thy hand" (verse 16–17).

P.J. Hyatt has suggested, *en passant,* that the prophet may have used wooden writing tablets and joined them together in the form of a diptych, i.e. a two-leaved "book."

WAX. It has long been known that wax writing surfaces were employed in Egypt, Greece, and Italy during the Classical period. In addition to much pictographic evidence, especially from Italy, a school text from Fayyum, Egypt, from 250 b.c.e. was found that had a red wax surface and on the reverse one in black. Properly treated, wax has the quality of being a lightweight substance that can be easily reused.

This surface is mentioned in older literary sources from Mesopotamia. An important discovery at ancient Calah during the 1950s were 16 ivory boards with the same number of wooden boards in a well in Sargon II's palace (717–705 b.c.e.). They were constructed so as to contain an inscription on wax. One of the tablets was still covered with beeswax, compounded with sulphite of arsenic or orpiment, bearing the text of a well-known astrological text *Enuma Anu Enlil.* Since these boards were tied or hinged together forming a diptych, triptych, or polyptych, they may be called the earliest known form of the book.

An Aramean scribe holding an oblong, book-shaped object, with ribbed markings at the edge for hinges, is clearly depicted on the stele of Barrakab, king of Samal. This picture predates the above Calah material by about a quarter of century and demonstrates the Western Semites' familiarity with this writing surface.

TATTOO MARKS. A more unusual writing surface was the human skin, originally incised with a slave mark indicating ownership, but occasionally with a sign demonstrating fidelity to a deity. It was done by cutting into the skin and filling the incision with ink or a dye. This method is already noted in the Mishnah: "If a man wrote [on his skin] pricked-in writing [he is culpable] .... but only if he writes it and pricks it in with ink or eye-paint or anything that leaves a lasting mark" (*Makkot* 3:6). The Bible categorically forbids this practice: "You shall not make gashes in your flesh for the dead or incise any marks *[ketovet ka'aka]* on yourselves; I am the Lord" (Leviticus 19:28). While this was generally the rule, there seem to have been cases where devotees of YHWH did incise His name on their arms. Isaiah may be referring to this custom when he says: "One shall say: 'I am the Lord's'; And another shall call himself by the name of Jacob; and another shall inscribe his hand 'Belonging to the Lord' . . ." (44:5) and perhaps figuratively: "Surely I have graven upon your palms: Thy sealings (!) are continually before me" (49:16). Furthermore in Elephantine, slaves of Jews were marked with the name of their owner, as was the general practice.

WRITING EQUIPMENT

PENS. Several different types of writing implements were employed in accordance with the different types of surfaces. Inscriptions on stone or metal required a chisel, whereas for clay or wax a stylus would suffice. In Mesopotamia, the stylus was made of reeds, hard-

An open segment of the Copper Scroll. J.M. Allegro.

wood, or even bone and metal. There is no pictographic evidence from ancient Israel nor is there any artifact that can be definitely identified as a stylus. The literary sources do mention at least two kinds of tools for writing on stone: an iron pen, *et barzel,* and a hard stone stylus, *ẓipporen shamir* (Jermiah 17:1; Job 19:24). The *ḥeret* may have been a tool for working on metal or wood (Exodus 32:4).

The Egyptians used a rush, cut obliquely and frayed at the end forming a brush, to write with ink on papyrus, hides, ostraca, and wood. A similar type of pen seems to have been used on the Samaria and Lachish ostraca. This instrument was probably called the scribe's pen, *et sofer* [*soferim*] (Jeremiah 8:8; Psalms 45:2), in order to differentiate it from the stone engraver's iron pen. Likewise, the *ḥeret enosh,* the common or soft stylus (Isaiah 8:1), is not the same as mentioned above.

At the end of the third century b.c.e., Greek scribes living in Egypt invented a new type of reed pen pointed and split at the end. The quill, used to this day by Torah scribes *(soferei setam)* was introduced during the Middles Ages in Ashkenazi communities.

INK. From earliest times, the Egyptians wrote in black and red ink. Black ink was made from carbon in the form of soot mixed with a thin solution of gum. This solution was molded and dried into cakes, which were mixed with water before use. In producing red ink, red ocher, or red iron oxide was substituted for carbon.

In Israel, a similar type of black ink was probably used, though the Lachish ostraca show traces of iron. The Hebrew word for ink is *deyo* (Jeremiah 36:18), a term whose etymology is uncertain. In at least one of its solutions, the ink did not easily penetrate the writing surface and could be erased with water (Numbers 5:23). Most of the Dead Sea Scrolls were written with a carbon ink, while the badly damaged *Genesis Apocryphon* was written with the metallic mixture.

CASES. The ancient Egyptians carried their brushes in a hollow reed case. They added to this a wooden palette containing two depressions for the cakes of black and red ink. This was joined by a cord to a small cup designed to hold water for moistening the ink. A stylized drawing of these three pieces became the hieroglyphic sign S.S., meaning "writing" or "scribe." Later the pen case and palette were combined and easily carried on the belt (cf. Ezekiel 9:2–3, 11). An Egyptian ivory pen case dating from the time of Ramses III was found at Megiddo. The biblical term for this item is *keset,* derived from the

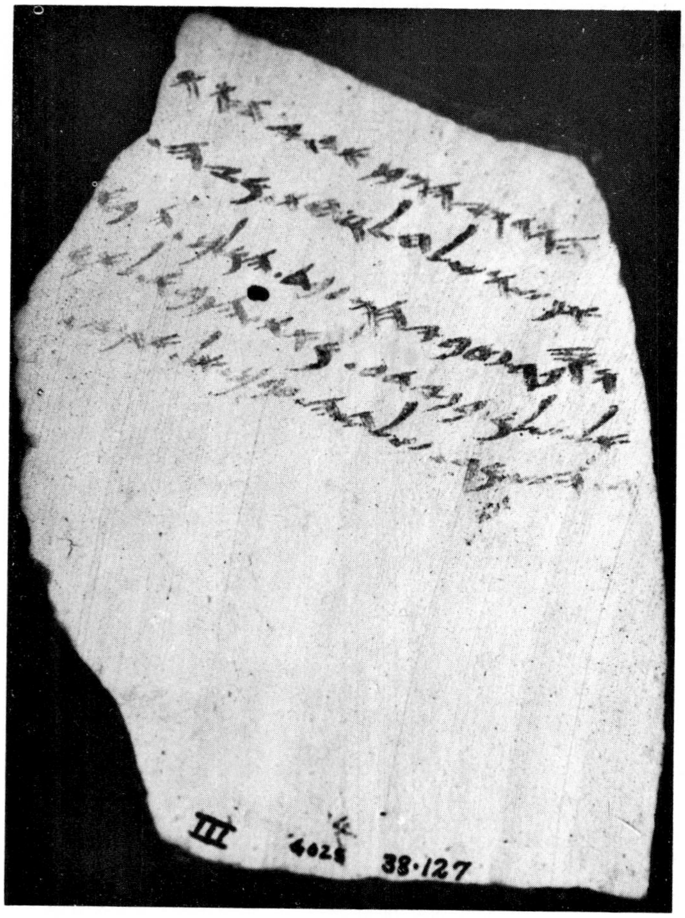

One of the 18 Lachish ostraca from 587/6 b.c.e. It is written with a reed pen in iron-carbon ink. Jerusalem, Israel Department of Antiquities and Museums.

Egyptian *gsti.* A razor for cutting leather or papyrus and probably a straight edge for ruling lines as well as a cloth or sponge for erasures completed the equipment required by the scribe.

TALMUD AND HALAKHAH

The tremendous importance attached by the talmudic sages to the art of writing is reflected, according to one interpretation, in Mishnah *Avot* 5:6, which includes among the "ten things which were created on the eve of the Sabbath" (of creation, i.e., which partake of the semi-miraculous) *ha-ketav ve-ha-makhtev* ("writing and the instrument of writing"). The usual explanation is that the phrase applies to the writing of the Decalogue, which is mentioned afterward, but another view is that it applies to the art of writing as a whole. On the other hand there was the realization that the committal of doctrine to writing had a possibly deleterious effect in that it introduced an inflexibility and a finality to doctrine which should re-

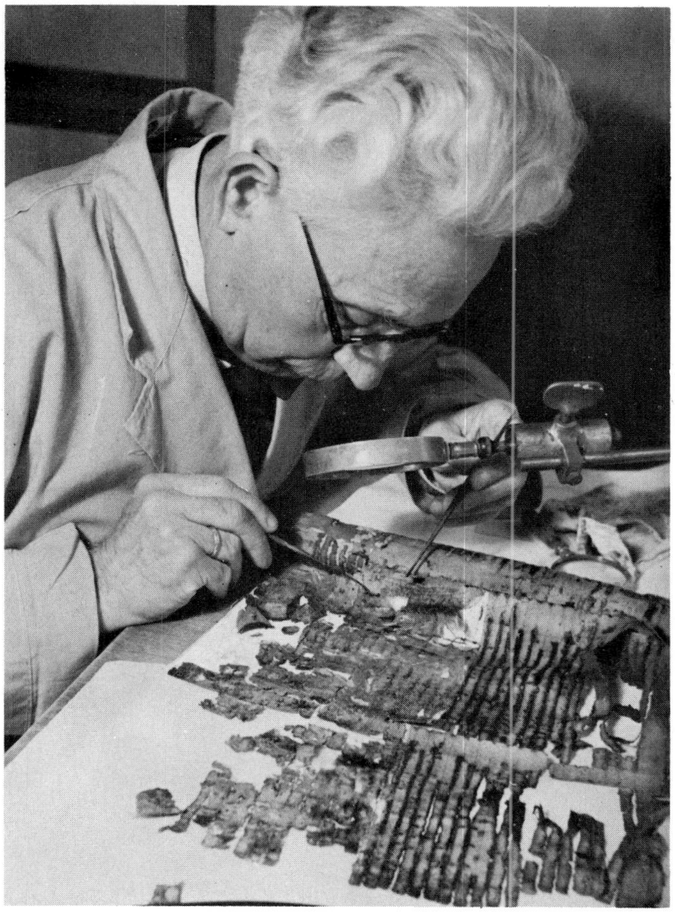

The opening of the Genesis Apocryphon, the oldest written Palestinian Pentateuch translation. Jerusalem, Israel Museum, Shrine of the Book.

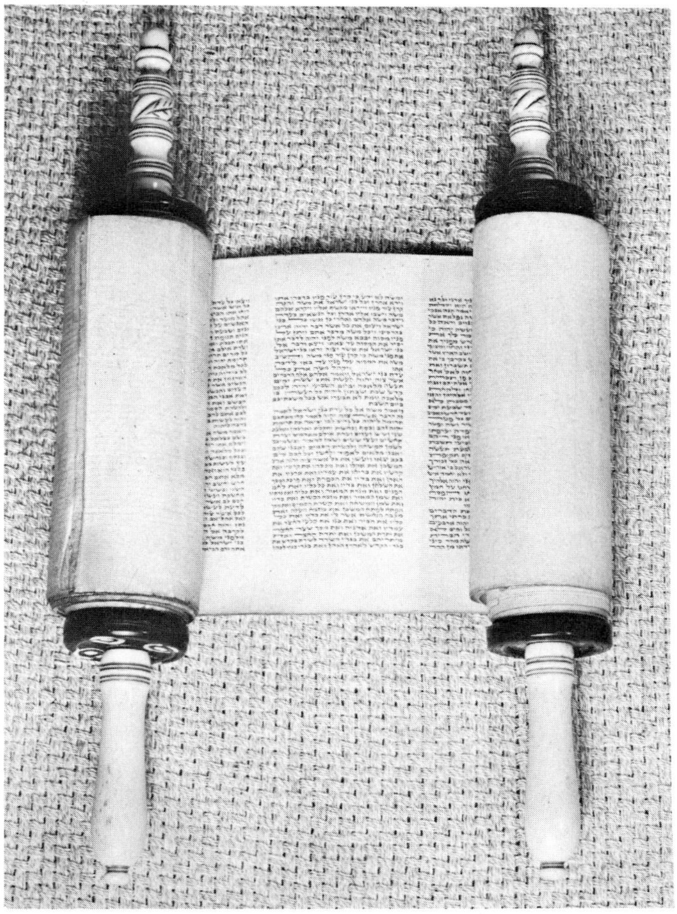

An 18th-century Polish *Sefer Torah*, handwritten in accordance with the special regulations pertaining to the writing of the scroll of the Law. Feinberg Collection, Detroit.

main flexible and elastic. According to one scholar it was this which lay behind the prohibition on committing the Oral Law to writing. The Written Law was final and decisive; its interpretation had to remain open to adjustment.

WRITING FOR RITUAL PURPOSES. Writing, its materials, its regulations, and its instruments play a prominent part in the *halakhah.* They are important in the laws of writing a *Sefer Torah, tefillin* and *mezuzot* (see below). An exception is the portion of the *sotah* (the woman suspected of adultery – Numbers 5:11–31), since the Bible explicitly states that the writing had to be erased in the bitter waters. There are different regulations for the writing of a bill of divorce, and lastly there is the prohibition of writing on the Sabbath, and the regulations as to what constitutes writing. It is almost entirely in connection with those laws that the many details concerning writing and writing materials occur (cf. especially *Shabbat* 12:3–5, *Gittin* 2:3–4 and the corresponding Tosefta and the relevant discussion in the Talmuds). Whereas for the writing of the *Sefer Torah* and other sacred writings only parchment made from the hide of permitted animals could be used, after the required treatment, bills of divorce could be written on paper made from papyrus. The prohibition of writing on the Sabbath applied to all permanent writing materials. A differentiation is made between permanent writing materials and non-permanent ones. In the former, the Mishnah enumerates olive leaves and a cow's horn, to which the Tosefta (*Shabbat* 11 (12):8) adds carob leaves or cabbage leaves. It is difficult to see how they could be used widely and their listing could be theoretical only. Non-permanent writing materials are given as leaves of leeks, onions, vegetables and the sorb apple tree.

Owing to the scarcity and the high cost of paper, particularly parchment, it was used more than once, by rubbing out the writing with stone and superimposing new writing. It is this palimpsest which is referred to in the dictum of Elisha ben Avuyah, who compares learning as a child to "ink written on clean

paper" and learning on one's old age to "ink written on erased paper" (*Avot* 4:20, *Gittin* 2:4, where erased paper is equated with *diftera,* hide which has been treated with salt and flour, but not with gall nuts).

A similar distinction is made between permanent and non-permanent inks. To the former belong ink proper *(deyo),* caustic, red dye, and gum (*Shabbat* 12:4; *Sotah* 2;4). The Tosefta (*Shabbat* 11 (12): 8) adds congealed blood and curdled milk, as well as nutshells and pomegranate peel, which were widely used for making dyestuffs. Ink was made from a mixture of oil and resin, which hardened and to which water was added. Any oil or resin could be used, but the best quality was of olive oil and balsam (*Shabbat* 23a, 104b). The most permanent ink, however, was made by adding iron sulphate or vitriol to the ink, which made it a deep black, and it was therefore also used as boot-blacking (*Gittin* 19a). This admixture made the ink completely indelible and was therefore prohibited for use in writing the passage of the *sotah* (*Eruvin* 13a). Non-permanent inks were made from "taria water" (juice of wine), fruit juices, and juice of gall nuts. There is an interesting reference to invisible

Above: Fragment from a *tefillin* scroll dating from the second century c.e. The parchment is well-preserved and the text of the *Shema* can still be read. It was found at Murabba'at near the Dead Sea. R. de Vaux, *Discoveries in the Judean Desert,* Oxford, 1961. Below: Three clay pen-cases (*kesatot*) from Qumran, near Jericho, either fourth century b.c.e. or first century b.c.e. to first century c.e. Jerusalem, Rockefeller Museum, Israel Department of Antiquities.

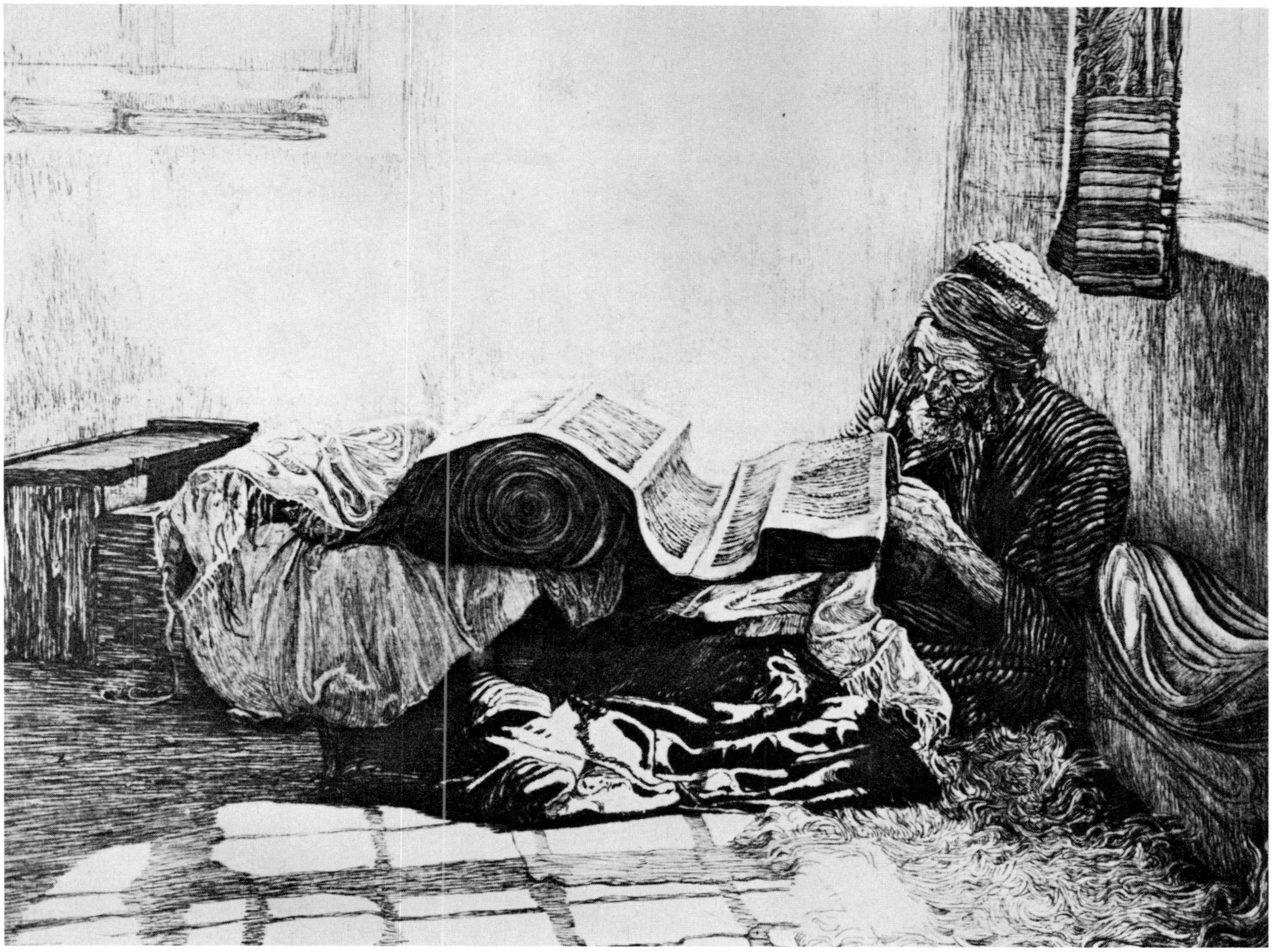

"The Torah Scribe." Etching by Ephraim Moses Lilien, Jerusalem. B.M. Ansbacher Collection.

writing: "These people of the East are very cunning. When one of them wishes to write a letter in secret writing to his friend he writes it with melon water and when the recipient receives it he pours ink over it and is able to decipher the writing" (TJ, *Shabbat* 12:4; TB, *Gittin* 2:3, 44b).

It would appear that originally the custom was to use gold lettering for the writing of the Torah scroll since the Midrash applies the verse "we will make thee circlets of gold, with studs of silver" (Song of Songs 1:11) to the writing and the ruled lined lines respectively. According to the Letter of Aristeas (176), the *Sefer Torah* presented by Eleazar the high priest to Ptolemy Philadelphus written in letters of gold. However, such ostentation was later forbidden and tractate *Soferim* (1:9) states, "it is forbidden to write [a *Sefer Torah*] in gold. It happened that in a *Sefer Torah* of Alexandria all the divine names were written in gold, and when it was brought to the notice of the sages they ordered it to be hidden away." There is also mention of Queen Helena of Adiabene having the passage of the *sotah* written on a gold tablet from which the text would be copied. Simeon ben Lakish, however, said that it referred only to the initials.

The professional scribe, the *livlar* (librarius) used a *kalmus* (calamus), a quill made of reeds. For ordinary writing the *makhtev,* a two pointed pin, or stylus was used, one end for writing and the other for erasing. The inkwell, called a *kalmarin,* was provided with an inner rim to prevent spilling. This inkwell was used by ordinary people. The inkwell of the scribe, called the *bet deyo* (ink container), had a cover and mention is made of the "inkwell of Joseph the Priest which had a hole in the side."

Pen, paper, and inkstand are referred to as "things of honor" in a peculiar context. Rabban Simeon ben Gamaliel states that any idol which bears something in its hand is forbidden. The Jerusalem Talmud makes an exception in the case of "something of honor" and specifies "paper, pen, and inkwell" (*Avodah Zarah* 3:1). Among the other instruments of the scribe were the *olar,* the pen-knife used for cutting the reed to make the quill; the *izmel,* a knife for cutting the paper; and the *sargel,* a sharp instrument for drawing the lines on the parchment or paper. For sacred writings the *sargel* had to be made from a reed. "Writer's sand" was used to dry the ink.

THE SCRIBE

The Hebrew term for "scribe" is *sofer,* a participle form of the root *spr,* meaning "to count." It is a Canaanite word, appearing in Ugarit as well as a loanword in an Egyptian text – *sofer yode'a,* i.e., "wise scribe" (Papyrus Anastasi I; late 13th century b.c.e.). It may be a cognate to Akkadian *šāpiru,* "secretary, official." The first biblical reference to *sofer* is found in the Song of Deborah (Judges 5:14). Another term used frequently is *shoter,* which probably meant "recorder." This functionary is associated with food rationing (Numbers 11:16; Joshua 1:10; cf. Proverbs 6:7), raising the levy (Exodus 5:6, et al; Deuteronomy 20:5, cf. II Chronicles 26:11) and the law courts (Deuteronomy 1:15; 16; 18). The root of *shoter* is derived from the cognate Akkadian *šatāru,* "to write," and reappears in later Aramaic and Hebrew in *shetar,* "a written document" (see also Job 38:33). The common Akkadian word for scribe was *tupšarru* which appears as *ti/afsar* in Nahum's prophesy of the destruction of Nineveh (3:17) and Jeremiah's words on Babylon's doom (51:27).

As in neighboring lands, the Israelite scribe learned his profession in family-like guilds (cf. "the families of scribes who inhabited Jabez," I Chronicles 2:5). A 15th-century b.c.e. text does indicate the existence of scribal schools in Canaan proper. It is a letter written by a teacher to a student's father living in Shechem asking for the long overdue tuition fee that could be paid in kind. The teacher describes his relationship to his students as that of a parent. W.F. Albright reads this important text:

> Unto Birashshena say:
> Thus Baniti – [Ashirat (?)]:
> From three years (ago) until now thou hast not caused me to be paid –
> is there no grain nor oil nor wine(?) which thou canst send?
> What is my offense that thou has not paid [me]?

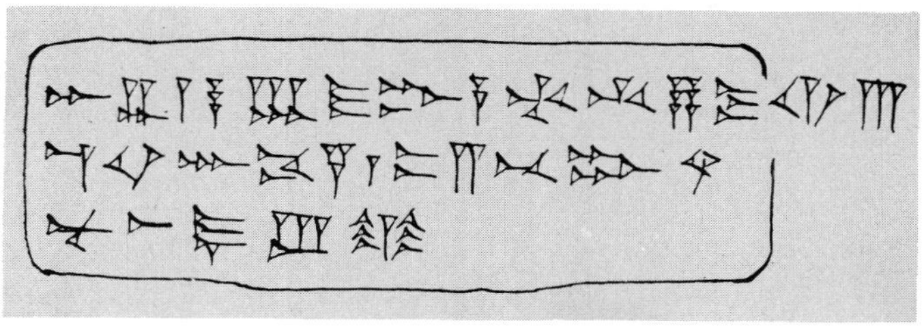

The Ugarit alphabet, from a tablet found at Ras Shamra, 14th century b.c.e.

> The children who are with me continue to learn – their father and their mother every [day] alike am I . . .
> Now [behold] whatever [there is] at the disposal of
> [my lord let him send] unto me, and let him inform me!

During the time of David, a certain Seraiah (II Samuel 8:17; also referred to as Sheva, II Samuel 20:25; Shisha, I Kings 4:3; Shabsha, I Chronicles 18:16) was appointed royal scribe. Both his sons Elihoreph and Ahijah followed him in Solomon's court.

Scribes of various degrees of competence were attached to all government and temple offices. Apparently there were also independent scribes who either served the public or were in the employ of men of means. The highest scribal post was that of royal scribe. It is difficult to determine his exact position among the king's other ministers, even if it is assumed that the various biblical lists follow the principle of order of importance. In the time of Hezekiah, the royal scribe seems to be of a lower rank than royal chamberlain, but higher than the official known as *mazkir* (Isaiah 22:15–25; 36:3; II Kings 18: 18,37 and also II Chronicles 34:8). Exactly what the duties of the royal scribe were is unknown. Besides fulfilling an advisory capacity, he seems to have been in charge of financial matters. This function may underlie the original meaning of the title, which may have been "accountant." Quite likely, other ministries had their own scribal service. The priesthood definitely needed literati and so did the chief of staff. Perhaps the youth of Judges 8:14 was a local scribe: "And he [Gideon] caught a young man of the men of Succoth, and inquired of him; and he wrote down for him the princes and elders of Succoth, seventy-seven men." City governments, as well, required lists of prominent landowners for purposes of taxation and army service (Judges 8:14). The public at large would also turn to a scribe to draw up documents of legal or religious character. Wealthy gentry could afford a per-

A school for scribes in the palace at Mari, Mesopotamia. From A. Parrot, *Mari, Editions Ides et Calindes*, Paris, 1953.

sonal secretary for their business affairs. Baruch son of Neriah served Jeremiah in this capacity, though the relationship may be better characterized as that of master and disciple (Jeremiah 32:12; 36:4,18; 43:3; 45; lff). Several inscribed seals from the Monarchy period bearing the title *sofer* have been discovered in and around Palestine.

SCRIBAL EDUCATION. The Israelite scribe had the easy task of learning the 22-letter alphabet, whereas his Egyptian and Mesopotamian counterpart had to master at least one system of hundreds of signs. Indicative of the conservative nature of the scribal art is the fact that the form of the letters in the three main alphabetic branches (Phoenician, Hebrew, and Aramaic) did not differ radically during the period between 1200 and 600 b.c.e. While mastering the forms, the apprentice scribe learned their order. The standard order of the characters is found already in the 30-letter abecedaries of the scribal schools of Ugarit (15th century b.c.e.). Minus eight letters, the series reappears in biblical acrostics (Psalms 119, 145; Lamentations 1–4), and is almost identicial with the sequence of the modern Hebrew alphabet. Probably in the ninth century b.c.e. the form and order of the letters were exported to the Greek islands as well.

It seems that Isaiah refers to an elementary class learning the alphabet in one of his prophecies (28:9–13): he describes the "first grade" lesson for the day when the children learned the letters *ẓadi* (צ) and *kof* (ק). During the excavations at Lachish, a list of the first five letters was found incised on one of the steps of an Israelite building, perhaps the work of a child practicing his alphabet.

The second stage of a scribe's training was the copying of short texts that may have been learned by heart and practiced at home. The Gezer Calendar

The Gezer Calendar. Replica in the Israel Museum, Jerusalem.

(tenth century b.c.e.) is a possible example of such an assignment. It divides the year into eight agricultural seasons, noting the main characteristics of each. Gezer had been an important Canaanite city, and during the tenth century it housed a levite community serving the Jerusalem administration. Perhaps it was in cities like Gezer that that Canaanite scribal traditions were conveyed to the Israelite.

The young student next learned epistolary and other administrative formulas. After much practice, he could easily produce the names of the city elders (Judges 8:14).

During the monarchy there was a standard tax form, as found in the Samaria Ostraca (mid-ninth or according to others mid-eighth-century b.c.e.) and as recently noted in the inscribed jar handles from Gibeon (late seventh century b.c.e.).

The local scribe had also to master the forms of deeds of sale, marriage contracts, and bills of divorce, as well as court pleas. The latter, however, may have been part of the responsibilities of the *shoter* or "court secretary."

The king's scribes received a broader and more cos-

Illuminated miniature at the opening of the Book of Proverbs, picturing the judgment of Solomon. From a 15th century Italian manuscript. Jerusalem, Israel Museum.

mopolitan education. They had to be competent in diplomacy and the exact sciences. Their knowledge of international diplomacy began with the study of Aramaic, the lingua franca of the period.

Because of the involvement of all the Israelite kings, from Ahab to Zedekiah, in regional politics, it was necessary that the royal scribes know the workings of the Assyrian, Egyptian, Aramean, and Phoenician courts. Several kings even appeared in person before their Mesopotamian suzerains. International law and treaty formulas, as well as far-reaching trade agreements were the scribes' normal business.

Simple arithmetic was probably learned in all formal systems of education. The Israelite court scribe, like his Egyptian and Mesopotamian counterparts, mastered the higher mathematics needed for solving problems of logistics and engineering. While astronomy is not specifically mentioned in Israelite sources, it was needed for the calendrical intercalations decreed by the central government. Cartography as well was a well-known ancient art.

In addition to diplomacy and the exact sciences, the court bureaucracy developed what might be termed a "scribal ethic." Wisdom literature, more specifically the collections now found in the Book of Proverbs, served as a primary text for character education; they focused on the individual's rather than on the national interest.

Like the comparative Egyptian material, and the Book of Ahikar (Aramaic), the Book of Proverbs was an outstanding example of court literature. The book was meant to serve in educating king and courtier (8:15–18) but especially the bureaucracy (22:29). The virtues stressed by these pedagogues were, among others, religious piety, proper family relations, honesty, industry, sagacity, responsibility, social virtues, and loyalty to the king.

Various literary methods were used as memory aids for the student. Key words (Proverbs 25:4–5; 30:11–14) and common ideas (25:2–3, 5–6) tied together independent statements. Similarly alliteration (*rash, rasha, ra,* 28:3–5) and repetition of the same or similar roots (25:18–20) served as learning devices. Other units might be formed as number series (30:15–33). Another mnemonic device was the alphabet acrostic (31:10–31).

The Book of Proverbs may be the closest thing to an actual school text from the biblical period. Its explicit pedagogic goal, as well as its employment of mnemonic devices, supports this contention. The centrality of secular, royal figures (Solomon, Hezekiah, King Lemuel of Massa, "The Wise") and its affinities to non-Israelite wisdom literature further argue for its

Section from a highly-decorated Dutch or Italian Scroll of Esther, dating from the 17th or 18th century c.e. London, Cecil Roth Collection.

role in the education of the officialdom.

IN JUDAISM. The term *soferim* later came to mean the body of scholars who lived after Ezra. These became the main teachers of the Oral Law and in rabbinic parlance they are often referred to as the *ḥakhamim,* the sages. In this sense, of course the description *sofer* is not a professional, technical term. Later the term *sofer* came to refer to a professional expert in the writing of Torah scrolls, *tefillin, mezuzot,* and bills of divorce. Scribes are, therefore, known as *sofer setam* סוֹפֵר סְתָ"ם, *setam* being composed of the Hebrew initials of *Sefer Torah, tefillin,* and *mezuzot.* These have to be written with a feather quill in indelible ink, in straight lines, and on specially prepared parchment. It is inferred from the Bible that every Jew should write for himself a Torah scroll (see Deuteronomy 31:19; *Sanhedrin* 21b). Expertness, however, being required in writing a Torah scroll, the commandment can only be fulfilled by ordering it from a scribe. The profession of scribe was indispensable to the Jewish community, and according to the Talmud a scholar should not dwell in a town where there is no scribe. In the talmudic period, scribes were poorly paid lest they become rich and desert their vocations, leaving the community without their services. The scribe writing a Torah scroll must devote attention and care to the writing; he is forbidden to rely on his memory and has to write from a model copy. His guide is the professional compendium for scribes, *Tikkun Soferim,* which contains the traditional text of the Torah, the specific rules concerning the decorative flourishes (*tagin,* "crowns") on certain letters, the regulations as to the spacing of certain Torah sections ("open" or "closed" pericopes), and the rules for writing Torah scrolls in which each column begins with the Hebrew letter *vav (vavei ha-ammudim).* Only the Scroll of Esther may be adorned with artistic illustrations but not the Torah scroll, although Alexandrian scribes are said to have gilded the name and appellations of God. When writing a Torah scroll a scribe must especially prepare himself so that he writes the names of the Lord with proper devotion and in ritual purity. It is, therefore, customary that he immerses himself in a ritual bath *(mikveh)* before beginning his work. This subject is treated at length in the following chapter.

Scribe re-inking a faded letter in the Book of Numbers, chapter 36, on a Torah scroll. He is working at Kibbutz Ḥafez Ḥayyim. Jerusalem, J.N.F.

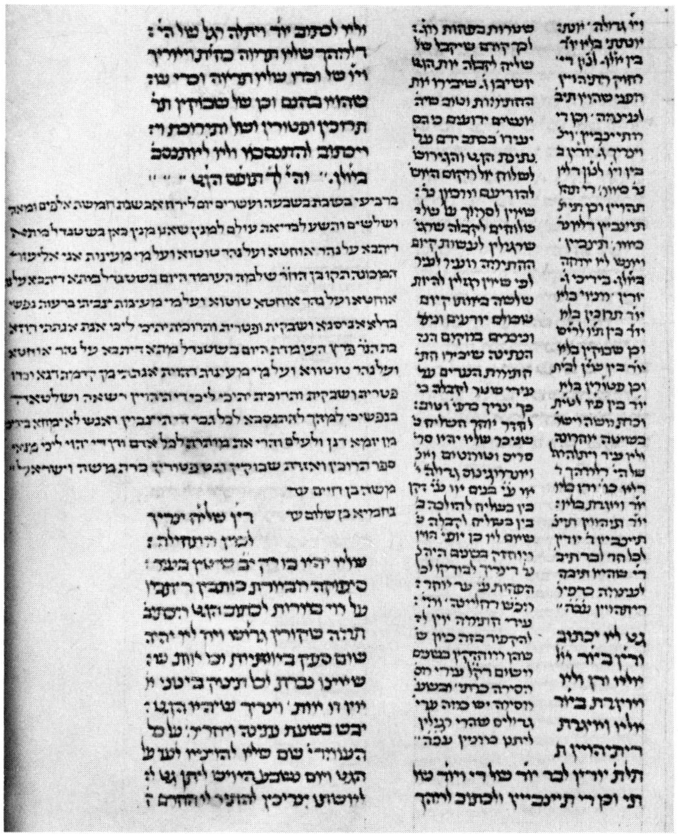

An example of the layout of a bill of divorce from *Sefer Mitzvot Katan* by Isaac of Corbeil, 1379. London, British Museum, Ms. Harl. 5584 fol. 746.

Scribes also acted as recording clerks and court secretaries of the *bet din* and were, therefore, also called *lavlar,* from the Latin *libellarius.* They wrote legal documents such as bills of divorce and contracts. In the *halakhah* there are established rules as to who pays the scribe's fee. The general principle is that the person who receives the greater benefit from a transaction has to pay the scribe, e.g., the buyer of property and the borrower of money. In modern times printed forms are used for most legal transactions and the only document that has to be written by an expert scribe is the bill of divorce.

2. the scroll

SCROLLS AS EARLY BOOKS

In antiquity, all books, Jewish or non-Jewish, were scrolls. The Torah, which was presented in the third century to Ptolemy II (Philadelphus) of Egypt by the high priest from Jerusalem so that it might be translated into Greek (the Septuagint), was unrolled before him. One of the Torah scrolls kept in the Temple (TJ, *Ta'anit* 4:2) was carried through Rome among the spoils in the triumphal procession of Titus, but the theory that it is pictured on the Arch of Titus is not tenable. The Talmud and Midrash speak mainly of scroll-books. The high priest on the Day of Atonement read from a scroll during the Temple service and then rolled it up, as was done after each reading of the Law. In talmudic times this was an honor reserved for the leader of the congregation. If a man received a Torah scroll in deposit to secure a loan or for some other purpose, he had to roll it open for airing once a year. A Torah scroll was rolled from both ends toward the middle, each end being attached to a cylindrical handle called *ammud* (pillar) or, in later times, *eẓ ḥayyim* (tree of life), enough parchment being left clear of writing for wrapping round the handle. Other scrolls had only one handle on the right end, while on the left enough parchment was left vacant for wrapping around the

A Jerusalem Yemenite scribe writing a Torah scroll. Courtesy Keren Hayesod, United Israel Appeal, Jerusalem.

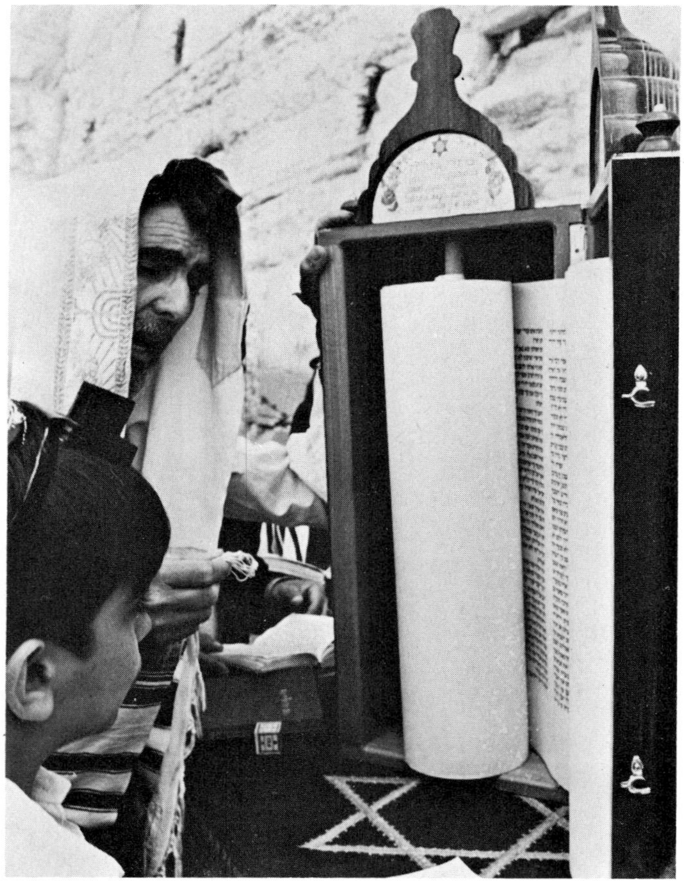

A bar mitzvah at the Western Wall in Jerusalem. The Torah scroll being read from is of the Sephardi type and the *ammud* around which the scroll is rolled is clearly shown. Photo: David Posner, Jerusalem.

A contemporary *megillah* in an olive wood case, carved with pictures of holy places.

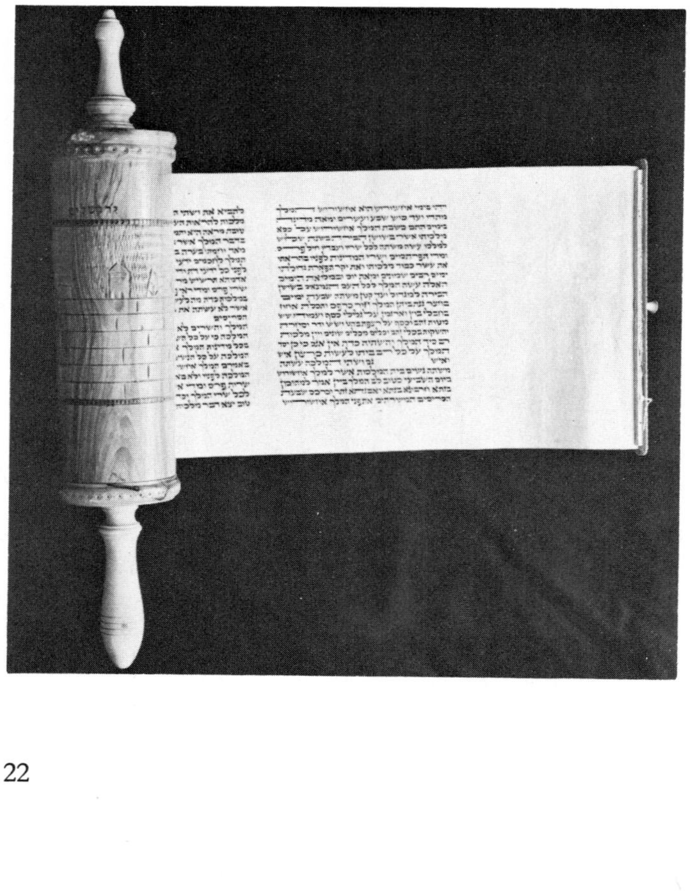

whole scroll. In the Septuagint the word for *megillah* (scroll) is the Greek for head-piece, referring to the handle, which thus is used to stand for the whole scroll. This shows that the handles were already in use in the last centuries b.c.e.

In any event, there is no reference in either biblical or talmudic literature to books in the form of codices with folded pages, unless the *pinkas,* which could have as many as 24 tablets (*Lamentations Rabbah* 1:14), should be regarded as its precursor (but see above, Chapter I, WOOD). The term *tomos* (volume, form Greek and Latin) is used in the Tosefta (*Shabbat* 13:4; *Bava Meẓia* 9:31) for which there is a Hebrew synonym *takhrikh;* but it is not clear whether some sort of codex is meant or the traditional scroll made of sheets sewn together. The Church Father Jerome (fourth century), who speaks of Hebrew Bibles in the posession of Christians, does not mention any Hebrew codex. However, by the fifth century most books, like the earliest Christian ones, are codices. Passages in such late talmudic works as tractate *Soferim* and in the minor tractate *Sefer Torah* have been interpreted as referring to codices.

SINGLE AND COMBINED SCROLLS. Biblical books certainly remained in scroll form, and those used in the synagogue have preserved this format. For liturgical use the five books of the Pentateuch had to be written on one single scroll (*Gittin* 60a). According to one tradition, the Torah consisted of seven scrolls, with a division of Numbers at chapter 10:35–36, these two verses making a separate book (*Shabbat* 115b–116a). The division of the books of the Bible was largely determined by the size of the scroll. Samuel and Kings were probably originally one book but were divided and subdivided because of size. The Book of Psalms too was divided into five books at an early date. Ezra, Nehemiah, and Chronicles were originally one book, as suggested by the identity of the last two verses of Chronicles with the first two of Ezra-Nehemiah. Smaller books, such as the two parts of Isaiah and of Zechariah, were combined into one scroll. The fact that the Minor Prophets were called the Twelve Prophets as early as Ben Sira 49:10 (third-second centuries b.c.e.) proves both their separate and combined entity.

SCROLLS IN THE TALMUD. Talmudic sources reflect the existence of scrolls containing both single and combined books of the Bible. Single books (Psalms, Job, Proverbs), though much worn, could be given to a widow in payment or part payment of her marriage settlement according to the Talmud. The combination of single books into Pentateuch, Prophets, and Hagiographa respectively is discussed as a halakhic problem. Whether those three could be combined or written in one scroll – at least for liturgical use – was controversial, but the *halakhah* was decided in the affirmative (*Bava Batra* 13b). According to one opinion Baitos (Boethos) ben Zonin had the eight prophetic books fastened together with the approval of Eleazar ben Azariah; while Judah ha-Nasi reports that his court's approval was a given for a complete Bible in this form *(ibid).* Heirs who had inherited biblical books were not allowed to divide a single scroll between them but could do so if they were separate ones *(ibid).* The five books: Song of Songs, Ruth, Lamentations, Ecclesiastes, and Esther are called *megillot* (scrolls), the last one known as "the *megillah*" in Mishnah and Talmud, because it had to be read publicly from a parchment scroll. Like the *Sefer Torah,* the Scroll of Esther retains the scroll form today. At a later stage the custom arose – and is still current – of reading the other four *megillot* on special occasions, in some communities also from scrolls.

For special purposes excerpts from the biblical books were written in separate scrolls or on one or more sheets *(pinkas).* The most important example is the *Sefer Aftarta,* the collection of weekly prophetic readings in the synagogue (*Gittin* 60a), which in some communities is still used today. In the same talmudic passage the use of *Sifrei Aggadeta* (homiletical books) is mentioned as well as the question whether *megillot,* meaning excerpts form the Pentateuch, could be written for teaching purposes. Though the conclusion is negative, it was the practice to copy the *Shema* and the *Hallel* psalms for this purpose.

In the Talmud, genealogical tables current in Temple and talmudic times were called *megillot* or *Sefer Yuḥasin,* and these are also mentioned by Josephus. The Mishnah mentions heretical books under the collective name of *Sefarim Ḥiẓonim* (i.e., external books), and this term has been variously interpreted in Talmud and Midrash (*Sanhedrin* 100b). Similar books were found among the Dead Sea Scrolls. These discoveries, the oldest Hebrew (or Aramaic) manuscripts in existence – some belonging to the second century b.c.e. – have considerably increased knowledge of this field. Y. Yadin has established that the Dead Sea Scrolls generally conform to the talmudic rules for the writing of sacred scrolls. Though the writing down of the Oral Law was strictly forbidden, this was circumvented by the notes taken down on so-

The Samaritans maintain the office of High Priest. Here the present incumbent is pictured raising the Scroll of the Law on high on the seventh day of Passover. Photo: Binyamin Zedaka, Holon.

The Thanksgiving Psalm of the Dead Sea Scrolls before it was unrolled. The Dead Sea Scrolls generally conform to the talmudic rules for the writing of sacred books. Jerusalem, Israel Museum, Shrine of the Book.

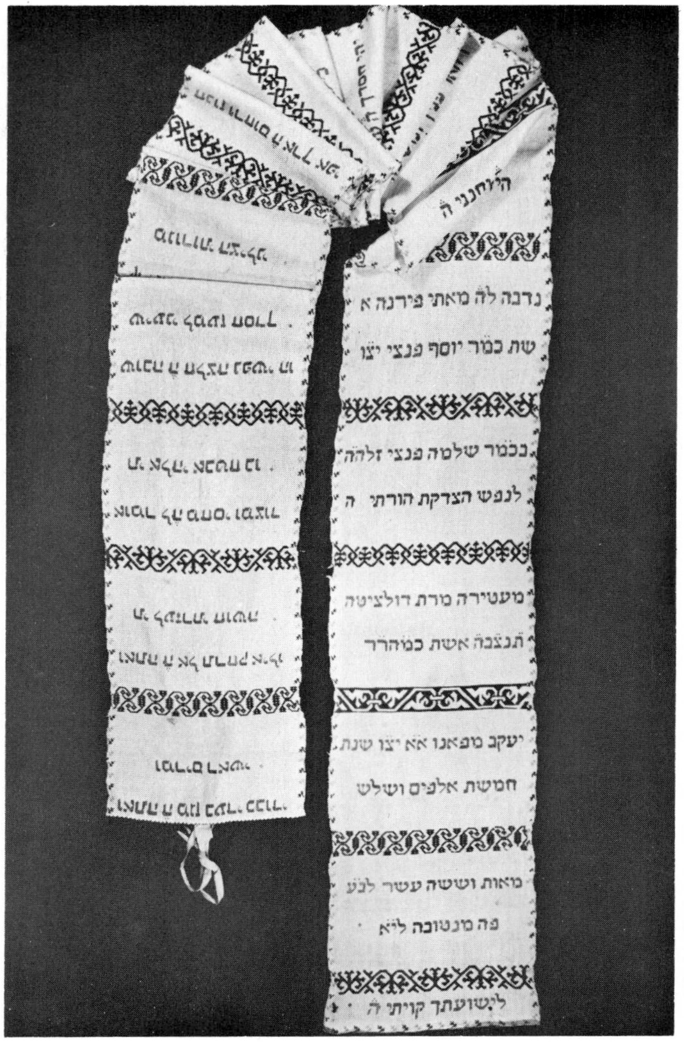

Linen Torah wrapper from Mantua, Italy, 1556. It is embroidered in red and blue with phrases from prayers. Cleveland, Ohio. Joseph B. Horwitz Judaica Collection.

called *megillot setarim,* i.e. private notebooks or such as the *Sifrei Aggadeta* mentioned above.

SIZE OF BOOKS. From the description in the Mishnah of the reading from the Torah by the high priest on the Day of Atonement (*Yoma* 7:1) and by the king on the occasion of the *Hakhel* ceremony, a national convocation which took place every seven years (*Sotah* 7:8), this Temple scroll cannot have been unduly large. The measurements mentioned in the Talmud are 6 by 6 hand-breaths (44 x 44 cm.) and the scroll was to be of equal height and width, a requirement which was admittedly difficult to achieve. The script had to be correspondingly small – the Torah alone consists of over 300,000 letters. Jerome (*Prologium ad Ezeckielem,* 20) complained that the Hebrew Bible text could hardly be read by daylight, let alone by the light of a lamp, but diminutive script was widely used in antiquity, and Jews were familiar with the Bible from childhood.

KEEPING OF SCROLL BOOKS. Scrolls, being valuable, were kept with care. Sacred books had to be wrapped in *mitpaḥot* (sing. *mitpaḥat*) and it was forbidden to touch them with bare hands. The wraps were made of linen, silk, purple materials, or leather. Today's embroidered Torah mantle thus has a long history. Some Dead Sea Scrolls were found preserved in linen wrappings. Books were kept in chests, alone or with other things; the synagogue Ark is a survivor of these chests. Earthenware jars were also used as receptacles for books from Bible times, and such containers have preserved for posterity the treasures of the Dead Sea caves, the Elephantine Letters, etc. Baskets too were used for keeping books.

GENIZAH. Worn sacred books had to be reverently "hidden away" – in a *genizah* – and were eventually buried. This accounts for the fact that so few Torah or Bible fragments have been preserved from antiquity, as parchment, let alone papyrus, decays in

Torah scrolls in modern velvet mantles in the Ark of New York's Central Synagogue.

Fragment of the Jerusalem Talmud from the treasure trove of the Cairo *Genizah*. Cambridge University Library.

the ground. Where the *genizah* was limited to storing away, it made possible such treasure troves as those from the Dead Sea caves and the Cairo *Genizah*. Heretical books too were condemned to *genizah,* and these included almost anything not admitted to the Bible canon.

OWNERSHIP OF BOOKS. While books were costly and rare in antiquity, by the second century b.c.e. some Jews possessed their own copies of biblical books. During the persecution preceding the Hasmonean revolt, those caught possessing sacred books were burned with them (I Maccabees 1:56–57; 3:48). On the Day of Atonement the burghers of Jerusalem could each produce their *Sefer Torah* for the admiration of all (*Yoma* 70a). True wealth was books, and it was charity to loan them out (*Ketubbot* 50a commenting on Psalms 112:3). Special laws applied to the finding, borrowing, and depositing of books, whether and under what circumstances it was permitted to sell them. The provocative query as to whether a room filled with Torah scrolls requires a *mezuzah* at its door is put by the aggadic legend into the mouth of Korah. Sacred books were above all owned by municipalities and synagogues. Schoolchildren, too, usually had their own books. Mention is also made of books being written and owned by gentiles, heretics, and Samaritans.

THE SEFER TORAH

The most sacred written item in the Jewish religion is the scroll containing the Five Books of Moses. This scroll is used for public reading in the synagogue and great care must be taken that the text is exactly according to the tradition. This tradition was fixed by the Masoretes as the scholars of the *Masorah* ("[text] tradition") are known. The text followed today is that of Aaron Ben-Asher who worked, presumably in Tiberias, in the first half of the tenth century, but there were other slightly divergent versions. The text of the Torah scroll includes a number of diacritical signs such as dots above certain letters as well as some scribal peculiarities such as outsized and small letters and, between sections, inverted letters. The text is composed of consonants only; neither the vowel signs nor the cantillation marks are written in the scroll.

WRITING THE SEFER TORAH. The tools and materials used by the scribe are parchment, quill, ink, stylus and ruler, and *tikkun* (guide), a book with the exact Torah text. The Torah is written on parchment manufactured from specified sections of the hide of a kosher animal. The hide consists of three layers, but only the flesh side of the inner layer and the outer side of the hairy layer may be used for Torah parchment. The method of cleaning and softening the hide, which must be of the best quality, has changed throughout the centuries. During talmudic times, salt and barley flour were sprinkled on the skins which were then soaked in the juice of gallnuts. There is, however, a reference to the use of dogs' dung for this purpose. Nowadays the skins are softened by soaking them in clear water for two days after which the hair is removed by soaking the hides in limewater for nine days. Finally, the skins are rinsed and dried and the creases ironed out with presses. The processor must make a verbal declaration when soaking the skins that his action is being performed for the holiness of the *Sefer Torah.* Whereas reeds were used as pens in the days of the Talmud, quills are used today, the quill of the turkey feather, which is sturdy and long lasting, being preferred. The *sofer* cuts the point of the feather to give it a flat surface, which is desirable for forming the square letters, and then slits it lengthwise.

The ink must be black, durable, but not indelible. During talmudic times a viscous ink was made by heating a vessel with a flame the fuel of which was olive oil; the soot thus produced on the sides of the vessel was scraped off and mixed with oil, honey, and gallnuts (*Shabbat* 23a). Ink is now made by boiling a mixture of gallnuts, gum arabic, and copper sulfate

A scribe in Jaffa, Israel, working on an old Yemenite Torah scroll. He has mixed and boiled the special ink he needs to fill in the erased sections on the scroll. Tel Aviv, Government Press Office.

A skin being dried and "ironed" on a wooden frame at Meron. Tel Aviv, Government Press Office.

Masoretic lists by Aaron Ben-Asher from a tenth century manuscript written in Egypt and found in the Cairo *Genizah.* London, the British Library Board.

Goatskin curing at Meron, Israel, 1950. The skins are dipped first in clear water and then in limewater. Tel Aviv, Government Press Office.

A synagogue in Aden, 1949. The congregation stands respectfully while the *Sefer Torah* is removed from the holy ark for public reading. Jewish Agency Photo Archive.

crystals. Some scribes also add vinegar and alcohol. To ensure that the letters will be straight and the lines equally spaced, 43 thin lines are incised across the width of the parchment with a stylus and ruler. Two additional longitudinal lines are incised at the end of the page to ensure that all the lines end equally. To enhance the appearance of the printing on the parchment a four inch margin is left at the bottom, a three inch margin at the top, and a two inch margin between the columns.

Although there is no law regulating the number of pages or columns a Torah should have, from the beginning of the 19th century a standard pattern of 248 columns of 42 lines each was established. Each column is about five inches wide since by tradition there must be space enough to write the word לְמִשְׁפְּחוֹתֵיהֶם (Genesis 8:19), the longest occuring in the Torah, three times.

Intention. Before the *sofer* begins his daily work, he performs ritual ablution in a *mikveh.* To avoid mistakes talmudic *soferim* copied from another scroll, and according to one tradition there was a copy of the Torah kept in the Temple which scribes used as the standard (TJ, *Shekalim* 4:3). Before commencing, the scribe tests the feather and ink by writing the name "Amalek" and crossing it out, thus symbolically "blotting out Amalek" (cf. Deuteronomy 25:19). He then makes the declaration, "I am writing the Torah in the name of its sanctity and the name of God in its sanctity." The scribe then looks into the *tikkun,* reads the sentence aloud, and proceeds to write it. Before writing the name of God the *sofer* repeats, "I am writing the name of God for the holiness of His name."

Script. The Torah is written in the square script known as *Ketav Ashuri,* of which there are two different types: the Ashkenazi, which resembles the script described in the Talmud, and the Sephardi, which is identical with the printed letters of the Hebrew alphabet currently used in sacred texts. The thickness of the letters varies and it is often necessary for the *sofer* to make several strokes to form a letter. The scribe holds the feather sideways to make thin lines, and flat, so that the entire point writes, to make thick lines. Particular care must be given to those letters that are similar in appearance (e.g. *dalet* and *resh*) so that they can be easily distinguished. Each letter must be complete, with the exception of the "split *vav*" in the word *shalom* in Numbers 25:12. Although Hebrew is read from right to left, the action of writing each individual letter in the *Sefer Torah* is from left to right. Six letters are written particularly small (e.g. the *alef* in the first word of Leviticus 1:1) and 11 letters are written very large (e.g. the *bet* in the first word of Genesis 1:1). There must be a space between the letters, a greater space between the words, and a nine letter gap between the portions. A four line separation is made between each of the Five Books of Moses.

Tagin. Seven of the 22 letters of the alphabet have special designs on the upper left hand corner of the letter called *tagin.* Shaped somewhat like the letter *zayin,* three such *tagin* are placed above the letter just touching it. The center *tag* is slightly higher than the two on the ends. The Torah contains no vowels or punctuation marks. However, there are a number of dots over several words (e.g. Deuteronomy 29:28). There are two *shirot* or songs in the Torah which are

את משנה תורת משה אשר
כתב לפני בני ישראל וכל
ישראל וזקניו ושטרים ושפטים
עמדים מזה ומזה לארון נגד
הכהנים הלוים נשאי ארון
ברית יהוה כגר כאזרח חציו
אל מול הר גרזים והחציו אל
מול הר עיבל כאשר צוה משה

הים הגדול אל מול הלבנון החתי
והאמרי הכנעני הפרזי החוי
והיבוסי ויתקבצו יחדו להלחם
עם יהושע ועם ישראל פה
אחד: וישבי גבעון
שמעו את אשר עשה יהושע
ליריחו ולעי ויעשו גם המה
בערמה וילכו ויצטירו ויקחו

Above: An example of Sephardi square script, an alternative Torah script. This section is from the Book of Joshua and dates from 1207. Paris, Bibliothèque Nationale, Ms. 2235, heb. 82, fol. 10. Below: Earliest surviving example of the fully developed Ashkenazi square script, one of the scripts in which the Torah is written. It dates from 896 c.e. This section is from Malachi 3:18.

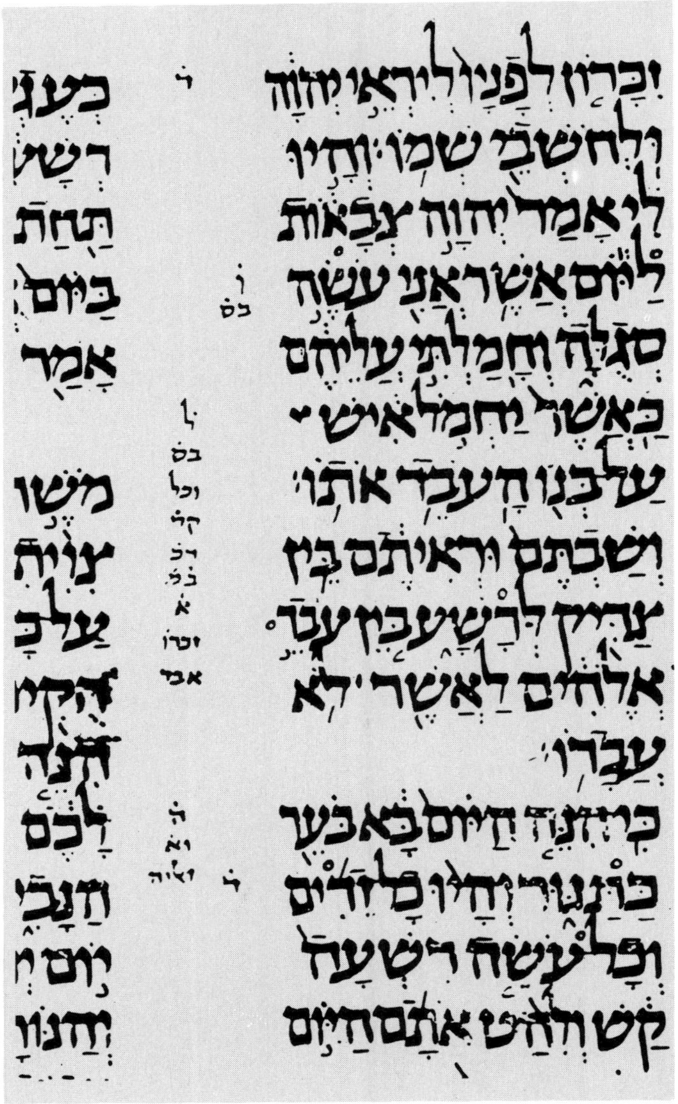

זכרון לפניו ליראי יהוה
ולחשבי שמו: והיו
לי אמר יהוה צבאות
ליום אשר אני עשה
סגלה וחמלתי עליהם
כאשר יחמל איש
על בנו העבד אתו:
ושבתם וראיתם בין
צדיק לרשע בין עבד
אלהים לאשר לא
עבדו:
כי הנה היום בא בער
כתנור והיו כל זדים
וכל עשה רשעה
וקש ולהט אתם היום

written in unique fashion. *Shirat ha-Yam* (Exodus 15:1–19) has a nine letter gap in the middle of each sentence, and these gaps are so spaced that they appear like "half bricks set over whole bricks" (*Megillah* 16b). *Shirat Ha'azinu* (Deuteronomy 32:1–43) also contains a nine letter separation in the middle of each sentence, but these blank spaces form a single space down the center of the entire column.

SEWING. After the copying of the Torah has been completed, the sheets of parchment are sewn together with *giddin*, a special thread made of tendon tissue taken from the foot muscles of a kosher animal. Every four pages are sewn together to form a section or *yeri'ah*. These sections of parchment are sewn on the outer side of the parchment, with one inch left unsewn both at the very top and bottom. To reinforce the *giddin*, thin strips of parchment are pasted on the top and bottom of the page. After connecting the sheets the ends are tied to wooden rollers, *aẓei ḥayyim*, by inserting the *giddin* in the holes in the rollers. The *eẓ ḥayyim* consists of a center pole, with handles of wood and discs to support the rolled-up scroll. Besides serving as a means of rolling the scroll, the *aẓei ḥayyim* also prevent people from touching the holy parchment with their hands. In Oriental and some Sephardi communities, the discs are not employed since the Torah scrolls are kept in an ornamental wooden or metal case.

INVALID SIFREI TORAH. Mistakes in the Torah scroll can generally be corrected, since the ink can be erased with a knife and pumice stone. However, a mistake in the writing of any of the names of God cannot be corrected since the name of God may not be erased, and such faulty parchments must be discarded. When a mistake is found in a *Sefer Torah,* the wimple is tied round the outside of its mantle as a sign that it should not be used for the statutory synagogue reading until the mistake has been corrected. According to the Talmud a *Sefer Torah* which has less than 85 correct letters is to be discarded (*Yadayim* 3:5). This number is the number of letters in Numbers 10:35–36, which is sometimes regarded as a separate book. However, it was later laid down that too extensive corrections rendered the scroll unsightly and therefore invalid. If a scroll is beyond repair, it is placed in an earthenware urn and buried in the cemetery; in Talmud times it was customary to bury such scrolls alongside the resting place of a prominent rabbi. The Mishnah (*Gittin* 4:6) permits the purchase of a *Sefer Torah* from a non-Jew at its market value and the Talmud (*ibid.,* 45b) even records that Rabban Simeon ben Gamaliel permitted the purchase of those written by a non-Jew. Another tradition, however, laid it down that a scroll written by a non-Jew must be stored away, while one written by a heretic must be burned since it is feared that he may have maliciously altered the text (*ibid.*).

THE DUTY TO POSSESS A SEFER TORAH. It is regarded as a positive biblical commandment for

ויהי בימי אחשורוש הוא אחשורוש המלך
מהדו ועד כוש שבע ועשרים ומאה מדינה
בימים ההם כשבת המלך אחשורוש על
כסא מלכותו אשר בשושן הבירה בשנת
שלוש למלכו עשה משתה לכל שריו
ועבדיו חיל פרס ומדי הפרתמים ושרי
המדינות לפניו בהראתו את עשר כבוד

Beginning of the Scroll of Esther with *tagin* on the appropriate letters. Courtesy L.I. Rabinowitz, Jerusalem.

A scribe working on the Book of Genesis in Jaffa, Israel, February 1960. He gives his full attention to his precise and exacting task. Tel Aviv, Government Press Office.

Shirat ha-Yam from the Book of Exodus, set out in traditional manner. The decoration of splayed dots is an unusual embellishment. Jerusalem, Jewish National and University Library.

הבאים אחריהם בים לא נשאר בהם עד אחד ובני ישראל הלכו
ביבשה בתוך הים והמים להם חמה מימינם ומשמאלם ויושע
יהוה ביום ההוא את ישראל מיד מצרים וירא ישראל את מצרים
מת על שפת הים וירא ישראל את היד הגדלה אשר עשה יהוה
במצרים וייראו העם את יהוה ויאמינו ביהוה ובמשה עבדו

אז ישיר משה ובני ישראל את השירה הזאת ליהוה ויאמרו
לאמר אשירה ליהוה כי גאה גאה סוס
ורכבו רמה בים עזי וזמרת יה ויהי לי
לישועה זה אלי ואנוהו אלהי
אבי וארממנהו יהוה איש מלחמה יהוה
שמו מרכבת פרעה וחילו ירה בים ומבחר
שלשיו טבעו בים סוף תהמת יכסימו ירדו במצולת כמו
אבן ימינך יהוה נאדרי בכח ימינך
יהוה תרעץ אויב וברב גאונך תהרס
קמיך תשלח חרנך יאכלמו כקש וברוח
אפיך נערמו מים נצבו כמו נד
נזלים קפאו תהמת בלב ים אמר
אויב ארדף אשיג אחלק שלל תמלאמו
נפשי אריק חרבי תורישמו ידי נשפת
ברוחך כסמו ים צללו כעופרת במים
אדירים מי כמכה באלם יהוה מי
כמכה נאדר בקדש נורא תהלת עשה
פלא נטית ימינך תבלעמו ארץ נחית
בחסדך עם זו גאלת נהלת בעזך אל נוה
קדשך שמעו עמים ירגזון חיל
אחז ישבי פלשת אז נבהלו אלופי
אדום אילי מואב יאחזמו רעד נמגו
כל ישבי כנען תפל עליהם אימתה
ופחד בגדל זרועך ידמו כאבן עד
יעבר עמך יהוה עד יעבר עם זו
קנית תבאמו ותטעמו בהר נחלתך מכון
לשבתך פעלת יהוה מקדש אדני כוננו
ידיך יהוה ימלך לעלם ועד כי
בא סוס פרעה ברכבו ובפרשיו בים וישב יהוה עלהם את מי
הים ובני ישראל הלכו ביבשה בתוך הים

ותקח מרים הנביאה אחות אהרן את התף בידה ותצאן כל הנשים
אחריה בתפים ובמחלת ותען להם מרים שירו ליהוה כי גאה גאה
סוס ורכבו רמה בים ויסע משה את ישראל מים סוף
ויצאו אל מדבר שור וילכו שלשת ימים במדבר ולא מצאו מים
ויבאו מרתה ולא יכלו לשתת מים ממרה כי מרים הם על כן קרא

Torah scrolls from the Lemnoria synagogue desecrated during the pogroms in Kishinev, Russia, in 1903. Jerusalem, JNUL. Memorial album of the Kishinev pogrom.

Silver Torah pointer dated 1883. It is embossed with an eagle, a stag and a lion, after the verse in the Ethics of the Fathers, "Be light as the eagle, skillful as the stag and strong as the lion." Prague, State Jewish Museum.

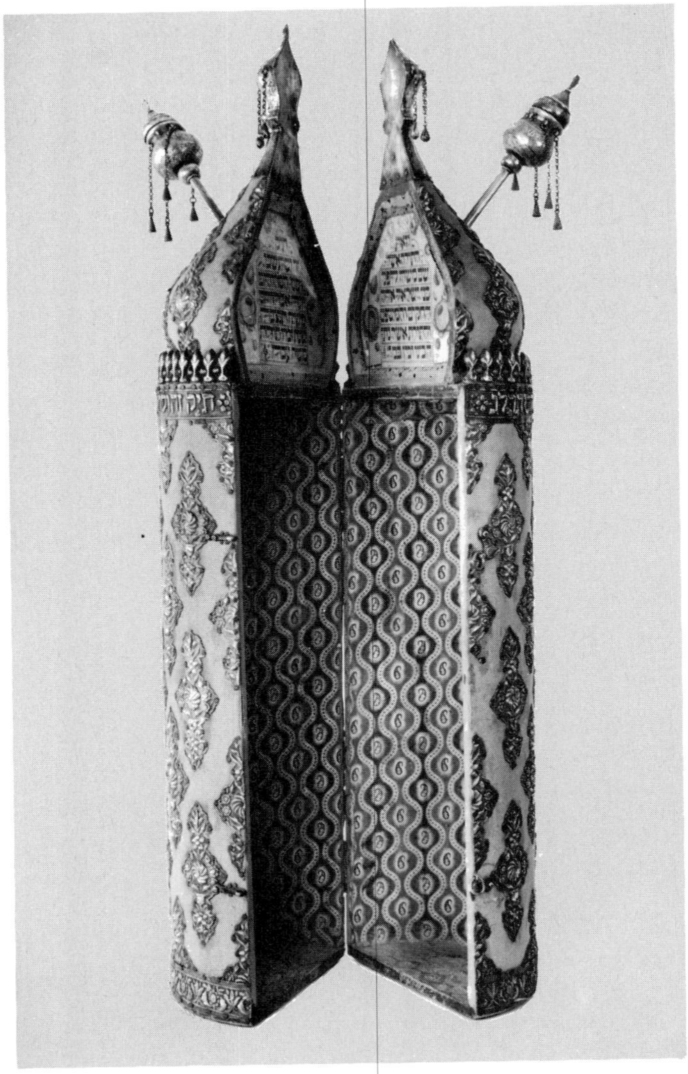

A 19th-century Sephardi Torah case. It is made of leather, silver and cloth and comes from Persia. Jerusalem, Israel Museum.

every Jew to possess a *Sefer Torah;* the word "song" in Deuteronomy 31:19, "now therefore write this song for yourself," was interpreted as applying to the Torah as a whole. Even if he has inherited one from his father a man is still obliged to have one of his own according to the Talmud. He may write it himself, or have it written on his behalf by a *sofer,* or purchase one, but "he who writes it himself is regarded as though it had been given to him on Mt. Sinai."

On the basis of the statement of the Talmud (*Menaḥot* 30a) to the effect that he who merely corrects even one letter in a *Sefer Torah* is regarded as though he had himself written it, a custom has developed which both gives every Jew a portion in a *Sefer Torah* and symbolically regards him as having fulfilled the command of writing one. The *sofer* writes only the outlines of the words in the first and last passages of

Torah scrolls carried through West 16th Street in New York City, at the dedication of a new Young Israel synagogue.

Earthenware urns found at Masada. It was customary to bury Torah scrolls that were beyond repair in urns such as these. Courtesy Yigael Yadin, Jerusalem, Israel Museum.

the *Sefer Torah* and they are completed at a ceremony known as *Siyyum ha-Torah* (the completion of the Torah). Those present are honored by each being invited to fill in one of the hollow letters.

THE SANCTITY OF THE SEFER TORAH. The *Sefer Torah* is the most sacred of all Jewish books. A valid *Sefer Torah* must be treated with special sanctity and great reverence. Its sanctity is higher that that of all other scrolls of the books of the Bible, and therefore, though one *Sefer Torah* may be placed on top of another, or on the scroll of another book, another scroll must not be placed on it.

It is obligatory to stand in the presence of a *Sefer Torah* (*Kiddushin* 33b) both when it is revealed when the ark is opened and when it is being carried, and it is customary to bow reverently or kiss it when it passes. The bare parchment must not be touched with the hand. So insistent were the rabbis on this that they declared "He who touches a naked *Sefer Torah* will be buried naked," although the statement was modified to mean either "naked of good deeds" or

The *Sefer Torah* is ceremoniously raised during a service at the Western Wall, Jerusalem. Photo: David Posner, Jerusalem.

"naked of the reward for good deeds" which he would otherwise have had from reading it. For this reason the *yad* ("pointer") is used for reading and the Sephardim cover the outside of the parchment with silk for the same reason.

It was forbidden to sell a *Sefer Torah* except to provide the means for marrying, studying, and for the ransom of captives. Should a *Sefer Torah* accidentally fall to the ground, the whole congregation is obliged to fast for that day. It was permitted and even enjoined to disregard the Sabbath in order to save not only the *Sefer Torah* but even its case from destruction, and should it be burnt one had to rend one's garment as an act of mourning; if one saw it torn one had to rend the garment twice, "once for the writing and once for the parchment." The *Sefer Torah* must not be carried about unless for religious purposes, and even for the purpose of reading from it at services held at a temporary place of worship, such as a house of mourning, it may not be taken unless it is read there on at least three occasions. When it is transferred to a permanent site it is usually done with full ceremonial. The *Sefer Torah* is carried through the streets under a canopy and the procession is accompanied by songs and dances.

Among the Sephardim before the reading of the law, and among the Ashkenazim at the conclusion, the *Sefer Torah* is ceremoniously held aloft, its writing exposed to the congregation, who recite "and this is the Torah which Moses set before the children of Israel (Deuteronomy 4:44), according to the commandment of the Lord by the hand of Moses." One must make every effort to acquire a beautiful *Sefer Torah*. Unless it is corrected, a text of the *Sefer Torah* that is in error may be kept only 30 days.

3. the manuscript

The term Hebrew Manuscript includes religious and secular books, as well as letters and documents written on papyrus, parchment, hides, and paper in Hebrew characters, sometimes using them for the writing of languages other than Hebrew, such as Aramaic, Yiddish, Ladino. Hebrew manuscripts have been preserved in archives and public and private libraries. It has been estimated that there are about 60,000 manuscripts (codices) and about 200,000 fragments in existence; most of the latter have come from the Cairo *Genizah* and a certain number from the finds in the Judean Desert.

NON-ILLUMINATED MANUSCRIPTS

500 B.C.E. – 500 C.E. Documents and letters, some with accurate dates, have been preserved from the period of 500 b.c.e. to 500 c.e. The most important of them are a collection of papyri from Elephantine and Assuan in Egypt (494–407 b.c.e.); papyri from Edfu, also in Egypt, are thought to belong to the third century b.c.e., as are parts of the Book of Jeremiah and fragments of II Samuel among the Dead Sea Scrolls. The other scrolls from the Judean Desert are regarded as dating from the second century b.c.e. to the Bar Kokhba War (132–135 c.e.), including some written or dictated by Bar Kokhba himself.

David Kimḥi's commentary to the Book of Psalms (opening page). The page comes from the *Corinaldi Bible,* Ferrara, 1396. Florence, Biblioteca Medicea Laurenziana, fol. 672.

500 – 1500. No material is available which can be proven with any certainty as belonging to the first centuries of this period. The oldest manuscripts of the period date from the end of the ninth century although information has been published on a biblical manuscript in Leningrad dated to 846. On the other hand, some of the fragments found in the Cairo *Genizah* belong, without doubt, to the beginning of this period and possibly even to the end of the previous one. The development of Hebrew paleography will presumably make it possible to determine with greater accuracy the dates of these of these most valuable fragments.

BIBLE AND BIBLE EXEGESIS. The oldest dated biblical manuscripts are: the Prophets vocalized by Moses Ben-Asher, which was found in the Karaite synagogue of Cairo and written in Tiberias in 895 (figure 3); the Latter Prophets, with the Babylonian system of punctuation, in the Saltykov-Shchedrin Library in Leningrad which was copied in 916; and a Pentateuch which was copied by Solomon ben Buya'a (who also prepared, according to a note at its end, the so-called *Keter Aram Ẓova,* later vocalized by Aaron Ben-Asher ; figure 4) in 929 and vocalized by his brother Ephraim ben Buya'a (it appears that both were active in Tiberias). The *Keter Aram Ẓova* (*keter,* "crown," is an appellation for a Bible codex; *Aram Ẓova,* "Aleppo") is at the Ben-Zvi Institute, Jerusalem. There are biblical manuscripts in the Saltykov-Shchedrin Library and others, which, according to their colophons, were written during the tenth century, but doubts have been raised as to the reliability of these colophons. Finally, there is the Bible manuscript in Leningrad which was written in 1009 in Egypt. The text is complete and the date appears to be authentic.

MISHNAH, TOSEFTA, TALMUD, AND HALAKHIC MIDRASHIM. The oldest dated manuscripts of the Mishnah are: Paris Manuscripts 328/9, the complete text with Maimonides' commentary and written and vocalized by Joab ben Jehiel, known as the "Physician of Beth-El," from the province of Cesena (Italy), between 1399 and 1401. Individual orders *(sedarim)* written and vocalized (in part) from 1168 (*Zera'im, Nezikin, Kodashim*) are in Oxford (nos. 393, 404), and *Mo'ed* of the same set is in the Sassoon Library (no. 72). Not dated but definitely early works are: Kaufmann Number 50 (facsimile edited by G. Baer, 1929; figure 5) and Parma Number 138. The oldest Tosefta manuscripts are Erfurt Number 159, which was thought to have been written in 1150, and

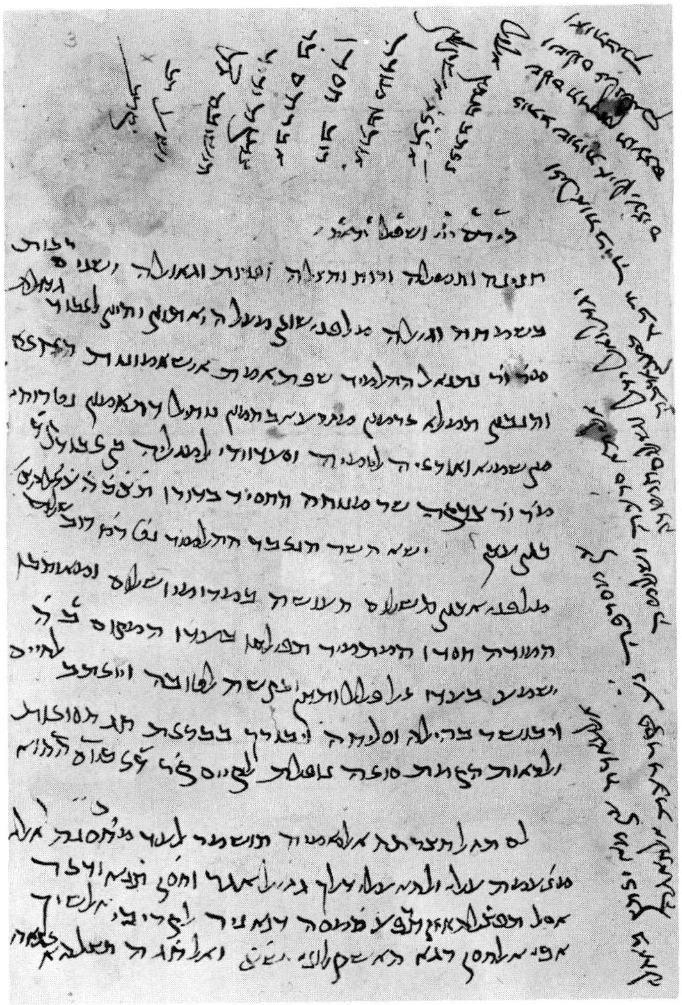

Figure 1. Letter written in Palestine in 1114 c.e. Cambridge University Library T-S 13-J 13/3.

Figure 2. Legal document of Palestine, 1021 c.e. Oxford, Bodleian Library Ms. Heb. b. 12 fol. 24r.

Figure 3. A page from the Prophets, vocalized by Moses Ben-Asher, in one of the oldest dated biblical manuscripts, 895 C.E.

Figure 4. A page from *Keter Aram Ẓova.* Jerusalem, Ben-Zevi Institute.

Vienna Number 46. The oldest dated halakhic Midrashim are: Sifra of 1073 (Vatican Library, no. 31) and Sifra of 1291 (Oxford, no. 151), which also includes the *Mekhilta.* The only manuscript of the Jerusalem Talmud, which was written in 1299 by Jehiel ben Jekuthiel ben Benjamin, the Physician, is at Leyden. There is also only one complete extant manuscript of the Babylonian Talmud (Munich, Bayerische Staatsbibliothek, Cod. Heb. 95; figure 6). It was written "on the twelfth of the month of Kislev, in the year 103 of the sixth millennium" (1342) by Solomon ben Samson, probably in France (facsimile edited by H. Strack, 1912). At the end of this manuscript several minor tractates are added. Individual tractates from 1176 and after have been preserved in the Library of Florence, as well as a manuscript from 1184 in the Hamburg Library and in the Jewish Theological Seminary of America Library.

AGGADIC MIDRASHIM. Among the extant manuscripts of aggadic Midrashim are *Genesis Rabbah* and *Leviticus Rabbah* from 1291 *(Bibliothèque Nationale* of Paris, no. 149). There is a manuscript from the same year of the *Pesikta de-Rav Kahana* in the Bodleian. The Parma Library possesses a manuscript from 1270 (no. 1240) which contains *Song of Songs*

Figure 5. Page from a manuscript of the Mishnah written between 12th and 14th centuries, listed as Kaufmann No. 50. Budapest, Library of the Hungarian Academy of Sciences, Kaufmann Collection.

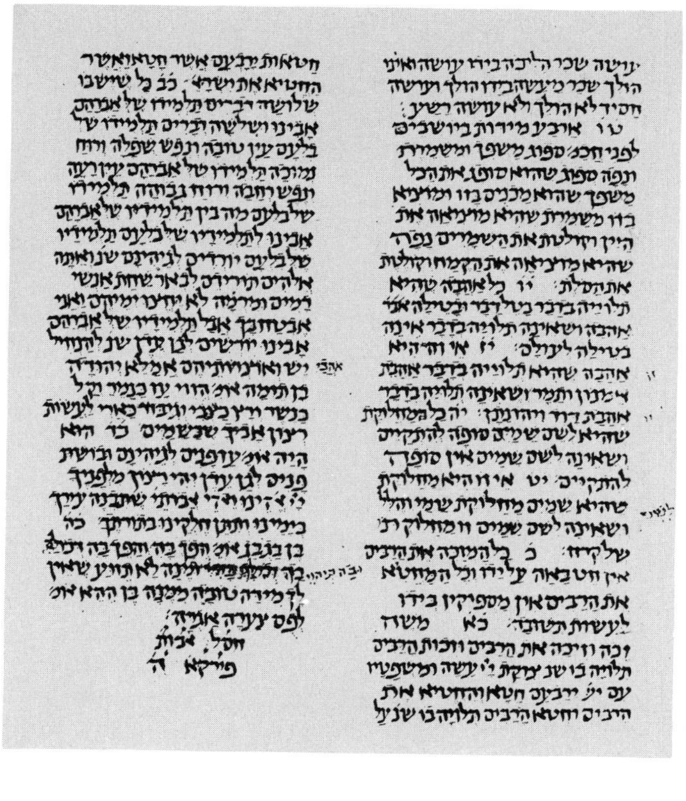

COLLECTIONS OF HEBREW MANUSCRIPTS

PLACE	NUMBER AND OTHER DETAILS	CATALOG
AUSTRIA		
Vienna:		
Nationalbibliothek	216; 308 fragments	A. Z. Schwarz, 1925
Bibliothek der Isr. Kultusgemeinde	215: 40 transferred to the Jewish Historical Institute, Warsaw	A. Z. Schwarz-Oesterreich, 1932
DENMARK		
Copenhagen:		
The Royal Library	244	N. Allony-E. Kupfer, 1964
ENGLAND		
Cambridge:		
Trinity College Library	160	H. Loewe, 1926
University Library	1,000; 100,000 fragments	S. Schiller-Szinessy, 1876
Westminster College Library	3,000 fragments	
Leeds:		
University Library	371	C. Roth (Alexander Marx Jubilee Volume, 1950)
Letchworth:		
D. S. Sassoon Collection	1,220	D. S. Sassoon, 1932
London:		
Bet Din and Bet Ha-Midrash	161	A. Neubauer, 1886
British Museum	2,467; 10,000 fragments, includes the first part of the Gaster Collection	G. Margoliouth, 1899–1935
Jews College Library	580; Montefiore Collection	H. Hirschfeld (JQR, 1902–03)
Manchester:		
John Rylands Library	750; 10,000 fragments; second part of the Gaster Collection	E. Robertson, 1938–62 (only the Samaritan Mss.)
Oxford:		
Bodleian Library	2,650; 10,000 fragments	A. Neubauer-A. E. Cowly, 1886–1906
FRANCE		
Paris:		
Bibliothèque de l'Alliance Universelle	338; 4,000 fragments	M. Schwab (REJ, 1904, 1912); B. Chapira (REJ, 1904)
Bibliothèque Nationale	1,459	H. Zotenberg, 1886
Ecole Rabbinique de France	172	M. Abraham (REJ, 1924–25)
Strassbourg:		
Bibliothèque Nationale et Universitaire	176; 292 fragments	S. Landauer, 1881
GERMANY		
Berlin:		
Preussische Staatsbibliothek	510	M. Steinschneider, 1878–97 N. Allony-D. S. Loewinger, 1957
Frankfort:		
Stadt- und Universitats-bibliothek	400; 10,000 fragments; 10,000 Geniza fragments lost during World War II	R. N. N. Rabbinowitz, 1888; N. Allony–D. S. Loewinger. 1957; includes the Merzbacher Collection
Hamburg:		
Stadtbibliothek	476	M. Steinschneider, 1878; includes the Levy Collection
Munich:		
Bayerische Staatsbibliothek	476	M. Steinschneider, 1895; E. Roth, 1966
HUNGARY		
Budapest:		
Hungarian Academy of Sciences	595; 600 fragments; Kaufmann Collection	M. Weisz, 1906; D. S. Loewinger-A. Scheiber, 1947
Library of the Jewish Theological Seminary	315; 400 fragments	D. S. Loewinger, 1940
ITALY		
Florence:		
Biblioteca Mediceo Laurenziana	187	A. M. Biscioni, 1757
Leghorn:		
Talmud Torah	134; part transferred to Jewish National and University Library, Jerusalem	C. Bernheimer, 1915
Mantua:		
Communita Israelitica	167	M. Mortara, 1878
Milan:		
Biblioteca Ambrosiana	183	C. Bernheimer, 1933; N. Allony-E. Kupfer (*Areshet*, 1960)
Parma:		
Biblioteca Palatina	1,552	G. B. De-Rossi, 1803; P. Perreau, 1880

Rome:		
Biblioteca Casanatense	230	G. Sacerdote, 1897
Biblioteca Apostolica Vaticana	(See Vatican below)	
Turin:		
Biblioteca Nazionale	247; a great part destroyed by fire in 1904	B. Peyron, 1880
ISRAEL		
Jerusalem:		
National and University Library	6,000	G. Scholem, 1930; B. Joel, 1934
N. Ben-Menahem	120	
Hechal Shlomo	150	J. L. Bialer, 1966–69
Mosad ha-Rav Kook	1,000	N. Ben-Menahem (*Areshet,* 1959)
Ben-Zvi Institute	1,100	
Schocken Library	400	
Ramat Gan:		
Bar-Ilan University Library	750; Margulies Collection	
Tel Aviv:		
Bialik House	200	
NETHERLANDS		
Amsterdam:		
Portugeesch Israelitisch Seminarium Etz Haim-Livraria D. Montezinos	160	N. Allony-E. Kupfer, 1964
Universiteitsbibliotheek	305; Rosenthaliana	M. Roest, 1875; N. Allony-E. Kupfer, 1964
Leiden:		
Bibliotheek der Universiteit	118	M. Steinschneider, 1858
POLAND		
Warsaw:		
Jewish Historical Institute	1,500	E. Kupfer-S. Strelcyn (Przeglad Orientalisticzny, 1954–55)
Wroclaw (Breslau):		
Jewish Theological Seminary of Breslau	405; partly transferred to the Jewish Historical Institute, Warsaw	D. S. Loewinger-B. Weinryb, 1965
SWITZERLAND		
Zurich:		
Zentralbibliothek	238	L. C. Wohlberg, 1932; N. Allony-E. Kupfer, 1964
U.S.A.		
Cincinnati:		
Hebrew Union College Library	1,500	
Los Angeles:		
University Library	400; Rosenberg Collection from Ancona; third part of the Gaster Collection, etc.	
New Haven:		
Yale University Library	300	L. Nemoy (Journal of Jewish Bibliography, 1938–39)
New York:		
Columbia University	1,000	
Jewish Theological Seminary	10,000; 25,000 fragments	E. N. Adler, 1921 JTS Registers, 1902 ff.
Jewish Institute of Religion—Hebrew Union College	200	
Jewish Teachers Seminary Library	120	
R. H. Lehmann Collection	400	
The New York University, Jewish Culture Foundation Library	114	
Yeshiva University	1,000	
Yivo Institute for Jewish Research	1,200	
Philadelphia:		
Dropsie College for Hebrew and Cognate Learning	256; 500 fragments	B. Halpern, 1924
San Francisco:		
California State Library	167; Sutro Collection	W. M. Brinner, 1966
U.S.S.R.		
Leningrad:		
M. S. Saltykov-Shchedrin State Library	1,962; 15,000 fragments; includes the Firkovich Collection	A. Harkavy-H. L. Strack, 1875; A. I. Katsch, 1957–58; 1970
Asiatic Museum	2,347	
Moscow:		
Lenin State Library	2,000; Ginzburg Collection	
VATICAN:		
Biblioteca Apostolica Vaticana	801	U. Cassuto, 1956; N. Allony-D. S. Loewinger, 1968

Figure 6. Page from the earliest complete manuscript of the Babylonian Talmud, copied by Solomon ben Samson in 1342, probably in France. It is known as the Munich Codex. Munich, Staatsbibliothek, Cod. Heb. 95 fol. 248r.

Rabbah, Lamentations Rabbah, Tanḥuma, Pesikta Rabbati, Midrash Proverbs, and others.

MISCELLANEA. Thousands of medieval manuscripts in the fields of philosophy and Kabbalah are extant; these are as numerous as those in medicine, astronomy, astrology, geography, and other natural sciences. A considerable number of these manuscripts are translations from Greek, Arabic, and other languages spoken and written in the countries of the Diaspora. Polemics, poetry, philology (grammar, dictionaries, *masorah*), history, sectarian literature, *halakhah* (responsa, novellae, codes, ritual compendiums), ethics, and homiletics are well represented, as is liturgy (*siddurim* and *maḥzorim*). Due to their constant use many tens of thousands of them were stored away in *genizot* after being worn and damaged. Occasionally autographs were also preserved, i.e., either manuscripts from the hand of the author, such as Maimonides' Mishnah commentary and miscellaneous writings (ed. S.D. Sassoon, 1966), or confirmations of the correctness of the copy as the one added by Maimonides to a copy of his code: "Corrected from my [original] copy, I, Moses, son of Maimon of blessed memory" (Oxford Ms. 577).

1500–1970. Manuscripts of this last period are also extant; some of them have been published, some not. A considerable number of the manuscripts of this period were written in countries where there were no Hebrew presses (e.g. the Yemen). They were either contemporary works or those of earlier periods, but some were copied from printed works which had reached them from Western countries and are therefore of no original value. Manuscripts written by the authors themselves are of special importance because of their corrections. They make it possible to reconstruct the original text and compare it with other copies, either handwritten or printed editions. Early authorities, who wrote in the early years after the appearance of printing, made use of manuscripts of classic books and commentaries. In later centuries this practice naturally waned.

OWNERS AND COLLECTIONS. At the beginning and the end of manuscripts it was customary to note the name of the owner, with a formula such as "a man should always sign his name in his book lest a man from the street come and say it is mine." Owners, who usually were scholars, often added notes of their own to the text. At times, the names of several generations of a single family appear in these lists, and well-known names in Jewish literature and history are found among the owners, e.g. a manuscript of Maimonides' *Guide* (1472, Parma 660) belonged successively to David, Abraham, and Moses Provencale (father, son, and grandson).

Modern manuscript catalogs generally register these notes and lists in detail. The same pages were also used to commemorate family and general events, and documents which are sometimes of great historical value were also copied on them, although they may have no connection with the contents of the manuscript. Among this material are lists of books describing whole or parts of private collections. Such lists shed light on the cultural standards of various periods and environments. The prices of the manuscripts which are mentioned in them are of particular interest.

COLLECTION OF THE MATERIAL. The Institute for the Photography of Hebrew Manuscripts was founded in 1950 by the Israel Government (Ministry of Education and Culture) in order to enable a comparative processing and registration of all possible

אסרוחנ בעבותי ס ע ל
קרנות המזבח ש את ה
ואורך שהי ארום מ ך
לי כי
ט מ כי
ל שי חסד

כל מעשיד וחסיריך
וצריקים עשיר צונך

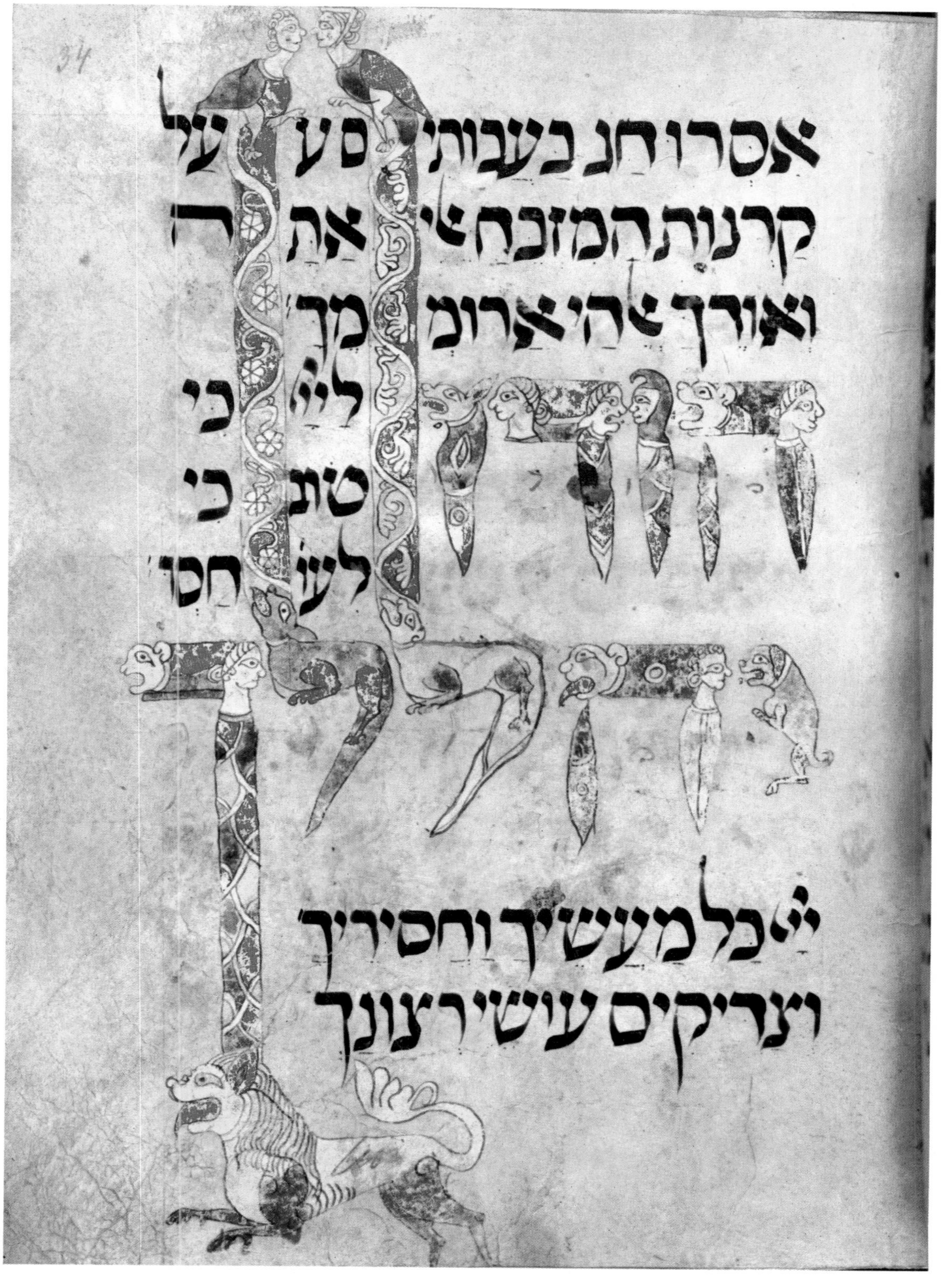

Plate 7. Part of the *Hallel* prayer from the *Haggadah* in the *Hamilton Siddur,* Spain, 13th century. The initial words are composed of painted zoo- and anthropomorphic letters. Berlin, Preussische Staatsbibliothek, Ms. Ham. 288.

Plate 8. A decorated text-page of Psalm 102:5-26 from the *First Gaster Bible,* written in verse form across a double column. The page is decorated with gold lotus bud scrolls in the lower margin, remnants of two large palmette motifs in the outer margin, and stylized scrolls as line fillers. Egypt, 10th or 11th century. London, British Museum, Or. Ms. 9879, fol. 23v.

Plate 9. A page from the *Copenhagen Moreh Nevukhim,* Barcelona, 1348 – Maimonides' *Guide of the Perplexed* translated into Hebrew by Samuel ben Judah ibn Tibbon. Shown is an astronomer holding an astrolabe and discussing the laws of nature and the attributes of God with his fellow philosophers. Copenhagen, Det Kongelige Bibliotek, Cod. Heb. 37, fol. 114

אז לא אבוש בהביטי אל מ

מצותיך

כל המצות שנתנו לו למשה בסיני בפירושן נתנו שנא'
ואתנה לך את לוחת האבן והתורה והמצוה. תורה זו
תורה שבכתב ומצוה זו פירושה וצונו לעשות התורה
על פי המצוה ומצוה זו היא הנקראת תורה שבעל פה.
כל התורה כתבה משה רבנו קודם שימות בכתב ידו
ונתן ספר לכל שבט ושבט וספר אחד נתנהו בארון
לעד שנא' לקוח את ספר התורה וגו' והמצוה שהיא
פירוש התורה לא כתבה אלא צוה בה לזקנים
וליהושע ולשאר כל ישראל שנא' את כל הדבר
אשר אנכי מצוה אתכם אותו תשמרו לעשות' וגו'
ומפני זה נקראת תורה שבעל פה' ואע"פ שלא נכתבה
תורה שבעל פה למדה משה רבנו כלה בבית דינו
לשבעים זקנים ואלעזר ופינחס ויהושע שלשתם
קבלו ממשה וליהושע שהוא תלמידו של משה
רבנו מסר לו תורה שבעל פה וצוהו עליה וכן יהושע
למד כל ימי חייו על פה' וזקנים רבים קבלו מיהושע
וקבל עלי מן הזקנים ומפינחס' ושמואל קבל מעלי
ובית דינו' ודוד קבל משמואל ובית דינו' ואחיה
השילוני מיוצאי מצרים היה ולוי היה ושמע ממשה
רבנו והיה קטן בימי משה והוא קבל מדוד ובית דינו
אליהו קבל מאחיה השילוני ובית דינו' ואלישע קבל
מאליהו ובית דינו' ויהוידע הכהן קבל מאלישע ובית
דינו' וזכריה קבל מיהוידע ובית דינו' והושע קבל
מזכריה ובית דינו' ועמוס קבל מהושע ובית דינו'
וישעיה קבל מעמוס ובית דינו' ומיכה קבל מישעיה
ובית דינו' ויואל קבל ממיכה ובית דינו' ונחום קבל
מיואל ובית דינו' וחבקוק קבל מנחום ובית דינו'
וצפניה קבל מחבקוק ובית דינו' וירמיה קבל מצפני'
ובית דינו' וברוך בן נריה קבל מירמיה ובית דינו ועזרא
ובית דינו קבלו מברוך ובית דינו' בית דינו של עזרא
הם הנקראים אנשי כנסת הגדלה והם חגי' זכריה
מלאכי ודניאל וחנניה ומישאל ועזריה ונחמיה בן
חכליה ומרדכי בלשן וזרבבל והרבה חכמים עמהם
תשלום מאה ועשרים זקנים האחרון מהם הוא

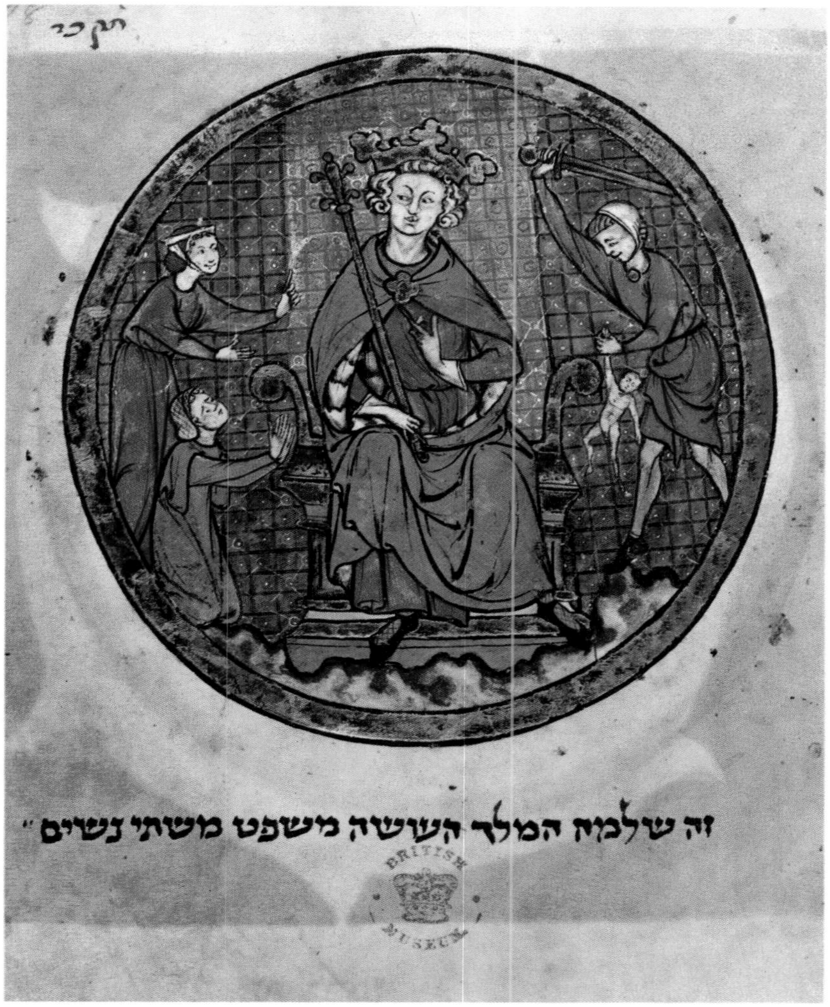

Plate 11. Two full-page miniatures from the *British Museum Miscellany,* Troyes (?), c. 1280. Left: "This is Solomon the King who passes judgment on the two women" (fol. 518). Below: "This is the *menorah* [candelabrum] and Aaron who pours oil into the lamps" (fol. 114). London, British Museum, Add. Ms. 11639.

Plate 10 (opposite). A decorated opening page to the general introduction of the *British Museum Mishneh Torah,* Portugal, 1472. London, British Museum, Harley Ms. 5698.

Plate 12 (above). Two miniatures illustrating a *piyyut* for Ḥanukkah from the *Hamburg Miscellany,* Germany, c. 1427. In the top one Hannah is lamenting her sons who were killed for refusing to bow to idols. The bottom one depicts a Jewess immersing herself in a *mikveh* (ritual bath) before going to her husband who is awaiting her in bed. According to legend the Syrian king forbade the use of *mikva'ot* and, in order to keep Jewish women from sin, God supplied them with secluded ritual baths. Hamburg, Staats- und Universitaetsbibliothik, Cod. Heb. 37.

Plate 13 (opposite). Initial-word panel in a typical page from the *Jerusalem Mishneh Torah,* copied in Spain, 14th century, illuminated in Perugia, Italy, c. 1400. Jerusalem J.N.U.L., Ms. Heb. 4°1193.

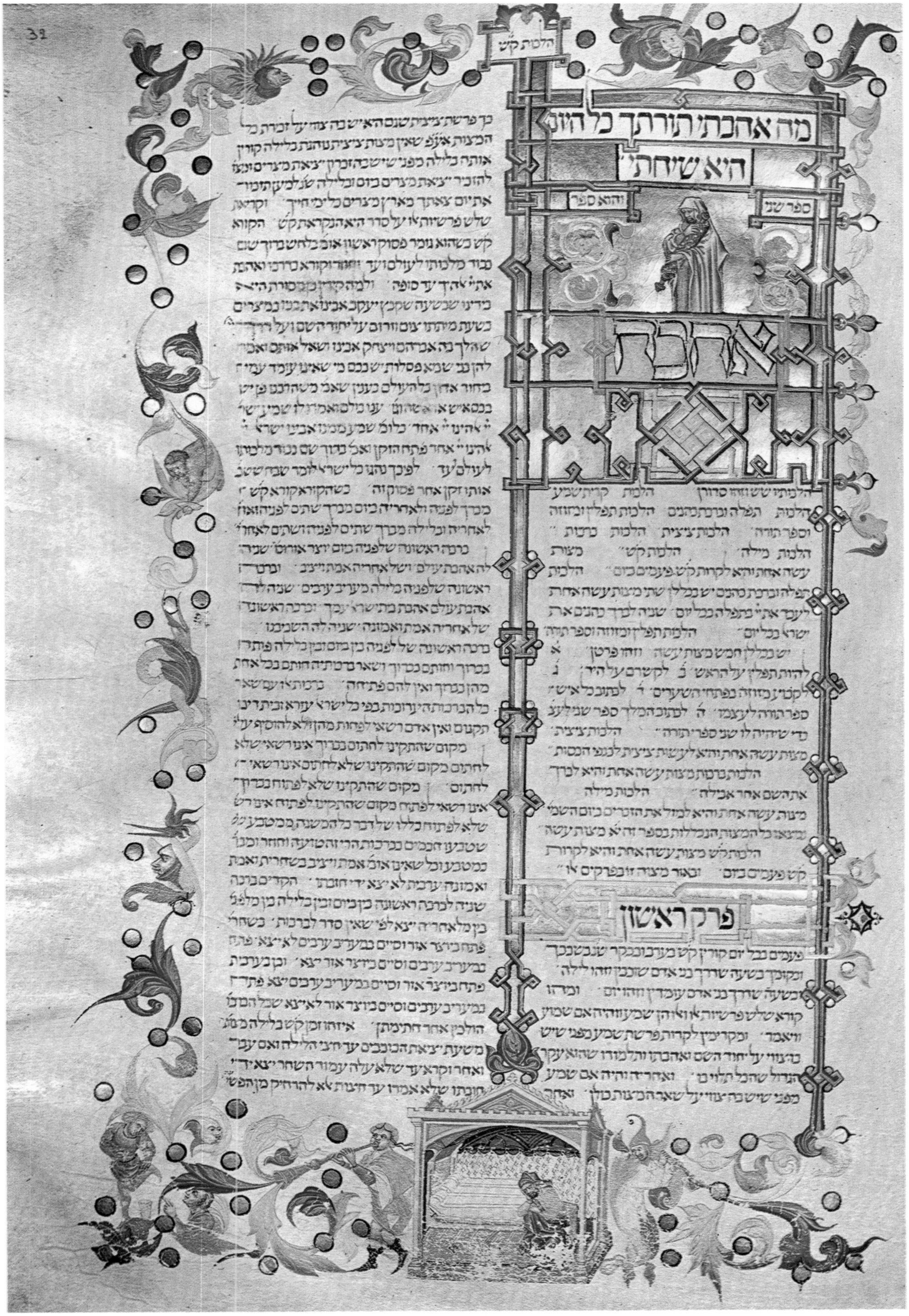
32
הלכות ק״ש
מה אהבתי תורתך כל היום
היא שיחתי
ספר שני והוא ספר
אהבה
פרק ראשון

Plate 14. A page with a decorated title-panel of *Sefer Madda* from Maimonides' *Mishneh Torah,* South Germany, 1310. Budapest, Hungarian Academy of Sciences, Kaufmann Collection, Ms. A. 78, Vol. I, fol. 8v.

material. In 1962 the institute was placed under the authority of the Hebrew University and became affiliated with the National and University Library. During its 24 years of activity the Institute has photographed — mainly in the form of microfilms — approximately half of the collections of manuscripts and fragments scattered throughout the libraries of the world. The most important works which had not been previously published in the form of facsimiles were enlarged by the Institute, as were all the fragments which reached it. Some of the material has been listed in the publications of the Institute. The Jewish Theological Seminary of America houses the Louis Ginzberg Microfilm Collection, which aims at the microfilming of important Hebrew manuscripts from all over the world. The list on pages 36-37 includes all libraries containing over 100 Hebrew or Samaritan manuscripts. The numbers of the manuscripts and fragments are given as well as the names of the authors of the catalogs and the year of their publication. The numbers of the manuscripts given here are not always identical with those which are classified in the catalogs, as additions were acquired after the catalogs were published.

ILLUMINATED MANUSCRIPTS

HELLENISTIC TIMES. It is impossible to state with any degree of certainty how far back in history the tradition of the illuminated Hebrew manuscripts began. The oldest extant specimens belong to the Muslim environment, in the ninth century; but it is out of the question that the practice began at this period, and indications are not lacking which suggest a longer history. It may well be, in fact, that the illumination of Hebrew manuscripts goes back even as far as the Hellenistic period, although no specimens have survived.

During recent years, archaeological discoveries have revealed that it was the practice in the Roman period to adorn synagogues in Palestine with mosaic floors which embodied not only decorative features and animal figures but also graphic representations of biblical scenes and personalities; the walls might be covered with frescoes depicting in great detail entire cycles of Bible history, with possibly some special symbolic significance, such as have survived in the third-century synagogue at Dura-Europos (figure 8). If this was considered legitimate in the actual place of worship, notwithstanding the ostensibly stringent biblical prohibition of "graven images," it is hardly possible that a greater degree of anti-iconic strictness was observed as regards objects such as manuscripts, which were intended for domestic use. According to some, Dura-Europos frescoes were based on pictorial versions which adorned manuscript texts of the Bible.

EARLY CHRISTIAN MANUSCRIPTS. The earliest extant Christian illuminated manuscripts of the Bible are, as it happens, of Old Testament books, such as the so-called *Vienna Genesis* (figure 9), and are conjectured by some scholars to have been based on Jewish prototypes. It is significant too that the favorite topics for early Christian religious art, in churches, catacombs, sarcophagi, and minor objects, were based on Old rather than New Testament subjects (the sacrifice of Isaac, the story of Jonah, and so on), again perhaps suggesting Jewish prototypes, and it is

Figure 7. A fragment of a ninth-century mercantile document in Persian, written in Hebrew characters. London, British Museum, Ms. Or. 8212 No. 166.

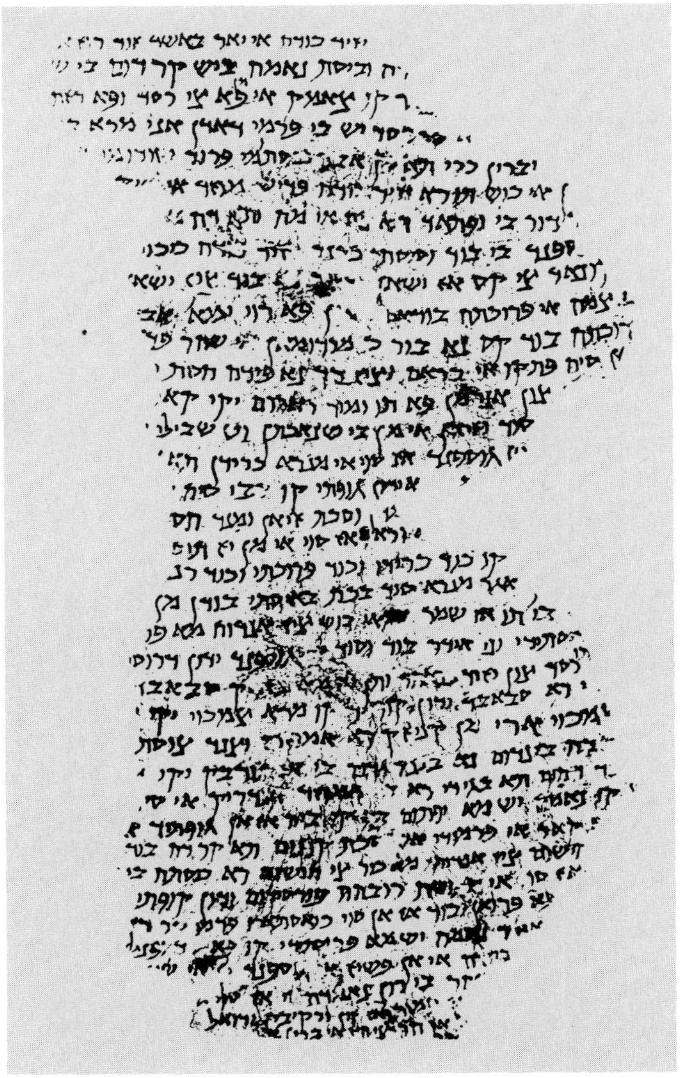

Figure 8. Fresco from the synagogue at Dura-Europos depicting the childhood of Moses. E.R. Goodenough, *Jewish Symbols in the Greco-Roman Period*, Vol. II, Bollingen Foundation, New York.

noteworthy that precisely these subjects reemerge (rather than emerge) as favorite topics in the Jewish manuscript and religious art of the Middle Ages. Christian illuminated Bible manuscripts in the medieval heyday often elaborate the plain narrative with materials reflecting rabbinic legend; and it is a moot point whether this resulted from an antecedent Jewish art or from the common store of medieval folklore. An illustration in the seventh-century Latin *Ashburnham Pentateuch* (figure 10) shows Adam and Eve dressed in animal skins, standing under a booth which, according to the Jewish Midrash, had been built for them by God. Such Jewish legends appear as early as the third century, on the walls of the Dura-Europos synagogue; in the episode of the finding of Moses, for instance, Jochebed and Miriam, Moses' mother and sister, are identified with Shifrah and Puah, the two midwives.

Furthermore, there are certain motifs in the illuminated medieval Hebrew Bibles – a tradition going back to the tenth or eleventh century – which seem to carry on the tradition of very remote antiquity, reflected both in the early Jewish monuments of the classical period on the one hand, and in Christian illuminated codices on the other. The outstanding example of this is the conventional representation of the sanctuary and its vessels which are represented also in the seventh-century Latin *Codex Amiatinus* (Florence, Laurenziana, Ms. Amiat. 1) – confessedly based on an oriental prototype – and in early Jewish monumental art. There are indications that the conventional figure of the Evangelist prefixed to early

Figure 9. "Jacob foretelling the destinies of his sons." From the *Vienna Genesis*, one of the earliest surviving Christian illuminated manuscripts of the Bible. Austrian National Library, Vindobon Theol. Gk. 31.

Latin and Greek texts of the Gospels may also have a Jewish antecedent: indeed, the parallel figure in the *Codex Amiatinus* (figure 11) shows not an Evangelist but Ezra the scribe, apparently wearing the Jewish phylactery, a feature hardly imaginable in a Christian archetype. The Hellenistic Jewish biblical illustrations need not have been attached to a complete Hebrew Bible. It is probable that they illustrated a narrative paraphrase, including many legends, of some books of the Bible, like the Pentateuch, Joshua, Judges, and Kings. The paraphrase may have been in Greek, Aramaic, or Latin, and not necessarily in Hebrew, somewhat like Josephus' *Jewish Antiquities.*

However, J. Gutmann in 1966 opposed the hypothesis of the existence of Hebrew illuminated manuscripts in antiquity by stressing that none survived and by pointing out the fact that the Church Fathers were conversant with midrashic literature and used Jewish legends in their writings. There are, however, no such early Christian illuminated manuscripts, and it is hardly likely that Christian artists went around searching for Jewish legends to illustrate their Bibles. They probably found them in Jewish illuminated paraphrased Bibles, since lost. Jewish wanderings, coupled with the wholesale destruction of Hebrew books by Christian censors, may be responsible for the disappearance of the entire body of evidence. But another adverse element was the periodic triumph among the Jews of anti-iconic principles.

DECORATED TORAH SCROLLS. Some literary evidence of decorated Torah scrolls may indicate their existence in antiquity; this was referred to above in Chapter 1 but deserves brief mention here. The Letter of Aristeas, describing the translation of the Bible by the 72 sages (the Septuagint) states that among the gifts brought to King Ptolemy was a scroll of the Law written entirely in gold. According to the Talmud ". . . if one writes the [Divine] Name in gold, they [the scrolls] must be hidden." This prohibition suggests that Torah scrolls decorated in this fashion did exist. The tractate *Soferim* (1:8) mentions an instance of a Torah scroll belonging to the Alexandrians in which the Names of God were written in gold throughout. Unfortunately, none of the biblical manuscripts found among the Dead Sea Scrolls contains any illustrations.

While there is no conclusive evidence for the existence of Hebrew illuminated manuscripts during the Hellenistic period, there is definite indication of their existence in the East during the Middle Ages, although the exact dates of their origin are not known. The influence of oriental motifs is apparent in all succeeding schools of Hebrew illumination. In Europe, the earliest surviving Hebrew illuminated manuscripts stem from 13th-century Germany. There are a considerably larger number from the 14th century, while their existence during the 15th century is evenly spread thorughout Europe. By the end of the 15th century, the invention of printing caused the decline of all manuscript illumination, including Hebrew, although thereafter a few schools of Hebrew illumination continued to appear, the most important of them in Central Europe in the 18th century.

Figure 10. Illustration from the seventh-century Latin *Ashburnham Pentateuch* showing Adam and Eve dressed in animal skins, standing under a booth built for them by God. Paris, Bibliothèque Nationale, fol. 6 N.A.L. 2334.

Figure 11. Illustration from the *Codex Amiatinus* picturing the scribe, Ezra, wearing *tefillin*. Florence, Biblioteca Laurenziana (f 5 r). From *The Medieval World* by P. Kidson.

THE CHARACTER OF HEBREW MANUSCRIPT ILLUMINATION. Throughout its history, the style of Hebrew illuminated manuscripts was basically dependent on contemporary schools of illumination in each region. Thus, the oriental school is similar to the Muslim, Persian, or Egyptian schools in style as well as motifs, while each of the European regional schools has stylistic and decorative elements directly influenced by the Latin or Greek illumination of the period. However, particular elements became traditional in Hebrew illumination and survived in Europe despite the change in general style during the late Middle Ages. As a result, the style of Hebrew illuminated manuscripts, particularly those executed by minor artists who tended to follow their models more closely, was often outmoded. Although more accomplished artists might use traditional Jewish motifs in their illuminations, they tried to conform to the latest fashion in contemporary styles. Thus it is most difficult to define a Jewish style in any of these schools, even where distinctively Jewish motifs can be found.

Undoubtedly most of the illuminators of the Hebrew books were Jewish. A few of their names are known to us from their colophons, such as Joseph ha-Ẓarefati, the artist of the 1300 c.e. *Cervera Bible* (figure 13) and Joseph ibn Ḥayyim, the artist of the *Kennicott Bible* of 1476 (figure 14). Another Sephardi artist, Joshua ben Abraham ibn Gaon, a masorete and illuminator, specialized in adding illuminated calendars and carpet pages to Bibles (Paris n. 21). The most famous of Ashkenazi artists was Joel ben Simeon, who directed a workshop of scribes and illuminators in Germany and Italy in the second half of the 15th century (figure 15). Other names appear in contracts for book illuminations. In one such example, from Palma de Majorca in 1335, Asher Bonnim Maymo undertakes to copy and illuminate a Bible and two books by Maimonides for David Isaac Cohen. In the 15th century a Portuguese Jew, Abraham ibn Ḥayyim, compiled a treatise on the art of illumination. In Italy Jews were sometimes admitted to the guild of illuminators, as happened in two instances in Perugia, in 1507–08. Most of the artists of the 18th-century schools centered around Bohemia and Moravia are known by name.

GRAVEN IMAGES. The Second Commmandment, prohibiting the making of "graven images" for idolatry, did not restrain Hebrew illumination during the Middle Ages. In fact, whenever Jewish illuminators opposed representational art during the Middle Ages, it was mainly the result of the stricter attitude of their general environment. For instance, the Jews in Muslim countries refrained from depicting human figures in sacred books because of the Muslims' pro-

Figure 12. An example of an illuminated manuscript from 15th century Germany. This is a page from the first *Nuremberg Haggadah.* The initial word is decorated with both human and animal heads, and dragons, a ram, a rabbit and a stag. Jerusalem, Schocken Library ms. 2710 b fol. 14.

Figure 13. Colophon of Joseph ha-Ẓarefati, composed of zoomorphic letters. From the *Cervera Bible*, Spain, 1300. Lisbon, National Library Ms. 72 fol. 449.

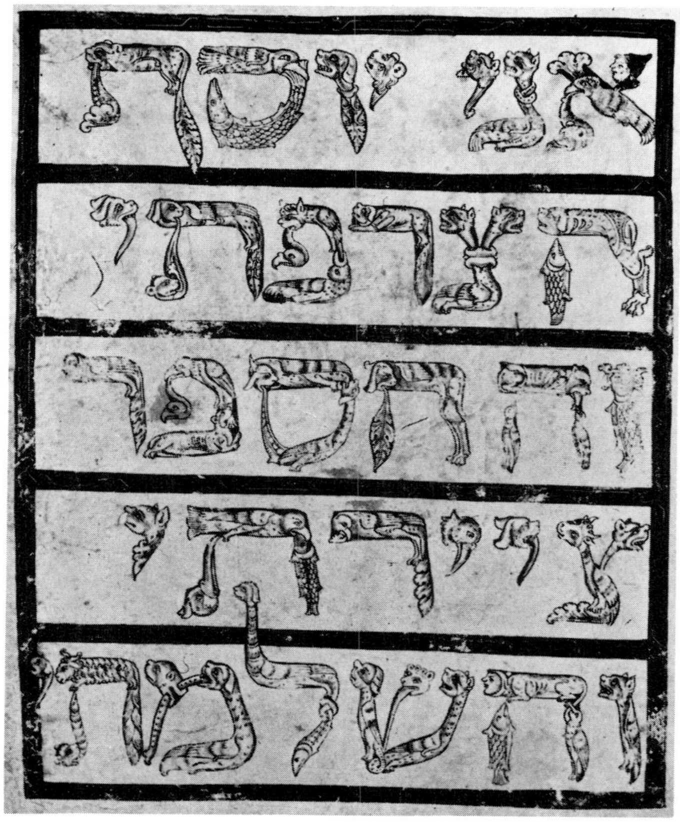

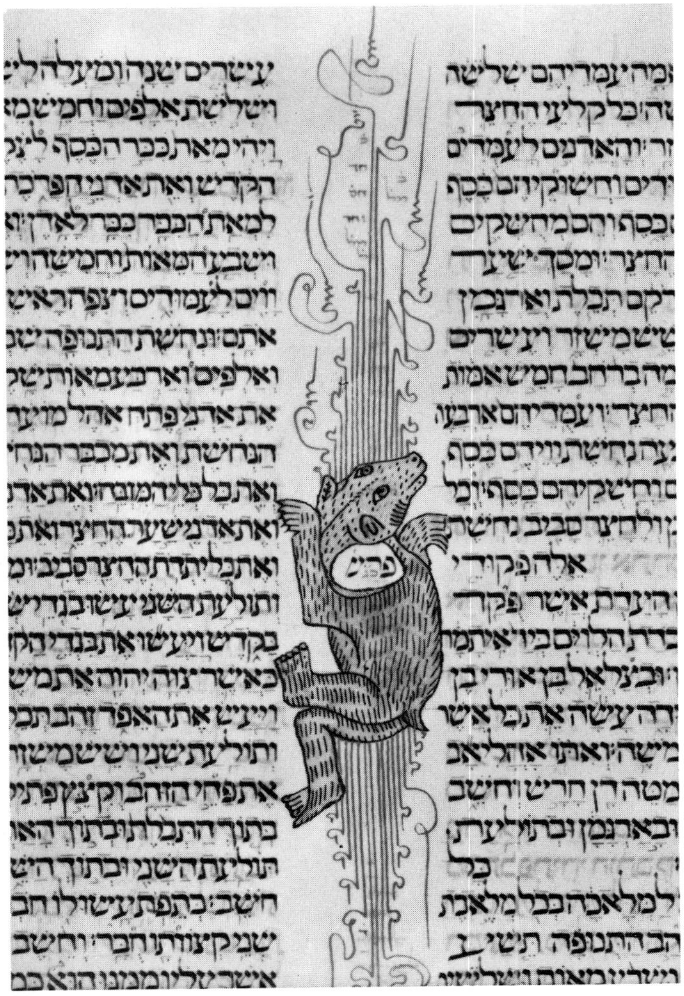

Figure 14. A page from the *Kennicott Bible,* illustrated by Joseph ibn Ḥayyim. Oxford, Bodleian Library, ms. Kennicott 1 f. 58r.

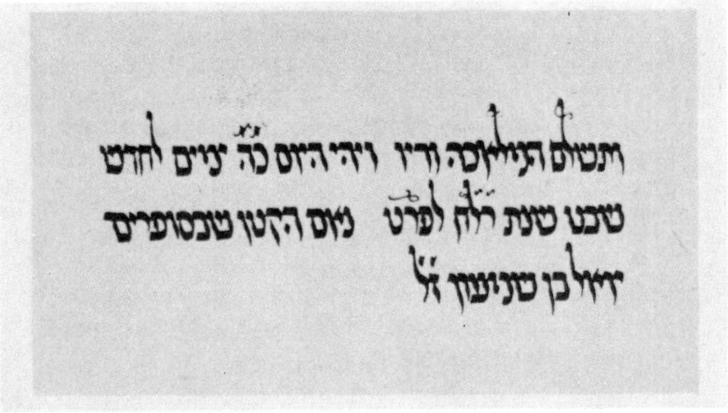

Figure 15. Colophon of the *Washington Haggadah* by the Ashkenazi artist Joel ben Simeon. Washington D.C., Library of Congress *Washington Haggadah* fol. 34v.

Figure 16. The *Dayyeinu* hymn from the *Birds' Head Haggadah,* Southern Germany, 1300. Jerusalem, Israel Museum ms. 180/57.

hibition against such illustrations. In the Byzantine Empire, during the period of iconoclasm (726–843), Jewish artists may also have completely abstained from illuminating Hebrew manuscripts. A further example of restricted representation of the human form developed in Germany during the 13th century. Under the influence of the ascetic Christian movement in the south of Germany and northern Italy during the 12th and 13th centuries, a similar Jewish asceticism developed. This caused Jewish illuminators to introduce a new motif into their art, indicating their iconophobic tendency by depicting distorted figures, such as human bodies with animal heads. Although pagan, Christian, or Muslim in origin, animal-headed figures became one of the main Jewish motifs in south German Hebrew illumination of the 13th and 14th centuries (figure 16). However, Rabbi Meir of Rothenburg, the leader of the Jewish communties in Germany at the end of the 13th century, disapproved of illustrating prayer books because of the distraction the illustrations might cause the reader, rather than because of the Second Commandment's prohibition.

CAPITAL LETTERS. Another characteristic aspect in Hebrew illuminated manuscripts was a direct outcome of the absence of capital letters in the Hebrew script, like other Semitic languages. Since initials did not lend themselves to decoration, they were replaced by decorated "initial words" (figure 17) or sometimes whole decorated verses, as in illuminated Arabic Korans. This characterictic survived throughout the Middle Ages in Europe as well as in the East. Where illuminated initial letters did develop in Europe, they were influenced directly by Latin illumination.

MICROGRAPHY. Another element peculiar to Jewish illumination was the use of micrography (minute script) to form geometrical or floral designs surround-

Figure 17. Initial words in a *siddur* of 1470 decorated with a dove and leaf and floral motifs. Jerusalem, Israel Museum, Rothschild ms. 24 Miscellany fol. 137b.

Figure 18. First page of the Book of Exodus from the 13th-century German *Reuchlin Bible*. The initial word is surrounded by figurated micrography which is also the Masorah text. Karlsruhe Badische Landesbibliothek Cod. Reuchlin 1 fol. 77r.

ing a page of conventional script or to form a whole carpet page. The most common examples are the marginal lists of irregularities in writing, spelling, and reading the Bible which constitute the so-called Masorah Magna. In oriental and Spanish Bibles, the Masorah is written in micrography in decorated carpet pages, and masoretic micrography outlines the design, for example, the oriental *Second Leningrad Bible*, the *Damascus Keter* from Spain, and the *Lisbon Bible* from Portugal. In Ashkenazi Bibles the masoretic micrography decorates initial-word panels and also the margins of text pages. Unlike oriental and Spanish Bibles, the micrography decorations contain animals and grotesques and sometimes text illustrations (figure 18). In accordance with tradition, the Masorah apparatus, though not necessarily legible or comprehensible, had to be written in the Bible codices.

MOTIFS. In subject matter, too, Jewish illumination had its peculiar characteristics. The main inspiration of the Jewish illuminator was in the Bible, and therefore he tended to choose biblical episodes as subject matter for illumination in manuscripts of every description. Important supplements to the biblical sources were legendary episodes based on midrashic commentaries found in all European schools as early as the 13th century. Some of these episodes, e.g., Abraham being thrown into the fire of the Chaldeans by order of King Nimrod, appear simultaneously in far-removed areas, as in the *Golden Haggadah* (British Museum, Ms. Add. 27210; figure 19) from Spain and the *Leipzig Maḥzor* from Germany (Leipzig University Library, Ms. V. 1102), indicating the existence of an earlier common European prototype.

The iconography of some subjects is specifically Jewish, as distinct from the general Christian or Muslim representations. For instance, in Christian art, a picture of the creation of the world will include the image of the Creator; in a Jewish work, however, only the Hand of God or rays will indicate the existence of the Supreme Power, as in the *Sarajevo Haggadah* (figure 20). Jewish customs and rituals, both domestic and synagogal, are depicted in most liturgical manuscripts; a favorite subject was the implements of the Temple. These illustrations must have been created by Jewish artists and fashioned ad hoc from available models. Since Hebrew illumination is directly related in style to the general schools of illumination, it serves as an important link with the history of non-Hebrew illuminated manuscripts. Moreover, in areas where the only dated illuminated manuscripts are Hebrew, this may become important evidence for dating and placing a certain style. For example, the date (1348) of the Copenhagen *Moreh Nevukhim* helps in dating other manuscripts and paintings from Catalonia where it was executed.

MATERIALS AND TECHNIQUES. While most Hebrew manuscripts were written on sheepskin parchment, the skins of other animals were also used; sometimes cowhide for large manuscripts, both in Europe and in the East; goatskins were used in the East; calfskin vellum, of which the finest, called "uterine vellum," came from embryos and still-born calves, was more expensive and therefore used only for costly manuscripts. The simplified process of parchment production in Europe during the 13th century enabled the scribes to use cheaper skins. All parchments were chalked before use, the Italian ones the most thickly, with the result that they have a greater stiffness. In most manuscripts, both sides of the parchment were used, except for the full-page miniatures, for which artists tended to use the flesh side, leaving the hair side blank. This practice prevailed mainly in Spain. Paper was also used for writing and decorating, but since it is not as durable as parchment few examples have survived.

Most of the colors were extracted from natural compounds, and the more durable ones were a mixture of well-pounded minerals or colored stones. The binding material might be a mixture of gypsum, sometimes egg, in solution with water. Gold was applied in two ways: either pounded and mixed with ocher or yellow and painted with a brush or in the form of gold leaf, applied on a base of gypsum mixed with minium and then burnished. The volume and texture of colors

Figure 19. The Chaldeans cast Abraham into the furnace by order of Nimrod. From the *Golden Haggadah,* Spain, 14th century. London, British Museum, Add. 27210, fol. 10v.

Figure 20. Abraham's sacrifice of Isaac (top) and Isaac encounters Rebekah (bottom). Full page illustration from the 14th-century Spanish *Sarajevo Haggadah*. Sarajevo National Museum fol. 8.

differed from one school to the other and from one period to the next, generally reflecting the local school of illumination. Some of the basic decorations of the page were done by the scribes themselves. In addition to planning the layout of the page, the scribe was responsible for placing the illustration, the initial-word panels, and linear decorations (figure 21). Other craftsmen were assigned the rest of the decoration. The vocalizer was in most cases responsible for most micrography decoration. Joshua ibn Gaon, the scribe, vocalizer, and illuminator, signed his name in the wings of a dragon drawn in micrographic Masorah (figure 22). The illuminator illustrated the manuscript according to the chief scribe's direction, using sketchbooks from his workshop or other illuminated manuscripts as models. The final process, the addition of color and gold, was carried out by an apprentice. The scribe was responsible for the entire manuscript and therefore, in most cases, is the only craftsman mentioned in the colophon. The illuminator, regarded as the minor craftsman, hardly ever signed his name.

THE MAIN SCHOOLS OF ILLUMINATION.

Oriental School. The earliest-known school of surviving oriental Hebrew illuminated manuscripts dates from the ninth century and probably originated in Mesopotamia, later spreading to Syria, Palestine, and Egypt. An offshoot of this school developed in Yemen during the 15th century. Most of the Hebrew illuminated manuscripts originating in the East between the ninth and 13th centuries have survived through the Cairo *Genizah.*

Examples of the various oriental styles from the ninth to the 13th centuries exist in Hebrew manuscripts. In most cases of dated manuscripts, the style corresponds to general Muslim art of the same period. The geometrical interlacing interwoven with foliage scrolls and palmettes typical of Persian, Syrian, or Egyptian Arabic Koran illumination may also be found in the Hebrew Bible manuscripts. In the tenth century, the delicately gold-tinted open flowers seen from above, arranged one next to the other within undulating scrolls to form a rhythmic pattern, are the most typical decoration in carpet pages of Korans and Bibles alike. Light blue, green, and red, which fill the background of the palmette motifs, are similarly common, e.g., the two carpet pages in a tenth-century fragment of a Hebrew Pentateuch written in Arabic characters (figure 23). In the 11th and 12th centuries, dark outlines were applied to the interlacings and flowers, usually on a panel of gold background decorated with deeper colors, as may be seen clearly in the 1008 or 1010 *Second Leningrad Bible* (figure 24). During the 13th century, Persian floral motifs penetrated into the decoration of most schools of art throughout the Muslim empires. The cartouche and palmette motifs in illuminated Bibles such as the *Second Gaster Bible* (British Museum, Or. Ms. 9880)

Figure 21. Opening page from the *Farḥi Bible,* arranged to include two columns of print, micrographical decoration, and margin illustrations. Provence, 1368–83. Letchworth, England, Sassoon Collection Ms. 368 p. 194.

Figure 22. Colophon of Joshua ben Abraham ibn Gaon in the lower margin of a page from a Hebrew Bible, Spain (Soria), 1301. Paris, Bibliothèque Nationale, Cod. heb. 20 fol. 69.

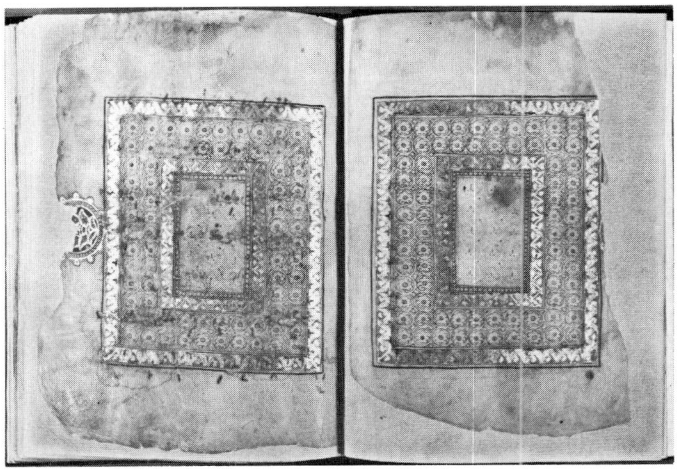

Figure 23. Double carpet page with palmette motif from a 10th-century Karaite Bible. London, British Museum. Or. ms. 2540 fols. 2v and 3r.

Figure 24. Carpet page from the *Second Leningrad Bible,* Egypt, 1008–10. Leningrad Public Library ms. B 19A fol. 746v.

are good examples of this kind of decoration. By the 14th century, there was a decline in the art of Hebrew illumination in the Eastern schools of Persia, Syria, Palestine, and Egypt, although the Arabic schools continued to flourish.

The Yemenite School, surviving examples of which date from the end of the 14th century and later, developed to its fullest capacity only in the second half of the 15th century. Yemenite Bibles were embellished with floral carpet pages and micrography in

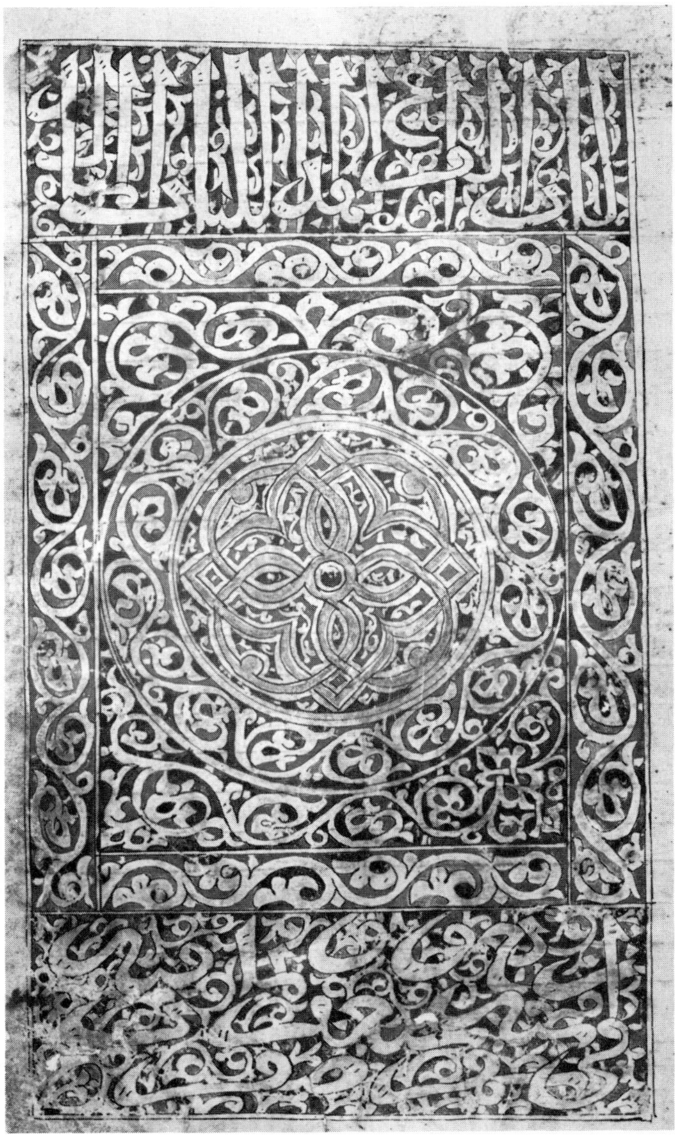

Figure 25. Carpet page from a Yemenite Pentateuch, San'a, 1469, embellished with floral and geometric designs. London, British Museum, Or. Ms. 2348 fol. 155r.

geometrical forms (figure 25). These Bibles contain no text illustrations, but the decorations on the text pages are similar to, and probably derived from, the earlier oriental type. Roundels bearing palmette motifs and other floral designs were used as fillers for incomplete lines or as section indicators (e.g., British Museum, Or. Ms. 2348 of 1469). Oriental illumination has some peculiar identifying features. First, there is a complete lack of human figures and a paucity of text illustrations. The oriental type of floral and geometrical decoration in carpet pages and panels is the most definitive indication of Hebrew illuminated manuscripts from the East. Although the motifs and the idea of carpet pages in Hebrew Bibles may derive from Islamic illumination, the Jewish workshops developed their own characteristically

Figure 26. Tenth century Oriental textbook for teaching children their alphabet. Opposite the opening page with its representation of a *menorah* are the first three letters of the Hebrew alphabet and some of the vowels. Cambridge University Library T-S K. 5.13.

Figure 27. Two pages from the *piyyut* of *Dayyeinu* from a 12th century Oriental *Haggadah*. The initial letter of each verse is written in line to form a decorative column. Cambridge University Library T-S 324.

Jewish version. This, in turn, may have influenced other schools of illumination in Europe. Most of the illuminated manuscripts of oriental origin are Bibles, although there are also some children's textbooks, decorated marriage contracts *(ketubbot),* and a few fragments of liturgical and scientific books. Of the illuminated Bibles, only very few are complete manuscripts; these sometimes contain colophons giving the date and place of execution, the name of the scribe, and the patron for whom they were made, as in the *Second Leningrad Bible.* In most cases these sumptuously decorated Bibles belonged to the Karaite communities in Palestine and Egypt. Decorative elements similar to those in Bibles adorned small booklets containing single sections of the Pentateuch. There is evidence that these booklets may have been

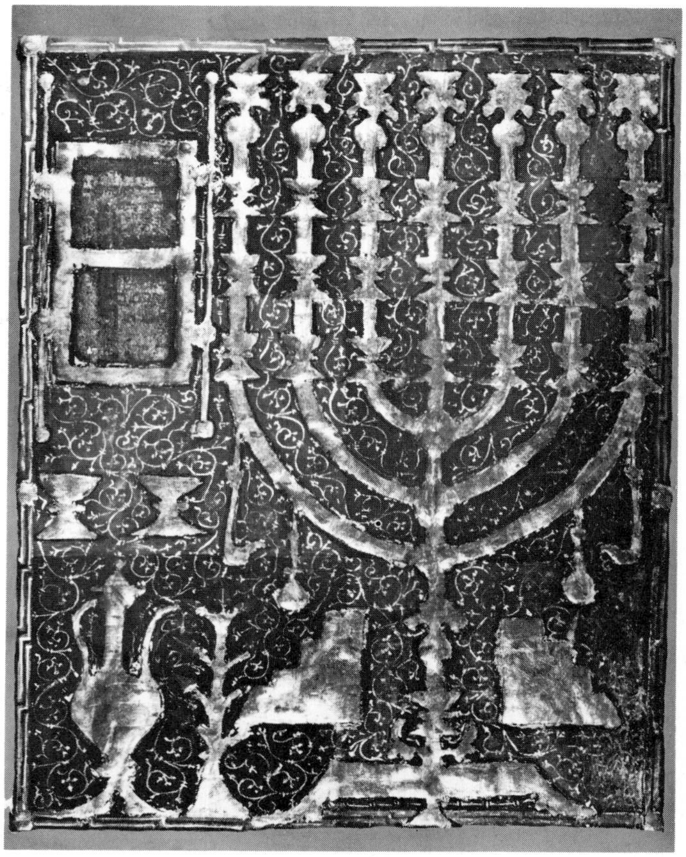

Figure 28. The seven-branched *menorah* and various Temple implements in a Hebrew Bible from 14th-century Spain. London, British Museum, Harley Ms. 1528, fol. 7v.

fashionable as bar mitzvah and wedding gifts. The *Parashat Shelaḥ Lekha* manuscript of 1106–07 is the most complete example of such a booklet. It has carpet pages at the beginning and at the end, its colophon page is framed, and the Masorah is written in decorative forms. The head of the first two text pages is decorated with gold bars, while roundels and palmette motifs indicate the sub-sections.

From the tenth to the 13th centuries, textbooks for teaching children the alphabet were also decorated. The letters were outlined in ink and filled with different colors. After the colored and vocalized letters, there followed a section of the Pentateuch, usually Leviticus 1:1–7, which was regarded as the most suitable text for a child's initial study. An opening carpet page was usually added to these books, denoting their distinct relation to the Bible. One example in the Cambridge University Library depicts the seven-branched *menorah* on its opening carpet page (figure 26). Liturgical books were also decorated in the East. The *Haggadah* conventionally had illustrations of the round *mazzah* wafer and the *maror.* Initial words were written in a special way, as in the

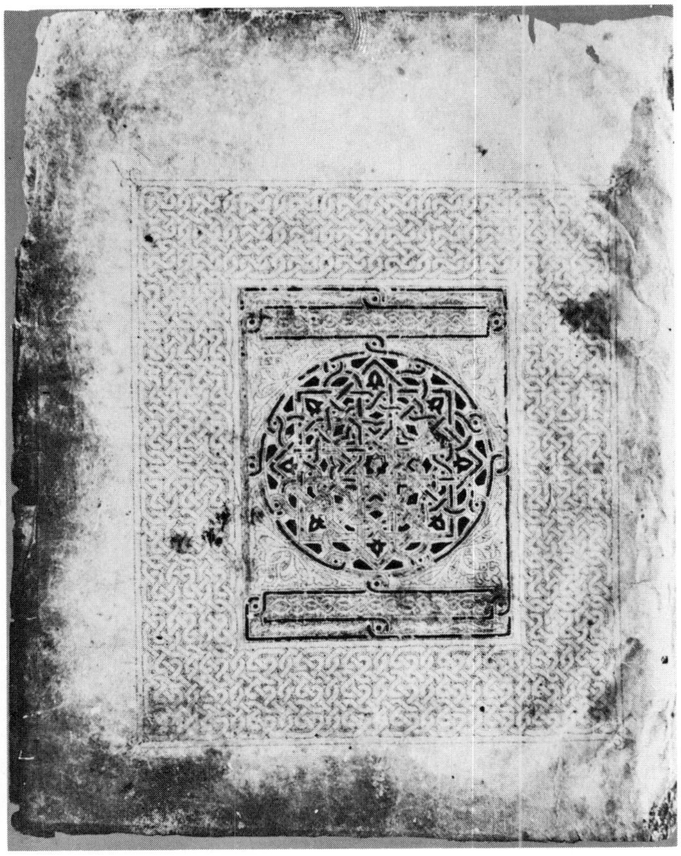

Figure 29. Carpet page from a 14th-century Spanish Bible, with foliage decoration resembling Muslim arabesques. Paris, Bibliothèque Nationale, Cod. heb. 1314 fol. 3v.

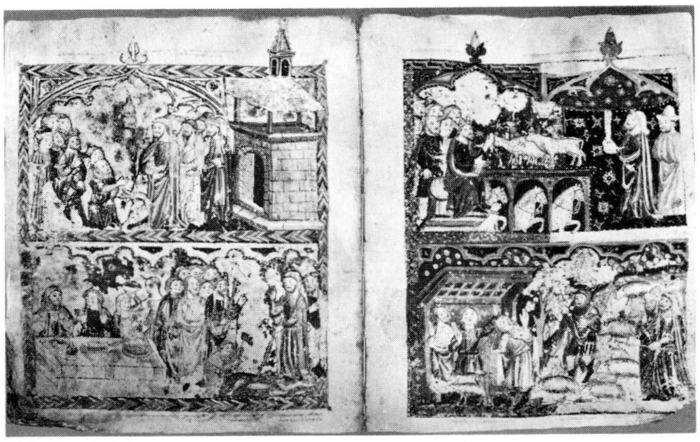

Figure 30. Some of the Ten Plagues (right) and part of the Moses and Aaron cycle (left) on two pages of the *Kaufmann Haggadah,* showing the Italian influence on 14th century Catalonian illumination. Budapest, Library of the Hungarian Academy of Sciences, Kaufmann Collection ms. A422 fols. 5v and 6.

poem of *"Dayyeinu"* ("It Would Have Sufficed"), in which the repeated initial word in each verse is written one beneath the other to form a decorative column (figure 27). Some fragments of decorated scientific books originating in the East have survived; they have geometrical and floral motifs, with colored roundels, squares, foliage scrolls, and ornamental script used as section headings and line fillers.

Spanish Illumination. The Spanish and Provençal schools of Hebrew illumination, which were greatly influenced by oriental decoration, reached their peak during the 14th century. The style and iconography of the Spanish school derive from both the Orient and the Occident. The existing Spanish illuminated manuscripts belong to the Christian Conquest period and reveal a strong link with the oriental type of illumination. Spanish Bibles, like oriental ones, have mainly Egyptian decorative elements, such as carpet pages, the Temple implements (figure 28), micrography, decorated Masorah *parashot* indicators, and, at the end of each book, decorated frames indicating the number of verses. There is a theory that these elements were assembled and modified from the eighth to the 13th centuries in Hebrew manuscripts of Muslim Spain. Since no Spanish Hebrew illuminated manuscripts of this period have survived, this assumption cannot be verified. The few existing dated Hebrew manuscripts from the Iberian Peninsula are mainly Bibles. They are stylistically so different from the illustrated *haggadot* and from the non-illustrated, liturgical, legal, and scientific books that it is very difficult to make a comparative study.

The northern Spanish school, directly related to Provence and influenced by the northern French school, is the earliest Spanish style still extant. It is characterized by Bibles of a large format. Their foliage decoration, comprised of interlacing scrolls, is reminiscent of Muslim arabesques (figure 29). The typical *mudejar* (Arabs under Christian rule) filigree ornament of thin, elegant, undulating scrolls, with paisley and round flower designs, remained in fashion in other Spanish schools up to the 15th century.

The Catalan and Castilian schools of Hebrew illumination in the 14th century were probably directly influenced by the traditional elements of local Spanish and northern French style. Italian influence was more pronounced in the Kingdom of Majorca and in Catalonia. It is evident in the use of darker colors, Byzantine modeling, and fleshy leaves, in Bibles, *haggadot,* and other Hebrew illuminated manuscripts. The Byzantine and Italianate elements are evident in the coffered ceilings of the miniatures in the *Golden Haggadah* (British Museum Add. Ms. 27210), as well as in the style of the figures in its "Sister" (British Museum Or. Ms. 2884). The combination of French and Italian gothic style in the *Golden Haggadah* resembles the style of the miniatures in a Catalan legal manuscript (c. 1320) now to be found in Paris (Bibliothèque Nationale Cod. Lat. 4670A). The Italianate style of Catalonia can be seen in the 14th-century *Copenhagen Moreh Nevukhim* from Barcelona (color plate 9). The highlights and shadows of the figures, as well as the crispness of the multi-colored leaves entwining the stem, are two of the Italianate elements. The spread of Italian elements to Castile came a generation later, and the traditional French gothic style prevailed even in the middle of the 14th century. The *Rashba Bible* of 1383 (from Cervera) in the Sassoon collection (Ms. 16) has typical Franco-Spanish decorations in the frames of the carpet pages and arcades, though it has delicate Italianate scrolls as section indicators and book openings. The style of figures and decorative motifs of the undated *haggadot* can be related to the dated Bibles. The zoomorphic and anthromorphic letters of the *Hamilton Siddur* are somewhat similar to those of the *Cervera Bible* of c. 1300 (Lisbon National Library

Figure 31. Carpet page from the *Farḥi Bible*, Provence, 1366–83, framed by sayings pertaining to the importance of Bible study, and by a grammatical dictionary of Hebrew roots and words. Letchworth, England, Sassoon Collection ms. 368 p. 42.

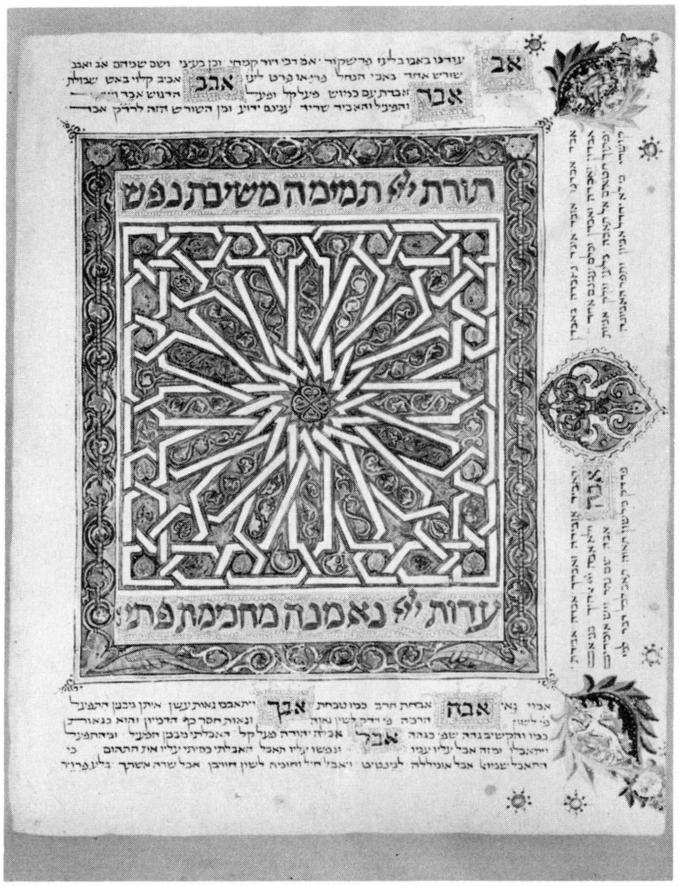

Figure 32. Opening page of the Book of Joshua from the *Lisbon Bible,* 1482, with wide, decorative border typical of the Portuguese school of manuscript illumination. London, British Museum Or. Ms. 2627 fol. 1v.

Figure 33. Two pages from the *Hispanic Society Bible,* Portugal, late 15th century. On the right is the last page of the Book of Kings, and on the left, the beginning of Isaiah. In the lower righthand border is the combined coat of arms of Castile and Leon. New York, Hispanic Society of America, ms. B 241 pp. 288-9.

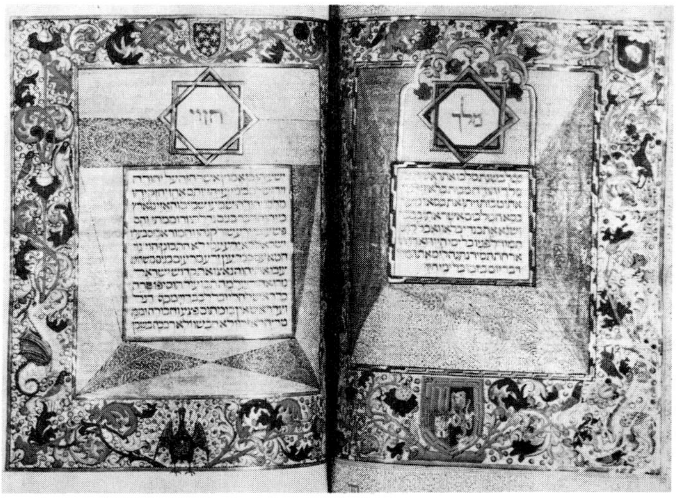

Ms. 72), while the linear filigree work within the letters of the *Hamilton Siddur* may, like its bright colors, indicate an even earlier date. The *Sassoon Spanish Haggadah* and the *Barcelona Haggadah* are somewhat related to the *Golden Haggadah* and to the Catalan Bibles of the first quarter of the 14th century. The *Rylands Spanish Haggadah* and its "Brother" are, like the *Kaufmann Haggadah* (figure 30), more Italianate, and must therefore be of the second half of the 14th century. The *Sarajevo Haggadah,* retaining some French-gothic elements, may be of Catalan origin dating from the middle of the 14th century. The *Farḥi Bible* (figure 31) of 1383–86 serves as evidence that the Hispano-Provençal school still existed in the 14th century. Its scores of arabesque carpet pages are still Spanish gothic style, though the fleshy foliage motif extending form the corners is more Italianate.

The destruction of most of the Jewish communities in the kingdoms of Castile and Aragon in 1391 brought to an end some of the most important schools of Hebrew illumination in these areas, and many illuminated manuscripts were destroyed. During the 15th century, however, new schools developed – some in the above-mentioned kingdoms, though in different population centers. One of these new centers was Seville, in the south. Two Bibles from the middle of the 15th century, in the Sassoon collection, are good examples of this school. The earlier one, from 1415 (Ms. 499) is only barely decorated with micrography. The later one, from 1468 (Ms. 487) has many micrographic decorations of full pages, panels, arcades, and borders. Though most of the motifs are traditional, the predominant southern Spanish Muslim feeling prevails. A Bible from Berlanga of 1455 (Bodleian Library, Ms. Can. Or. 77) is also related in decoration to the south Spanish school of the mid-15th century. In Corunna, northern Spain, the *First Kennicott Bible* of 1476 was probably not a unique example. Similar in style is a Pentateuch from 1479, now in Dublin (Trinity College Ms. M 2.5).

The most important school in the Iberian Peninsula at the end of the 15th century was the Portuguese. Most of the manuscripts of this school are Bibles, though it also produced a few prayer books like the *siddur* (from Lisbon) of 1484 (Paris Bibliothèque Nationale Cod. heb. 592) and some copies of Maimondes' *Mishneh Torah.* The manuscripts of the Portuguese

Figure 34. A page from the *British Museum Mishneh Torah.* London, British Museum, Harl. 5698, fol. 2526.

Figure 35. A miniature from the *British Museum Miscellany,* London, British Museum, Add. Ms. 11639 fol. 523b.

school, centered in Lisbon, are decorated with wide border frames on their opening pages, grammatical treatises, and masoretic variations. Initial words are mainly written in gold within very large panels decorated with *mudejar* filigree work. The two most important manuscripts of this school are the *British Museum Mishneh Torah* of 1472 and the *Lisbon Bible* of 1482 (figure 32). Most of the Portuguese manuscripts have no text illustrations. The *Bible of the Hispanic Society of America* can be attributed to the Portuguese school because of the typical decorative motifs in the frames of the opening pages of the books (figure 33).

The expulsion of the Jews from the Kingdom of Spain in 1492 and from Portugal in 1496–97 resulted in their spreading throughout Europe and into North Africa. The Spanish Jews brought their illuminated manuscripts to all these areas. In style, and especially in the system of illumination, the Spanish schools influenced Hebrew illuminated manuscripts in Italy, Turkey, Tunisia, and Yemen. Despite the invention of printing, some examples from these countries are extant from as late as the beginning of the 16th century.

As well as the magnificent Bibles and *haggadot* legal books, the most common of which was Maimonides' *Mishneh Torah,* were also illuminated in Spain. This treatise usually has an entire framed page at the beginning of each of its 14 books. Text illustrations in the *Mishneh Torah* appear only in Book Eight, accompanying the description of the Temple and its implements. Most *Mishneh Torah* manuscripts, in Spain as well as in Germany and Italy, have a diagram of the Temple that indicates the proper position of each of the implements. The *British Museum Mishneh Torah* (Portugal, 1472; Harley Ms. 5689–99; figure 34) is one of the most elaborately and delicately decorated examples of Spanish illumination. Maimonides' philosophical treatise, *Moreh Nevukhim (Guide of the Perplexed)* was another popular choice for illumination. Divided into three parts, it has only title page decorations and infrequent illustrations. The *Copenhagen Moreh Nevukhim* (Barcelona, 1348; Royal Library, Heb. 37) is an exception, as the initial-word panels of each of the three parts contain an illustration related to the text. Other philosophical treatises, such as Levi ben Gershom's *Sefer Milḥamot Adonai* of 1391 (Bodleian Library, Ms. Poc. 376), contain decorated title pages. Some scientific treatises have diagrammatic or instructional paintings. The Hebrew translation from the Arabic of the astronomical text *Almagest* by Ptolemy (Sassoon Ms. 699) has hundreds of diagrams as well as painted panels. Another astronomical manuscript in the Sassoon collection (Ms. 823) contains treatises by many authors. The part composed by Ptolemy has pictures of the heavenly constellations, signs of the zodiac, and cosmological diagrams. Jews were the expert astronomers in Spain and prepared many nautical maps.

The French School. Side by side with the Sephardi culture, which developed in Spain, Provence, and later in North Africa, Ashkenazi culture spread through Germany, northern France, England, and the Low Countries. It reached Italy in the 15th century, when German Jews entered the north of the country. By that time Ashkenazi influence was prevalent in Eastern Europe. Italy, however, retained a somewhat special vitality.

The northern French school of Hebrew illumination seems to have been one of the most important in the Ashkenazi communities. Of the few surviving illuminated French manuscripts most are sparsely decorated; however, some are sumptuous and reveal the high quality and sophistication of French illumination. The *British Museum Miscellany* (Ms. Add. 11639; possibly from Troyes, c. 1280; figure 35) is one of the best examples. The text contains scores of books and treatises, including the entire Bible and liturgy for the whole year. Almost every page is illuminated with floral, animal, and grotesque motifs, but the *Haggadah* is the only comprehensively illustrated text. The most significant are the four groups of full-page miniatures, which are not altogether an integral part of the manuscript and some of which may even have been later random additions. The lack of uniformity and the repetition of certain subjects, such as Aaron lighting the *menorah* (fols. 114 and 522v), indicate that they are not the work of one artist. It appears that Benjamin, the scribe of the manuscript – who had his name illuminated in several places (e.g. 142v, 306v) – gave directions to the illuminator in the lower margins of some pages. In one instance (fol. 219v) (figure 36), the scribe wrote *shalshelet* ("chain") in the lower part of the page and the artist accordingly decorated the side margin near the text with an undulating chain ornamented with animal grotesques. Most of the full-page miniatures are biblical, others are midrashic or eschatological.

Few illuminated Bibles and *haggadot* have survived from France. Common to the northern French Jewish communities were small manuscripts containing the Psalter. Though most of these are merely decorated,

Figure 36. The *shalshelet* page from the *British Museum Miscellany.* London, British Museum, Add. ms. 11639 fol. 219r.

one in the Bodleian Library (Oxford, Or. Ms. 621) opens with a a half-length representation of David playing the harp. Legal books of French origin are primarily copies of Moses of Coucy's *Sefer Mitzvot Gadol;* they are mainly decorated, but a few contain illustrations.

From the end of the 14th century, some illumination developed in Southern France (properly Provence) where the Jews were allowed to remain after the expulsion. Bibles, prayer books, philosophical treatises, such as Levi ben Gershom's *Sefer Milḥamot Adonai,* and scientific and medical treatises have survived. Southern French illumination of this period is closer in style to Italian and Spanish schools than to those of northern France.

The German School. The earliest surviving European Hebrew manuscripts are from Germany. A manuscript containing the biblical commentary by Rashi, written by Solomon ben Samuel of Wuerzburg

Figure 37. Rashi's commentary on the Book of Daniel, copied by Solomon ben Samuel of Wuerzburg, 1233. Munich, Bayerische Staatsbibliothek, Cod. heb. 5 vol. II fol. 209r.

Figure 38. The faces of Joseph and of his mourners have deliberately been left blank. A panel from the end of Genesis/ beginning of Exodus from the *Ambrosian Bible,* South Germany, 1236–8. Milan, Ambrosian Library, ms. B 30 Inf. fol. 182v.

in 1233 (Munich, Cod. Heb. 5; figure 37), is the earliest dated of these illuminated manuscripts. The style, which is directly related to the south German school of Latin illumination, shows no specifically Jewish characteristics apart from the featureless human faces. While the reason for this is not definitely known, it may be connected with other means of distorting the human form common in southern Germany during the 13th century, such as covering human faces with crowns, wreaths, kerchiefs, or helmets; depicting them from behind; or replacing them with animal or bird heads. All of these devices are employed in the *Ambrosian Bible* of the south German school, which was written for Joseph ben Moses of Ulm between 1236 and 1238 (figure 38). Z. Ameisenowa has suggested that people with animal heads designate holy men, righteous people, evangelists, or deacons. This practice, which may have originated in Muslim and Persian motifs, was borrowed by Christian as well as Jewish artists. The Jewish school of illumination in southern Germany adopted this motif and used it not only for righteous people and angels, but also sometimes to portray gentiles. Since there was no direct official prohibition against the depiction of the human form in illuminated manuscripts, it would appear that the south German Jews imposed this restriction upon themselves out of some iconophobic notion that may have developed here in the 12th century from the pietistic movement headed by Judah and Samuel he-Ḥasid. The movement of Ḥasidei Ashkenaz was ascetic, restricting embellishments in private or public life and forbidding any sort of decoration in manuscripts, even to the extent of prohibiting decoration with micrographic Masorah.

The south German school of illumination was the most prominent and prolific of the Ashkenazi schools. It is also probably the most closely related in style to the contemporary local south German Latin illumination. From the beginning, the only Jewish motif in Hebrew illumination from southern Germany was the distortion of the human face. The soft undulating drapery, bright colors with dark outlines, expressive gestures, and acorn scrolls with large leaves and open composite flowers seen from above are but a few of the south German stylistic features to be found in Hebrew as well as in Latin illumination of the 13th and 14th centuries, like the Aich Latin Bible and the gradual of St. Katharinental of 1312. This school survived during the 14th century. A good example is the *ketubbah* from 1392 (Vienna,

Figure 39. Page from the *Erna Michael Haggadah,* South Germany, c. 1400. Jerusalem, Israel Museum, IM 180/58.

National Library, Cod. Heb. 218), the style of which is similar to that of the *Erna Michael Haggadah* of about 1400 (figure 39).

The mid-Rhenish school of illumination was influenced in style by south German as well as by the northern French illumination. Thus, the *Hamburg Miscellany* from Mainz reflects both of these elements. The lower Rhine area shows the most French influence of all German schools, as can be seen from the *Kaufmann Mishneh Torah* (figure 40). During the 15th century, Italian influence is evident in manuscripts executed in southern as well as central Germany, such as the *Darmstadt Haggadah* and the *Siddur of the Rabbi of Ruzhin* (figure 41).

Very few names of artists from medieval Germany are

Figure 40. Opening page of the *Kaufmann Mishneh Torah.* The French-Gothic influence is clear: in the center is the initial word panel, *kol ha-mitzvot,* and below Judah Maccabee is depicted as a jousting knight. Budapest, Library of the Hungarian Academy of Sciences, Kaufman Collection, ms. A 77/1, vol. 1 fol. 2r.

known. Joel ben Simeon, sometimes called Feibush Ashkenazi, is famous because he signed so many manuscripts executed in his workshop. Active in Germany and Italy in the second half of the 15th century, he was of German origin, probably from Cologne or Bonn, but established a workshop in northern Italy. It was possibly due to the influence of the Italian Renaissance that the artist felt secure enough to sign his name not only as a scribe but also as an illuminator. Other names found on illuminated manuscripts are mainly of the scribes. The *nakdanim* ("punctuators") who were also the masoretes of Bibles, were responsible for all the pen drawings, and micrographic decorations in Ashkenazi manuscripts. Of these, as well, only a few names are known.

Figure 41. Page from the illuminated *Siddur of the Rabbi of Ruzhin,* south or east Germany, c. 1460. The framed miniature with landscape background reveals an Italian influence on German illumination. Jerusalem, Israel Museum, IM 180/53.

Aside from the *maḥzorim* (the most important innovation of the German school), Bibles, and *haggadot,* there were illuminated legal books, the most common of which are copies of Maimonides' *Mishneh Torah.* As in similar manuscripts from Spain, the only illustrations are plans of the Temple and its implements. The initial-word panels are sometimes elaborately decorated, but hardly ever illustrated. Secular illuminated Hebrew manuscripts from Germany are very rare. One of the more common is the *Meshal ha-Kadmoni* by the 13th-century Spanish poet Isaac ben Solomon ibn Abi Sahula. This lengthy rhymed collection of exemplary tales was usually illustrated with a set of pictures at the opening of each chapter. Since each picture has a rhymed inscription by the author, it is assumed that the manuscript was, from its inception, intended to be illustrated; however, no Spanish example has survived. It must have been a highly popular book in southwest Germany during the 15th century, for several complete copies are extant, as well as a few fragments.

The Italian School. Italian Hebrew illumination may have been one of the earliest schools in Europe, just as the Jewish community in Italy was one of the oldest and culturally most developed in Europe from the early Middle Ages. Hebrew illuminated manuscripts from Italy are most varied in their style and type. A good number of them were executed by the finest Italian artists. As they originated in various schools from the end of the 13th to the beginning of the 16th century, they vary widely in their mode of

Figure 42. Opening page of Isaiah, from an ornate 15th-century North Italian Bible, by Attavante degli Attavanti of Ferrara. The text is framed by a fenentella-like arch with the initial word panel *Ḥazon* ("vision") between two *putti* above the tympanum. On the floor beneath the arch, *putti* are playing with a monkey. The arch is framed by borders, which include foliage scrolls, vases, grotesques, *putti* and strange-looking people. In the right and left borders, in the center, are cartouches, the one on the right containing a lion and on the left, two deer. In the top and bottom borders are panels containing masoretic notes. Paris, Bibliothèque Nationale. Ms. heb. 15 fol. 251.

illustration, which ranges from marginal illustrations through initial-word panels to full-page decorations and miniatures.

The system of illuminating each type of book differed from school to school, though some elements are common to all, influenced by Ashkenazi as well as Sephardi illumination. Most Italian Hebrew manuscripts are decorated with initial-word panels at the openings of sections, sometimes with the entire opening page (figure 42), or at least the first text column, decoratively framed. This decoration may be a simple foliage scroll surrounding the text, or a stage-like arcade elaborately decorating the frontispiece. Bibles, *maḥzorim* and *siddurim,* literary texts, books of *halakhah,* and secular works of philosophy, science, and medicine are all usually decorated with framed openings of books, prayers, chapters, or sections. Some manuscripts have text illustrations in the margins and in miniatures within the text or as full pages. The Italian *haggadot* follow the Ashkenazi system of marginal illustration and initial-word panels (figure 43).

13th-century Schools of Rome and Central Italy. The *Bishop Bedell Bible* in Emmanuel College, Cambridge (Ms. 1.1.5–7; figure 44), dating from 1284, is a typical example of the Roman-Jewish school of illumination at the end of the 13th century (figure 44). Similar arcades and painted scrolls are to be found in another Bible, from about 1300, and also in a *Sefer Mitzvot* by Maimonides from 1285. All these manuscripts are Roman, and like the *Bishop Bedell Bible,* were written and decorated by Abraham ben Yom Tov for his patron, Shabbetai ben Mattathias. In central Italy, similar illuminations were used in Bibles. A two-volume Bible in the British Museum (Harl. Ms. 5710–11,54), from about 1300 (and certainly from before 1340, when it was sold) still preserves both techniques of decoration – watercolor pen drawings and painted illuminations. Another delicately painted manuscript of Emilian style, from the end of the 13th century, is a psalter in the Biblioteca Palatina in Parma (MS. 1870; De'Rossi 510). Many of the chapter openings have small initial-word panels with grotesques and animals in the margins. Some illustrate the text: weeping people, with their violins hung upon a willow, illustrate Psalm 137. Another manuscript from the same district is a *Moreh Nevukhim* copied by Solomon of Rome in Viterbo in 1273 (British Museum, Add. Ms. 14763).

14th-century Schools. A school illustrating legal books developed in Bologna in the second half of the 14th century, probably under the influence of the Bolognese Latin school, which specialized in papal decrees, urban laws, and other legal documents. A fine example is a manuscript containing the halakhic decisions of Rabbi Isaiah of Trani (13th century) which was copied in Bologna in 1347 (British Museum Or. Ms. 5024). Among the most interesting text illustrations are a man lighting a Hanukkah lamp (fol. 19), woodcutter stoned for working on a festival day (fol. 64v), a Tabernacle and a man carrying the symbolic fruits of Sukkot (fol. 79v), carpenters working with stolen wood (184v), a merchant selling a ship (fol. 225v; figure 45), and a judge (fol. 241). The heavy figure drawing of the text illustration and the style of the marginal decorations resemble the school of Niccolo di Giacomo da Bologna.

Stylistically akin to these illustrated legal books is a manuscript of Maimonides' *Mishneh Torah,* now in the Jewish National and University Library in Jerusalem (MS. Heb. 4° 1193), copied in Spain or in Provence in the first half of the 14th century and partially illuminated in Perugia around 1400 in the school of Matteo di Ser Cambio. Apart from border decorations, the *Jerusalem Mishneh Torah* has some text illustrations in initial-word panels and in the margins of the first 40 pages. These are the earliest extant *Mishneh Torah* illustrations. The beginning of the *Sefer Ahavah,* "Book of Love [of God]" has a man hugging a Torah scroll within the initial-word panel and another reciting morning benedictions by his bed in the lower margin (color plate 13). Since it is unlikely that the Christian artist, Matteo di Ser Cambio, invented the system of illustrating a *Mishneh Torah,* it may be assumed that either there existed an

Figure 44. Opening pages of the *Bishop Bedell Bible.* In the center of the right-hand page is the Hebrew letter *shin,* the initial of the book's original patron, Shabbetai ben Mattathias. On the left-hand page an inscription reads, "Crown of Beauty: Pentateuch, Prophets and Hagiographa." Cambridge, Emmanuel College, Ms. I.I. 5–7 fol. IV–2.

Figure 43. Page from the *Washington Haggadah,* a 15th-century Italian work, with a decorative initial-word panel. Washington D.C., Library of Congress fol. 19v.

Figure 45. The sale of a ship as a marginal illustration in the manuscript collection of halakhic decisions of Rabbi Isaiah of Trani, Bologna, 1347. London, British Museum Or. Ms. 5024 fol. 225v.

Figure 46. A page from the Vatican Library manuscript of Jacob ben Asher's *Arba'ah Turim*. Vatican Library, Cod. Rossianna, Ms. 555 fol. 293.

earlier model, which has not survived, or that Matteo di Ser Cambio was instructed by a Jew.

Other schools are known to have existed in central and northern Italy at the end of the 14th and beginning of the 15th century. These schools were sometimes initiated by a single patron – a book and art lover who ordered illuminated manuscripts for his private use or as presents for friends and relations. One such school revolved around a physician named Daniel ben Samuel ha-Rofe. The tinted pen drawings which decorate these manuscripts are typical of Lombard work at the end of the 14th century.

Another group of manuscripts from the end of the 14th and early 15th century was executed for a father and son of the Bet El family. The father, Jeḥiel ben Mattathias, commissioned manuscripts at the end of the 14th century. A *Sefer Arukh ha-Shalem* written by Nathan ben Jeḥiel of Rome, executed in Perugia in 1396 (Parma, De' Rossi Ms. 180) and a *siddur* from Pisa of 1397 (Sassoon Ms. 1028) were both ordered by Jeḥiel. Many more manuscripts were ordered by his son, Jekuthiel, between 1415 and 1442. In style, this group of manuscripts is close to that of Daniel ha-Rofe. Although there are a few local elements, on the whole it is influenced by Lombardic tinted drawings.

15th-century Schools. An elaborately illuminated manuscript (from Mantua) dating from 1436 is the *Arba'ah Turim* in the Vatican Library (Cod. Rossiana 555; figure 46). It is similar in style to Mantuan Latin illumination of the first half of the 15th century. A single page belongs to the Mantuan school of the second half of the 15th century: this is a fragment of another copy of the same treatise, attached now to a different manuscript from 1457 in Vercelli, Seminario Vescovile. Another important manuscript from Lombardy, from either the school of Mantua or Ferrara, is the *Mishneh Torah* manuscript, formerly in the Frankfort Municipal Library.

One of the most elegant and delicately executed of Italian Hebrew illumination, the *Rothschild Miscellany* Ms. 24 is now in the Israel Museum (IM 180/51). The figure drawing in some of its miniatures

Figure 47. Initial word panel and a man praying. Illuminated page from the *Rothschild Miscellany*, northern Italy (Ferrara ?), c. 1470. Jerusalem, Israel Museum Ms. 24 IM 180/51.

and border decorations resembles the art of Taddeo Crivelli of Ferrara, one of the artists of the Bible of Borso d'Este. However, some of the decorations in the *Rothschild Miscellany* display a Venetian style, which may be due either to the prevailing influence of Venetian illumination at the time or to the collaboration of other artists trained in Venice (figure 47). Ferrarese style is evident also in a manuscript of *Sefer ha-Ikkarim* by Joseph Albo in the Biblioteca Silvestriana in Rovigo.

The famous medical handbook, the *Canon* of the physician-philosopher Avicenna (988–1037) now in the University Library of Bologna, is also illuminated in the Ferrarese style (figure 48). Another medical book, a miscellany now in the Cambridge University Library, is decorated by miniatures at the head of each of the various treatises. The style of the figures and of the decoration is very close to that of the Latin school of Padua. A *Halakhic Miscellany,* in the State and University Library at Hamburg (Cod. heb. 337), was written and illuminated in Padua in 1477, with later additions in Florentine style. Most of the treatises in it are by Isaac of Dueren. Illumination in the earlier Paduan style consists of some initial-word panels (e.g., fols. 44 and 50), one magnificent marginal illustration of an old man slaughtering a doe (fol. 6), and a full-page initial-word panel above a miniature (fol. 75v) illustrating a marriage ceremony within a landscape. The Florentine-style miniatures and initial-word panels illustrating the text at the beginning of the book (fol. 3v), and at the opening of the section by Rabbi Meir of Rothenburg, were added in 1492.

Figure 48. Miniature illuminating the opening of a Hebrew version of Book One of the *Canon* of Avicenna, Ferrara, 15th century. In the top panel, a physician instructs his pupils; at the bottom, other liberal arts are portrayed. The signs of the Zodiac form part of the border. Bologna, University Library, Ms. 2197 fol. 23v.

Figure 49. Page from the *Rothschild Maḥzor* by Abraham Judah ben Jehiel of Camerino, Florence, 1492. The initial word panel *nifla'im* (wonders) is illuminated in the center; at the foot of the page is the Norsa coat of arms. New York, Jewish Theological Seminary.

The 1480 *siddur* from Pesaro, in the Sassoon collection (Ms. 23), is related in style to the Ferrarese school, rather than to the Florentine.

The school of Florence, known to have created dozens of manuscripts, was one of the most important in Hebrew illumination in the 15th century.

Most of its products are decorated with delicate filigree work in initial-word panels and border decorations. To these are usually attached pen-drawn masks, profiles, and small animals. The favorite color in these pen decorations is a purple-blue. Painted illumination of the Florentine-school is also based on pen drawings. A good example is the *Rothschild Maḥzor,* in the Jewish Theological Seminary in New York (figure 49). Among other Florentine-style manuscripts with painted drawings are two *siddurim,* one in the George Weill collection in Strasbourg, and one in the Jewish National and University Library in Jerusalem. The more "painterly" style of the Florentine school is exemplified in a manuscript comprising Psalms, Job, and Proverbs, now in the Israel Museum (figure 50). The school of Naples was another important center of Hebrew illumination during the 15th century. The best-known example of its work is the *Aberdeen Bible* (University of Aberdeen, Ms. 23), possibly written in Naples in 1493 (figure 51).

POST-MEDIEVAL ILLUMINATION. Renaissance Italy produced the peak of Hebrew illuminated manuscripts. Throughout Europe, the spread of printing brought about the decline of hand-produced books, though some of the loveliest manuscripts belong to the end of the 15th century, when the printed book was already widely diffused. This tradition continued into the 16th century; a fine illuminated *Haggadah* formerly in the Stadtbibliothek in Frankfort, now in a private collection in New York, was executed in Bologna around 1510. Apart from this, the art of illumination was kept alive among Jews in two kinds of manuscripts which became widely diffused only after the invention of printing – the illuminated *ketubbah,* which was especially popular in Italy (figure 52; though an isolated 14th-century German specimen is known); and the illuminated Scrolls of Esther, found throughout Germany and Central Europe. Less common, but well-known in Italy, were illuminations of marriage poems, and the documents

Figure 50. Full page miniature of David beheading Goliath, as the opening to the Book of Psalms. The manuscript includes Job and Proverbs and was produced in Italy (Florence ?) in the 15th century. Jerusalem, Israel Museum, IM 180/55, fol. 4v.

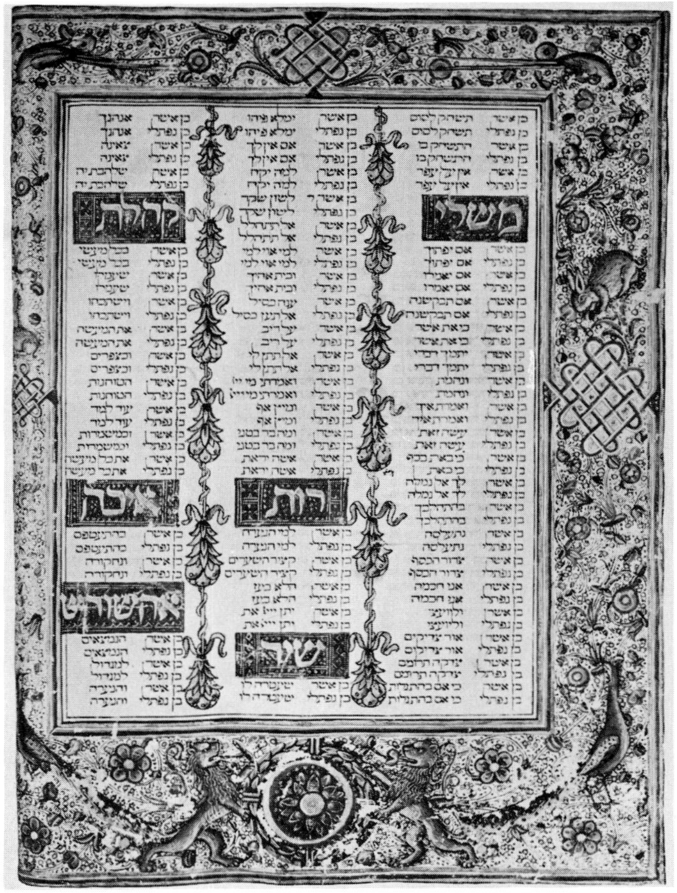

Figure 51. Illuminated page from the *Aberdeen Bible,* Naples (?), 1493. Aberdeen University Library, Ms. 23 fol. 7v.

Figure 52. Illuminated *ketubbah* from Ancona, Italy, 1784, with an illustration of the sacrifice of Isaac. Made for the marriage of Moses Judah of Senigallia and Diamante of Pacifico. London, Cecil Roth Collection, ms. 812.

for rabbinical ordinations and even licenses for *sheḥitah.* A series of manuscripts with illuminations, some of a very high quality, were executed in Italy in the course of the late 16th and early 17th century. From the mid-16th century illuminated manuscripts were also produced, usually in scroll form, comprising the Itineraries of the Holy Land, with naive depictions of the graves of the righteous.

From the closing years of the 17th century there was, however, a remarkable development in Germany and Central Europe, centering mainly on the Passover *Haggadah.* Although this ever-popular work was available in numerous lavishly illustrated printed editions, it was not unusual for practiced scribes to try their hands at imitating these in manuscript, or for wealthy householders to try to outdo their neighbors by having impressive handwritten copies. Hence from this period there began to appear once more on the market hand-written and hand-illuminated *haggadot,* generally expensively executed on vellum. In the first instance there was a tendency to reproduce somewhat slavishly illustrations from the popular Amsterdam printed editions; later, greater freedom and originality were shown. Sometimes these belated specimens of the illuminator's art were made as wedding presents, and even bore the bride's portrait. A distinctive feature of these late manuscripts, naturally not found in those of the Middle Ages, was the inclusion of impressive title pages, often depicting (in imitation of those in printed books) the figures of Moses and Aaron, and sometimes with vignettes illustrating the history of the biblical figure whose name was borne by the patron of the artist (figure 53). In due course, the scribes extended this newly found competence to other categories of domestic

Figure 53. Opening page of a *Haggadah* written and illustrated by Abraham of Eiringen in Alsace, 1740. Portrayed in folk-art style are David and Solomon, Moses and Aaron, and at the foot of the page a man washes his hands at the beginning of the *seder,* flanked by the sacrifice of Isaac and Jacob's dream. Paris, V. Klagsbald Collection.

Figure 54. Frontispiece of the Hebrew Union College *Haggadah, Sister* to the *Van Geldern Haggadah,* painted by Moses Leib Trebitsch, 1716–17. Cincinnati, Hebrew Union College.

liturgical manuscripts, e.g. the table hymns and readings for the Sabbath, the service for the circumsion ceremony, and later sometimes even the regulations of religious confraternities. Occasionally repetitive, naive, and even gross though certain of these manuscripts were, some of them manifest a fine artistic sensibility with vivid imagination, delicacy of execution, and sometimes even a half-suppressed sense of humor. Occasionally, these artists of Hebrew manuscripts were encouraged in other work by non-Jewish patrons and some, as in the case of the Fiorino family, became miniature-painters and artists in the wider sense.

The main center of this belated school of manuscript illuminators seems at the outset to have been in Bohemia and Moravia, the place of origin of Moses Leib Trebitsch, the artist of the *Van Geldern Haggadah* and its companion in the Hebrew Union College, Jewish Institute of Religion, Cincinnati (figure 54). At least a dozen of Trebitsch's works are known; equally prolific was Aaron Wolf of Gewitsch, who seems to have maintained an atelier in which assistants worked under his supervision. Later, an offshoot of this Moravian school established itself in and around Hamburg. The most important figure was Joseph ben David Leipnik, of Moravian origin, whose *haggadot* miniatures have the quality of small paintings. He was rivaled by Uri Phoebus Segal, whose illuminations, deliberately clothed in contemporary dress, have an unusual realistic quality. Scribes such as Aaron ben Moses, of Dublin and later London, carried something of the spirit of these illuminations as far as the British Isles.

In the revival of the art of manuscript illumination in the 20th century, artists such as Sol Nodel, Zeev Rabban, Ben Shahn, and especially Arthur Szyk based themselves on the medieval models rather than on the long-neglected 18th-century school.

Figure 55. Ben Shahn's Decalogue, illustration to the *Alphabet of Creation.* Schocken Books, New York, 1965.

Figure 56. "Tears of Rage and Blood." Illustration by Arthur Szyk in *Ink and Blood.* George Macy Companies Inc., New York, 1946.

4. the science of the hebrew book

Abraham Yaari (born in eastern Galicia 1899; died in Israel 1966). J.N.U.L., Schwadron Collection, Jerusalem.

Today as in the past Hebrew bibliography is faced with four main tasks: 1) to provide a tool for scholars of Judaism with which they can further the state of knowledge in their respective fields of scholarship (professional bibiliography); 2) to assist the student — and the scholar outside his own field of specialization to find his way to revelant material (applied bibliography); 3) to study the history of the Hebrew book with respect to content, as an aspect of cultural history in its own right (programmatic bibliography); 4) to study the printing of the Hebrew book, its physical appearance (technique and typography), as a subject in its own right in the material aspects of cultural history (physical bibliography). The general pattern formed by these four tasks is not unique to Hebrew bibliography; the various components are not in competition or in opposition, but rather serve to complement each other and are all of equal importance. However, because of the comparatively infant state of Jewish scholarship, with the study of most periods and problems only in its early (or more advanced) stages, the third and fourth of the tasks listed above have been allotted third and fourth place in order of priority.

As stated, scientific research in Jewish studies is still in its youth, and bibliographical assistance has been and remains very much in demand for the first two purposes; we have not yet arrived at scientific study of Hebrew book production as a subject in its own right. This is reflected clearly in the curriculum of studies at institutes of higher learning in Israel and abroad. No important Jewish university yet has a department for studying the third and fourth branches of bibliography, nor is instruction in these subjects given in any other department of studies. Academic activity in these areas, to the extent that it exists, is carried out privately, not in the universities. Moreover, the schools of librarianship which have recently been set up in the large universities and granted complete academic recognition, are only concerned with teaching the fundamental principles required for applied bibliography (the second task listed above); only recently have voices been raised in support of including advanced studies, for a third degree, which will provide training for the scientific pursuit of the third and fourth branches of bibliography. A similar situation is reflected in published scholarship. Professional bibliography exists (though there is less than there should be); applied bibliography exists to a greater extent (though a similar reservation must be made); there are far fewer programmatic bibliographies; and study of the physical aspects of the Hebrew book is in effect completely non-existent. An exemplary pioneering study of great value in this field, is the recently published work of Herbert Zafran *Dyherenfurth and Shabbetai Bass, A Typographical Profile* included in the *festshrift* presented to Yiẓḥak Kiev (New York 1972); it deals at length with the fundamental problem and warns of its neglect.

JOURNALS

A further expression of the state of bibliographical studies today is provided by the professional journals available in the field. There is in effect only one journal devoted exclusively to the study of the Hebrew book, *Kirjath Sepher,* now in its 49th consecutive year of publication since its founding in 1924. Over the years some very important studies of the Hebrew book have been published in this journal, but in large measure (about 80%) this journal is devoted to an ongoing bibliographical listing of Hebrew books published today, source books, new editions and facsimile editions, accompanied by selected critical essays. This important enterprise serves the first two tasks listed above, which, as pointed out, constitute the main bibliographical activity. It should be noted

Moritz Steinschneider (born in Prossnitz, Moravia, 1816; died in Berlin, 1907). J.N.U.L., Schwadron Collection, Jerusalem.

that through this work the journal continues a worthy tradition established by the principal bibliographical journals which preceded it, Steinschneider's *Hamazkir* which appeared in 21 volumes between the years 1859 and 1882, and its sequel – *Hebraeische Bibliographie* – edited by H. Brody and later by A. Freidman, which appeared in 23 volumes between the years 1896 and 1920. These journals, too, devoted considerable space to ongoing listings – mainly for commercial reasons, a factor in the history of Hebrew bibliography which we shall go into in more detail later – as well as some most important, fundamental studies in pure bibliography. Today this tradition is continued without any economic motivation, out of an understanding of the importance of ongoing listing as a tool of research at all levels and especially as an aid for librarians in the great research institutions abroad. Presumably, with the development and improvement of computers on the one hand and the ongoing information "explosion" on the other, this kind of listing in a journal will cease completely. At all events, *Kirjath Sepher* is the only journal in Hebrew in the field, and in English also there is only one single journal, *Studies in Bibliography and Book Lore* published by the Hebrew Union College. Other journals devoted to the study of the Hebrew book have appeared at certain periods, and in particular mention should be made of the annual *Areshet*, five important volumes of which appeared between the years 1959 and 1973, though various reasons combined to put an end to publication within a fairly short period. Despite the diversity of reasons, they all have their roots in the fact that the number of scholars ready and able to make a scientific contribution in the field of Hebrew bibliography has always been small, and those who did exist saw no personal fulfillment in systematic professional engagement in bibliography. It should be remembered that the existence of a regular journal, at a high level of scholarship, whose appearance at regular intervals is guaranteed, is an essential precondition for progress in any branch of science; it provides an instrument for transforming the achievements of the individual into the legacy of all and thus guaranteeing the continued progress of research. In the absence of such a journal, any branch of science is doomed to stagnation and a vicious circle is created from which there is no escape. In what follows we shall outline briefly the main achievements of Hebrew bibliography to date – and they are by no means inconsiderable – and indicate its limitations. We shall also pay attention to several topics which have not been included up to now within the scope of activity of Hebrew bibliography; even though the time may not yet be ripe for full and comprehensive treatment, they should not be ignored entirely.

CATALOGS

BODLEIAN LIBRARY AND THE BRITISH MUSEUM. Modern Hebrew bibliography begins with the catalogs of the two great Jewish libraries in England: the Bodleian Library in Oxford and the library of the British Musuem in London. There is a great difference between these two catalogs. The Jewish department of the Bodleian collection was listed in detail, with annotations and from a deep knowledge of history of medieval sciences by the father of Hebrew bibliography – and its outstanding exponent to this day – Moritz Steinschneider, during the years 1852 to 1860. In 1867 Joseph Zedner printed the Hebrew catalog of the library of the British Museum in London. Zedner maintained close contact with Steinschneider and provided him with very important bibliographical information that came into his possession – at first as a member of the well-known Berlin firm of booksellers, Asher, later as an independent bookseller and finally as librarian of the Hebrew department of the British Museum (between the years 1845 and 1869). These first two catalogs are classics of Hebrew bibliography, among its finest achievements to this day, and both have been reprinted for the benefit of scholars in recent years – in photographed form which does not easily allow correction. They also illustrate in diametrically opposed ways the problems and concerns of professional bibliography. Zedner is one of those who are content with the minimum. His listing is brief, concentrated, uniform, very precise and never strays to details which have no place on the frontispiece of the book. Were it not for the high reliability, completeness and professional clarity of the entries, we would think we were dealing with a commercial catalog (without prices); this impression is strengthened on reading the incidental notes scattered here and there concerning the physical condition of the book. Undoubtedly, Zedner's close contacts with the world of commercial booksellers had considerable effect on his method of work; this is meant solely as a compliment. By contrast, the vast catalog of Steinschneider represents a desire to see the study of the Hebrew book as a firm basis for a general advance in Jewish scholarship, with the frontispiece of the Hebrew book providing an entry into the palace of Hebrew culture. Steinschneider's spirit, and his ambitions within the field of Jewish cultural history, knew no bounds; his greatness lies in the wisdom with which he restricted himself to the petty – on the face of it! – details of bibliography, and the triviality of scanning the frontispieces of innumerable books. In the Bodleian catalog accurate bibliographical listing, dry and technical, frequently serves as a springboard for plunging into the historical and cultural details connected with the book or author in question. But everything in brief, in hints, with abbreviations, and – above all – in Latin (so economical as compared with German!). Nevertheless, the ratio of bibliographical detail to historical and cultural material remains on the average of five to one.

FRIEDLAND COLLECTION AND ROSENTHAL LIBRARY. Between these two extremes, Zedner the pedestrian bibliographer and Steinschneider the maximalist, exist many intermediate attempts, some of them of the first importance such as the list of Hebrew books in the Asiatic Museum in St. Petersburg (the Friedland Collection), *Kehilat Moshe,* edited by Samuel Wiener (letters *Alef* to *Lamed*). This library is unique for the great number of books from Eastern Europe that it contains, including Yiddish, and the work of Wiener, almost without precedent in his excellent sense of bibliographical discipline, is characterized by his notes which, unlike those of Steinschneider, are mainly bibliographical: earlier and later editions, evidence concerning further editions which are not extant, etc. His bibliographical annotations, phrased with extreme brevity, are so much to the point that to this day it is generally possible with their aid to identity "difficult" problematic volumes as if Wiener's own copies were lying in front of us.

These three catalogs – the "beginnings" of modern Hebrew bibliography – constitute most of what we possess in the way of description of the great collections of Hebraica in the world (for printed books; the position is different for manuscripts). One should also note the catalog of the Rosenthal library in Amsterdam, the work of an excellent bibliographer, Roest (printed in 1875), and a few others here and there. Recently several of the great Jewish libraries in the world have photographed their card catalogs, and distributed them to their sister libraries throughout the world. Among the libraries which have done this one should note those of the Hebrew Union College in Cincinatti, the New York Public Library and the Jewish Theological Seminary in New York. Use of these photographed catalogs obviously means visiting the libraries where they are held, and is therefore restricted.

CATALOGS FOR PUBLIC SALE. To this type one should add the (few) important catalogs, both historically and practically, which were prepared by well-known bibliographers for the purpose of public sale of famous libraries. To this day these catalogs provide an important source of information; in their day they were distributed among dealers in antiquities, collectors and great public libraries to awaken their interest in acquisitions from the collection. Among the classics of this genre one should name the catalog of the Van Biema library, edited by Samuel Zeligman (1905), and the catalog *Ohel Avraham* made by the bibliographer Raphael N. Rabbinovicz (1888), a "list of the books assembled and collected . . . by Abraham Merzbacher." Although the compiler – Rabbinovicz – stated that he edited the work on the basis of notebooks, and that it was not as accurate or as systematic as it should have been, and although it was not compiled – according to Rabbinovicz – for commerical purposes but to inform the public of the greatness of the collection, this catalog is quite unique since it was Rabbinovicz himself who purchased and collected the great collection for Merzbacher, his patron and benefactor, who intended in this way to provide bibliographical (and financial) assistance for the *Dikdukei Soferim* of Rabbinovicz. The first of the Hebrew catalogs designed for the purposes of a public sale is that of the fabulous library of Rabbi David Oppenheim (first printed in 1764, with an enlarged edition in 1782, and a more complete version *Kohelet David* in 1826). This library was the basis of the Bodleian collection in Oxford (which purchased the whole vast collection for a paltry sum in 1829). The books are in any case included in Steinschneider's list quoted above. There are many commercial catalogs extant, but the great majority of them were compiled by men without sufficient (or even, in some cases, the basic) knowledge, and frequently placed only obstacles and difficulties in the way of study of the Hebrew book.

THE FIRST CATALOGS. According to the recognized division of Jewish studies into periods, which we ourselves have followed, Steinschneider is the father of modern, scientific Hebrew bibliography; this is absolutely beyond doubt. At the same time, however, it is very difficult to accept the conventional view concerning the nature of the innovation which Steinschneider introduced into the profession. It is conventional to state that he was the first among Jewish scholars to establish the study of the Hebrew book as a scientific discipline in its own right, but actually the reverse is true: Steinschneider was the first Jewish scholar to turn knowledge of the history of the Jewish book (in manuscript and in print) into a lever with which to give the whole of Jewish studies a great thrust forward. The simple fact is that prior to Steinschneider all Hebrew bibliographical study, from the pioneering work of Shabbetai Bass in his book *Siftei Yeshenim* to the important bibliographical section (about 100 pages) included by Zunz in his book *Zur Geschichte und Literatur* published in 1845, deals with knowledge of the Hebrew book *for its own sake,* as an independent discipline. Undoubtedly the motives for research changed from the time of Shabbetai Bass to that of Zunz, as did the tools of bibliography and the demands made upon it, but the approach to the discipline remained fundamentally the same: knowledge of the Hebrew book and its history were their own justification. In the opinion of Rabbi Shabbetai Bass knowledge of the names of books and their authors could be useful – in mystical fashion – to men who knew nothing about the contents of the books, and could stand them in good stead in the world to come. Shabbetai Bass went on to say that knowledge of books was also of practical use in this world, helping men to distinguish when there had been changes between different editions of a book, and when a single book had several names or the same name referred to different books, besides several other simpler uses, e.g., to prevent an author calling his book a name already used for another book. These, of course, were not the purposes of Zunz. He had a broader historical perspective, which included henceforth not only the books but also the history of the art of printing. His list of contents clearly shows the direction of his research into the matter: printers and typography in Mantua from 1476 to 1662, the Hebrew press in Prague from 1513 to 1657, and a chapter on the dates included in books, a precursor of the change about to take place.

Steinschneider was the first to realize the true importance of bibliography as a preliminary tool and a basic method in the general study of the history of culture and thus he was the first to emphasize the tremendous gap between what existed and what was needed in Hebrew bibliography. He came to teach and remained to learn. In trying to lay the foundations for comprehensive, objective research in the history of Jewish studies and Jewish literature, he was compelled to make a proper listing of everything available in these areas (in print and in manuscript) and as he became engaged in this gigantic enterprise he became aware of the full extent of the bibliographical problems; it was like an open field which first had to be fenced before one could enjoy its fruits.

Raphael Nathan Nata Rabbinovicz (born in Novo-Zhagory, Kovno, 1835; died in Kiev, 1888). J.N.U.L., Schwadron Collection, Jerusalem.

A catalog of the books offered for sale by "Abraham Boukabza and Company," who were book dealers and petit-publishers of popular Hebrew books in Arabic characters 1885–1888. After that date Boukabza took up some other business. This rare catalog lists some 200 books and from it a great deal can be learned about what books were in demand in Algiers at the end of the 19th century, as well as about Hebrew printing there. Many of the books printed in Algiers – particularly the small popular Arabic books printed in Hebrew letters – no longer exist. The list lacks the place and date of publishing.

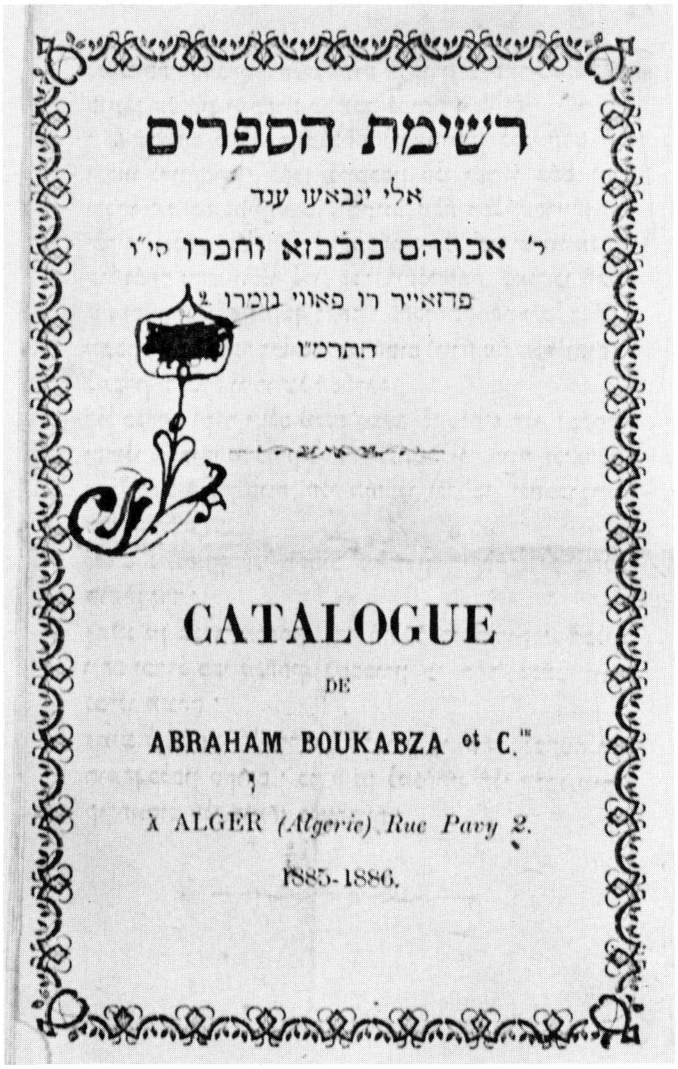

רשימת הספרים

אלי ינבאעו ענד

ר' אברהם בוכבזא וחברו הי"ו

פרזאייר רו פאווי נומירו 2

התרמ"ו

CATALOGUE

DE

ABRAHAM BOUKABZA et C.ie

À ALGER *(Algerie)* Rue Pavy 2.

1885-1886.

Since that time, Steinschneider's innovative approach has almost disappeared, because of the unusual breadth of knowledge it required, and Hebrew bibliography has returned to its original, more restricted format. A most important exception is the bibliographical work of Gershom Scholem in the field of Kabbalah. This scholar, who was the first to place research into mysticism on a scientific basis, established by himself the bibliographical groundwork required in this broad field, as an integral part of his overall research in the area. This comprehensive bibliographical enterprise has not been published in full, in professional form, except for a small part – mainly the *Bibliographia Kabbalistica* (1927), *Hebrew Kabbalistic Manuscripts in the National University Library of Jerusalem* (1944), and several essays and special publications. However, its tremendous scope is evident on reading and studying his hundreds of published works in the field of Jewish mysticism, scattered over dozens of publications, all with considerable space devoted to bibliographical notes. Particulaly impressive is the productive interaction between bibliographical endeavor and academic research. Academic research helps in the solution of bibliographical problems, and bibliographical investigation for its part furthers academic studies. There is no doubt that the lack of a general bibliography of Ḥasidism is a symptom – both cause and effect – of the general state of research in this area, just as the existence of detailed bibliographies of Braslav Ḥasidism (by G. Scholem) and Ḥabad Ḥasidism (by A. Haberman) reflects the relative progress of research in these branches of Ḥasidism. One could not imagine the great progress in the study of Hebrew poetry without the magnificent work of A. Davidson *Oẓar ha-Shirah ve-ha-Piyyut*(I–IV, 1925–1933), nor progress in the study of the Haskalah Movement – historically parallel and contemporary with Ḥasidism – without the fundamental bibliographical work of W. Zeitlin, *Bibliotheca Hebraica post-Mendelssohniana* (1891–1899); there are many more examples, positive and negative.

Ḥayyim Joseph David Azulai (1724–1806), one of the greatest rabbinical authorities of the 18th century. The Ḥida (as he is known from the initials of his name) was a multi-faceted character whose literary activity was extremely varied. Of the more than 40 of his books that were printed, his *Shem ha-Gedolim* was the most famous. This work is a lexicon of all the great rabbis up to and including his own time. The second part is an alphabetical listing of all the Hebrew books – both printed and in manuscript – of which he had heard. Although some 200 years have passed since that part appeared it is still of great importance for Hebrew bibliography because of its author's wide knowledge, helpful notes and bibliographical instinct.

THE PRELIMINARY PAGES

Besides the historical value of a book's contents – the main if not the only bridge between the past and present – a considerable amount of very valuable material is to be found in the pages printed before the main body of the book, and generally including the following: the title page, the introduction by the author and the publisher, forewords, *haskamot* (approbations), and warnings of various kinds, and the pages added at the end of the book including generally the following: the colophon, the names of the workers, comments of the proofreader, short poems, etc. These diminutive "literary genres" on the whole characteristic to printed works, constitute an invaluable source of information on a wide range of topics, sometimes in directions difficult to foresee in advance. In their introduction, the authors and/or the publishers generally say a little – or a lot – about their personal histories and wanderings, and describe events, personalities, places and periods for which they sometimes constitute the only source. Most of the *haskamot* are by Jewish sages of greater or lesser fame, and their words of recommendation have independent value as minor works of "occasional" literature. We also can learn from them where various rabbis held office and can establish with accuracy the chronological sequence of their rabbinates, since most

Plate 15 (above) and **Plate 16** (right). Scribes at work. Photo: Werner Braun, Jerusalem.

Plate 17 (above, left). The *mezuzah* scroll, being sacred, has to be written with a feather quill in indelible ink, in straight lines, and on specially prepared parchment. The 19th-century East European *mezuzah* case shown, which protects the scroll, is carved from wood. Mishkan le-Omanut, Kibbutz Ein Harod.

Plate 18 (above, right). An aspect of the careful handling of sacred scrolls is to wrap them in *mitpaḥot* like these three linen wrappers from Germany, 18th and 19th centuries. Mishkan le-Omanut, Kibbutz Ein Harod.

Plate 19 (below). The Torah scroll binder was customarily presented to the synagogue when a child was brought there for the first time. The binder usually had the following formula embroidered on it in Hebrew: "A, son of B, born . . . May the Holy One, Blessed be He, cause him to grow up to study His Law and to perform the Commandments and to enter beneath the marriage canopy." This last phrase was sometimes illustrated by a representation of the wedding scene. This example is of London origin, 1733. The Jewish Museum, London.

Plate 20 (opposite). The embroidered Torah mantle evolved because it was forbidden to touch the sacred scrolls by hand. Pictured is an English mantle for the Scroll of the Law. It was made of Italian tissue for the Hambro Synagogue in London – probably on the occasion of the opening of its first permanent home in 1727. Three red velvet orphreys, exquisitely embroidered in gold and silver thread, with parts raised in the manner of "stump work," represent in miniature the Altar, the Candelabrum and a fully equipped Scroll. The Jewish Museum, London.

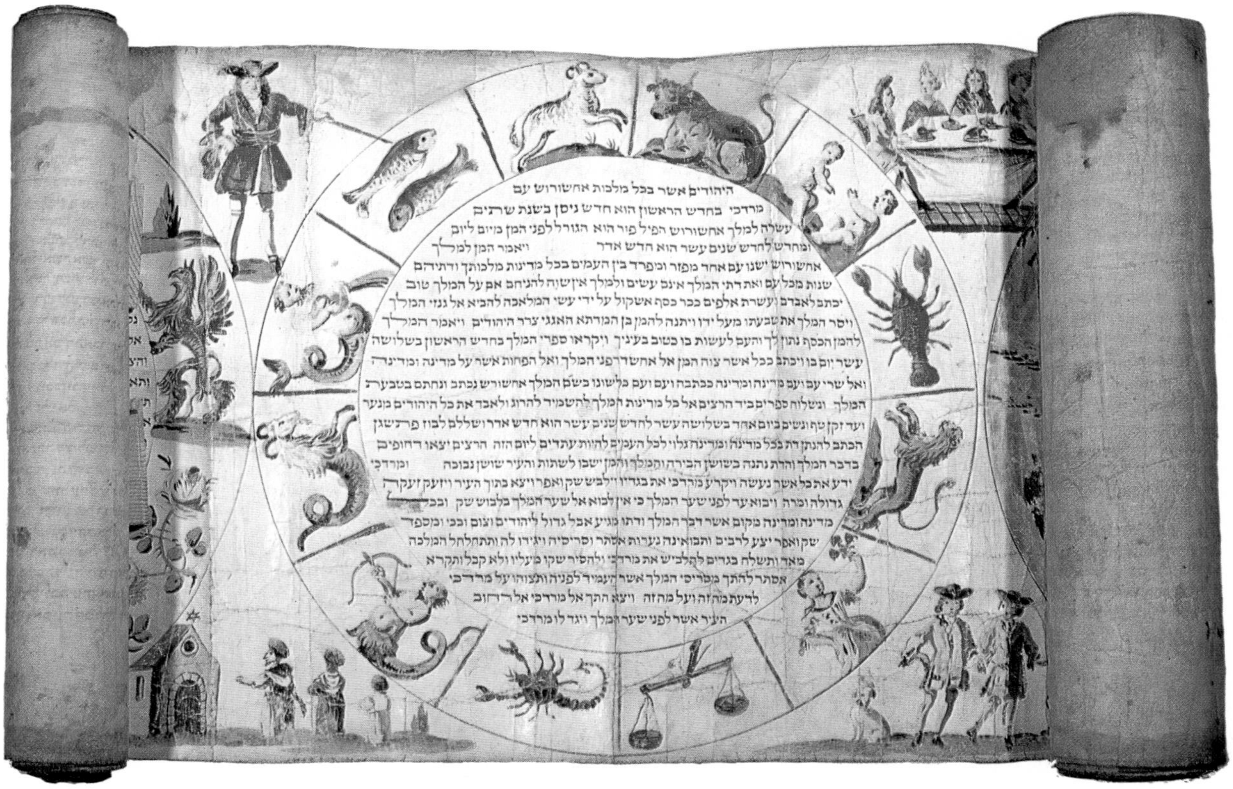

Plate 21 (above). Unlike the Torah scroll, the Scroll of Esther may be adorned with artistic illustrations. In this one, from Alsace, c. 1730, the text is written in a series of decorated circles. This section is illustrated by signs of the zodiac. Other illustrations include Purim scenes, human and animal figures, birds, and flowers. Jerusalem, Israel Museum.

Plate 22 (left). North African Torah ornaments, 19th century, including a velvet mantle, embroidered with silver and gold thread, backed with leather. Jerusalem, Israel Museum.

Gershom Scholem (born in Berlin, 1897, came to Ereẓ Israel in 1923). Courtesy Hebrew University of Jerusalem. Photo Meyerowitch.

of the *haskamot* are printed with the exact date clearly given in full. This, too, is of importance as a source of information on the battles between the *Mitnaggedim* and the *Ḥasidim* and their rabbis. The *haskamot* and warnings refer to the copyright of the writer, the printer and the publisher, to problems of censorship (especially the standard announcement that the nations mentioned in the book are not the nations of the contemporary world — an announcement whose development is still awaiting study) and to grateful acknowledgements to men of standing who had provided financial assistance towards the printing of the book, etc. The full list of workers' names at the end of the book — a feature characteristic mainly, though not solely, of the last 200 years in the history of printing, in Eastern Europe only — is an important source of information on the history of Jewish craftsmanship, and the comments of the proofreader are frequently important for establishing the text. The short poems have their own honorable place in the study of Hebrew poetry. The greatest value has been ascribed to the title page and the colophon. Apart from the historical information provided by almost every line of the colophon and the title page — the name of the author, his lineage, the printing arrangements, the place of printing, the year of printing, the owners of the press, and the authorities under whose patronage the book was printed, etc. — the title pages of books are also a significant source of information concerning the art of illustration among Jews from the end of the 15th century. The title pages are usually illustrated and decorated with etchings, woodcuts, printed symbols, graphic devices and "technical" ornamentation; their study is a rewarding source of information in the field of Jewish art. We have not included any reference to the artistry of the bookbinding which is so common and constitutes another chapter of great interest in the history of Jewish art. Further reason for bibliographical effort is the fact that differences are frequently found between individual copies of the same edition of a book, and the differences are likely to occur in any of the aforementioned "literary genres" at the beginning or end of a printed book. There are always valid reasons, sometimes known and sometimes unknown, for these differences and understanding them contributes greatly to the advancement of knowledge. An important problem in bibliography is the forged title page — to be distinguished from the forged book — and here too the interest lies in the historical and cultural circumstances which gave rise to the forgery. From the books — and from them alone — we may learn the history of the printing families, their rise and fall, their wanderings and problems, and this knowledge has historical importance from various points of view, social and cultural.

It should however be pointed out that this rich and diverse material has not yet been exploited except incidentally and unsystematically. Special and exceptional approbations have been singled out by scholars, and a number of comprehensive lists of approbations by particular sages have been compiled, including a recent study of Rabbi Moses Sofer, known after his books as the "Ḥatam Sofer." *Mafteaḥ ha-Haskamot*, "A Key to the Forewords," by Leopold Lowenstein, printed in facsimile in a limited edition in the year 1923, in no way meets the need, though it is a pioneering effort in this field. The question of "warnings" concerning authors' copyright and the commercial rights of printers and publishers has received a certain amount of attention in recent research, but though a serious beginning has been made, there is nothing more. The same holds for the rest of the historical material included in the pages "at the front and the back."

20th CENTURY

There is one difference in the landscape of Hebrew bibliography in the 20th century as compared with the 19th, when most Hebrew bibliographers were connected in one way or another with the book trade: as sellers – and this is true even of such a first-rank bibliographer and scholar as R.N. Rabbinovicz – as buyers (collectors!) or as both.

With the establishment of institutions of Jewish research in Israel and America, and the creation of great public libraries in these centers, a generation of bibliographers has arisen whose production is connected with their work as librarians and as directors of these libraries. And though bibliography, in contrast to most other branches of the humanities, has in all periods been known for the great importance ascribed to the personal attachment of the scholar to the subject of his research, i.e., the Hebrew book – such a relationship of love and affection as would be liable to detract from scholarship in any other field of research – yet this difference is highly significant. The simple fact is that the number of books acquired by these libraries (in Jerusalem, Tel Aviv, New York and elsewhere) is immense – after all, the ambition of these libraries is to reach completion! – and if such a library has importance for the scholars who read there, how much greater is its value for the bibliographer-librarian who devotes all his energies to the study of the Hebrew book. Bibliography is one of the few professions where quantity becomes quality, not only because of the great value of accumulated experience but also, and mainly, because each additional detail contributes greater clarification of the picture and thus leads to greater progress in bibliography as a whole.

The great libraries also serve as excellent means for developing and perfecting the productive skills of talented bibliographers. Among the most important of these in this century have been the brothers Alexander and Moses Marx, Aron Freimann, Isaac Rivkind, Aryeh Tauber, Abraham Yaari and Ḥayyim Liberman. They have all done their work by virtue of the posts they held in great Jewish libraries throughout the world, in Europe, Jerusalem and New York. The major achievements of study in the Hebrew book in the 20th century have been in two fields of study which at first sight appear very far removed from each other: the incunabula and printing in Italy in the second half of the 16th century, and books printed in Hebrew in the Middle East and in Eastern Europe since the middle of the 18th century (altogether four fields of study, not two). Though they seem at first glance very far apart, these fields of study do share an interesting common denominator: the books required for research in these areas are rare and very precious, the former because of their remoteness in time and the latter because of the trials and tribulations of the communities there and the catastrophes they suffered. Here too there has been mutual interaction: the library provides the librarian with the materials and circumstances required for research – books, time and sustenance – and the librarian guides the acquisition policy of the library along certain cultural channels, to meet their joint needs. It would be impossible to imagine any progress in these four great areas of study without the resources at the disposal of the great public libraries, and it is not surprising that it is in these areas that the greatest progress has been made in the 20th century. However, one must also point out that the listing of

Title page of *Sefer Midrash Rabbah,* Part I, printed in the townlet of Minkowitz in the region of Podolia. This edition was printed in 1800 and is quite rare. Only about 30 books were printed in Minkowitz between 1786 and c. 1820.

ספר
מדרש רבות
על ספר בראשית
עם כל המפרשים · שנדפסו מקדמת דנא ; ואלה שמותם ; הרב מתנות כהונה · והי"ב ידי משה ; וקצור יפה תואר · כאשר היו בדפוס פרנקפורט דאודרא · ומשנת רבי אליעזר ; ופירש זרע אברהם ·
במינקאוויץ
תחת
כשנת לך אני הושיעני כי פקודיך דרשתי לפק

printers in the east has been made possible basically thanks to the collection of the Sassoon family, in whose possession many of the books were concentrated. In addition to these areas of study, an important beginning has been made in the 20th century to the study of the Hebrew illustrated book.

The prime virtue of Hebrew bibliography in the 20th century as compared with the 19th – its close association with the great Jewish public libraries, with their financial resources and interest in research – has paradoxically been the cause of one of its major defects: inadequate sensitivity to bibliographical variance. Since the sheer volume of acquisition in the great public libraries deprives the librarian of the opportunity to carry out an autoptic examination (personal inspection) of all the books, he identifies them by means of the catalog, on the assumption that the catalog will suffice for a clear and complete identification of the book in question. In most cases it would seem that this is actually so but in a considerable proportion of antique volumes there have been internal changes, both during printing and after, for a great variety of reasons, and this fact usually succeeds in evading normal bibliographical listing. Clearly it is of particular interest to track down such books in order to determine the nature and scope of the changes and especially the reason for them, something which cannot usually be ascertained on the basis of a catalog identification. Every collector knows, from his own experience in his own field of interest, of dozens of such instances among the books in his possession, instances which would not be revealed by the catalogs of the great libraries. As we have said, this drawback stems from the very nature of the great public library and its method of work, and it can therefore be assumed with certainty that the private collections of hundreds of collectors throughout the world will always play a most important role in the furtherance of the study of the Hebrew book. It should be remembered that when private collections are bequeathed to the great libraries, they generally lose their unique character, since private collectors do not usually make catalogs, and even when the collection is listed separately in its new home the comparison with copies held by the library is made by means of the catalog.

Side by side with the various great catalogs, there began to develop in the middle of the 19th century a comprehensive, almost national bibliography, to judge by the ambition of its compilers. The huge undertaking by Isaac Benjacob, *Oẓar ha-Sefarim,* first printed in Vilna in 1880 after the death of its com-

Three title pages of *Sha'arei Kedushah* by the kabbalist Ḥayyim Vital, printed in Kapust in 1836. Although nos. 2 and 3 appear to be identical, they are not; no. 2 contains 24 pages whereas no. 3 has 26 pages. The internal order is also completely different. The only indication of a difference is the lack of the decorative lines in no. 2 and the fact that its Cyrillic lettering is smaller.

ספר
שערי קדושה
זה השער לה' צדיקים יבואו בו, להיישיר נוכח ה' דרכי איש, וזה הדרך אשר ילך בה, לדבק נשמתו במקום קדושה חוצבה, במקורה העליון, ואת המעשה אשר יעשון, ליישר האדם לעבודת בוראו ית' ויתעלה:
הועתק מכתבי הקודש, כתיבת יד הרמה והנשאה, המקובל אלהי, כמוהר"ר
חיים וויטאל
זלה"ה, בארץ מצרים, תלמיד מובהק לאיש אלהים קדוש הוא האר"י לוריא זלה"ה:
נדפס ע"י מ' שבתי במ' שמעון סלאוין ז"ל.
сеферъ шаре кедуша
т. е. святы враша
въ КОпысь
Въ типографіи шобсела славина
1836
בקאפוסט
בשנת תקצ"ו לפ"ק
1

ספר
שערי קדושה
זה השער לה' צדיקים יבואו בו, להיישיר נוכח ה' דרכי איש, וזה הדרך אשר ילך בה, לדבק נשמתו במקום קדושה חוצבה, במקורה העלין, ואת המעשה אשר יעשון, ליישר האדם לעבודת בוראו ית' ויתעלה:
הועתק מכתבי הקודש, כתיבת יד הרמה והנשאה, המקובל אלהי, כמוהר"ר
חיים וויטאל
זלה"ה, בארץ מצרים, תלמיד מובהק לאיש אלהים קדוש הוא האר"י לוריא זלה"ה:
נדפס על ידי הרבני מ' שבחי במ' שמעון סלאווין
С феръ шаре кедуша
т. е. Святы враша
Вь КопыСь
Въ Типографіи ш. славина
1836
בקאפוסט
בשנת תקצ"ו לפ"ק
2

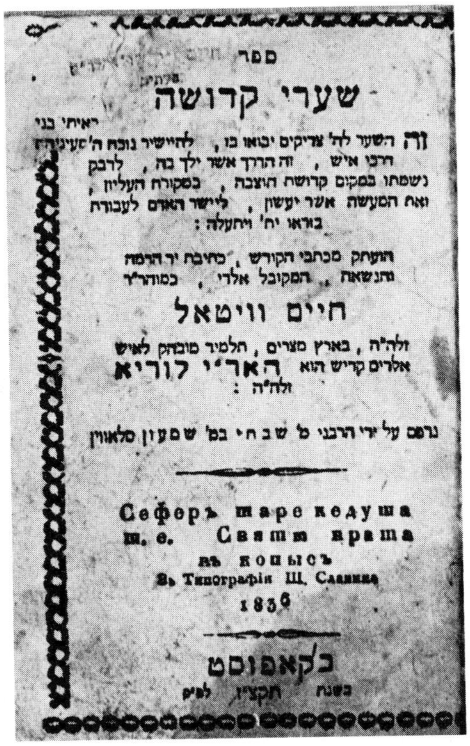
ספר
שערי קדושה
זה השער לה' צדיקים יבואו בו, להיישיר נוכח ה' דרכי איש, וזה הדרך אשר ילך בה, לדבק נשמתו במקום קדושה חוצבה, במקורה העליון, ואת המעשה אשר יעשון, ליישר האדם לעבודת בוראו ית' ויתעלה:
הועתק מכתבי הקודש, כתיבת יד הרמה והנשאה, המקובל אלהי, כמוהר"ר
חיים וויטאל
זלה"ה, בארץ מצרים, תלמיד מובהק לאיש אלהים קדוש הוא האר"י לוריא זלה"ה:
נדפס על ידי הרבני מ' שבחי במ' שמעון סלאווין
Сеферъ шаре кедуша
т. е. Святы враша
въ копысь
Въ Типографіи Ш. Славина
1836
בקאפוסט
בשנת תקצ"ו לפ"ק
3

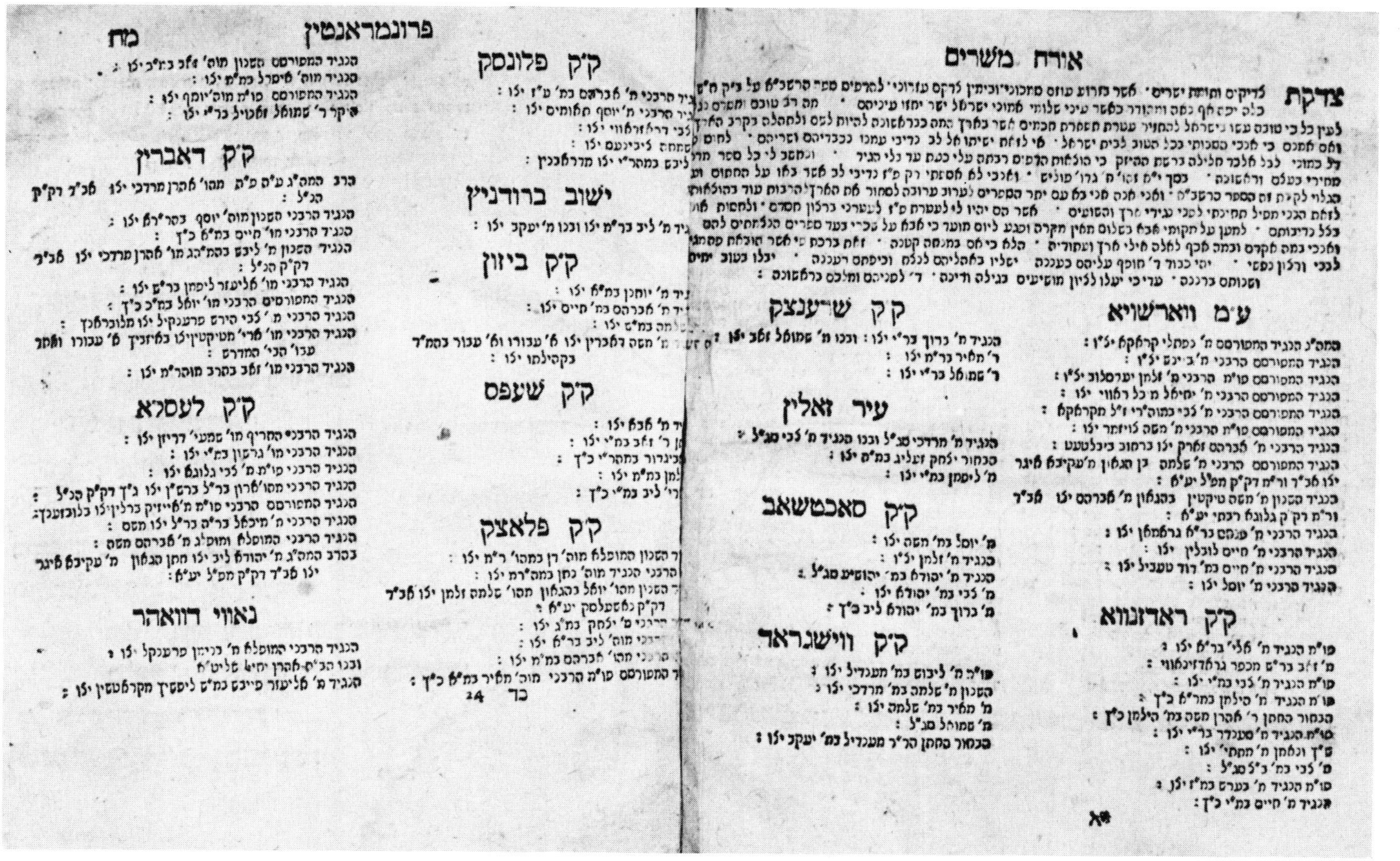

The last two pages of the second part of the novellae of Rashba (Solomon ben Abraham Adret) on the talmudic tractate *Bava Kamma* printed in Nowy Dwor in 1805. These are lists of people in various Polish towns and villages who "subscribed" to the book before it was printed and paid the publisher completely or partly in advance. Such lists are an important historical source for the personal history of the subscribers and for their places of residence. Of particular interest here is Solomon, the son of Rabbi Akiva Eger, a well-known scholar who was to play an important role in Jewish communal life in Poland; at the time he was 19 years of age and living in Warsaw. In the list for the town of Laslow the son-in-law of Rabbi Akiva Eger is mentioned. This is one of the first such detailed lists to appear; they became very common, particularly in Poland and Russia, until the Holocaust.

piler, is the first attempt to list all the books printed in Hebrew characters, with all their editions, from the establishment of the first printers to the date of the compiler (who died in 1863), and all books extant in manuscript only, mainly from the libraries of Europe. This bibliography lists 15,000 entries (not editions – although the title page promises 17,000) of which 7,000 are printed books, 3,000 are manuscripts, 2,000 are doubtful and another 3,000 are duplications. The details listed include principally the name of the book, its author, full and ordered contents, place and time of printing, and format. For manuscripts the style of handwriting is also given. This pioneering enterprise is still valuable and has not lost any of its importance. The author, one of the most important scholars of the Haskalah in Lithuania, "shook the dust" – in the words of his son, Jacob, who printed the book – "from all the books of the catalogs of all time," besides the vast number of books which he saw with his own eyes during 20 years of activity as publisher, author and dealer in ancient books, and besides the immense help given him by Steinschneider both in criticism and in supplementary information. This unique project remains awe-inspiring to this day, not merely because of its scope but mainly because of its meticulous accuracy and the striving for perfection in every single entry; this is most conspicuous in those books where Benjacob suspected that the information given on the frontispiece was incorrect or only partly correct. In such cases the listing is accompanied by short notes which draw the reader's attention to the existence of the problem. In 1965, M.M. Zlatkin published corrections to 4,000 of the entries, based on the finding of recent bibliography. He also added an index of names and authors, and called his work *Ozar ha-Sefarim Part II*.

In the first half of the 20th century, the pioneering

enterprise of Benjacob found its successor in the monumental work of H.D. Friedberg, *Bet Eked Sefarim.* This great scholar undertook to amend and complete the work of Benjacob as regards printed books, relying mainly on the wealth of scholarly – and other – literature but also on direct examination. His importance lies mainly in completing the study of everything printed from about 1850 – the last date included in *Oẓar ha-Sefarim* – to 1950, the year that *Bet Eked Sefarim* (in a second, much-enlarged edition) was handed to the printers. Despite the various criticisms leveled against this book, there is nothing better or more useful, and the critics themselves – fellow bibliographers who did not spare him either their stingy criticism or their narrowness of vision – made constant, sometimes unacknowledged, reference to it. No significant approximation can yet be made of what is missing from the book, either in entries or in editions, nor what percentage of errors it includes. The principal weakness of his work – by contrast with Benjacob's – lies in his excessive reliance on whatever book listings he could find, and his preference for a superfluous entry to an omission – a highly dubious principle even though at first glance it might seem correct. Moreover, Friedberg apparently paid insufficient attention to the fundamental importance of autopsy – direct examination – and consequently did not even consider it

The two title pages of *Tashbeẓ,* the responsa of Simeon ben Ẓemaḥ Duran, one of the greatest rabbinical authorities of North Africa in the 14th–15th century. The title page, decorated with depictions of Moses, Aaron, David and Solomon, is a copper engraving and bears the date 1741. The other, with the lions, is a wood carving and is dated 1738. Bibliographical tradition has it that the first edition was almost completely destroyed in a fire at the press and that the book was reprinted three years later. However, this seems to be legend and copies with both title pages are equally available. There can be no doubt that the difference in dates stems from the time it took to print this very large book; one title page was made at the beginning of the work and the other at the end.

necessary to take the elementary step of indicating by an asterisk any volume which he had seen (or not seen) with his own eyes. Regular users of Friedberg's book are convinced they can usually tell by various indications whether a book has been directly examined by Friedberg, but this is "blind" discrimination, usually quite unreliable.

Friedberg took the raw material which he accumulated on this project and reworked it in the form of historical sketches, using it for his books – the only ones of their kind – on "the history of Hebrew printing" mainly in Germany, Poland and Italy.

During the last 15 years, work has been carried out at the National Library in Jerusalem on "the Hebrew Bibliographical Project," under the joint auspices of the Hebrew University, Mossad Bialik and the Ministry of Education and Culture, whose aim is "to realize the dream of an all-inclusive national bibliography based as far as possible on the resources of the great libraries, private and public, in Israel and abroad, listing the books on the basis of direct inspection, with a full and accurate description, in accordance with the best internationally accepted cataloging practices" (from the introduction by Gershom Scholem to the "Specimen Brochure" of the project published in Jerusalem, 1964). This project, first initiated by Dr. Israel Mehlman, one of the greatest collectors of Hebrew books in this generation, should bear fruit towards the end of the century.

An important development in Hebrew bibliography in the 20th century has been the attention paid to the practical aspects of the work; the systematization of library work has been improved, principles of classification for Jewish studies have been established (here too the guiding spirit has been Gershom Scholem), the Hebrew catalog has been improved and rules laid down (linked to the principles of classification), and huge efforts have been made to achieve greater ease of access to the vast amount of bibliographical information which over the years has become dispersed among hundreds of publications. The climax of this attempt is represented by the *Mafteaḥ ha-Mafteḥot* by S. Shunami, a bibliography of the bibliographies published up to 1968, the year of the second edition of *Mafteaḥ ha-Mafteḥot* which includes 5,000 bibliographical entries on 27 subjects, of which the main ones are the following: Encyclopaedias, bibliographies, catalogs, manuscripts, religion, Hebrew, Bible, rabbinic literature, prayers and the synagogue, Jewish literature, Yiddish, Ladino, Israel and the nations, sociology, sects, Zionism, the Land of Israel, secular sciences, history, countries, the Holocaust, biographies, and Hebrew printing.

METHODS

The standard method of Hebrew bibliography, from its beginnings to the present day (with the exception of the vast and unique projects described above) has been that of geographical or local listing. Lists of books according to the widely dispersed towns where they were printed have been the most common kind of Hebrew bibliography, together with lists of books that trace the activities and wanderings of families of printers. In these two areas one can see the principal achievements of Hebrew bibliography to date. For Central and Eastern Europe the work has generally been carried out by rabbis, scholars, book lovers and professional bibliographers who either came from the towns or were actually living there. Works of outstanding importance in this area in recent years include *The History of Hebrew Printing in Poland* by H.D. Friedberg (second enlarged edition, Jerusalem 1950), *Hebrew Printing in Jerusalem* (till 1890) by Shoshana Halevi, an outstanding book (Jerusalem, 1962), *Die Basler Hebraeischer Drucke* ("Hebrew Printing in Basle", Freiburg, 1964) by Joseph Prijs, and *Hebrew Printing in Constantinople* by A. Yaari, printed after his death (Jerusalem, 1967). The arbitrariness of choice is well evident even within the field of the "standard method" in Hebrew bibliography. Besides books printed in Constantinople, Yaari also listed books printed in Smyrna, but those printed in Salonika – a most important topic in the study of printing in the East – have not yet been systematically listed and only partial lists exist. As an example of the histories of printers, one may cite A.M. Haberman's book on the Soncino family of printers (1933). Next in line quantitatively, though certainly not qualitatively, come the professional bibliographies, among which the following excellent works should be noted: An Index of Wills and Funeral Eulogies by B. Wachstein, *Sarei ha-Elef* edited by Dov Mandlebaum and Menaḥem M. Kasher, which covers all the rabbinic literature composed during the 1,000 years between the completion of the Talmud (about 500 c.e.) and the time of Joseph Caro, author of the *Shulḥan Arukh*. *A Bibliography of the History of the Jews in North Africa* compiled with exemplary thoroughness by A. Hatal (Jerusalem 1974), containing all relevant material on the topic,

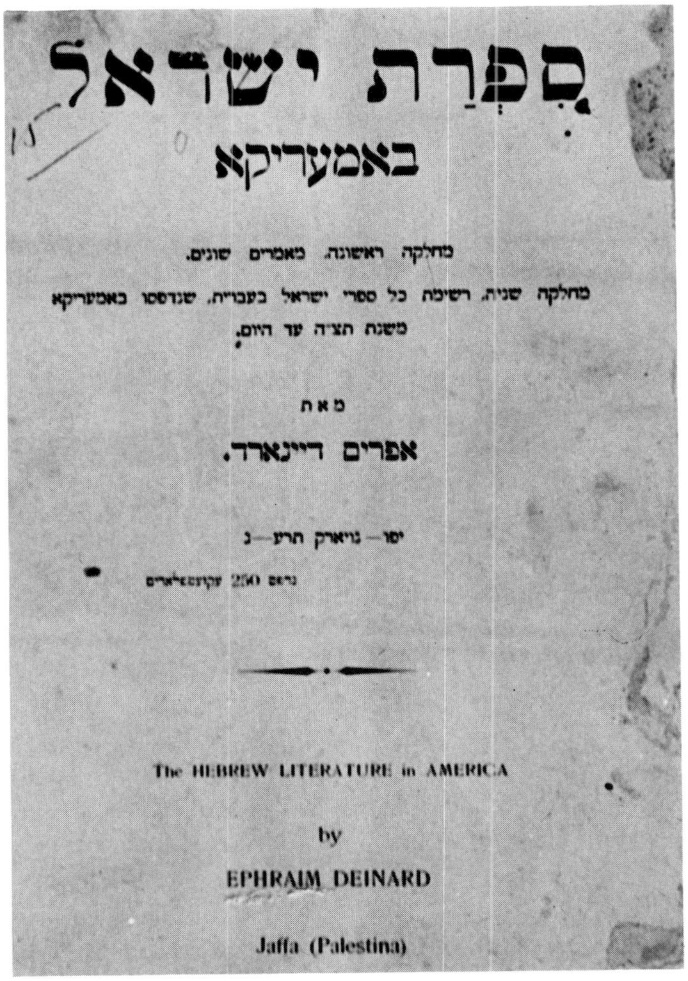
ספרת ישראל
באמעריקא
מחלקה ראשונה. מאמרים שונים.
מחלקה שניה. רשימה כל ספרי ישראל בעברית, שנדפסו באמעריקא משנת תצ״ה עד היום.
מאת
אפרים דיינארד.
יפו — נויארק תרע—ג
נדפס 250 עקזעמפלארים

The HEBREW LITERATURE in AMERICA
by
EPHRAIM DEINARD
Jaffa (Palestina)

A list of Hebrew books printed in America since 1735, compiled by Ephraim Deinard. It was printed in two parts, one in New York in 1910 and the other in Jaffa in 1913. This was Deinard's second effort in this field, and it contains 571 items. In 1926 he improved the book; the second edition printed in St. Louis listed 989 items because, among other reasons, it covered an additional 13 years. The first edition, which was only printed in 250 copies, was totally destroyed by fire in the riots instigated by Gamal Pasha in Jaffa in 1914 at the start of World War I. According to Deinard in the introduction to the second edition, only 17 copies survived because they had been sent to the U.S. This bibliography is very "personal" and selective, a fact which Deinard's many antagonists were not loath to stress.

with no restrictions in time, and in ten languages (about 5,650 entries), and the *Bibliography of Jewish Art,* published (posthumously) by Leo Meir.

These few examples have been chosen merely to illustrate the range of topics. To summarize, we can only quote the words of S. Shunami in his introduction to the *Mafteaḥ ha-Maftehot* (page xviii): "Nearly 5,000 entries are included in this book. Nevertheless, there are some topics in Jewish studies which have not received bibliographical treatment. And there are some fields of study where the bibliographies that have been compiled are inadequate even by minimal standards. For some of our great writers and scholars there is no proper bibliography which is either complete or of an appropriate standard."

FUTURE TASKS

Hebrew bibliography today is faced with a number of heavy tasks which have so far not even been broached. We shall mention only those which will lead to a deepening of our knowledge of the history of the Hebrew book itself, topics which will serve to place the profession of bibliography on a firmer foundation both programmatically and technically, apart from their contribution to other fields of study.

The title page of the responsa of Israel of Brunna, one of the great rabbinical authorities of 15-century Germany. The first edition (shown here) was printed in Salonika in 1798. This edition is very rare because most of the copies were destroyed in a fire at the press. The book was printed again at Stettin in 1860 and at Jerusalem in 1965. This copy belonged to Dr. A. Jellineck.

PREDIGER IN WIEN
ספר שו״ת
שלמה קאמונדו
משה בצלאל
שמואל
יחיאל יעקב אליקים
סאלוניקי
סילים
החכמה והדעת
שבתי

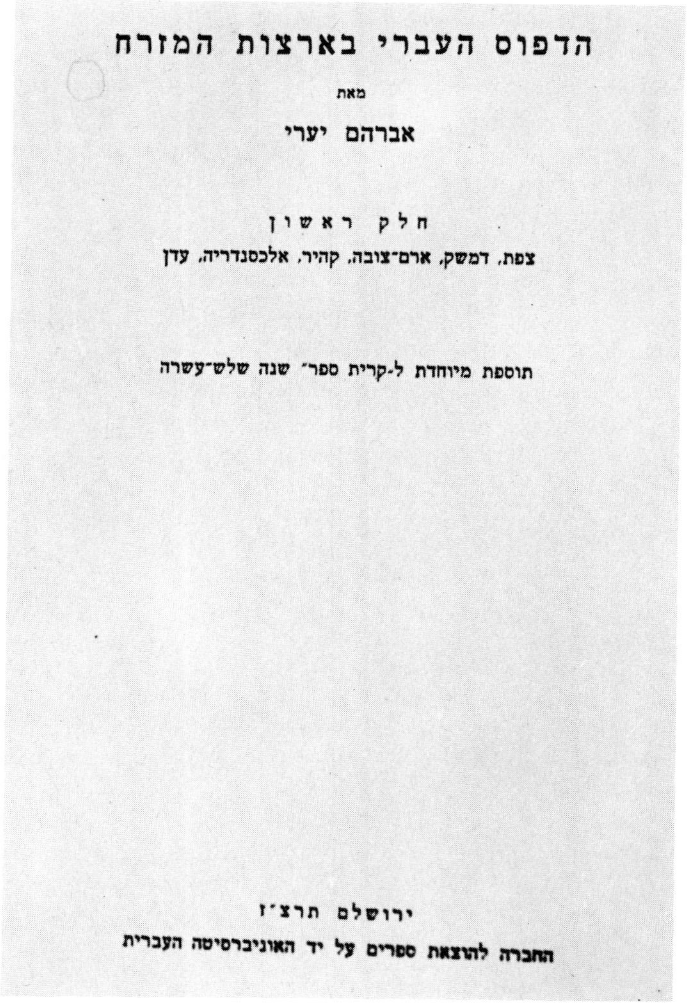
הדפוס העברי בארצות המזרח

מאת

אברהם יערי

חלק ראשון

צפת, דמשק, ארם־צובה, קהיר, אלכסנדריה, עדן

תוספת מיוחדת ל״קרית ספר״ שנה שלש־עשרה

ירושלם תרצ״ז

החברה להוצאת ספרים על יד האוניברסיטה העברית

The title page of Abraham Yaari's monumental study of Hebrew printing in Syria, Egypt, Aden and Safed. This was the first part of what the author intended to be a comprehensive study of Hebrew printing in the Orient. The second volume treated Iraq and India and the fourth, Constantinople. The third volume, on Jerusalem, was never printed. Yaari also published a study of Hebrew printing in Izmir (Istanbul) in the journal, *Areshet,* I, 1959. The book pictured was printed posthumously.

LOST BOOKS. The most difficult task is the listing of all Hebrew books which have disappeared over the years and failed to survive even in manuscript. Sometimes not even quotations from such books have survived but only their names. This important project should be regarded as complementary to the National Bibliography described above, and as its natural and indispensable counterpart. Our assumption is – though obviously it cannot be proven – that the number of lost titles will not be much smaller than the number of extant works listed in the National Bibliography. It should be noted that even books extant in manuscript are "lost" if we know for certain that they were printed and the printed edition has not survived in even a single copy. One must distinguish between books which survived in name only, books from which quotations have been preserved either as originally written or in paraphrase, and books which survive in manuscript though lost in their printed form. Such a bibliography will need a special set of rules both as regards contents and as regards form and listing. The literary sources on which such a bibliography must be based are extremely varied: lists of books, starting with those from the Cairo *Genizah* and extending to the endpapers in books on which the owners were wont to write down the lists of books in their possession; lists of books which had been seen by the censors, especially in Italy from the second half of the 16th century; the evidence of writers and printers who referred to earlier printings or manuscripts in their possession; polemical works which were usually accompanied by the destruction of opposing literary efforts great or small; memoirs and biographies; and in general all Hebrew literature in existence today in print or in manuscript, which must be thoroughly combed and searched for all evidence relevant to the listing of lost books. It is difficult to exaggerate the importance of this work and the contribution it can make to the study of Jewish culture, as it will cast a new light on the spiritual horizons of our civilization, both quantitatively and qualitatively. Such a list would also be illuminating for the general listing of printed books and would help to solve many bibliographical riddles.

ANONYMOUS BOOKS. Another task is the systematic bibliographical listing of all Hebrew books published anonymously. Such an enterprise would be immeasurably smaller than the previous one, but in no way less important. Anonymous literature includes books attributed in manuscript or in print, in error or deliberately, to other writers, and books written by a group of authors (generally anonymous, e.g., the literature of Mayence) as well as normal anonymous literature whose authors concealed their identity entirely or obscured it by using pseudonyms and initials, or whose anonymity has resulted from the passing of time. A full listing of such books, in all their editions and variants, would isolate a literary problem of the first magnitude and would facilitate a comprehensive study of the topic. It would also answer one of the main questions in this field of research: Is there any common factor – of geography, content or period – and can the working of an implicit law be discerned in the light of which the operation and significance of this phenomenon can be explained?

ART OF PRINTING. A further task of an entirely different character is the study of the craft (or art – in both senses) of printing, both technically and professionally. The kinds of type face, the size of the letters, the length of the lines and the space between them, the arrangement of the lines (in one, two or three columns per page) and the general layout of the page, the arrangement of vertical and horizontal margins, the combination of large and small letters, the inventory of letters available, the paper, the ink, the printing press, the proofreading, etc. – none of these has as yet been granted even minimal listing. There does not exist today any bibliographical catalog on such topics, which would describe the situation in the various towns where printing took place from these points of view, and the authenticity of books in which place of origin is not indicated or whose details have been forged cannot be bibliographically established except by guesswork or from long experience of day to day handling of such books. An accurate catalog on these topics would make possible unequivocal – or, at least, more reliable – ascriptions and would immeasurably improve the general National Bibliography, since the place of printing is one of the most important details about which the reader must be informed. Clearly this technical study, which lies at the heart of bibliography in the exact meaning of the word, will make a substantial contribution to our understanding of the history of Jewish typography, a subject whose importance it is hard to overestimate, and to our knowledge of the wanderings of printers and their printing presses from town to town and from state to state. A byproduct of this project would be a full listing of all the books which lack a place or year of publication, a subject of great importance in its own right; concealment of the place and time of publication was never without very good reason, and an understanding of the nature of these reasons is important for the study of the history of Jewish culture.

ספר

טהרת הכסף

מהדורא בתרא

ולוה הטעיות על קצת ספר זבחים שלמים וכסף אחר · עם קצת פסקים לקוחים מספר ש״ות כת״י המחבר · והסכמות חכמי ורבני הדור על הספר הנזכר אשר כתבו לסתור את דברי המשיג עליו ומחרחר · להראות לכל באי עולם לידע ולהודיע משפט עובר לסוחר · ותהי האמת נהדרת הדור הדור כל יאחר · מידי אביר בתורה · נושא ונותן באמונה · הני קראי דתנה · ויהי לפנינה · דין הוא הדר הרב המובהק כמוהר״ר אברהם אנקאווא נר״ו יאיר :

פה ליוורנו יע״א

שנת יחל ישראל אל ס׳ לפ״ק

בדפוס חדש של החכם רש״ל

אליהו בן אמוזג וחבריו הי״ו

מדפיסים ומוכרי ספרים

In the year 1858 in Leghorn a book was printed entitled *Zevaḥim Shelemim* which contained, inter alia, the commentary of R. Abraham Anakawah, the book's publisher, on Maimonides' laws of *sheḥitah* (ritual slaughter). The book was sharply attacked by a group of North African rabbis and became the cause of a violent controversy there. Rabbi Anakawah was forced to compose a small work in his own defense, *Toharat ha-Kesef,* which was also printed in Leghorn in 1860. It contains a collection of rabbinic opinions favorable to this earlier work, his explanations of the points which caused the controversy, and also an attack against his critics and the way they behaved.

ANALYTICAL BIBLIOGRAPHY. A most important aim which faces workers in the field of Hebrew bibliography today is the analytical listing of Hebrew literature of all periods. Very often a book on *halakhah,* or any sacred book, will include large or small sections dealing with groups of responsa or individual responsa by a particular rabbi who is not the author of the book named on the frontispiece. This is a very common occurence, but in the present state of Hebrew bibliography there is no possible way of investigating it or establishing its dimensions. In effect there is not one of the great Jewish sages whose literary work can be described in full. All that can be done is to list the books in which his name appears as author on the title page. As far as the great Jewish authorities are concerned, the greater their fame and importance in their own time, the more their responsa were solicited by lesser rabbis who generally included these responsa in their own books and basked in the reflected glory. Though these responsa not infrequently deal with communal and social problems, and knowledge of them is of great value, our purpose here has been to stress the lack of analytical bibliography from the purely technical point of view, without reference to its usefullness for historical and social studies, etc. However, the goal of collecting and listing all the works of every single author, wherever they appeared and in whatever genre (books, pamphlets, individual responsa, forewords, poems, letters, etc.) must be seen as one of the major goals with top priority in the field of bibliography. Such an enterprise clearly calls for cooperation between bibliographers and scholars in the various fields of literature; a professional bibliographer alone, without outside help, could not cope with the task.

A common factor in all the tasks listed so far has been the fact that they are bibliographies which must go beyond the title page. Their execution requires meticulous study of the body of the book – though not as far as content is concerned! – and the adoption of an appropriate and effective method of work.

BOOKS UNDER ATTACK. Another important task is the complete and accurate listing of all books known to have been proscribed, burnt, or confiscated. This does not mean books which were so completely destroyed that not a single copy has survived. The listing of such works has been described above, in the paragraph dealing with lost books. The reference here is to books which have survived in a limited number of copies, and which can therefore be given complete and accurate bibliographical listing. It is a matter of concentrating all such books in one list, a kind of professional bibliography of controversy and dispute. Such a record would in any case cover all the important trends within Judaism, and would demonstrate the central importance of the book as a social instrument, and the battles fought against books which were regarded as objects capable, as it were, of spreading poison and infection to the public danger. The number of books which would appear in such a list may well turn out to be surprisingly large, covering an extremely broad range of topics, from such important intellectual and religious trends as Kabbalah, Ḥasidism and messianism to petty personal disputes on quite marginal problems which seemed in their time to be of the highest national, religious or social importance. Such a list would also help to preserve these rare books. The list of books which have been persecuted and have perished would be supplemented by a list of the polemical works directed against them, which explained the motives for the persecution, the danger in the persecuted books, their error, etc. And of course the books on the other side, those meant to defend and justify the persecuted books. This is the literature of polemic and disputation, the list of books written against other books. It is an extremely complex and difficult project, if only for the simple reason that most of the basic bibliographical data provided by the title page is incorrect, characterized by camouflage and a good deal of concealment. But the importance of this project is as great as its difficulty. This topic is dealt with – albeit briefly, superficially and with insufficient accuracy – in Moshe Carmilly's book *Sefer ve-Sayif* (Jerusalem, New York, 1967), whose sub-title is *Freedom of expression and thought among the Jewish people.*

ISOLATED PAGES. A subject which so far as is known has not been treated at all up till now is the bibliographical listing of "isolated pages." Considered estimates have placed their number in the thousands, perhaps as many as ten thousand, and they are of great importance both for knowledge of Jewish culture and for knowledge of the history of the Jewish press. These pages are generally connected with disputes between leaders of the community and their rabbis, family quarrels, migrant rabbis, polemical discourse, etc. Those pages which were hung or pasted on the walls of ghetto houses or synagogues etc. have for the most part been lost and only in exceptional cases has anything survived. This brand of literature has special value in connection with the disputes within Ḥasidism and those against the *Mitnaggedim.* One should also include in this genre posters and leaflets up to our own time, including leaflets from the anti-Hitler underground in Europe and from the opposition to the Mandate in Palestine, leaflets of the Neturei Karta and many more besides. Also printed on isolated pages were charms and talismans, advertisements, isolated recommendations, etc. and short folk tales confined to one page.

FURTHER OMISSIONS. In order to demonstrate how unsatisfactory is the state of Hebrew bibliography after one hundred and fifty years of activity and research along regular conventional lines, it should be pointed out that to date we do not possess any comprehensive bibliographical listing of any one of the basic works of Jewish culture: the prayer book, the Pentateuch, the Mishnah, the Midrashim (most of which have not even been partially listed), the *Shulḥan Arukh,* etc. Exception must be made for the Talmud (Babylonian and Jerusalem) and the *Zohar.* An example of what needs to be done is provided by the bibliography of the Passover *Haggadah,* in which

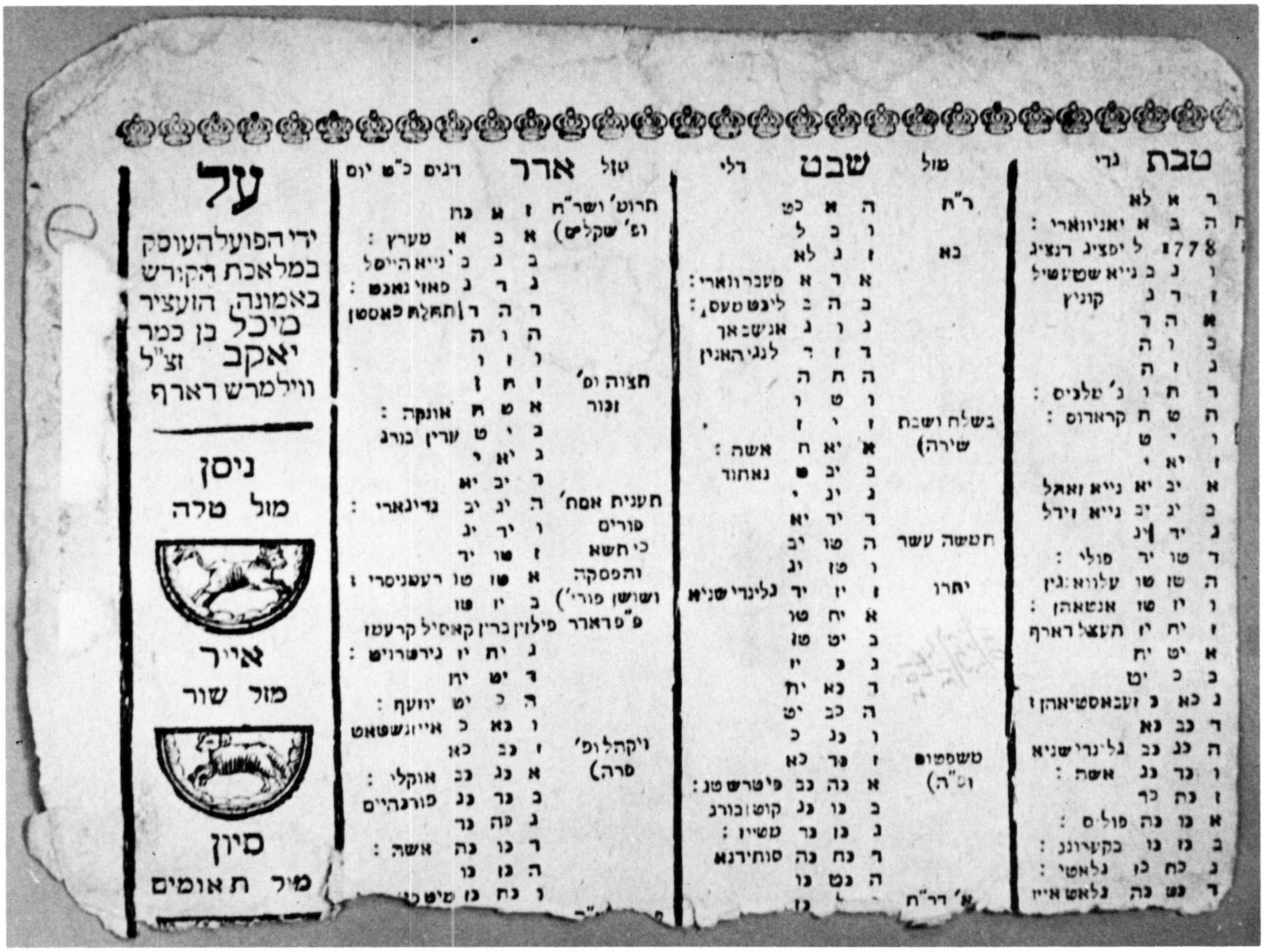

A page from a wall calendar printed in Wilmersdorf in 1778 by the worker Michal ben Jacob. The calendar lists the Hebrew date opposite the secular date with the weekly Torah readings to the right and secular holidays and market days to the left. The signs of the zodiac are in the outer border. This fragment survived as part of the binding of a book.

an unusual amount of bibliographical effort has been invested in recent years, thanks to the affection in which it is held by collectors. The history of this bibliography makes an exciting story. Prominent bibliographers began work on the project at the end of the last century and the beginning of this; in 1960 Abraham Yaari tried to summarize the tremendous efforts that had been devoted to the project up till then, and added a good deal of his own. The indefatigable Yaari listed about 2,700 Passover *haggadot* and since then many bibliographers have added well over a thousand further entries, and still the work remains incomplete. This enormous effort well illustrates both the principal weakness of Hebrew bibliography today and its strength. The choice of topic and the work of recording have been quite unplanned; each scholar worked at whatever library happened to be at hand. The material has been printed in many literary periodicals, and anyone today who wants to identify a *haggadah* in his possession by reference to published research can have no idea where to look, or even once he has succeeded in identifying the *haggadah,* what parallel and matching entries exist in the different lists. There is undoubtedly a need for further work, collating all the existing bibliographies of Passover *haggadot*, thus facilitating the task of revision and completion. It hardly needs to be said that from the point of view of scientific research or general cultural studies, there is no special interest in the Passover *haggadah* or in the commentaries upon it (why not the Book of Esther, for example?); immeasurably more important would be a similar endeavor – systematic and coordinated – with respect to the prayer book, the Pentateuch, the

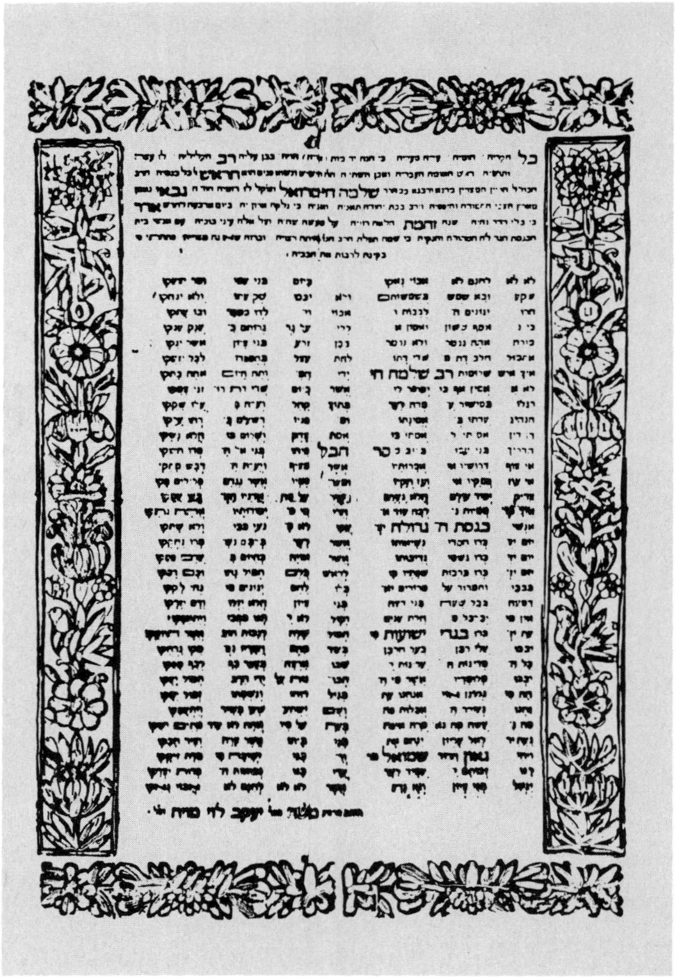

An elegy by Moses ben Jacob Levi Moya on the death of the Venetian scholar and rabbi Solomon Hai ben Nehemiah Saraval, who passed away on the fourth of Adar, 1692. It consists of one page which includes a preamble in prose and then the poem itself which is laid out in seven columns. The poem also expresses words of consolation to the bereaved family, and extends good wishes to a certain dignitary, Samuel, apparently the rabbinical successor of the deceased. The whole text is enclosed in a floral border whose right and left panels include a dove. It was composed and printed in Venice, 1692. Cecil Roth collection.

The Wise, the Wicked, the Just, and the Simple.
King David Praying before the Altar.

A page from a Passover *Haggadah* which was printed in London in 1836. A non-illustrated edition appeared in London in 1833 and in 1836 the publishers re-issued it with pages of illustration and an illustrated title page. This edition is not listed. The engravings were done by a non-Jew and some of the Hebrew words are so badly written as to be unrecognizable.

Mishnah, etc. with all their commentaries – the most valued possessions of Jewish culture. According to Shunami, in the introduction quoted above (page xiv): "most of the compilers of bibliographies are not experts in the field, a fact which is clearly evident in their publications. At the same time it is surprising what a high proportion of those lacking in expertise have reached a proper standard of bibliography, both in editing and in reliability and accuracy."

NEED FOR ORGANIZED ACADEMIC RESEARCH. There is a tradition in Hebrew bibliography for projects that require team work and institutional and financial organization to be carried out by individuals "with a bee in their bonnet"; this is a good illustration of the state of affairs in the profession. What is needed to accomplish the tasks listed above is a breakthrough on the part of the academic bodies engaged in study of the Hebrew book. The schools of librarianship at the various universities must open their doors to advanced research in this field, theoretical research designed to train not merely librarians and library technicians but scholars engaged in bibliographical research as historians and students of literature. To this end the schools must make it possible for work to be presented as doctoral dissertations, and the various departments that constitute "Jewish studies" in the universities must encourage their students to engage in theoretical bibliographical research. It is difficult to understand why there can be scholars working in the field of legal theory who are not expected to engage in drafting legislation or in the judicial process, yet all scholars of the Hebrew book are obliged to compile catalogs and deal with borrowers. On this matter a complete change of values is essential.

The development and improvement of studies in Hebrew bibliography at the universities and academic institutions is vital not only for the advancement of research but also organizationally. Appropriate institutions must determine orders of priority and logical organization of research, avoiding any possible duplication and wasted effort. Each academic institution will determine the kinds of research appropriate to the scale and special character of its library, and the research potential available. This will also guarantee the continued existence of journals that provide an outlet for results and direct research into new channels; it will also guarantee appropriate forums, written and oral, for the exchange of ideas and clarification of problems by different scholars. In other words, this will pave the way for Hebrew bibliography to achieve the same opportunities as the rest of the branches of study found within the framework of academic institutions, and presumably as a result its development will become more rational and less dependent on chance. Books are considered to be among the things that are subject to luck. The same seems to be true of their study.

Part of the campus of the Hebrew University, Jerusalem. Straight ahead is the Jewish National and University Library, which also houses the School of Librarianship of the Hebrew University. Photo W. Braun, Jerusalem.

5. printing

INTRODUCTION

The first mention of Jews in connection with printing is found in Avignon c. 1444 (before Johann Gutenberg) when a Jew, David de Caderousse, studied the new craft. The first Hebrew books were printed within, at most, 35 years of the invention of printing — the first dated ones being Rashi's commentary on the Pentateuch and Jacob ben Ashers's *Arba'ah Turim* of 1475. This new and wonderful invention was called the "crown of all science," and its practice, like that of the writing of sacred books, *melekhet shamayim* ("the work of heaven" or "a divine craft," see *Eruvin* 13a) or *melekhet ha-kodesh* ("a sacred craft," cf. Exodus 36:4). It was regarded as a means to realize Isaiah's prediction (11:9) that "the earth shall be full of the knowledge of the Lord." There were, on the other hand, interested parties such as the copyists, who feared for their livelihood and who opposed the innovation, as did those monk-copyists who described it as the "work of the devil." Printing raised variegated halakhic problems as shown by contemporary responsa, the major ones being whether the *halakhah* concerning the writing of sacred books and the care and respect due to them was applicable to printed books as well and whether, in particular, items that required "writing" such as *Sifrei Torah, tefillin, mezuzot,* bills of divorce, among others, could be printed.

The Gutenberg press depicted in a 15th century engraving. Photo: Werner Braun, Jerusalem.

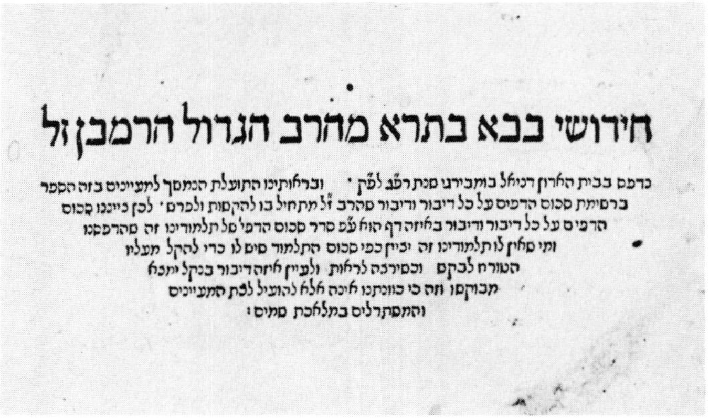
חידושי בבא בתרא מהרב הגדול הרמבן זל

The novellae of Naḥmanides (d.c. 1270) on the talmudic tractate *Bava Batra* printed by Bomberg in Venice, 1523. It was only possible to print novellae separate from the Talmud text (unlike Rashi and *Tosafot* which were printed on the Talmud page together with the text) after Bomberg had, in one operation from 1520 to 1523, printed the entire Talmud. The fact that Bomberg fixed a unified layout for each page of the Talmud created the possibility of referring to each page in the novellae he printed separately. Before that, each edition of each tractate had different pagination, with the result that the student could not locate the section the novellae was referring to.

Printing had a revolutionary influence on the religious and cultural life of Jewish communities everywhere: on books and their distribution, on learning and education, and on synagogal rites. The order and division of the books of the Bible, which today differ from both the talmudic and masoretic traditions, and the division into chapters in particular, are the result of printing. The printing of the Bible popularized it, while dictionaries and grammars, now easily obtainable, contributed greatly to its comprehension. The same is true for the Talmud. A standard pagination originated in the first complete Bomberg edition (1520–23), and the study of the Talmud became easier and far more widespread. The printing alongside of the text, in addition to Rashi's commentary, of the *Tosafot* of Touques gave talmudic learning a new direction which led to the development of the novellae literature and of *pilpul.* The widespread use of printed prayer books reduced the importance and relative freedom of the cantor; minor prayer rites were eliminated in favor of the major ones.

Earlier (1477), the word דְּפוּס, *defus,* (talmudic: frame, mold) was used as a noun for printing, alliterating to the Latin *typus.* To describe the activity, the same word as for writing כָּתַב, *katav,* or engraving חָקַק, *ḥakak,* was chosen, from which was derived מְחוֹקֵק, *meḥokek* for the printer; but also הֶעְתִּיק, *ha'atek,* (to copy) which led to the noun הֶעְתֵּק, *he'etek,* for the copy of a printed book. The noun מַטְבֵּעַ, *matbea* (mint), is also found, standing for "press." Occasionally there are such circumscriptions as "writing with many pens" (cf. *Yoma* 38b) or "writing without a pen." By the 16th century the derivatives from *defus* in the verb-forms of הִדְפִּיס, *hidpis,* and נִדְפַּס, *nidpas,* and מַדְפִּיס, *madpis,* for the printer, which are the accepted Hebrew terms today, were in common use though some of the early terminology such as *meḥokek* survived in Germany and Eastern Europe for a considerable time.

INCUNABULA

The term incunabula (or "cradle books") denotes books printed before 1500, including broadsheets, or other typographical products printed from letterpress composed of movable type. The first book known to have been printed by Gutenberg in Germany dates from 1445. Jews were denied the opportunity of learning the art of printing as long as it was exclusively practiced within Germany, for the strict rules of German guilds forbade the admission of apprentices who were not proven to be legitimately born sons of Christian citizens.

In 1465 Conrad Sweynheym and Arnold Pannartz, two immigrant printers from Germany, established themselves at Subiaco, near Rome, printing books in Latin. It can be assumed that they were the teachers, instructors, or foremen of an industrious group of Jewish printers (or typesetters) supposed to have been active in Rome or its vicinity c. 1470.

QUANTITIES. It has been estimated that approximately 50,000 incunabula editions were published, some 35,000 of them still represented by copies fully or partially preserved. Included in this total are the 175 editions printed with Hebrew letters known from copies preserved in public collections. It is in no way certain that this is a complete list of all books printed in Hebrew during the 15th century. During the 19th and 20th centuries the interest in, and knowledge of, Hebrew incunabula increased considerably. While G.B. de Rossi listed 60 items in 1776 and 86 in 1795, J. Jacobs in 1906 enumerated 102 (*Jewish Encyclopaedia,* VI: 778–9), and A.M. Habermann in 1950 had 153 titles (*Encyclopaedia Hebraica,* II: 984–5). H.M.Z. Meyer (A. Freimann and M. Marx, *Thesaurus . . .* (1969²), supplement to pt. 1) listed 185 incunabula, of which ten were considered doubtful. The number of "lost" incunabula has been estimated as one-third of the number of "confirmed" editions. The scarcity of incunabula – and the high prices they command – though natural enough in

Plate 23. Laws of the festival of Sukkot from the *Weill Maḥzor*, Italy, 15th century. The illustrations show several aspects of the festival. Strasbourg, G. Weill Collection. Photo: Communaute, Paris.

Plate 24. The Creation of the World as depicted in two pages from the *Sarajevo Haggadah,* Spain, c. 1400. Right-hand page: top right panel — the earth unformed and void; top left — the division of light and darkness (first day); bottom right — the division of the waters (second day); bottom left — the creation of vegetation (third day). Left-hand page: top right — the creation of the sun and the moon (fourth day); top left — the creation of living creatures (fifth day); bottom right — the creation of man (sixth day); bottom left — the Sabbath, illustrated by a man resting. Throughout, the power of God is represented by rays of light. Sarajevo, National Museum, fols. 1 and 2.

view of the small editions printed and the lapse of time, is also due in a certain measure to the inroads of Church censorship and book burnings in Italy, and in Spain to the Inquisition and expulsions.

FORMAT. Of the incunabula, 106 appeared in folio format against 40 in quarto and 29 in octavo or smaller formats. As to the number of leaves, it is impossible to account for those of the 70 incunabula which are only partially preserved. An analysis of the 105 complete editions reveals: 2 folios and 2 quartos (each containing 1–16 leaves); 8 folios and 10 quartos and 3 smaller sizes (each containing 17–96 leaves); 28 folios and 14 quartos and 5 smaller sizes (each containing 97–192 leaves); 23 folios and 3 quartos (each containing 193–400 leaves); 6 folios and 1 smaller size (each containing 401–626 leaves).

A page from Maimonides' *Yad* (no. 156 in the incunabula list; see Chapter 5) which, according to the accepted opinion, was printed in Rome before 1480. The names of the printers appear at the end of *Sefer Zera'im.* This is, apparently, the first known printing of this book although it is not at all clear if it really antedates the Spanish editions (at least four) which were printed before the expulsion in 1492.

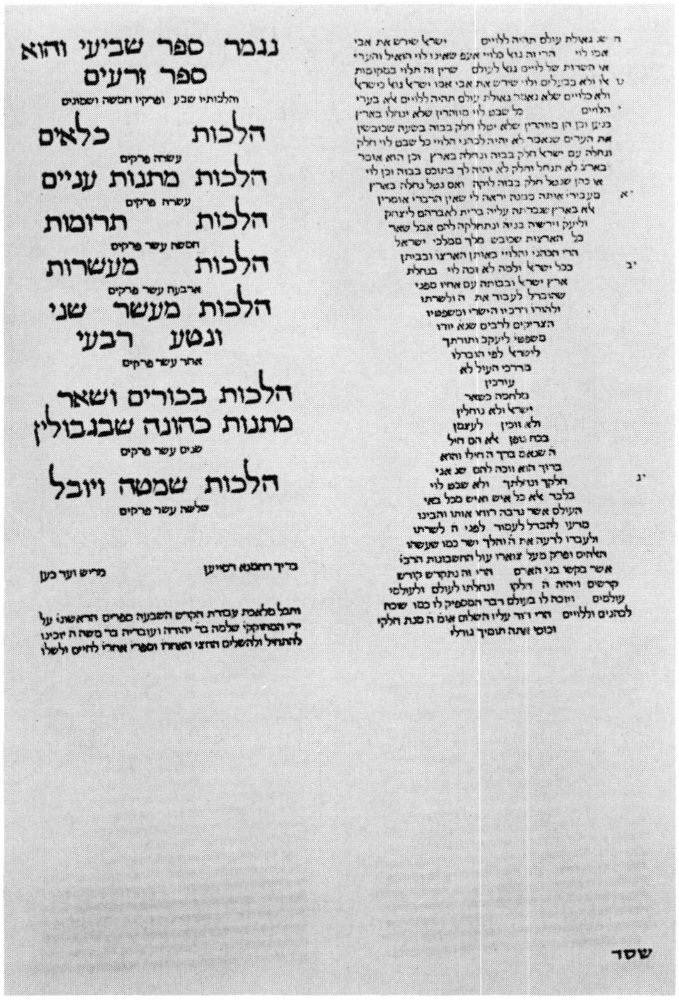
נגמר ספר שביעי והוא
ספר זרעים
הלכות כלאים
עשרה פרקים
הלכות מתנות עניים
עשרה פרקים
הלכות תרומות
חמשה עשר פרקים
הלכות מעשרות
ארבעה עשר פרקים
הלכות מעשר שני
ונטע רבעי
אחד עשר פרקים
הלכות בכורים ושאר
מתנות כהונה שבגבולין
שנים עשר פרקים
הלכות שמטה ויובל
שלשה עשר פרקים
ששר

EDITIONS. Owing to the scarcity of paper and the complicated manual work involved in the operation of the printing presses, editions were relatively small. During the 1470s, many Latin books appeared in editions of 100 or 125 copies; Sweynheym and Pannartz produced only 275 to 300 copies of each of their 28 publications. Hebrew printers, too, occasionally reported on the size of their editions: 300 copies of the 1477 edition of the Book of Psalms (no. 40 in the accompanying list of incunabula); 380 of *Ḥoshen Mishpat* in 1480 (no. 136); and 400 of David Kimḥi's commentary on the Latter Prophets (no. 148). It is possible that Abraham Conat limited his *Tur Oraḥ Ḥayyim* to 125 copies.

PRINTERS. Twenty-two Hebrew printing shops are known to have been working during the 15th century, 12 of them in Italy, nine in the Iberian Peninsula and one in Constantinople (present day Istanbul) – though many scholars correct the dating of this "incunabula" (no. 26) from 5254 [=1494] to 5265 [=1504]. For 18 of these presses, their places of printing are mentioned in the colophons of the books produced by them. While the location of three more printing houses may be assumed with a certain degree of probability, it is impossible to place four of the printers on the map. On the other hand, the books printed for the "patrons" at Faro, Portugal, do not indicate the names of their printers. There are, finally, five more or less completely preserved books (nos. 86, 88, 89, 111, and 149 in the incunabula list) which contain no colophon or any other means of identification of the printer, the place of printing, or the date.

The following is a complete list of printers based on the documentary evidence of the colophons in books preserved:

ITALY

1. Obadia (ben Moses?), Manasseh, and Benjamin, of Rome (colophon of no. 163). A comparison of the measurements of their book pages with the size of other contemporary productions has led to the assumption that they had learned the trade from Conrad Sweynheym and Arnold Pannartz, the two German master printers working from 1465 at Subiaco, a monastery in the neighborhood of Rome, and in Rome itself (see above). It has been assumed, therefore, that Rome was the place of Hebrew printing sometime between 1469 and 1472. Examination of the typographical material used led to the conclusion that the books recorded as nos. 145, 150, 153, 155, 156, 163, 167, and 170 also origi-

ABBREVIATIONS USED:

Goff Heb = F. R. Goff (ed.), *Incunabula in American Libraries* (1964), 316–25;

Thes = Freimann-Marx, *Thesaurus Typographiae Hebraicae*... (1967–69[2]); signatures in parentheses refer to vol. 2 in preparation;

S-T.C. = Short-title catalog in *Supplement, ibid.*

THE FOLLOWING LIST IS ALPHABETICAL FROM NO. 106

1. THE HOLY BIBLE—Complete Edition. Pentateuch, Prophets and Hagiographa. [In Spain or Portugal], printer unknown [1480?]. Folio.
Goff Heb 12; Thes (B.50); S-T.C.256.

2. (–.–) [?] Unvocalized text in 2 columns, 28 lines to a full page. [Spain], printer & date unknown. Folio.
Goff Heb 16, 6; Thes (B.54); S-T.C.257.

3. (–.–) [?, or Pentateuch only]. Unvocalized text, one column, 28 lines to a full page. [Spain], printer & date unknown. Folio.
Goff Heb 16, 3; Thes B.38; S-T.C.258.

4. (–.–) [?] Unvocalized text in one column of 30 [?] lines to a full page. [Spain], printer & date unknown. Folio.
S-T.C.259.

5. (–.–) [?, or Prophets only]. Text with vowels & accents, 2 columns, 27 or 29 lines to a full page. [Spain], printer & date unknown. Folio. Probably "Portugal, 1487."
S-T.C.260.

6. (–.–). Corrected by Abraham b. Ḥayyim dei Tintori. Soncino, Joshua Soncino, Iyar 11, 5248 (= April 22, 1488). Folio.
Goff Heb 8; Thes A.45; S-T.C.49.

7. (–.–) With Targum Onkelos. [Hijar, Eliezer Alantansi], no date.
S-T.C.229.

8. (–.–) [Naples, Joshua Soncino, 1491 or 1492]. Folio.
Goff Heb 9; Thes A.75; S-T.C.69.

9. (–.–) [? or Pentateuch only]. [Leira, Don Samuel D'Ortas], date unknown.
S-T.C.253.

10. (–.–) Brescia, Gershom Soncino, Sivan 19–25, 5254 (= May 24–30, 1494). Octavo.
Goff Heb 10; Thes A.81; S-T.C.89.

11. (–.–) [? or Prophets & Hagiographa only]. Vocalized text, two columns, 32 lines to a complete page. [Naples?], printer unknown, [1495?] Quarto.
S-T.C.110.

12. (-) PENTATEUCH With Targum Onkelos and Rashi. ∴ for the name of God and ה for Elohim. [Italy?], printer unknown, [1480?]. Folio.
S-T.C.109.

13. (–.–) With Targum Onkelos and Rashi. Corrected by Joseph Ḥayyim b. Aaron Strasbourg Ẓarefati. Printed for Joseph b. Abraham Caravita. Bologna, Abraham b. Ḥayyim dei Tintori, Adar I 5, 5242 (= January 26, 1482). Folio.
Goff Heb 18; Thes A.15; S-T.C.22.

14. (–.–) With Targum Onkelos, Megillot, and Haftarot. Corrected by Joshua bar Jekuthiel, typesetting by Isaiah and Judah, sons of Samuel Raphael Ha-Rofe, and by Benjamin and Joseph, the sons of Elhanan bar Eliezer, and Solomon bar Solomon. [Northern Italy], Isaac b. Aaron d'Este and Moses b. Eliezer Raphael, [1480–1490]. Folio.
Goff. Heb 13; Thes B. 40; S-T.C. 27.

15. (–.–) Printed by order of Don Samuel Gacon. Faro, printer unknown, Tammuz 9, 5247 (= June 30, 1487). Folio.
Thes B.14; S-T.C.233.

16. (–.–) With Megillot and Haftarot. [Hijar], Eliezer ibn Alantansi [1487–88?]. Folio.
Goff Heb 14; Thes B.12; S-T.C.227.

17. (–.–) With Targum Onkelos and Rashi. Corrected by Abraham B. Isaac b. David. Printed for Solomon b. Maimon Zalmati. Hijar [Eliezer ibn Alantansi], Av 5250 (= July 19,–August 17, 1490). Folio.
Goff Heb 19; Thes B.11; S-T.C.228.

18. (–.–) With Megillot and Haftarot. [Hijar, Eliezer ibn Alantansi], date unknown. Octavo.
S-T.C.230.

19. (–.–) With Targum Onkelos, Rashi, and a poem by David ben Joseph ibn Yaḥya. Corrected by Joseph Calphon. Lisbon, Eliezer Toledano [probably in collaboration with Judah Gedaliah], Av 5251 (= July 8–August 6, 1491). Folio.
Goff Heb 20; Thes B.20; S-T.C.240.

20. (–.–) Vocalized text with accents. 19 lines to a full page. [Naples, Joshua Soncino, 1491?]. Quarto.
Thes A.70a; S-T.C.61.

21. (–.–) With Rashi, Megillot, Haftarot and Megillat Antiochus. Naples, Benei Soncino, 5251 (= 1491). Folio.
Goff Heb 21; Thes A.70; S-T.C.63.

22. (–.–) With Haftarot. [Naples, Joshua Soncino], date unknown. [Between 1490 and 1492]. Folio.
Goff Heb 17; Thes A.98; S-T.C.64.

23. (–.–) [Naples, Joshua Soncino], date unknown. [Between 1490 and 1492?]. Octavo.
Goff Heb 16, 1; Thes A.99; S-T.C.65.

24. (–.–) With Megillot and Haftarot. Brescia, Gershom Soncino, Shevat 24, 5252 (= January 23, 1492). Quarto.
Goff Heb 15; Thes A.78; S-T.C.84.

25. (–.–) Vocalized text with accents. 32(?) lines to a full page. [Lisbon?], Eliezer [Toledano?], before 1492. Folio.
S-T.C.245.

26. (–.–) Vocalized text with accents. 17 lines to a full page. [Leiria?, Don Samuel d'Ortas or his sons?, between 1492 and 1495?]. Octavo.
S-T.C.262.

27. (–.–) Vocalized text with accents. Megillot and Haftarot. Brescia, Gershom Soncino, Kislev 15, 5254 (= November 24, 1493). Octavo.
Thes (A.79); S-T.C.85.

28. (–.–) With Haftarot. 2 columns, 25 or 26 lines to a full page. [At a unknown place in Spain or Portugal, printer and date unknown]. Folio.
Thes (B.55); S-T.C.261.

29. (–.–) With Haftarot. Unvocalized text. 18–19 lines to a full page. Place, printer and date unknown [Spain or Portugal?]. Quarto.
Goff Heb 17, 2; Thes (B.39); S-T.C.263.

30. (–.–) Vocalized text with accents. Place [Spain or Portugal], printer, and date unknown. Folio.
Goff Heb 16, 5; Thes B.49; S-T.C.264.

31. (–.–) Vocalized text with accents. 2 columns, 15 lines to a full page. Place [Spain or Portugal], printer, and date unknown. Folio.
Goff Heb 16, 4; Thes B. 48; S-T.C.265.

32. (–.–) Corrected according to the Hilleli codex. With Megillot and Haftarot. 1 or 2 columns, 32 lines to a full page. Printed somewhere in Spain or Portugal, printer and date unknown. Folio.
Goff Heb 16, 2; Thes B.30; S-T.C.266.

33. (–) Former Prophets. With commentary by David Kimḥi [Soncino] Joshua Soncino, Ḥeshvan 6, 5246 (=October 15, 1485). Folio.
Goff Heb 22; Thes A. 31; S-T.C.36.

34. (–.–) With Targum Jonathan and commentaries by Levi b. Gershom and D. Kimḥi. Leiria [Don Samuel d'Ortas and his] three sons, Shevat 19–21, 5254 (=January 26–28, 1495). Folio.
Goff Heb 23; Thes B.27; S-T.C.254.

35. (–) Latter Prophets. With commentary by D. Kimḥi [Soncino], Joshua Soncino [1486?]. Folio.
Goff Heb 24; Thes A.39; S-T.C.42.

36. (–.–) [Hijar, Eliezer ibn Alantansi, 1486–7?].
Thes (B.10); S-T.C.223.

37. (–.–) Isaiah and Jeremiah with commentary by D. Kimḥi. Lisbon, Eliezer Toledano [probably together with Judah Gedaliah], 5252 (= 1491–92). Folio.
Goff Heb 25; Thes B.21; S-T.C.242.

38. (–) Hagiographa with commentaries by D. Kimḥi on Job, by Joseph b. Simeon Kara on Lamentations, and by Rashi on the remaining books. [Corrected or typeset by] Samuel b. Samuel of Rome. Naples [Joseph Gunzenhauser], Tishri 9, 5248 (=September 26, 1487). Quarto.
Goff Heb 26; Thes A.59; S-T.C.72.

39. (–.–) Unvocalized text; 30–31 lines to a full page. [Spain or Portugal], printer and date unknown.
Goff Heb 27; Thes (B.56); S-T.C.267.

40. (–) Psalms. With commentary by D. Kimḥi. [Bologna], Meister Joseph, Neria [his son?] Ḥayyim Mordecai and Hezekiah Montro of Ventura, Elul 20, 5237 (=August 29, 1477). Folio.
Goff Heb 28; Thes A.13; S-T.C.24.

41. (–.–) Unvocalized text. 19 lines to a full page. Without indication of place, printer, or date [pl. and pr. as in No. 40; 1477?]. Duodecimo.
Thes A. 14a; S-T.C.25.

42. (–.–) With an index for 149 psalms and Grace after Meals. [place and printer as in no. 40; between 1477 and 1480]. Duodecimo.
Thes A.14a; S-T.C.26.

43. (–.–) With commentary by D. Kimḥi edited by Jacob Baruch b. Judah Landau. Naples, Joseph Gunzenhauser, Nisan 4, 5247 (= March 28, 1487). Quarto.
Goff Heb 29; Thes A.57; S-T.C.70.

44. (–.–) [Naples, Joshua Soncino, 1490?]?
Goff Heb 31, 3; Thes A.91; S-T.C.58.

45. (–.–) Together with Job and Proverbs. Naples [Joshua Soncino], Kislev 29, 5251 (=December 12, 1490). Quarto.
Goff Heb 32; Thes A.68; S-T.C.60.

46. (–.–) [Spain, Shem Tov ibn Ḥalaz and his son Judah], date unknown. 32mo.
S-T.C.247.

47. (–.–) [Spain, or Portugal, printer unknown, 1491?]. 32mo.
Goff Heb 126, 3; Thes B.32A; S-T.C.268. [Perhaps identical with no. 46].

48. (–.–) [Naples, Joshua Soncino, 1490–1492?]. Duodecimo.
Goff Heb 31, 1 and 2; Thes A.100; S-T.C.66.

49. (–.–) Brescia, Gershom Soncino, Tevet 7, 5254 (=December 16, 1493). Duodecimo.
Goff Heb 30; Thes A.80; S-T.C.86.

50. (–.–) With ד for the name of God. 16 lines to a full page. [Brescia, Gershom Soncino], date unknown. Duodecimo.
Thes A.80A; S-T.C.87.

51. (–) Proverbs with commentary by Immanuel b. Solomon of Rome. Corrected [or typeset] by Ḥayyim b. Isaac ha-Levi Ashkenazi. [Naples, Joseph Gunzenhauser, 1487]. Quarto.
Goff Heb 34; Thes A.58; S-T.C.71.

52. (–.–) With the commentary *Kav ve-Naki* by David b. Solomon ibn Yaḥya. [Lisbon, Eliezer Toledano], date unknown. Folio.
Goff Heb 35; Thes B.23; S-T.C.244.

53. (–.–) With Targum Onkelos and commentaries by Menahem ha-Meiri and Levi b. Gershon. Typesetting by Abraham b. Samuel d'Ortas. [Leira], Don Samuel d'Ortas, Av 1 5252 (=July 25, 1492). Folio.
Goff Heb 33; Thes B.26; S-T.C. 252.

54. (–) The Five Scrolls. Esther with commentary by Abraham ibn Ezra, the other books with Rashi. [Bologna, Abraham dei Tintori, 1482]. Folio.
Thes A.16; S-T.C.23.

55. Mishnah. Mishnayot with commentary by Maimonides. Naples, Joshua Soncino and Joseph ibn Peso. Iyar 11, 5252 (=May 8, 1492). Folio.
Goff Heb 82; Thes A.73; S-T.C.68.

56. (–) Unvocalized text without commentary. 30–31 lines to a full page. [Spain or Portugal, printer and date unknown].
S-T.C.269.

57. (–) Avot. With commentary by Maimonides. Translated from the Arabic by Samuel b. Judah ibn Tibbon. [Soncino, Joshua Soncino, 1488 (?)]. Folio.
Goff Heb 83; Thes A.41; S-T.C.43.

58. Babylonian Talmud. Berakhot, with Rashi, Tosafot, Piskei Tosafot, and the commentaries of Maimonides and Mordecai b. Hillel. Corrected by Gabriel b. Aaron of Strasbourg. Soncino, Joshua Soncino, Tevet 20, 5244 (=December 19, 1483). Folio.
Goff Heb 102; Thes A.26; S-T.C.28.

59. (–) Berakhot with Rashi. [Guadalajara, Solomon ibn Alkabeẓ, after 1482]. Folio.
Goff Heb 103, 2; Thes B.5; S-T.C.212.

60. (–.–) [Faro, Don Samuel Gacon, 1494 or 1496]. Folio.
Goff Heb 103, 1; Thes B.16; S-T.C.235.

61. (–) Shabbat, with Rashi and Tosafot. [Soncino, Joshua Soncino, about 1484]. Folio.
Goff Heb 11; Thes A.29; S-T.C.31.

62. (–) Eruvin, with Rashi. [Guadalajara, Solomon ibn Alkabeẓ, after 1482]. Folio.
Thes (B.6); S-T.C.213.

63. (–) Yoma, with Rashi. [Guadalajara, Solomon ibn Alkabeẓ, after 1482]. Folio.
Goff Heb 119; Thes B.74; S-T.C.214.

64. (–) Beẓah, with Rashi. [Guadalajara, Solomon ibn Alkabeẓ, after 1482]. Folio.

Goff Heb 105; Thes B.58; S-T.C.215.

65. (–.–) With Rashi, Tosafot, Piskei Tosafot and commentaries by Maimonides and Mordecai b. Hillel. Corrected by Gabriel b. Aaron of Strasbourg. Soncino, Joshua Soncino, Adar I 6, 5244 (=February 2, 1484). Folio.

Goff Heb 104; Thes A.28; S.-T.C.30.

66. (–.–) [Brescia, Gershom Soncino, 1493]. Folio.

Thes A.88; S-T.C.88.

67. (–) Ta'anit. [Guadalajara, Solomon ibn Alkabeẓ, after 1482]. Folio.

S-T.C.216.

68. (–) Megillah with Rashi, Tosafot, etc. [Soncino, Joshua Soncino, 1485(?)]. Quarto.

Thes A.33; S-T.C.24.

69. (–) Ḥagigah, with Rashi. [Guadalajara, Solomon ibn Alkabeẓ, after 1482]. Folio.

Goff Heb 108; Thes (B.7); S-T.C.217.

70. (–) Ketubbot, with Rashi. [Guadalajara, Solomon ibn Alkabeẓ, after 1482]. Folio.

Goff Heb 112; Thes B.7B; S-T.C.218.

71. (–.–) With Rashi, Tosafot and Piskei Tosafot, edited by Samuel b. Meir Latif. Soncino [Joshua, Soncino], Kislev 20, 5248 (= December 5, 1487). Folio.

Goff Heb 111; Thes A.43; S-T.C.46.

72. (–) Gittin, with Rashi and Tosafot. Soncino [Joshua Soncino], Adar 6, 5248 (=February 19, 1488). Folio.

Goff Heb 106; Thes A.44; S-T.C.47.

73. (–.–) With Rashi. Faro, printed for Don Samuel Porteira, Tevet 15, 5257 or Tevet 11, 5257 (=December 12, 1496 or December 16, 1496). Folio.

Goff Heb 107; Thes B.15; S-T.C.234.

74. (–) Kiddushin, with Rashi. [Guadalajara, Solomon ibn Alkabeẓ, after 1482]. Folio.

Goff Heb 113; Thes B.6; S-T.C.219.

75. (–.–) With Rashi, Tosafot and Piskei Tosafot. [Soncino, Joshua Soncino, 1489]. Folio.

Goff Heb 114; Thes A.51; S-T.C.52.

76. (–) Bava Kamma, with Rashi, Tosafot and Piskei Tosafot. Corrected by David b. Elezar ha-Levi. [Soncino, Joshua Soncino, 1489(?)]. Folio.

Goff Heb 100; Thes A.49; S-T.C.50.

77. (–) Bava Meẓia, with Rashi and Tosafot. [Soncino, Joshua Soncino, 1489]. Folio.

Goff Heb 101; Thes A.50; S-T.C.51.

78. (–) Sanhedrin, with Rashi and Tosafot. [Somewhere in Italy], Gershom Soncino, Kislev 21, 5258 (=November 16, 1497). Folio.

Goff Heb 116; Thes A. 84; S-T.C.93.

79. (–) Shevu'ot with Rashi. [Faro, for Don Samuel Gacon or Don Samuel Porteira, 1494 or 1496]. Folio.

Goff Heb 118; Thes B.17; S-T.C.236.

80. (–) Middot, with Rashi. [Guadalajara, Solomon ibn Alkabeẓ, after 1482]. Folio.

Thes B.7.D; S-T.C.220.

81. (–.–) Ḥullin, with Rashi. [Guadalajara, Solomon ibn Alkabeẓ, after 1482]. Folio.

Goff Heb 110; Thes B.57; S-T.C.221.

82. (–.–) With Rashi, Tosafot and Piskei Tosafot, edited by David b. Eleazar ha-Levi (Pizzighetone), corrected by Mordecai b. Reuben Ẓarefati of Basle. [Soncino, Joshua Soncino], Tammuz 15, 5249 (=June 14, 1489). Folio.

Goff Heb 109; Thes A.53; S-T.C.53.

83. (–.–) [Spain or Portugal], printer and date unknown. Folio.

Goff Heb 110, 2; Thes B.35; S-T.C.221.

84. (–) Niddah, with Rashi, Tosafot and Piskei Tosafot, edited by David b. Eleazar ha-Levi, corrected by Mordecai b. Reuben Ẓarefati of Basle. [Soncino, Joshua Soncino], Av 25, 5249 (=July 23, 1489). Folio.

Goff Heb 115; Thes A.54; S-T.C.54.

85. Prayer Books. Various prayers, according to the German rite. [Soncino, Solomon Soncino, 1490(?)]. Quarto.

Goff Heb 121; Thes A.87; S-T.C.100.

86. (–) Siddur. Daily prayers, German rite. [Italy, printer and date unknown]. Octavo.

Goff Heb 122; Thes A.97; S-T.C.107.

87. (–.–) Tefillat Yaḥid, the so-called *Sidurello*. Daily prayers, Roman rite. Soncino [Joshua Soncino], Iyar 2, 5246 (=April 8, 1486). Octavo.

Goff Heb 121; Thes A.35; S-T.C.39.

88. (–.–) Roman Rite. [Italy, printer and date unknown]. Duodecimo.

Thes A.95; S-T.C.106.

89. (–.–) Various prayers according to the Roman rite. [Italy, printer and date unknown]. Printed at Naples(?) or Mantua, 1513 (?). Octavo.

Goff Heb 123; Thes A.96; S-T.C.108.

90. (–.–) Seder Tefillot. Daily prayers according to the Spanish rite. A poem by Moses b. Shem Tov b. Ḥabib. Printed for Ben Porat [=Joseph (probably Gunzenhauser)]. Naples, Joshua Soncino, Sivan 5, 5240 (=May 25, 1490). Quarto.

Goff Heb 124; Thes A.90; S-T.C.57.

91. (–.–) Spanish rite. [Naples, Joshua Soncino, date unknown.] Octavo.

Goff Heb 126, 1; Thes A.92; S-T.C.59.

92. (–.–) Seder Me'ah Berakhot, Spanish rite, with musical signs for the sounds of the *shofar*. [Lisbon, Eliezer Toledano, 1490(?)]. Octavo.

Goff Heb 125; Thes B.44; S-T.C.239.

93. (–.–) Spanish rite, 13 lines to a full page, [Spain or Portugal, printer and date unknown]. Octavo.

Thes B.43; S-T.C.27.

94. (–.–) Spanish rite. ,י, for the name of God, 11 lines to a full page. Octavo.

S-T.C.272.

95. (–.–) Spanish rite. ,י, for the name of God; 15 lines to a full page. [Spain or Portugal, printer and date unknown]. 16mo.

Goff Heb 126, 4; Thes B.46; S-T.C.273.

96. (–.–) Spanish rite. 18 lines to a full page. [Spain or Portugal, printer and date unknown]. 16mo.

Goff Heb 126, 5; Thes B.47; S-T.C.274.

97. (–.–) Of an undetermined rite. [Brescia, Gershom Soncino, 1485.] Duodecimo.

Goff Heb 127; Thes A.102; S-T.C.90.

98. (–) Seliḥot, German rite. [Piove di Sacco, Meshullam Cusi's sons, 1475]. Folio.

Thes A.3; S-T.C.12.

99. (–.–) German rite. [Soncino, Joshua Soncino, 1485(?)].

Thes A.34; S-T.C.38.

100. (–.–) German rite. Vocalized text. Sarco, Gershom Soncino, Tishri 8, 5257 (=Sept. 15, 1496). Folio.

Goff Heb 96; Thes A.83; S-T.C.92.

101. (–) SEDER TAḤANUNIM. Roman rite. Soncino [Joshua Soncino], Iyyar 23, 5247 (= May 16, 1487). Quarto.

Goff Heb 99; Thes A.40; S-T.C.44.

102. (–) MAḤZOR Minhag Roma, Soncino and Casalmaggiore, Benei Soncino, Tishri–Elul 20, 5246 (Sept. 10, 1485–August 21, 1486). Folio.

Goff Heb 73; Thes A.37; S-T.C.41.

103. (–.–) le-Yom ha-Kippurim. [Montalban?, Juan de Lucena, his daughters Theresa and Juana, together with Diego de Monbel and Inigo de Gurcos, 1475(?)]. Octavo.

Goff Heb 72; Thes B.53; S-T.C.201.

The identification of the printing house is questionable.

104. (–) PASSOVER HAGGADAH; together with tractate Avot, German rite. [Soncino, Joshua Soncino, approx. 1485]. Quarto.

Thes A.38; S-T.C.35.

105. (–.–) [Soncino, Joshua Soncino, 1486]. Duodecimo.

Goff Heb 42; Thes A.36; S-T.C.40.

106. AARON B. MESHULLAM HA-KOHEN OF LUNEL, ORḤOT ḤAYYIM. [Spain or Portugal], printer and date unknown. Folio.

Goff Heb 2; Thes B.37; S-T.C.275.

107. ABUDRAHAM, DAVID B. JOSEPH B. DAVID, Perush ha-Berakhot ve ha-Tefillot. Lisbon, Eliezer Toledano [probably with the collaboration of Judah Gedaliah], Tevet 1, 5250 (= November 25, 1489). Folio.

Goff Heb 36; Thes B.19; S-T.C.238.

108. ADRET, SOLOMON B. ABRAHAM (Rashba). Responsa. [Rome(?), Obadiah, Manasseh, and Benjamin of Rome, between 1469 and 1472]. Octavo.

Goff Heb 95; Thes A.25; S-T.C.6.

109. ALBO, JOSEPH, Sefer ha-Ikkarim. Soncino, Benei Soncino, Ḥeshvan 22, 5246 (= December 29, 1485). Folio.

Goff Heb 64; Thes A.32; S-T.C.37.

110. ALFASI, ISAAC, Halakhot. [Hijar, Eliezer Alantansi, between 1485 and 1490]. Folio.

Goff Heb 44; Thes B.34; S-T.C.231 and 276.

111. (Anonymous) LU'AḤ, Calendar for the year 5257 [Barco, Gershom Soncino, 1496.]

Goff Heb 3; Thes A.82; S-T.C.91.

112. (–) Sefer Kol Bo. [Italy (or Naples), printer unknown, 1485(?)]. Folio.

Goff Heb 67; Thes A.94; S-T.C.105.

113. (–) Megillat Antiochus, Aramaic text with Hebrew translation; Judah Halevi, Mi Khamokha; and: Tefillat ha-Derekh; Benedictions for different occasions; Passover Haggadah; Ḥaruzim (rules and calculations for the calendar). [Guadalajara(?), Solomon ibn Alkabeẓ(?), 1482(?)]. Folio.

S-T.C.209–211.

114. (–) Petaḥ Devarai. [Naples, Joshua Soncino], Adar II 1, 5252 (= February 28, 1492). Quarto.

Goff Heb 91; Thes A.72; S-T.C.67.

115. AVICENNA, The Canon. Translated from the Arabic by Joseph b. Judah al-Lorki and Nathan b. Eliezer ha-Me'ati. Corrected by Abraham b. Jacob Landau, typesetting by Asher b. Perez Minz. Naples, Azriel Gunzenhauser, Kislev 7, 5252 (= November 9, 1491). Folio.

Goff Heb 4; Thes A.71; S-T.C.103.

116. BAḤYA B. ASHER, commentary on the Pentateuch. Edited by Samuel b. Abraham Perez. Without indication of place [Spain], Shem Tov ibn Ḥalaẓ and his son Judah, Ḥeshvan 17, 5252 (= October 21, 1491). Folio.

Goff Heb 5; Thes B.31; S-T.C.246.

117. (–.–) Edited by Solomon b. Pereẓ Bonfroi Ẓarefati. Corrected by Samuel b. Hezekiah ha-Levi. Naples, Azriel Gunzenhauser, Tammuz 8, 5252 (= July 3, 1492). Folio.

Goff Heb 6; Thes A.74; S-T.C.104.

Published for Abraham and Jacob Pax (not Falcon).

118. BAḤYA B. JOSEPH IBN PAQUDA, Ḥovot ha-Levavot. Translated from the Arabic by Judah b. Saul ibn Tibbon. Corrected by Solomon b. Perez [Bonfroi Ẓarefati] [Naples], Joseph Gunzenhauser, Kislev 25, 5250 (= November 19, 1489). Quarto.

Goff Heb 7; Thes A.63; S-T.C.76.

119. ELDAD HA-DANI, Sefer Eldad. Together with various halakhot and responsa. [Piove di Sacco, Meshullam Cusi and sons, 1480?]. Quarto.

Goff Heb 41; Thes A.6; S-T.C.15.

120. FINZI, MORDECAI, Luḥot (astronomical tables). [Mantua, Abraham Conat, between 1476 and 1480]. Quarto.

Thes A.9; S-T.C.18.

121. GABIROL, SOLOMON IBN, Mivḥar ha-Peninim. Translated from the Arabic by Judah b. Saul ibn Tibbon with commentary, edited by Solomon b. Perez Bonfroi Ẓarefati. [Soncino]. Joshua Soncino, Shevat 17, 5244 (= January 14, 1484). Quarto.

Goff Heb 98; Thes A.27; S-T.C.29.

122. IBN EZRA, ABRAHAM, commentary on the Pentateuch, edited and corrected by Moses b. Shem Tov b. Ḥabib of Lisbon. Naples, Joseph Gunzenhauser and his son [Azriel], 36th day of Omer (= Iyyar 18, 5248 = April 29, 1488). Folio.

Goff Heb 1; Thes A.60; S-T.C.73.

123. IMANNUEL B. SOLOMON B. JEKUTHIEL OF ROME, Sefer ha-Maḥbarot. Brescia, Solomon Soncino, Ḥeshvan 26, 5252 (= October 30, 1491). Quarto.

Goff Heb 43; Thes A.77; S-T.C.83.

124. JACOB B. ASHER, Arba'ah Turim. Piove di Sacco, Meshullam Cusi and sons, Tammuz 28, 5235 (= July 3, 1475). Folio.

Goff Heb 47; Thes A.2; S-T.C.11.

125. (–.–) [Soncino], Solomon Soncino [1490]. Folio.

Goff Heb 48; Thes A.56; S-T.C.99.

126. (–.–) Edited by Elijah b. Benjamin ha-Levi. Constantinople, David and Samuel ibn Naḥmias, Tevet 4, 5254 (= December 13, 1493). Folio.

Goff Heb 49; Thes C.1; S-T.C.301.

127. (–.–) Oraḥ Ḥayyim. Mantua, Abraham Conat, Sivan 14, 5236 (= June 6, 1476). Folio.

Goff Heb 50; Thes A.4; S-T.C.13.

128. (–.–) Hijar, Eliezer ibn Alantansi, Elul 5245 (= August 12–September 9, 1485). Folio.

Goff Heb 51; Thes B.8; S-T.C.222.

129. (–.–) [Leiria, Abraham b. Samuel d'Ortas], Sivan 10, 5255 (= June 2, 1495). Folio.

Goff Heb 53; Thes B.29; S-T.C.255.

130. (–.–) [Italy, Gershom Soncino, 1497]. Quarto.

Goff Heb 54; Thes A.85; S-T.C.94.

131. (–.–) [Spain or Portugal, printer and date unknown]. Folio.

Goff Heb 52; Thes B.33; S-T.C.277.

132. (–.–) Yoreh De'ah. [Mantua, Abraham Conat] and Abraham b. Ḥayyim at Ferrara, Av 15, 5237 (= June 25,

1477). Folio.

Goff Heb 55; Thes A.5; S-T.C.14.

133. (–.–) [Guadalajara, Solomon ibn Alkabeẓ, 1482(?)]. Folio.

Goff Heb 52; Thes B.2.A.; S-T.C.207.

134. (–.–) Hijar, Eliezer ibn Alantansi, 5347 (= 1487). Folio.

Goff Heb 56; Thes B.9; S-T.C.226.

135. (–.–) *Even ha-Ezer.* [Guadalajara, Solomon ibn Alkabeẓ, 1482(?)]. Folio.

Goff Heb 58; Thes B.2; S-T.C.208.

136. (–.–) *Ḥoshen Mishpat.* Guadalajara, Solomon ibn Alkabez, Shevat 20–28, 5241 (= December 24–30, 1480). Folio.

Goff Heb 59; Thes B.3; S-T.C.205.

137. (–.–) [Hijar, Eliezer ibn Alantansi, between 1485 and 1490]. Folio.

Goff Heb 60; S-T.C.225.

138. Jedaiah ha-Penini, *Beḥinat ha-Olam* [Mantua], Estillina, the wife of Abraham Conat, assisted by Jacob Levi from Tarascon [Between 1476–1480]. Quarto.

Thes A.11; S-T.C.20.

139. (–.–), with a short commentary. Soncino [Joshua Soncino], Kislev 24, 5245 (= December 12, 1484). Quarto.

Goff Heb 61; Thes A.30; S-T.C.33.

140. (–), Bakkashat ha-Memin with: Moses Kimhi, *Mahalakh Shevilei ha-Da'at;* Joseph b. Ḥanan Ezobi, *Ka'arat Kesef; Mishlei Ḥamishim Talmidim.* Soncino, [Gershom Soncino], Av 13, 5248 (= July 21, 1488). Octavo.

Thes A.46; S-T.C.79.

141. Joseph b. Guryon, *Sefer bin Guryon,* the so-called *Josippon* [Mantua], Abraham Conat, the 49th day of Omer (= 5 Sivan), no year. Quarto.

Goff Heb 65; Thes A.8; S-T.C.278.

142. Joshua b. Joseph ha-Levi, *Seder Halikhot Olam,* with Jonah b. Abraham Gerondi, *Sefer ha-Yirah ve-sod ha-Teshuvah* [Somewhere in Spain or Portugal, printer and date unknown]. Quarto.

Goff Heb 63; Thes B.28; S-T.C.278.

143. Judah bar Jehiel (Rofeẓ), *Sefer Nofet Ẓufim.* [Mantua], Abraham Conat, [no date], Quarto.

Goff Heb 62; Thes A.7; S-T.C.16.

144. Kalonymus b. Kalonymus, *Even Boḥan.* Edited by Yom Tov b. Perez Ẓarefati. Naples, Joseph Gunzenhauser, Elul 28, 5249 (= August 25, 1489). Quarto.

Goff Heb 66; Thes A.62; S-T.C.75.

145. Kimḥi, David b. Joseph (Radak), *Sefer ha-Shorashim.* [Rome?, Obadiah (b. Moses?), Manasseh; and Benjamin of Rome, between 1469 and 1472]. Folio.

Goff Heb 38; Thes A.24; S-T.C.5.

146. (–.–) Naples [Joshua Soncino], Shevat 30, 5251 (= February 10, 1491). Folio.

Goff Heb 40; Thes A.69; S-T.C.62.

147. (–.–) Corrected by Samuel b. Meir Latif. Naples [Azriel Gunzenhauser], Elul 5250 (= August 18—September 15, 1490). Folio.

Goff Heb 39; Thes A.66; S-T.C.101.

148. (–) Commentary on Latter Prophets. Guadalajara, Solomon ibn Alkabeẓ, 5242 (= 1482). Folio.

Goff Heb 37; Thes B.1; S-T.C.15.

149. Landau, Jacob Baruch b. Judah, *Sefer Agur* and *Sefer Ḥazon.* [Naples, Azriel Gunzenhauser, 1490 (?)], Quarto.

Goff Heb 68; Thes A.67; S-T.C.102.

150. Levi b. Gershom (Ralbag), commentary on Daniel. [Rome(?), Obadiah, Manasseh and Benjamin of Rome(?), between 1469 and 1472]. Quarto.

Goff Heb 71; Thes A.22; S-T.C.4.

151. (–) Commentary on the Pentateuch. [Mantua], Abraham Conat with the help of Abraham Jedidiah ha-Ezraḥi of Cologne, [between 1476 and 1480]. Folio.

Goff Heb 69; Thes A.10; S-T.C.19.

152. (–) Commentary on Job. Edited by Nathan of Salo. [Ferrara], Abraham b. Ḥayyim dei Tintori, Sivan 4, 5237 (= May 17, 1477). Quarto.

Goff Heb 70; Thes A.12; S-T.C.21.

153. Moses b. Jacob of Coucy, *Sefer Mitzvot Gadol* [Rome(?), Obadiah, Manasseh, and Benjamin of Rome, between 1473 and 1475]. Folio.

Goff Heb 84; Thes A.19; S-T.C.7.

154. (–.–) [Soncino], Gershom Soncino, Tevet 15, 5249 (= December 19, 1488). Folio.

Goff Heb 85; Thes A.48; S-T.C.80.

155. Moses b. Maimon (Rambam), *Moreh Nevukhim.* Translated from the Arabic by Samuel b. Judah ibn Tibbon. With a table of contents by Judah b. Solomon al-Ḥarizi. [Rome(?), between 1473 and 1475]. Quarto.

Goff Heb 80; Thes A.18; S-T.C.8, where a name of a printer has been erroneously inserted.

156. (–) Mishneh Torah. [Rome(?)], Solomon b. Judah and Obadiah b. Moses [1475]. Folio.

Goff Heb 76; Thes A.1; S-T.C.9.

157. (–.–) [Hijar, Eliezer ibn Alantansi, date unknown]. Octavo.

S-T.C.232

158. (–.–) Edited by Eliezer b. Samuel. Soncino, Gershom Soncino, Nisan 1, 5250 (= March 23, 1490). Folio.

Goff Heb 77; Thes A.55; S-T.C.81.

159. (–.–) [Somewhere in Spain or Portugal], Moses ibn Shealtiel, [1491?]. Folio.

Goff Heb 78; Thes B.32; S-T.C.248.

160. (–.–) [Spain or Portugal, printer and date unknown]. Folio.

Goff Heb 79, 1; Thes B.36; S-T.C.279.

161. (–.–) [Spain or Portugal, printer and date unknown]. Folio.

Goff Heb 79, 2; Thes B.41; S-T.C.280.

162. (–.–) *Hilkhot Sheḥitah.* [Lisbon, Eliezer Toledano, 1492?]. Duodecimo.

Goff Heb 75; Thes B.22; S-T.C.243.

163. Moses b. Naḥman (Ramban). Commentary on the Pentateuch. [Rome(?)], Obadiah, Manasseh, and Benjamin of Rome [Between 1469 and 1472]. Folio.

Goff Heb 86; Thes A.20; S-T.C.1.

164. (–.–) [Naples]. [Joseph Gunzenhauser], Tammuz 13, 5250 (= July 2, 1490). Folio.

Goff Heb 88; Thes A.65; S-T.C.78.

165. (–) *Sha'ar ha-Gemul.* Naples, Joseph Gunzenhauser, Adar I 1, 5250 (= January 29, 1490). Quarto.

Goff Heb 89; Thes A.64; S-T.C.77.

166. (–) *Ḥiddushei ha-Torah* and letter sent from Jerusalem to his son. Lisbon, Eliezer Toledano, Av 18, 5249 (= July 16, 1489). Folio.

Goff Heb 87; Thes B.18; S-T.C.237.

167. Nathan ben Jehiel, *Sefer ha-Arukh.* [Rome(?),

Obadiah, Manasseh, and Benjamin of Rome, between 1469 and 1472]. Folio.

Goff Heb 90; Thes A.23; S-T.C.2.

168. SAHULA, ISAAC B. SOLOMON IBN, *Mashal ha-Kadmoni.* [Brescia, Gershom Soncino, 1491]. Quarto.

Goff Heb 45; Thes A.76; S-T.C.82.

169. (–.–) [Somewhere in Italy], Gershom Soncino [1497]. Quarto.

Goff Heb 46; Thes (A.86); S-T.C.95.

170. Solomon b. Isaac (Rashi), commentary on the Pentateuch. [Rome(?). Obadiah, Manasseh, and Benjamin of Rome, between 1469 and 1472]. Quarto.

Goff Heb 92; Thes A.21; S-T.C.3.

171. (–.–) Reggio di Calabria, Abraham b. Garton. Adar 10, 5235 (= February 18, 1475). Folio.

Goff Heb 93; Thes A.1; S-T.C.10.

172. (–.–) [Guadalajara, Solomon ibn Alkabez], Elul 16, 5236 (= September 1476). Folio.

Goff Heb 94; Thes B.4; S-T.C.202.

173. (–.–) [Soncino, Joshua Soncino], Sivan 14, 5247 (= June 6, 1487). Folio.

Thes A.42; S-T.C.45.

174. (–.–) Zamora, Samuel b. Musa and Immanuel, 5247, or [5]252 (= 1487 or 1492). Folio.

Thes B.13; S-T.C.25.

175. TREVOT, PEREZ, *Makrei Dardekei.* [Naples, Joseph Gunzenhauser], Elul 1, 5248 (=August 8, 1488). Folio.

Goff Heb 81; Thes A.61; S-T.C.74.

INDEX TO DATES OF PUBLICATION

INDEX TO PLACES OF PUBLICATION

COLLECTIONS OF INCUNABULA

Cambridge, University Library (29);
Cincinnati, Hebrew Union College (65);
Copenhagen, Det Kongelige Bibliotek (50, mostly from the Lazarus Goldschmidt Collection);
Frankfort on the Main, Stadt- und Universtaetsbibliothek (49, formerly 59);
Jerusalem, Jewish National and University Library (65, mostly from the S. Schocken Collection);
Leningrad, Bibliotheca Friedlandiana (34);
London, British Museum;
New York, Jewish Theological Seminary (143);
Oxford, Bodleian Library;
Paris, Bibliotheque Nationale (34);
Parma, Bibliotheca Palatina (Collection de Rossi);
Turin, Biblioteca Nazionale (25);
Vienna, Kultusgemeinde (28).

nated from this printing shop. Obadiah may be identical with his namesake under 2 (below).

2. **Solomon ben Judah and Obadiah ben Moses** (colophon of no. 156). The place of printing and the dating are conjectures based on typographical comparison.

3. **Abraham ben Garton ben Isaac**, first completely identifiable Hebrew printer. He produced Rashi's commentary on the Pentateuch completed at Reggio di Calabria on February 17, 1475. This is the first Hebrew book to appear with a full statement of all the three important bibliographical facts. Although this book bears the earliest date, it was not necessarily the first Hebrew book printed, as it may have been – and probably was – preceded by others which have disappeared or bear no date of publication. The only extant copy of the book, in the De' Rossi Collection in the Palatine Library, Parma, Italy, is slightly defective; it is in folio and contains 116 pages of 37 lines each. De' Rossi formerly owned another copy which was lost in transit. Abraham's country of origin is unknown, but it is conjectured that he came from Spain. No other book from his press is known.

David Kimḥi's introduction to his commentary on Psalms, printed in Bologna, 1477 (no. 40 in the incunabula list). This was the first printing of the book, which was very popular, and was thus selected for printing so early in the history of the craft. It was reprinted in Naples in 1487 (no. 43 on the list) but from a different manuscript, and there are differences between the two editions. Kimḥi's introduction did not appear in the Naples edition.

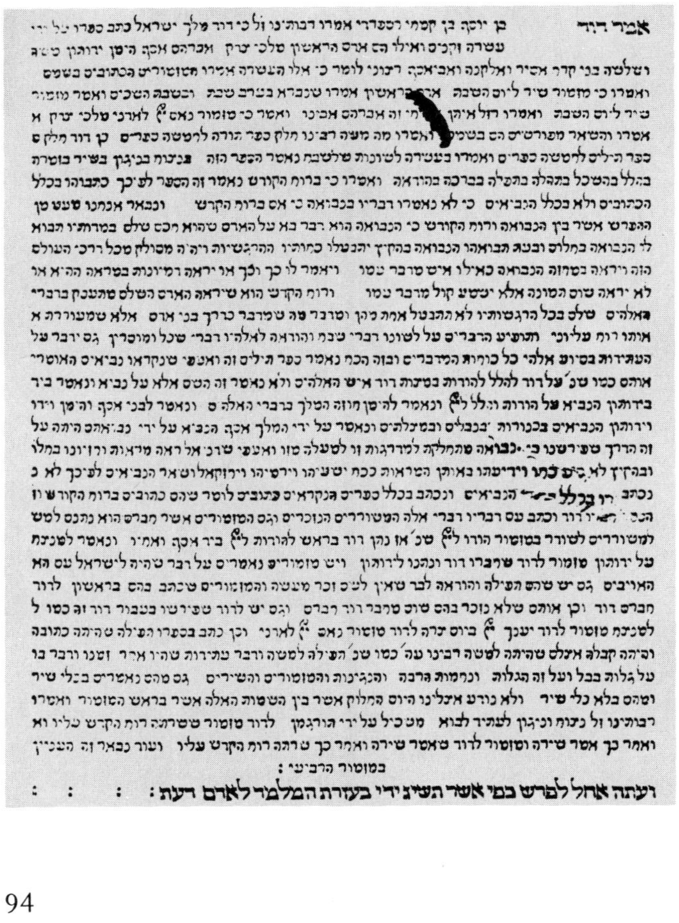

4. **Meshullam Cusi and his sons**, printers at Piove di Sacco; their first-known work (no. 124) was published on July 3, 1475. The sons are supposed to have printed no. 98, using the typographical material belonging to their father's estate.

5. **Abraham ben Solomon Conat of Mantua**, Italian physician and one of the earliest printers of Hebrew books. Conat was probably of Ashkenazi origin. He lived in Mantua, where he may have been active as early as 1475. June 1476 and June 1477 are two dates recorded in the colophons of books originating from his press; his name is mentioned in nos. 127, 141, 143, and 151, the place of printing in no. 127, and the dates in nos. 127, and 132. Printers employed by him were Abraham Jedidiah ha-Ezraḥi of Cologne and Jacob Levi of Tarascon, as well as his wife Estellina. The printing of no. 132 began at his presses but after the first 31 leaves Abraham ben Ḥayyim dei Tintori of Ferrara took over and printed the remaining 60 leaves, which suggests Conat died c. 1477. Conat's work is particularly beautiful, and his type has been imitated in modern luxury editions. He was assisted by his wife Estellina, who was responsible for the printing of *Beḥinat Olam.*

6. **Abraham ben Ḥayyim die Tintori ("the Dyer")**, Italian pioneer of Hebrew printing from Pesaro. Though Abraham may have been active in Hebrew typecasting and printing by 1473, his name as a printer appeared for the first time in two books printed in Ferrara in 1477 – Levi ben Gershom's commentary of Job, and Jacob ben Asher's *Tur Yoreh De'ah,* the first third of which Abraham Conat had printed in Mantua. Ferrara had become a printing center with the arrival in 1471 of André of Belfort and other Frenchmen. Five years later (1482) at Bologna, Abraham printed a Pentateuch with Targum Onkelos and Rashi's commentary. In the colophon, Joseph Ḥayyim praises Abraham as "unequaled in the realm of Hebrew printing and celebrated everywhere." Israel Nathan Soncino and his son Joshua Solomon secured Abraham's services for the work on the first printed Hebrew Bible – with vocalization and cantillation – which left the press at Soncino in February 1488. The edition of the Psalms, with David Kimḥi's commentary of 1477, as well as the Five Scrolls, with Rashi and with Abraham ibn Ezra's commentary on Esther (1482–83?), may also have been printed by Abraham.

A page from *Meshal ha-Kadmoni* by Isaac ibn Sahula, probably printed in Brescia by Gershom Soncino, 1491. The book includes a large collection of animal fables and aphorisms from which one can learn human moral characteristics. This was the first book printed with decorations and illustrations.

7. Joseph, his son Ḥayyim Mordecai, and Hezekiah Montero of Ventura. Joseph bears the title "Meister," probably because he was the apprentice of a German master printer. It has been suggested that his son was called Ḥayyim Mordecai and that the name Neriah is only based on a typographical error (ונריה instead of ובריה; Aram., "and his son"). No. 40 was finished in his printing shop on August 24, 1477, but no place of printing is mentioned in the colophons; some bibliographers assume that the work was done at Bologna. Nos. 41 and 42 are ascribed to this press.

8. Isaac ben Aaron d'Este and Moses ben Eliezer Rafael. Only one book is known to have been printed by this firm (no. 14). The colophon of their work gives no indication of the place or date of printing, but mentions the names of six co-workers employed.

9. Joseph ben Jacob Gunzenhauser (Ashkenazi) and his son, Azriel. Joseph's name is mentioned in nos. 43, 118, 144 and 165, first on March 28, 1487, and for the last time on January 29, 1490. Father and son are mentioned together in no. 122, and the son alone in nos. 115 and 117 (November 9, 1491, and July 3, 1492). They printed at Naples, as stated in the colophons of nos. 38, 43, 114, 117, 122, 144, 146, and 165. It is most probable that the first book printed by Joshua Soncino at Naples (no. 114) was produced by order of Joseph, because the name Ben Porat, mentioned in the colophon as the initiator of this work, is a synonym for Joseph (cf. Genesis 49:22). The names recorded as Gunzenhauser's collaborators or employees are: Jacob Baruch ben Judah Landau, author of no. 149, who also edited no. 43, the first book to be printed by Gunzenhauser; his son Abraham, who corrected no. 114; Ḥayyim ben Isaac ha-Levi Ashkenazi (no. 51); Samuel ben Samuel of Rome (no. 38); Moses ben Shem Tov ben Ḥabib of Lisbon (no. 122); Samuel ben Meir Latif (no. 147), mentioned above as a member of Soncino's staff; Asher ben Pereẓ Minz (= *Min Ẓarefat,* from France), typesetter of no. 115; Samuel ben Hezekiah ha-Levi (no. 117); the brothers Solomon and Yom Tov ben Pereẓ Ẓarefati (nos. 117 and 144), who presumably were the brothers of the Asher ben Pereẓ, mentioned before. The Gunzenhausers maintained good relations with the Soncinos, as shown by the use of Soncino's woodcut in Gunzenhauser's book.

10. Soncino, various printers, see page 161.

SPAIN AND PORTUGAL

11. Juan de Lucena, a Marrano printer working at Montalban, Spain. The names of his co-workers are recorded in no. 103, but there is no proof that the book described under this number was really a product of his printing shop.

12. Solomon ben Moses ibn Alkabeẓ, a printer at Guadalajara, Spain. His name and place of residence are reported in nos. 136 and 148, the first having been finished during the last week of December 1480. Another book attributed to his press (no. 172) was published on September 5, 1476, while no. 148 was printed in 1482. Other books attributed to his presses, on the evidence of the typographical material used, are nos. 59, 62-64, 67, 70, 74, 80, 81, 113, 133, and 135.

13. Eliezer ben Abraham ibn Alantansi, owner of a printing shop and physician at Hijar, Spain. The name of the printer and the town are mentioned in the colophon of no. 134. Abraham ben Isaac ben David corrected no. 17, which was most probably printed by Eliezer for Solomon ben Maimon Zalmati. The books produced by Eliezer's presses are outstanding for their technical perfection and beautiful ornamentation. The frame printed in no. 16 is regarded as the most remarkable example of book illustration of this period. Most delicately incised animals, fruits, flowers, and ornamental lines enliven the black background, and the same balance between black and white is sustained in the composition of the initials. These metal engravings are the work of Alfonso Fernandez de Cordoba, a silversmith, type cutter, and printer in Valencia. Alfonso used the same frame, together with a suitable set of Latin initials, in the *Manuale Caesar Augustanum,* supposed to have been printed by him at Hijar in about 1487. But the relation between this book and Eliezer's publication is obscured by the fact that the Hebrew printing took place before and after the Latin printing, and that the frame shows proofs of wear and tear not to be found in the Hebrew books. This frame, together with the initial letters and other printing types used by Eliezer, can be traced to the books originating from the presses of Eliezer Toledano (see below no. 15) in Lisbon.

14. Printing shop at Faro, a town in the Portuguese province of Algarve. The identity of the printer(s) working at this town for Don Samuel Gacon (no. 15, finished on June 30, 1487) and for Don Samuel Porteira (no. 73, published on 12 (or 16) December 1494) is unknown. Nos. 60 and 79 are attributed to one or the other of these two patrons (or publishers).

15. Eliezer Toledano mentioned as printer in nos. 19, 25, 37, and 166: the same colophons show Lisbon as his place of work. The earliest date in his colophons is July 18, 1488, while 1491/2 appears in no. 37. Eliezer, like his namesake in Hijar (no. 13 above), was a physician and used in his books the frame, initial letters and printing types to be found in the works of the Hijar presses. It was therefore obvious to assume that these two printers were in fact one and the same person especially as the activities at Hijar ended at approximately the time the work at Lisbon began. The distance between Hijar and Lisbon is approximately 400 miles, with Toledo as the midway station; that the new arrival was called by a name different from the one he bore at his place of departure is not surprising; it can be paralleled by many examples from European Jewry during the Middle Ages down to the 18th century. But no definite assertions can be made until further facts come to light.

16. Shem Tov ibn Ḥalaz and his son, Judah. They printed one book (no. 116), finished on October 21, 1491, at an unidentified place in Spain or Portugal.

17. Moses ibn Shealtiel. The one book produced by him in Spain or Portugal (no. 159) contains no reference to place or date of printing.

18. Samuel ben Musa, together with Immanuel working as printers at Zamora, Spain; their names and place of work appear in the colophon of no. 174.

19. Samuel d'Ortas and his three sons, one of them named Abraham, printers at Leiria, Portugal. Their names are found in nos. 53 and 34, their place of work in no. 34 only. Their colophons are dated July 25, 1492 and January 26–28, 1495, (no. 129).

CONSTANTINOPLE

20. Naḥmias, ibn (15th-16th centuries), a family of Hebrew printers from Spain. David ibn Naḥmias, his brother Samuel, and David's son Samuel, left Spain in 1492 and made their way to Constantinople. There they published Jacob ben Asher's *Turim* in 1493 (5254). The accuracy of this date, written out in words in the colophon, has been doubted by scholars such as M. Steinschneider (*Juedische Typographie,* 1938, 17), who assume an error of ten years. More recently, the case for the 1493 date has been strongly defended. After an interval of over ten years, the Ibn

Naḥmias brothers printed a Pentateuch with Rashi, including *haftarot* with David Kimḥi's commentary, and the Five Scrolls with that of Abraham ibn Ezra (1505–06). Several other books followed, among them Alfasi's *Halakhot* and Maimonides' *Code* (both 1509) and three works by Abrabanel, the only ones printed in the author's lifetime. Samuel died in 1509 or 1510, and David ibn Naḥmias about a year later. David's son Samuel carried on, alone or with a partner, to 1518, when the press was leased to others. The first two works printed (*Turim* and Pentateuch) have as printer's mark a *Magen David* surrounded by leaves and flowers.

1500-1550

ITALY. The first half of the 16th century was in many ways the golden age of Hebrew printing, with Italy and the house of Soncino (until 1526) in a leading position. Gershom Soncino published mainly the Bible and its commentators, prayer books, and single Talmud tractates. His great competitor was Daniel Bomberg, the Christian printer from Antwerp, who from 1516 (or perhaps a few years earlier) to 1549 systematically issued the basic texts of Judaism in hitherto unequaled typographical perfection. With Bomberg, Venice became the capital of Hebrew printing until well into the 18th century: in this period the names of Agostino and Marco Giustiniani and Alvise (and later Giovanni) Bragadini were outstanding. Elsewhere in Italy Samuel Latif printed in Mantua (1513–15). In 1518 the sons of Avigdor of Padua were active in Rome, where Samuel Ẓarefati printed in 1540–45 and Antonio Blado in 1545–46; another son of Avigdor used German square type in a *siddur* issued in Trino in 1525. More important were the productions of the Jewish silkmakers in Bologna (1537–40), in the main beautifully finished prayer books of the Italian rite of which copies printed on parchment have survived.

CONSTANTINOPLE, SALONIKA AND FEZ. Next to Italy in importance were Constantinople and Salonika (1513) where Hebrew printing was introduced by exiles from Spain and Portugal; the Soncinos began their activity in Salonika in 1527–28 and in Constantinople in 1530. Iberian refugees also brought printing to North Africa. Hebrew books were printed in Fez with Lisbon type, 1516–22. See also below, page 111.

NORTHERN EUROPE. Hebrew printing in northern Europe began in Prague in 1512 with a group of printers who were later joined by Gershom ben Solomon Kohen, founder of a long and famous line of printers (the "Gersonides"). He used German square and a new cursive rabbinic type and many ornaments: angels, birds, lions, municipal coats of arms, and outspread hands, the priestly symbol of the family. To this group also belonged Ḥayyim Shaḥor, who left Prague in 1529 to print at Oels (1530), Augsburg (1533–44), Ichenhausen, and Heddernheim (1545). Apart from continuing in the Prague style of type and decoration, Shaḥor also used the smaller Italian type. In Poland, Cracow and Lublin became important centers of Hebrew printing.

HEBREW PRINTING BY AND FOR NON-JEWS. This was a special feature of the first half of the 16th

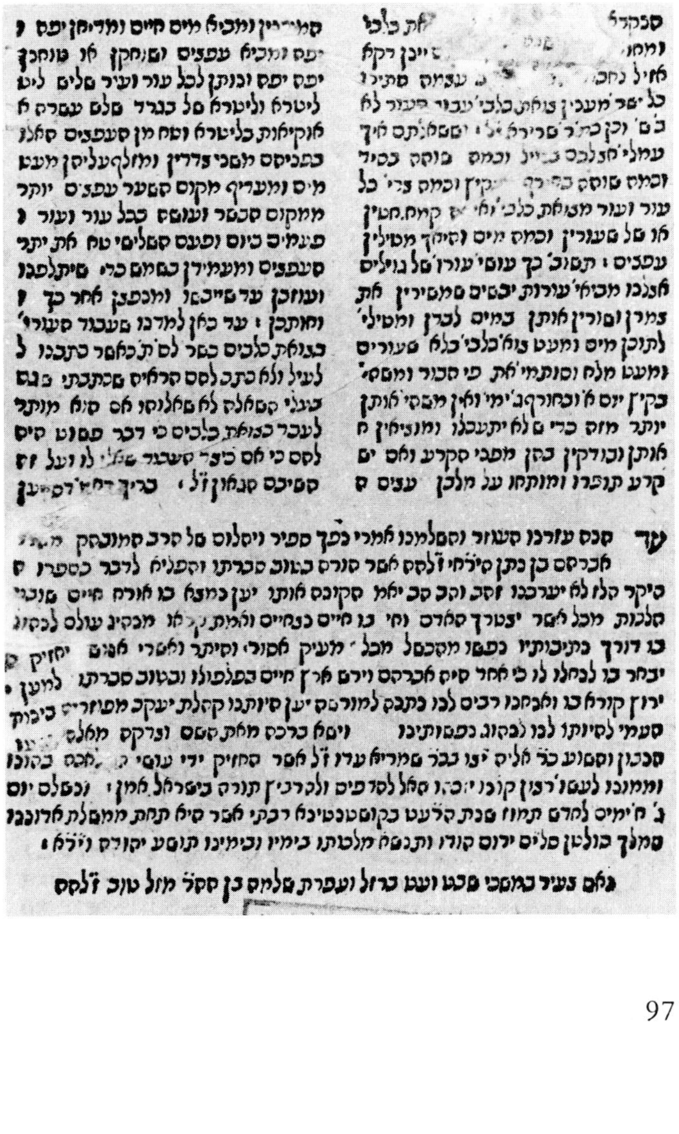

At the end of *Ha-Manhig* of Abraham ben Nathan of Lunel, the printer, Solomon ben Mazal Tov, attached a description of his work. In it he thanks God for having helped him to fulfill his desires and describes the value of the book and its usefulness. He makes honorable mention of Elijah ben Shemariah Iddo who financed the publication. At the end of this colophon the date of the completion of the work and its place are mentioned: Constantinople, 1519. The book is one of the most important in the *minhagim* literature and its author was active at the turn of the 13th century. This is the first edition of the book. J.N.U.L., Jerusalem.

century though it continued long afterward. In the ethos of Renaissance humanism enlightened Christian scholars became interested in the Hebrew Bible, its language, and grammar. Their demand was supplied by such men as Stephanus (Robert Estienne) in Paris (1508–?), who used his own rabbinic and square types which bore a resemblance to the Spanish ones. Only after 1542 did he go over to the Italian type. In Basle, Hebrew printing began in 1516 – and continued through the century; here a somewhat slanting German square type was used. Psalms, Hebrew grammars, and some Christian liturgical pieces in Hebrew, Latin, and Greek were printed in Lyons from 1520 by Andreas Gryphius, who utilized the same type. German cities in which Hebrew printing took place were Tuebingen (1511), Augsburg (1514), Cologne (1518), Wittenberg (1521), Leipzig (1533), Solingen (1538), and Mainz (1542). A special position was occupied by the Hebrew press set up in 1540 by the apostate Paulus Fagius in conjunction with Elijah Levita at Isny, Wuerttemberg, and later at Konstanz on the German-Swiss border, where some books were printed in separate editions for Jews and Christians (e.g. Levita's *Tishbi* of 1541–42). They used the German type for their meticulous productions.

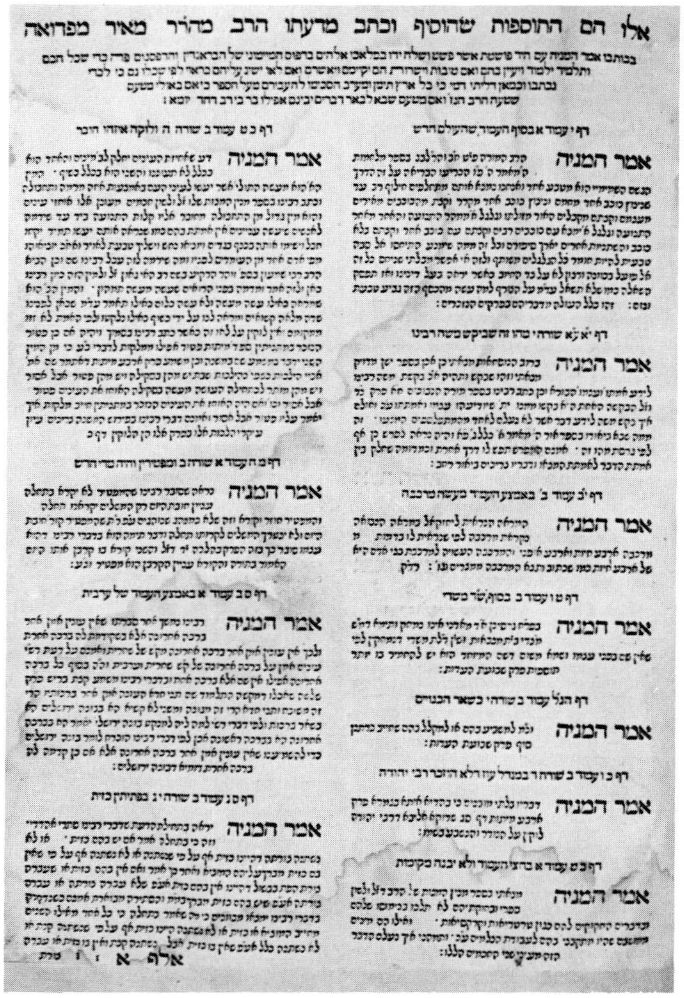
אלו הם התוספות שהוסיף וכתב מדעתו הרב מהור מאיר מפדואה

The last pages appended to Giustiniani's edition of Maimonides' *Mishneh Torah,* Venice 1550/1. This edition appeared immediately after a similar edition which was printed by another famous Venice printer, Bragadini, with whom Giustiniani was in competition. The pages contain the glosses of R. Meir of Padua which were sent by him especially to Bragadini to print in his edition, which was done. Giustiniani stole (or plagiarized) the text and printed it in his own edition, so as not to fall behind. But, as an introduction, he inserted four lines of ridicule (which also appear on the reverse side of the title page) saying, in effect, that these glosses are being presented in order to show their worthlessness. The outstanding halakhic authority, Moses Isserles, put Giustiniani's edition under ban. The vicious controversy the whole affair aroused led, after mutual slander, to the cessation of Hebrew printing in Venice for 10 years, and to the burning of the Talmud.

1550-1627

The single most influential event in the history of Hebrew printing in this period was the papal prohibition of Julius III and subsequent burning of the Talmud in 1553.

This catastrophe is closely connected with the unrestrained competition which lasted some time between the two non-Jewish printers, Bomberg and Bragadini, for the Jewish book market. The virtual monopoly of Venice on Talmud printing came to an end resulting in complete or partial Talmud editions in Lublin (1559), Salonika (1563), and Basle (1578). In Cracow and Constantinople, too, single tractates were printed at this time. In Italy itself the decentralization of Hebrew printing over many small presses occurred during 1550–68; and Venice reemerged as the center of Hebrew printing with the predominance of certain presses in the town from 1569 onward.

FERRARA, SABBIONETA, MANTUA, CREMONA AND RIVA DI TRENTO. In 1551 Samuel Ẓarefati, who had worked as a Hebrew printer in Rome, set up a press at Ferrara, which was taken over two years later by the Marrano, Abraham Usque. Simultaneously, Tobias Foa established a Hebrew press at Sabbioneta, near Mantua, with Joseph Shalit of Padua, Jacob ben Naphtali, and later Cornelio Adelkind (1553–55) as printers. The last-mentioned printed the last Talmud tractate *(Kiddushin)* before the prohibition, as well as an exemplary edition of Isaac Alfasi's Talmud-based code, the study of which was now substituted for that of the Talmud. In Sabbioneta, too, Salonika's influence was paramount, and the two types were so similar as to lead to confusion. The very small type used found its way to Mantua and later to Venice (De Gara, 1572; Bragadini, 1616). Sabbioneta productions are more lavishly decorated than those of Ferrara. Joseph Shalit and Jacob ben Naphtali continued printing at Mantua from 1556 at Tomaso Rufinelli's (1557–63). After a rather quiescent period (1563–90), of which only Azariah dei Rossi's *Me'or Einayim* of 1574 was noteworthy, more active printing was resumed at the Rufinelli press. A new one was set up in 1612 by Eliezer d'Italia, where besides smaller liturgical items, larger works such as Abraham Portaleone's *Shiltei ha-Gibborim* appeared. In 1622 the Perugia family took over this press which remained active for another 50 years. Mantua productions show little originality in their decorations. Jacob ha-Kohen first introduced a title page with a decorative border and the outspread hands of the priesthood. When he entered into partnership with Meir Sofer, the typical Mantua title portal with winding pillars made its appearance. They also used the various vignettes of Bragadini and De Farri and those of Sabbioneta. The Mantua illustrated *haggadot* with the big German type became famous. In Cremona, Vincenzo Conti printed, between 1556 and 1566, some 40 books, of which the most important was the *Zohar* of 1559. His assistants were Samuel Boehm, Zanvil Pescarol, and Vittorio Eliano. From 1558 works display the *cum licentia* of the "Superiori." Conti extended his activities to Sabbioneta, where Israel Zifroni printed several books for him in 1567. The last book printed in Cremona was

The title page of the *She'iltot* printed in Venice in 1546 at the press of Daniel Bomberg. To the left is the title page of *Bet Elohim* by the Safed scholar, Moses Mitrani, printed in 1576 in Venice by Juan Jara, "with the type of Bomberg," as stated on the page. However, not only was Bomberg's type used but also the entire *sha'ar* was his. Of interest is the fact that apart from the left column which was damaged between 1546 and 1576, the *sha'ar* is whole.

Yosef Lekaḥ by Eliezer Ashkenazi, issued by Solomon Bueno at Draconi's in 1576. Riva di Trento received its Hebrew press in 1558 when the physician Jacob Marcaria obtained a license from Cardinal Madruzzi. With the help of Rabbi Joseph Ottolenghi he first issued a reasonably priced edition of Alfasi for Ottolenghi's yeshivah students. This was followed by some philosophical and rabbinic works. The last of these, *Me'ir Iyyov* by Meir Arama, of 1562, had to be completed by Cavalli in Venice in 1566. Marcaria used mainly square types, among them a small one. His decorations are similar to those of Mantua in their title portals and decorated initials. Books of 1562 have their own vignette, later copied in Cracow.

VENICE. When in 1563 the printing of Hebrew books in Venice was once more permitted, most of the printers mentioned found employment with the houses of Gryphio (1564–67), Cavalli (1565–67), and Zanetti (1565–67), each using his own printers' mark. At that time mostly *Turim* with Caro's commentary and his *Shulḥan Arukh* came off the presses, taking the place of the prohibited Talmud. Eventually Di Gara and Bragadini emerged as the leading presses. Di Gara, whom some of the best printers had joined, aspired to continue the Bomberg tradition. He succeeded as far as externals were concerned until 1585, when new title pages, borders, and decorated letters gave the productions a different character. In the choice of books Di Gara followed in the footsteps of Bomberg. Di Gara also printed many homiletical works, mostly by oriental authors, such as Moses Alshekh, Solomon Alkabeẓ and Moses Almosnino. He was assisted in this by Isaac Gershon of Safed, as corrector. Bragadini resumed printing immediately after the repeal of the prohibition, with Meir Parenzo and, after the latter's death, his brother Asher as his managing printers. They published the first (1565) and two further editions of Joseph Caro's *Shulḥan Arukh* and a new edition of Maimonides' *Mishneh Torah* with Caro's commentary *Kesef Mishneh* (1574–75). From 1579 to 1600 Bragadini and Di Gara worked together. After a period of recession, there was a revival under Giovanni Cajon's management (c. 1615) which produced a new Bible (1617–18) under Leone Modena's supervision. From 1625, under Caleoni, several editions of the *maḥzor* and other liturgical items were printed, but with the rise of the Amsterdam and German presses, Bragadini's lost its impetus. A short-lived revival took place in 1710–15 as shown by the two-volume folio German *maḥzor*, printed with new, large type. Another

סוכה
עם פירוש רשי ותוספות ופסקי תוספות נדפס פה ק״ק לובלין הבירה

The title page of tractate *Sukkah* of the first Lublin edition of the Babylonian Talmud, printed in 1568. No complete set has survived. The text was proofread against a copy written by the famous rabbi, Shalom Shachna, who was the head of the *bet din* of Lublin. In advance of the printing, the heads of the yeshivot of the "three countries: Poland, Russia and Lithuania" came to an agreement that their academies would arrange their studies to fit the order of appearance of the individual tractates in order to help the printers and improve the quality of study in their own yeshivot by fixing a unified curriculum.

press active at Venice at the time was that of Zanetti, with Isaac Gershon as supervisor (1593–1608). Outside Venice, apart from Mantua, there was Padua, where Samuel Boehm printed at Lorenzo Pasquato in 1562–67, and Crivellari's press with two works, 1622–23. Some Hebrew and Judeo-German (Yiddish) books were issued at Verona by Francesco della Donne (1594–95).

CRACOW AND LUBLIN. Italian influence made itself felt in Cracow when Isaac ben Aaron Prostitz with the aid of Samuel Boehm set up his press in 1569. They had brought type and decorations with them from Italy and imitated the ornaments of most Italian presses. They printed, largely for local needs, the works of German and Polish authors as well as ethical and liturgical items in Hebrew and Yiddish.

From 1595 onward larger works were published. With Isaac ben Aaron's return to Prossnitz some Hebrew printing, such as an *Ein Ya'akov,* took place there (1603–05). In Lublin, where Kalonymus Jaffe was active from 1560, the influence of both Prague and Venice were at work. Jaffe printed, besides local authors, the Talmud and *Zohar* as well as some philosophical (or anti-philosophical) works. In Bistrowicz he prepared in 1592 a *Haggadah* with Isaac Abrabanel's commentary. His printers' mark was the Temple, which was also used in Prague and by Giustiniani.

PRAGUE, BASLE AND HANAU. The Kohen family in Prague continued to be active from 1566; in 1605 another printing family, the Baks, established themselves. They both continued the Prague tradition, Italian influence making itself felt only occasionally. The Prague productions were mainly in the liturgical and ethical field, both in Hebrew and Judeo-German (Yiddish). Israel Zifroni guided the Hebrew press of Frobenius in Basle, which hitherto had worked mainly for the Christian market, in a different direction by printing several rabbinic works, including an edition – censored – of the Talmud (1578–88) and without the "objectionable" tractate *Avodah Zarah,* which was, however, supplemented in Cracow (1580). Zifroni-Froben printed a few works in Freiburg-im-Breisgau as well (1583–84). The original Basle type gave way to the Italian one. Another Basle Hebrew press at the time was that of Konrad Waldkirch who, with the assistance of printers from Poland, issued among others a Bible (1618–19) and Joseph Solomon Delmedigo's *Ta'alumot Ḥokhmah* (1629–31). About this time Hebrew printing took place in Hanau (Hesse), where from 1610 to 1630 several important kabbalistic and Judeo-German works were issued. Their title pages showed the figures of Moses and Aaron – which set a fashion among later printers – and above was a representation of the *Akedah.*

TURKEY, EGYPT AND PALESTINE. The first Hebrew printing press – which was the first printing press in any language in the Ottoman Empire, the first book in Turkish being printed in 1728 – was set up in Constantinople in 1503 (or 1493) by David and Samuel ibn Naḥmias, exiles from Spain. Their first book was Jacob ben Asher's *Arba'ah Turim.* It was followed a year later by a volume of the Pentateuch with Rashi, *haftarot* with David Kimḥi's commentary, the Five Scrolls with the commentary of Abraham ibn Ezra, and the Antiochus Scroll. The Naḥmias family was active until 1518. In this early period of Hebrew printing in Constantinople (1504–30) more than 100 books of remarkable range and quality were published, among them, Midrashim, the *Aggadot ha-Talmud* (forerunner of Jacob ibn Ḥabib's *Ein Ya'akov*), geonic works, Alfasi, Maimonides' *Yad* – printed for the second time, but on the basis of another manuscript – and his *Sefer ha-Mitzvot* as well as his responsa and letters.

Title page of *Ma'aseh Bet David,* a loose translation into Yiddish of *Ma'aseh Bustenai* ("The Story of Bustenai"), *Ma'aseh Aseret ha-Shevatim ve-ha-Sambatyon* ("The Tale of the Ten Tribes and the Sambatyon River") and *Ma'aseh Melekh ha-Kuzarim* ("The Tale of the King of the Khazars"), printed at the press of Conrad Walkirche in Basle, 1599. The frame of the page is composed of four "columns" decorated with faces and petals. The book was translated and published by David Toeplitz from a Hebrew book of a similar nature by Isaac ibn Akrish which was printed in Constantinople, c. 1577.

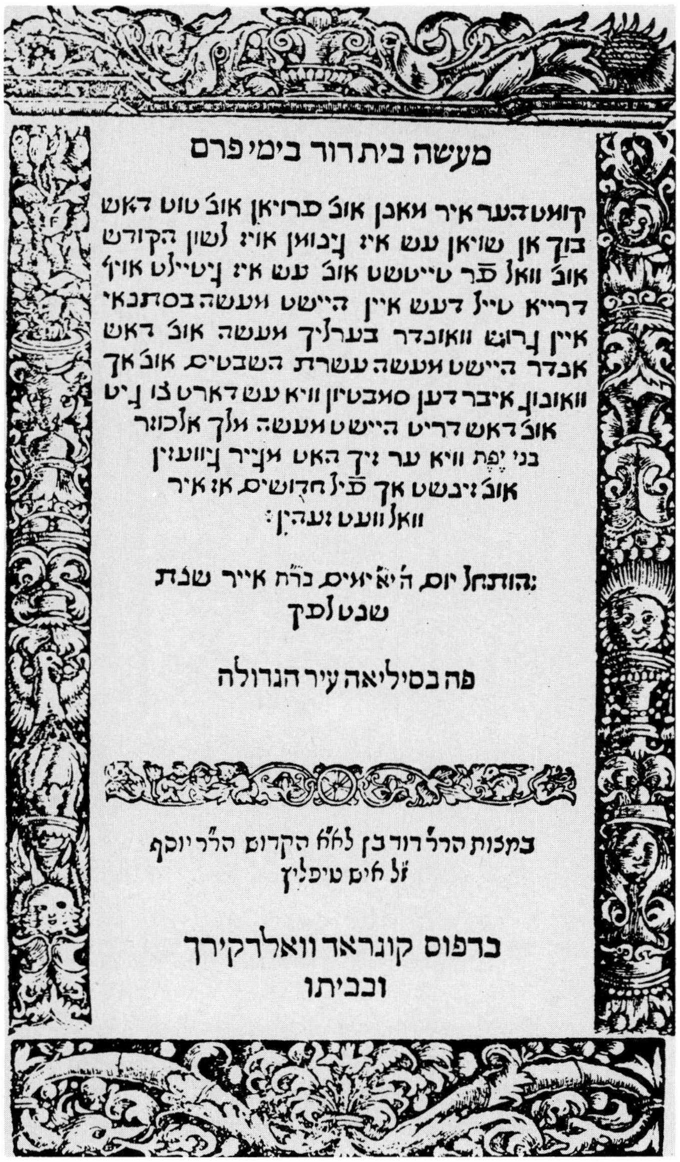
מעשה בית דוד בימי פרס

קומט הער איר מאנן אונ׳ פרויאן אונ׳ טוט דאש
בוך אן שויאן עש איז גנומן אויז לשון הקודש
אונ׳ וואל פר טייטשט אונ׳ עש איז גטיילט אין
דרייא טייל דעש איין הייסט מעשה בסתנאי
אין גרוש וואונדר בערליך מעשה אונ׳ דאש
אנדר הייסט מעשה עשרת השבטים אונ׳ אך
וואונן איבר דען סמבטיון ויא עש דארט צו גיט
אונ׳ דאש דריט הייסט מעשה מלך אלכוזר
בני יפת ויא ער זיך האט אנייר גוועזן
אונ׳ זיבשט אך פיל חדושים אז איר
וואל ווערט זעהין:

הותחל יום ה׳ י״א ימים בר״ח אייר שנת
שנט לפ״ק

פה בסיליאה עיר הגדולה

במצות הר״ר דוד בן לח״ח הקדוש הר״ר יוסף
ז״ל חים טיפליץ

ברפוס קונראד וואלדקירך
ובביתו

אגרת הקדש

ששלח המקובל
הגדול הגאון
הרמב"ן זצ"ל לח'
החברים בענין
חבור האדם אל
אשתו כדי לזכו'
לבנים בעלי
הוראה ראויים
לקבל עול מ"ש

בשאלוניקי

בשמ"חה לפ"ק

The decorated title page – without figures or faces – of *Iggeret ha-Kodesh*, attributed to Naḥmanides. It was printed in Salonika in 1599 and deals with the sanctity of marriage as well as the correct sexual behavior of the spouses.

Meanwhile, Gershom Soncino and his son Eliezer had arrived in Constantinople from Italy, and their press published over 40 books between 1530 and 1547, including a Pentateuch with Targum Onkelos, Rashi, and Saadiah's Arabic and Jacob ben Joseph Tavus's Persian translations (1545–46), followed by another Pentateuch edition, also with Targum Onkelos and Rashi, and translations into Greek and Spanish, both in Hebrew characters with vowel signs (1547). Eliezer also printed a Hebrew translation, by the physician Jacob Algabe, of the Spanish romance *Amadis de Gaula,* the first secular work in Hebrew to be printed in Constantinople. A former employee of the Soncinos', Moses ben Eliezer Parnas, continued printing on their press after Eliezer's death in 1548, publishing at least five books by 1553. Others active in printing in Constantinople during the period were the Halicz brothers, printers from Cracow, who publicly returned to Judaism in the city after having undergone baptism in Poland in 1537. Between 1551 and 1553 they printed a Hebrew Bible, Isaac of Dueren's halakhic compendium *Sha'arei Dura,* and a Hebrew version of the apocryphal, Book of Judith.

More important were the activities of Solomon and Joseph, the sons of Isaac Jabez from Spain, who arrived in Constantinople via Salonika and Adrianople. From 1559 until his death in 1593, Solomon, in partnership with his brother Joseph from 1570, printed such important items as the responsa of Elijah Mizraḥi (1559) and Joseph ibn Lev (1561) and, in particular, the larger part of the Talmud (1583–93). Eliezer ben Isaac (Ashkenazi) of Prague, a Hebrew printer from Lublin, went to Constantinople in 1575 with his equipment and printed geonic responsa and part of the *Maḥzor Romania.* After a dispute with his partner in this enterprise, David ben Elijah Kashti, the rest of the *maḥzor* was printed by Kashti at the press of Joseph Jabez. Under the patronage of Reyna, daughter of Dona Gracia, the widow of Joseph Nasi, Joseph ben Isaac Ashkeloni printed some 15 books, one of them in Ladino, of no great distinction, first at the palace of Belvedere at Ortakoy, 1592–94, and later at Kuru Tsheshme, 1597–99.

Early in the 16th century (c. 1512) Don Judah Gedaliah, his son Moses, and daughter arrived in Salonika having fled from Portugal. Gedaliah had previously managed the printing press of Eliezer Toledano in Lisbon; he brought at least some of the latter's typographical material with him, and later he had new types cut. Many of his productions, in the main liturgical works, have been lost, but some important items have survived: a Pentateuch with Onkelos and Rashi (1513); the first edition of Jacob ibn Ḥabib's *Ein Ya'akov* (1515–23); parts of Hagiographa with Rashi (1515); the tractate *Yoma*; *Tur, Oraḥ Ḥayyim*; a Pentateuch with Rashi's and Naḥmanides' commentaries (1520); *Yalkut Shimoni* on Prophets and Hagiographa (1521); and Solomon Molcho's sermons (1529). In 1525 Moses Soncino left Rimini (Italy) for Salonika, and in 1526 he issued the *Yalkut* on the Pentateuch and in 1527 a *maḥzor* of the Catalonian rite. His kinsmen Gershom and Eliezer arrived – also from Rimini – in 1526 and printed David Kimḥi's *Sefer ha-Shorashim-,* together with Abraham Bedersi's dictionary of biblical synonyms, *Ḥotam Tokhnit* (1527), and a *maḥzor* of the Aragonian rite (1529), before moving on to Constantinople.

Beginning in 1543 with Solomon and Joseph Jabez, refugees from Spain printed a great variety of Hebrew books in Salonika, among them a *maḥzor* of the Ashkenazi rite (1551–55). For a time, the enterprise had to be transferred to Adrianople (1555). Eventually Solomon Jabez went to Constantinople, whereas Joseph returned to Salonika in about 1560 and until about 1572 printed many works, notably a series of Talmud tractates based on the Bomberg and Giustiniani editions: works by Moses Almosnino; and translations into Judeo-Spanish and Provençal of parts of the Bible and prayer books. When he left, his typographical material was bought by David ben Abraham Azubib, who was active in printing from 1578 to 1588. About the year 1590, members of the Italian Bat-Sheva family settled in Salonika and set up a press, using Italian type and decorations. In Cairo a fourth-generation Soncino printed two Hebrew books in 1557 and 1562. The aforementioned Eliezer ben Isaac Ashkenazi printed several works in Safed during 1577–87, and the same type was used a generation later to print Josiah Pinto's *Kesef Nivḥar* in Damascus (1605).

Safed. In 1573 the well-known Hebrew printer Eliezer ben Isaac Ashkenazi and his son, Isaac of Prague, left Lublin for Ereẓ Israel, taking with them their printing tools, type, and decorations. After three years in Constantinople, where they printed some books, (described above) they proceeded to Safed. There they set up as printers in partnership with Abraham ben Isaac Ashkenaz, a resident of Safed who provided the funds necessary for the enterprise. Between 1577 and 1580 they issued three books. Then Abraham left for Yemen as an emissary of the

קמתי אני לפתח לדודי

ספר

פני רבה

והוא מפתח לפתוח ולהוציא ממסגר
אסיר ולהאיר עיני כל העלומה
בפירושים הנחמדים המפוארים
במדרש חמש מגילות רבה

עם מפתח קטנה למצא דברי חפץ
מעניני חמש מגילות רבה
בהם ימצא כל מעין ובפרט הדרשנים מרגוע לנפשם כי
בקשו אוכל למו

הוגה בעיון נמרץ
ונדפס בהוצאת הגבירים אפרים בואינו
ויונה אברבניאל יצו
באמשטירדאם
בבית מנשה בן יוסף בן ישראל זל
שנת צור חסיו בו

ונתתי מפתח בית דוד על שכמו ופתח ואין סגר

קמתי אני לפתח לדודי

ספר

פני רבה

והוא מפתח לפתוח ולהוציא ממסגר
אסיר ולהאיר עיני כל העלומה
בפירושים הנחמדים המפוזרים
במדרש רבה על כל ספרי
הקדש תורה נביאים
וכתובים והמש
מגילות
עם מפתח קטנה למצא דברי חפץ
מעניני חמש מגילות רבה
בהם ימצא כל מעין ובפרט הדרשנים מרגוע לנפשם כי
בקשו אוכל למו

הוגה בעיון נמרץ
ונדפס בהוצאת הגבירים אפרים בואינו
ויונה אברבניאל יצו
באמשטירדאם בבית מנשה
בן יוסף בן ישראל זל שנת צור חסיו בו

ונתתי מפתח בית דוד על שכמו ופתח ואין סגר

The *sha'ar* of *Penei Rabbah* written by Manasseh Ben Israel and printed at his press in 1628. The book, one of the first he printed, is an index of the biblical verses explained and elaborated on in the *Midrash Rabbah*. The author prepared two indices; one according to the Venice edition of the *Midrash Rabbah* and the other according to the "Ashkenazi editions" (Cracow, 1487) which were printed with the *Matnot Kehunah* commentary. In the *sha'ar*, Manasseh Ben Israel describes the value of the book for preachers who had to prepare weekly sermons based on the weekly Torah reading. The *Midrash Rabbah* on the Five Scrolls was indexed separately and has a separate *sha'ar*. The aesthetic progress made is easily recognizable as is how much a more intelligent layout of the text improves the general appearance of the page.

Tiberias yeshivah, selling his books at the same time. In 1587 Eliezer printed three more books; like the first three, they were all by Safed authors.

THE 17th AND 18th CENTURIES

AMSTERDAM. Hebrew printing followed the wanderings of the Jews. Fugitives from the Inquisition established the new Portuguese community in Amsterdam at the turn of the 16th century. Ignorant of Hebrew, they recited their prayers in Spanish, and prayer books in that language were printed in Amsterdam by 1604. When they became more proficient in Hebrew, Venice supplied prayer books in Hebrew, with or without translation. In 1626 Manasseh ben Israel set up the first Hebrew press in Amsterdam – a turning point in the history of Hebrew printing. He discarded Italian type, making himself independent of Venice, and had his own type cast which was destined to become dominant throughout Europe, even including Venice. Amsterdam productions were as much sought after as those of Venice had been earlier and they found imitators among Hebrew printers elsewhere. Amsterdam was at the time a great center of general printing, and in format, composition, and decoration Manasseh followed the Dutch style; thus he added the author's portrait to some works. Manasseh's press changed owners several times, though he remained connected with it. Simultaneous with this press another was set up by Daniel de Fonseca but only two works were issued: Meir Aldabi's *Shevilei Emunah* and Abraham de Fonseca's

Einei Avraham (1627). Manasseh found successors among his fellow Sephardim, among them Joseph Athias (1658–98) and his son Immanuel (died 1709). In externals such as vignettes and diagrams they adopted in some way the style of the famous Dutch printing house of Elsevier whose stock and equipment they bought up. Athias first used Manasseh's title pages, but later had one designed for himself depicting the biblical Joseph (his namesake) meeting his father Jacob. This was later adopted by the court preacher D.E. Jablonski in Berlin. He also added a neatly executed copperplate engraving to some of his productions, which found a number of imitators; one of them (*Shenei Luḥot ha-Berit,* 1698) was by the proselyte Abraham ben Jacob, who illustrated the famous *Amsterdam Haggadah* of 1695, produced by the German-Jewish printer Kosmann Emmerich. Another member (as it seems) of the Athias family, Abraham ben Raphael Hezekiah, printed some handsomely produced books during 1728–40. To the same Sephardi group belongs David de Castro Tartas, who learned the craft at Manasseh's press and often used Manasseh's borders. His frontispieces show scenes from the life of the biblical David. Of particular interest are his small-format liturgical items of 1666, dated year one of the new Shabbatean era and with an engraving of Shabbetai Ẓevi as king-messiah. Smaller entrepreneurs were Moses ben Abraham Mendes Coutinho, for whom Solomon Proops worked for some time; Isaac de Cordova (1688–1710), later in Hamburg; Moses ben Isaac Dias (1706–13); Isaac Templo (1714–34), who printed Neḥemiah Ḥayun's *Ha-Ẓad Ẓevi* (1744) but otherwise mainly liturgical items of the Sephardi rite; and Nethanel Foà (1702–15) who displayed as printers' mark the coat of arms of this well-known family. In addition to these printers, who produced mainly for their own community, there were those who endeavored to meet the needs of the German community established in Amsterdam in the course of the 17th century. Among these was Manuel (Immanuel) Benveniste, but his productions lack the finish of those of Manasseh, though his title page with the initials CVS was imitated by German, Italian, and even Salonika printers. Benveniste was succeeded by his former employee Uri Phoebus ben Aaron ha-Levi (1658–89), who worked even more for the German and also for the newly established Polish communities. From Manasseh he borrowed the title border and the vignettes. The title-pages in his Bibles and prayer books have engravings with motifs borrowed from Prague, Augsburg, and Hanau, showing Moses and Aaron on each side. This engraving was much copied by German presses. In 1692 he founded a Hebrew press at Zolkiew, thus bringing the Amsterdam type to Poland. Less important Ashkenazi printers in Amsterdam were Samuel ben Moses ha-Levi, who was active from 1650 to 1655, having for assistants Reuben ben Eliakim and Judah ben Mordecai; and Asher Anshel Shoḥet, who had worked with Uri Phoebus from 1663 to 1665 and printed some liturgical and popular items. The two Ashkenazi *dayyanim* (judges in a religious court) Joseph Dayyan and Moses Frankfurter printed some Talmud tractates, the latter in particular a large, four-volume Bible, *Kehillat Moshe* (1724–27). Of

The *sha'ar* of *Sefer ha-Emunot ve-ha-De'ot* of Saadiah Gaon, translated from the original Arabic into Hebrew by Judah ibn Tibbon, printed by Manasseh Ben Israel in 1648. From 1646 until 1648 the press was managed by Joseph, Manasseh's oldest son, and only his name appears on the title pages of books printed during that period. From 1649 until 1652 the press was managed by Manasseh's second son, Samuel, whose name appears on the books of those years. From 1653 until 1655 the press once again operated under Manasseh's name, although Manasseh's authority was also prime from 1648 until 1652. The edition presented was based on the first edition, of Constantinople 1562, but is inferior to it.

greater importance was the physician Naphtali Herẓ of Emden (1721–42, to 1768 with his son-in-law) who printed some fine books. Some Christians too, such as Kaspar Steen, engaged in the Hebrew printing in Amsterdam – employing Polish refugees. Albertus Magnus brought out a handsome *Seder Berakhot* with Spanish translation in 1687; G. Surenhuys printed a famous and impressive edition of the Mishnah with Latin translation and notes (1698–1703). In the 18th century the dominant figure in Amsterdam Hebrew printing became Samuel Proops (1704–34). He

A copper etching made for the *sha'ar* of *Shenei Luḥot ha-Berit* of Isaiah ha-Levi Horowitz printed by Immanuel Athias, Amsterdam 1698. The etching was the work of the proselyte Abraham ben Jacob who had formerly been a Christian pastor in Rhineland. His signature is in the right-hand lower corner. Of Abraham's other work the map of Ereẓ Israel in Hebrew which was attached to the Amsterdam *Haggadah* of 1695 is worthy of note. Athias' printing is outstanding for its beauty and advanced aesthetic taste. The *Shenei Luḥot ha-Berit* is one of the most beautiful Hebrew books.

printed mainly *siddurim* and *maḥzorim* of the various rites. From 1715 a list of his publications is advertised at the end of every copy. He was among the first to bring out a sales catalog of Hebrew books (*Appiryon Shelomo,* 1730). The press remained in the family until 1849 and was as important to Amsterdam as Bragadini was to Venice.

GERMANY. The unsettled conditions in Central and Eastern Europe – wars, frequent expulsions, raids, and fire, and, particularly the Chmielnicki pogroms (1648–49) in Poland from which thousands of refugees fled westward leaving behind everything including their books and libraries – had a profound influence on Hebrew book production. There was in particular an urgent need for copies of the Talmud and rabbinic literature in a period of unabated, passionate interest in these disciplines. This need was met by Amsterdam and the many Hebrew presses springing up in Germany. During the 18th century the Talmud was printed ten times, each edition in several thousand copies. Catastrophic events pro-

The decorated title page of a Passover *Haggadah* which contains two important commentaries. It was printed in Amsterdam by David Tartas in 1695. It is listed (number 60) in Abraham Yaari's bibliography of the *Haggadah*.

חדושי נדה
להרשב״א ז״ל
נדפס פה ק״ק אלטונא

Title page of the first edition of Solomon ben Adret's novellae to tractate *Niddah,* Altona, 1737. Rashba (as he is known from the initials of his name) was the outstanding rabbi of 13th-century Spain. Typographically this *sha'ar* is of great interest. The ornamental border is made up of more than 100 separate typographic units and yet retains its symmetry.

duced a desire among the less learned and the women for works of solace and edification, which accounts for the great increase in the publication of Yiddish literature. Printing became a profitable business besides being a pious enterprise, and large sums were invested, loaned or donated for these diverse reasons. In Central and Eastern Europe, Jews found it difficult to obtain the necessary printing licenses from feudal lords, and therefore had to associate with Christians as their nominal printers. On the other hand, economic considerations such as the needs of local paper-mills and fiscal expectations led many small princes or authorities to grant licenses, and to protect the new industry and their country's balance of payments by prohibiting the importation of Hebrew books. Large sums were involved: in about 1780 it was calculated that the Jews of Vienna spent 290,000 florins annually on books. Typographically the new Hebrew printers in Germany were at first dependent on Prague whence came most of the personnel. Gradually the influence of Amsterdam made itself felt, even in Prague. The German square type was increasingly discarded.

The Hebrew presses of Germany consisted of two groups: those with the Prague connection, such as Sulzbach, Wilhermsdorf and Fuerth; and those originating with the Ashkenzai printers of Amsterdam, such as Dyhernfurth, Dessau and Halle. Apart from Christian presses which issued Hebrew books sporadically only, and small, ephemeral Jewish printers, Germany produced a considerable number of important Hebrew presses. One of the most prominent Jewish agglomerations was the triple community of Altona, Hamburg, and Wandsbeck, which was reflected in printing as well. S. Poppert was active in Hamburg and Altona (1715–36); Ephraim Heckscher and his partner Aaron ben Elijah Kohen (1732–75); Abraham ben Israel of Halle, son of the printer at Offenbach, Homberg and Neuwied (1743–47). In 1745 Jacob Emden, the great rabbinic scholar and polemicist, set up his own press which printed mainly his own works, such as the three-volume *siddur, Ammudei Shamayim* (1745–48) and his polemics against the kabbalist Jonathan Eybeschuetz.

THE TWO FRANKFORTS, BERLIN, HALLE, ETC. In the ancient and influential community of Frankfort-on-Main no Jew could obtain a printing license from the guild-dominated city authorities, but Christians owned Hebrew presses: Johannes Wust (1677–1707), Blasius Ilsner (1682–?), the Andreas (1707–?), Nikolas Weinmann, and Anton Heinscheit. Of special importance was Johann Koelner (1708–28) from whose printing office came a five-volume *Arba'ah Turim* with Joel Sirkes' commentary (1712–16) and an excellent edition of the Talmud (1720–23) which became the basis for later editions. Aryeh Loeb, son of the Frankfort rabbi Joseph Samuel of Cracow, and later rabbi in Mattersdorf, was responsible for this enterprise. Aryeh Loeb had also prepared the second Amsterdam Talmud of 1714–17, the unacknowledged master copy for the later Berlin-Frankfort on the Oder edition. The Frankfort on the Oder Christian presses had issued Hebrew books before the end of the 16th century, but widespread printing began in 1695 with J.C. Beckmann and Michael Gottschalk, whose successors, F. Grillo, his widow, his daughter, and J.T. Elsner continued Hebrew printing until 1818. Gottschalk prepared the first Talmud edition in Germany (1697–99) which Behrend

The frontispiece of a *maḥzor* for the three pilgrim festivals with a Yiddish commentary, printed by Nathan ben Moses Mahah in Hamburg, 1793. The copper etching is extremely delicate and depicts scenes of (from right to left) Sukkot, Shavu'ot, Pesaḥ and Rosh Ha-Shanah. Above are the figures of Moses and Aaron. The non-Jewish engraver, T.N. Rolfsoen, signed his name in the lower right-hand corner.

Lehmann of Halberstadt financed, with 50,000 taler. A second edition, which Lehman first wanted to divert to the other Frankfort, was eventually printed (1715–22) in both Frankfort on the Oder and Berlin. Midrashim (*Rabba, Tanḥuma, Yalkut*) were also issued there. Gottschalk employed setters from Prague and Venice; his type and vignettes were of Amsterdam origin. In Berlin, D.E. Jablonski established a Hebrew press with Judah Loeb Neumark as manager. From 1708 to 1717 Baruch Buchbinder of Radow printed, among others, the *Ein Ya'akov* (1709) and several works of the Shabbatean writer Neḥemiah Ḥayun. Neumark's son Nathan had his own press from 1719 to 1727 on which he printed some Talmud tractates from 1723. His brother-in-law Aaron ben Moses Rofe was active for three decades from 1733. He printed the Talmud (1734–39) with the backing of Jablonski, whose type was used, and Grillo of Frankfort on the Oder; it was thus an undertaking of both cities. Aaron's press continued under his grandson Moses and his great-grandson Mordecai Landsberg. There was also Hebrew printing in Dessau (1694), Jessnitz (1718) and Koethen (1717) in the duchy of Anhalt. In Halle, the proselyte Moses ben Abraham of Nikolsburg and Prague was active from 1709 to 1714, after having worked with Hebrew printers in Amsterdam, Dessau, Berlin, and Frankfort on the Oder. In Dyhernfurth (Silesia), Shabbetai Bass of Prague, who had learned the trade with Uri Phoebus at Amsterdam, founded a press in 1689; his son Joseph took over in 1712 (till 1739). While his newly cast type and decorations were mostly of Amsterdam origin, Bass's employees came from Poland, among them Ẓevi Hirsch ben Ḥayyim. Neuwied (Rhineland) had Hebrew presses (Grat and J.B. Haupt), run by Israel ben Moses. Another printer there was Benjamin Solomon Kroneburg.

SOUTHERN GERMANY. In southern Germany and in the environs of Frankfort in particular, Hebrew was already being printed early in the 17th century in Hanau and was resumed from 1709, partly by Christian printers such as H.J. Bashuysen and J.C. Beausang. Among Jewish printers there was Seligman Reis (1710–30), who also had been active in Frankfort on the Main, Offenbach, and Homburg (1711–12). Aaron Dessau and partners set up a press in Homburg in 1736 (to 1757). In Offenbach, Seligmann Reis and his son Herz printed from 1714 to 1721. Bonaventura de Nannoy worked with the Jewish printer Israel ben Moses, who was also active in Neuwied and Homburg. In 1724 Israel acquired the press and worked it until 1733 and on his return from Neuwied in 1737 finished a Mishnah edition begun there in 1736.

SULZBACH, WILHERMSDORF AND FUERTH. In Sulzbach (Bavaria) an interesting and successful experiment in Christian and Jewish cooperation in the production of Hebrew books began in 1667, when Abraham Lichtenthaler, a Lutheran, set up a Hebrew press. He was assisted by Isaac ben Judah Loeb Yuedels, a Prague-trained printer, who had a license but no capital, and who was soon after in

The title page of *Naftali Seva Raẓon* (misprinted as *Roẓan*), sermons by Rabbi Naphtali Herz Ginzburg printed at the press of a non-Jew, Thomas Ruhyn; Hamburg, 1708. The word *Amsterdam* in the *sha'ar* stands out, giving the deliberate impression that the book was printed there. The text in small print, however, finishes with the phrase "in the letters of" meaning that the book is printed in an "Amsterdam-style face." The entire *sha'ar* clearly shows the influence of the Amsterdam title pages of 50 years earlier.

Wilhermsdorf. The patron of the project was Duke Christian August, an enthusiast of theosophy. Most early Sulzbach title pages have no decorations; only later did there appear simple border lines or illustrations engraved or on woodblocks. Some show a serpent winding round a tree (the Tree of Knowledge); others show crabs and fishes, or Moses and David on the right and Aaron and Solomon on the left. Some of these title pages were used in Fuerth and Dyhernfurth as well. The type was at first that of Prague, but for certain works the type of Amsterdam was used. Moses Bloch was succeeded by his widow and sons (1694–99) who printed some tractates as part of a plan to print the entire Talmud. Then Bloch's son-in-law Aaron Frankl took over, his first production being a two-volume folio *maḥzor,* attractively printed with decorated initials and a convenient arrangement of the prayers. Aaron was followed by his son Meshullam Zalman (1721–64), who printed a Talmud edition, 1755–63. His competitor, Proops of Amsterdam, obtained from the rabbinical assembly at the Four Council (autonomous Jewish council of Poland-Lithuania) meeting at Staro-Konstantinov (1755) an injunction, which was countermanded by the decision of a ten-member rabbinical court presided over by the rabbi of Fuerth, David Stanss. A similar controversy arose in the next century over the Talmud editions of Vilna and Slavuta. Meshullam Zalman's sons and grandsons continued the business into the middle of the 19th century, when it was carried on under the name of S. Arnstein and Sons (1818–51); their publisher's catalogs appeared from 1830. The firm founded by Moses Bloch had been active for 160 years, issuing about 600 works, among them many cheaply printed but popular liturgical items.

Another center of Hebrew printing in Bavaria was Wilhermsdorf, where Isaac ben Judah Loeb Yuedels set up a press in 1669 with staff recruited from Prague, among them his daughters as setters and a son-in-law as proofreader. Another Prague printer, Israel Meir, set up a press in 1712 but sold it the same year to Hirsch ben Ḥayyim of Fuerth, whose son worked later in Fuerth, printing until 1739. Hirsch cultivated book decorations: his printers' mark was the tree with the serpent, a crab and a lion on each side; the title page showed Moses and Aaron with angels hovering above them, and the last page a flower basket as vignette. Nearby Fuerth, a center of talmudic learning, had its first Hebrew presses by 1691. One was established by Solomon Shne'ur and

ספרי זרע ברך שלישי

חוט המשולש שחיבר אבר"ך בשנים אב"ר ור"מ הרב המופלג
הדרשן הגדול חריף ושנון כ"ש כמהר"ר ברכיה בירך נר"ו :

הסכמות המאור הגדול רבן של כל בני הגולה ונשיא בארץ ישראל ה"ה אב"ד
ור"מ דק"ק פראג וכל המדינה יצו' :

הסכמות הרב הגדול בעל המחבר מנחת יעקב ושבות יעקב וחק יעקב :

Title page of *Zera Berakh,* novellae on the Book of Genesis by Berechiah Berakh, which was printed by Moses ben Abraham the proselyte in Halle, 1714. This title page is unique – it includes two approbations *(haskamot).* The end of the book relates that the ruler of the city had the author imprisoned because he did not have a residence permit. For this reason the subsequent sections were not printed. In fact, all printing activity in Halle ceased as a result of this event. The author was the grandson of the famous preacher Berechiah Berakh the First.

his son Joseph with the help of the Cracow printer Moses Menaḥem Katz, and later continued under another son, Abraham, and a son-in-law Isaac Bing, and their sons or successors until 1730. This press printed some important rabbinic and Yiddish works. The other enterprise was that of Hirsch Frankfurter (till 1701), who had the backing of his brother-in-law, the Court Jew Mordecai Model of Ansbach, who had a license to print the Talmud. Another press was founded in Fuerth in 1737 by Ḥayyim ben Ẓevi Hirsch, son of the Dyhernfurth printer, and it continued under him and his widow until 1774.

ITALY, PRAGUE AND POLAND. In Venice, bereft of its former glory, Bragadini was still dominant at this period with Vendramini as its main competitor (from 1631) until they joined forces. Their activities were soon limited to *siddurim* and similar items. In Mantua, too, Hebrew printing continued, first under J.S. Perugia and his descendants, and from 1724 under the physician Raphael Ḥayyim d'Italia and his successor Eliezer Solomon d'Italia. From 1718 to 1723 Isaac Jare ben David and Jacob Ḥaver-Tov also printed in Mantua. A new center arose in Leghorn, where Abraham Ḥaver-Tov, one of Bragadini's best proofreaders, printed some important works in partnership with Jedidiah Gabbai. They used as printers' mark the three crowns – borrowed from Bragadini – with the addition of the coat of arms of the Medicis. Some Hebrew printing took place at Rossi's press in Verona during 1645–52, with the Amsterdam influence predominating. Such was the case in Venice from 1700 and, in particular, in Leghorn, where Israel da Paz, who had worked with Isaac Templo at Amsterdam, was active from 1740. In Prague Hebrew printing resumed, after an interval of two decades, at Jacob Bak's press. During the 17th century Prague preserved its own style, but in the 18th century the old German square type disappeared from the superscriptions and much was borrowed from Amsterdam. In 1746 the archbishop's press issued the Gospels in Hebrew, Yiddish, German, and Latin for missionary purposes. In Cracow Menaḥem N. Meisels established his press in 1631 and returned to the Prague style which replaced the Italian introduced by Isaac ben Aaron of Prossnitz. Meisel's manager was Judah Kohen of Prague, and there is a great similarity between their productions and those of Prague. Lublin too, where Hebrew printing took place with interruptions until 1678. remained under the Prague influence. Only when Uri Phoebus went to Zolkiew in 1692 did the Amsterdam style find a home in Poland.

Sha'ar of *Yalkut Re'uveni*, a collection of kabbalistic teachings arranged according to the order of the Bible, collected and edited by Reuben ben Hoeshke Katz. It was printed by Isaac ben Judah Loeb Yuedels in Wilhermsdorf, 1681. This is the first edition of this work, which is among the most important collections of kabbalistic teachings.

ילקוט
על התורה
נדפס פה קק ווילהרמרש דארף
שנת אמת לפק

TURKEY. Constantinople experienced an almost complete break in Hebrew printing from 1585 to 1638. In 1638 Solomon Franco set up his press, which his son Abraham continued until 1683 and where several refugees from the Chmielnicki massacres were employed.

Hebrew printing during the 18th century in Constantinople was dominated by Jonah ben Jacob Ashkenazi, his sons, and his grandsons. Between 1710 and 1778 they issued 188 works, employing at one time as many as 50 workers. Jonah designed and improved his type, and was among those who cast the first Turkish type in 1728. He traveled widely in search of worthwhile manuscripts. He printed such important works as the *Zohar* (1736–37); the first edition of the famous and influential book *Ḥemdat Yamim* (Smyrna, 1731–32; Constantinople, 1735–70); and a Bible with Ladino translation (in partnership with the Venetian Benjamin ben Moses Rushi). Altogether, his Ladino productions, originals or translations from the Hebrew, brought about a revival of Ladino literature and language.

In Salonika, a Marrano, Solomon ben David, revived the trade by printing Rashi's Pentateuch commentary in 1639. He was followed by his son Abraham and son-in-law Jacob ben Solomon Gabbai. They published mainly Sephardi authors, such as the responsa of Joseph ben Moses Trani (1641). They also published a *Midrash Rabbah* in the same year, a vowelled Mishnah text with the commentary *Kaf Naḥat* by Isaac Gabbai (1644–45), and other halakhic, homiletic, and kabbalistic literature.

A revival began in 1709 under Abraham ben David and Yomtov Canpillas, the latter printing alone from 1729 and with partners from 1732. They printed mainly rabbinic novellae, responsa, and homiletics. Salonika preserved in type, decorations, and even paper its own easily recognizable style. Jedidiah Gabbai's Leghorn press was transferred to Smyrna by his son Abraham in 1657. Jonah ben Jacob also printed there in 1729–41.

Shabbethai Mattathias Basevi (died 1601) acquired the Jabez press and he and his son issued various works until 1605, including a *Midrash Rabbah* (1594) an *Ein Ya'akov,* and a *Shulḥan Arukh Oraḥ Ḥayyim* (1595). The Salonika *talmud torah* administration printed a *maḥzor* of the Catalonian rite in 1695 and some Talmud tractates in 1707. This press passed through various hands in the 18th century when many works were printed. Between 1814 and 1941 eight more Hebrew printers worked in Salonika, among them the presses of Isaac Jahon; the Gemilut Ḥasadim Society, which was founded about 1870 and printed selections from the *Zohar*; and the Ez ha-Ḥayyim Society, which was founded about 1875 and printed *maḥzorim*. In Chufut-Kale, the printers Afda and Shabbetai Jeraka together with other partners set up the first Karaite press in 1734 (until 1741), working with types similar to that of Constantinople.

MODERN PERIOD

CENTRAL AND EASTERN EUROPE, 1760–1900. From the middle of the 18th century, the center of Hebrew printing shifted more and more to Central and Eastern Europe. States, large and small, in these regions wanted to prevent the importation of Hebrew books and the resulting drain on their capital resources. In addition, the increasing severity of the church-state censorship – more severe than it ever was in other parts of Europe, in a region that had not known such censorship before – made it desirable to the authorities to have Hebrew presses under their immediate supervision. For both these reasons the setting up of local Hebrew presses was encouraged. A more positive stimulus to the rise of these presses was the efflorescence of Talmud study in the growing number of yeshivot in Lithuania and Poland as well as of Ḥasidism and its literature, which created an ever larger demand for Hebrew books. The beginnings of Haskalah, (the Jewish Enlightenment movement), was another contributory factor. The shift to Eastern Europe resulted in a lowering of the standards of printing and book production.

Austria. The Hapsburg Empire was located in the center of Europe and its capital, Vienna, occupied a leading position in Hebrew printing of this period. Presses established in the last decade of the 18th

ספר
חדושי הרב
רבנו נסים ז"ל מחבר על מסכת גיטין
בקושטאנדינה

Sha'ar of *Ḥiddushei Rabbeinu Nissim,* novellae on the talmudic tractate *Gittin,* printed in Constantinople by Abraham Rosanes, 1711. Rosanes was the son-in-law of Abraham Franco whose press in Constantinople had operated for 40 years. Rosanes began to operate this press in 1711, after it had been idle for many years. No other book was printed on this press until 1719. The printer is mentioned on the reverse of the title page.

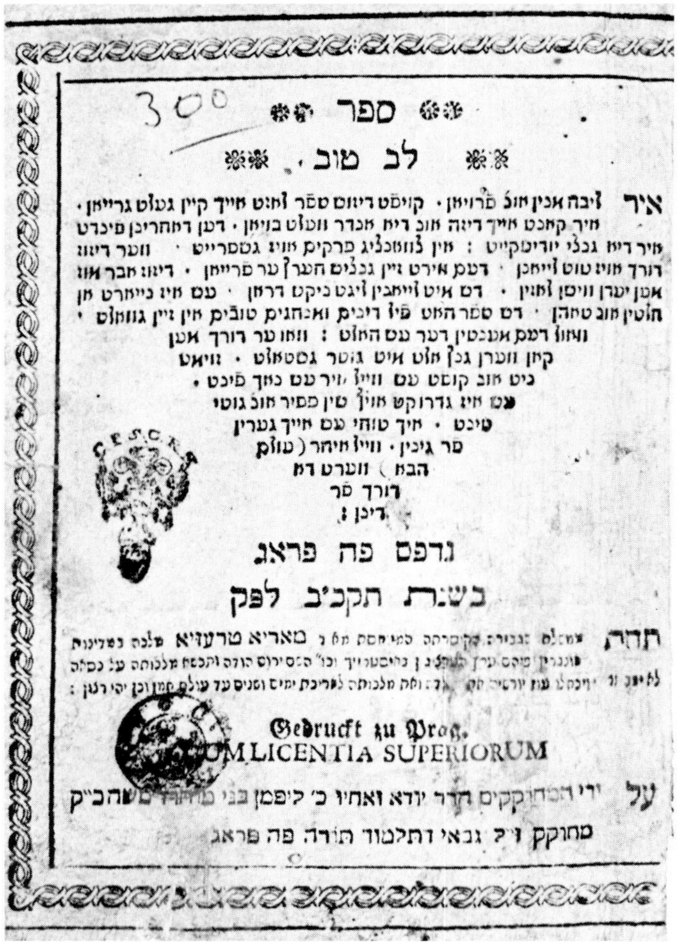
ספר
לב טוב
נדפס פה פראג
בשנת תקכ״ב לפק
Gedruckt zu Prag.
CUM LICENTIA SUPERIORUM

Sha'ar of *Lev Tov* printed at the Bak press in Prague during its brief renascence in 1762. This Yiddish book on laws and customs, written by Isaac ben Eliakim, was for non-Hebrew-speaking people who had no way of knowing the *halakhah* except by asking a rabbi or somebody else. Some rabbis raised great objections to this type of book; nevertheless, they were widely reprinted. *Lev Tov* itself went through about 50 reprintings between 1620 and 1840. This edition is very rare today.

century by the court printers Joseph Hrazchansky and Anton Schmidt succeeded the great Hebrew printing houses of Venice and Amsterdam. By 1850 they had issued five editions of the Talmud. Schmidt, who acquired a great part of the Bomberg and Proops presses, printed most of the classical texts, including Bibles and prayer books of all the rites. Later in the century and well into the 20th century Joseph Schlesinger was the leading publisher-printer of such liturgical items with translations into the main European languages. Over the provinces of the Austro-Hungarian monarchy which became Czechoslovakia, the old center of printing in Prague, the capital of Bohemia, never regained its former prominence. An attempt at revival by the Bak press from 1762 was stifled by severe censorship. A certain revival took place under Moses Landau (1820–50), who produced two Talmud editions and a good deal of Haskalah literature emanating from the Mendelssohn school. In Bruenn (Brno), capital of Moravia, a Hebrew press had been founded in 1754 on the initiative of the Moravian chamber by Joseph Neumann. Until 1802 it produced mainly liturgical items, works of edification in Yiddish for the local market and works of local authors. Another 18th century Bruenn Hebrew printer was Bezalel (Gottlieb) Jeiteles. In Pressburg (Bratislava), capital of Slovakia, where some Hebrew printing had taken place in 1789–90, Schmidt of Vienna set up a press in 1838 from which important items were issued. Joseph Schlesinger, too, printed there in the 1860s. In the Austrian-dominated parts of Poland (Galicia), Cracow retained its importance, with Naphtali Herz Shapiro and his sons active in 1802–22; Karl Budweiser (1863–74), who later moved to Lvov; and, in particular Joseph Fischer (1878–1914). The several small presses of Zolkiew were forced to transfer to Lvov in 1782, which led to the rise of that city as a center of Hebrew printing in the next century; in that century it accommodated the presses of Mann (Grossmann) Rosanes, Letteris, and, above all, Madfes – some as yet unsurpassed editions of the *Shulḥan Arukh* were produced there. In Zolkiew itself a new press was founded in 1791 by a certain Meyerhofer, where works of the local rabbi Z. H. Chajes appeared in 1840–50. In Czernowitz Hebrew printing took place from 1835. In the Rumanian capital of Bucharest the *Sifra* with the commentary by M.L. Malbim, then rabbi at Bucharest, was produced in a fine edition.

Poland and Russia. In Russia proper the first Hebrew book is said to have been printed in 1760 in Oleksinets (Y.L. Heller's *Berit Melaḥ*), where there was printing until 1776. The press of Slavuta, founded in 1792, issued three Talmud editions between 1800 and 1820; and one each (1816–28) in Kopys (founded 1807) and Grodno-Vilna (1835–54). The Shapira family of Slavuta continued in Zhitomir, printing fine editions of both Talmuds and the Zohar. Towards the middle of the 19th century Vilna became a great printing center – the Talmud editions of Romm, who also issued other standard rabbinic texts, were universally recognized as the best editions. Reproduction of these editions was continued until modern times. Romm's competitors in this field were printers like Samuel Orgelbrand and Rosenkranz-Schriftsetzer in Warsaw, where the first Hebrew book was issued in 1796, and which eventually became an

מסכת
ברכות
מן
תלמוד בבלי
עם כל המפרשים כאשר נדפס מקדם ועם הוספות
הרשות כמבואר בשער השני .
ווילנא
בדפוס והוצאות האלמנה והאחים ר״ם
שנת זאת הברכה לפ״ק
ТАЛМУДЪ ВАВИЛОНСКИЙ
Трактатъ Берахотъ
Съ Варшавскаго изданія 1876 г.
Съ прибавленіями.
Часть I.
1880 г.

important center of Hebrew printing. Following is a list of major places in Poland and Russia where Hebrew printing took place in this period:

Berdichev – Ukr. 1807
Boguslav – Ukr. 1819
Bratslav – Ukr. 1821
Dubno – Ukr. 1794
Dubrovno – Bel. 1802
Grodno – Bel. 1788
Hrubieszow – Pol. 1817
Jozefow – Pol. 1825
Kopys – Bel. 1807
Korets (Korzec) – Ukr. 1778
Medzhibozh – Ukr. 1817
Mezhorov – Ukr. 1789
Minkovtsy – Ukr. 1796
Minsk – Bel. 1808
Mogilev – Bel. 1825
Mogilev-Podolski – Ukr. 1809
Nowy Dwor – Pol. 1782
Odessa – Ukr. 1845
Oleksinets – Ukr. 1760
Ostraha – Ukr. 1793
Piotrkow – Pol. 1876
Polonnoye – Ukr. 1791
Poritsk – Ukr. 1786
Radziwillow – Ukr. 1814
Shklov – Bel. 1783
Slavuta – Ukr. 1792
Sudilkov – Ukr. 1817
Tarnopol – Ukr. 1813
Vilna – Lith. 1799
Warsaw – Pol. 1796
Zaslavl – Ukr. 1807
Zhitomir – Ukr. 1804

Ukr. = Ukraine
Pol. = Poland
Lith. = Lithuania
Bel. = Belorussia

The Russian Karaites too resumed printing in Chufut-Kale, 1804–06, and in Goslov-Yevpatoriya, Crimea, 1833–36, issuing prayer books and works of Karaite literature.

WESTERN EUROPE. In Germany Hebrew presses had not ceased working. In Berlin the *Orientalische Buchdruckerei* was founded in 1760. The apostate Julius Sittenfeld was active in the middle of the 19th century, producing a fine Talmud, 1862–68, for which N.A. Goldberg was responsible. Another Berlin printer from the second half of the century onward was H. Itzkowski. In Koenigsberg, where there had been sporadic printing during the 18th century, Gruebe and Longrein printed some fine rabbinic texts from 1858. To this group belongs Johannisberg, also in East Prussia, in the 1850s; Stettin, from 1859, where parts of the Talmud and a fine Mishnah were printed; Danzig (Mishnah with *Tiferet Yisrael* commentary, 1843); Hanover, at Telgeners, from 1828; Halberstadt from 1859 (Jeruham Fishel ben Ẓevi Hirsch); Leipzig; Breslau, from 1790; Lyck, east Prussia, where the weekly *Ha-Maggid* was printed, 1856–91, and the Mekiẓe Nirdamim Society brought

Opposite: *Sha'ar* of the Vilna edition of the Talmud printed by the Widow and Brothers Romm in 1880. This is the largest, most luxurious and most sophisticated edition of the Talmud that was ever printed. Dozens of early commentaries, the manuscripts of which were collected at great cost and effort, were printed for the first time in this edition. The novellae of many later authorities were also included mainly in the form of annotations. These included the novellae of David Luria, Samuel and Mattathias Strashun, Jacob Emden, Ẓevi Hirsch Chajes, Bezalel ha-Kohen of Vilna, the *Yefei Einayim* indicating parallel passages in the Jeruslaem Talmud and many others. This edition became the model for all subsequent editions of the Talmud and it was itself reprinted many times both from the original forms and by photo copying with the addition of more commentaries at the end. The actual printing of this edition took six years. J.N.U.L., Jerusalem.

The title page of the only book printed in Lyady, *Ammudei Golah* (known as a *Sefer Mitzvot Katan – Semak*) by the tosafist, Isaac of Corbeille. The book was printed in 1805 and contains an approbation from Schneur Zalman of Lyady, the founder of Ḥabad Ḥasidism.

The book of the Karaite Aaron ben Joseph (the First) who lived in Crimea between 1250 and 1320. It is a commentary on the Torah whose importance lies in the fact that the author draws heavily on early authorities both Karaite and Rabbanite including Saadiah Gaon, Jonah ibn Janah, Menahem ben Saruk and Abraham ibn Ezra. The book was printed in Goslov in 1835 which in that period (c. 1830-c. 1865) was a Karaite center and a main location for the printing of Karaitica, on the initiative of Abraham Firkovich.

out its early editions; Krotoszy, from 1834, with a fine Jerusalem Talmud; and in Posen from 1802. Of special importance is the press founded by Wolf Heidenheim in Roedelheim, near Frankfort on the Main, about 1800, where he issued his famous Pentateuch, *maḥzor,* and other liturgical texts. This tradition was continued by his successor, M. Lehrberger, later in Frankfort, who printed Seligman Isaac Baer's well-known liturgical texts. Karlsruhe had a Hebrew press both in the 18th and the 19th centuries.

In France Hebrew presses were established in Metz (c. 1760), Strasbourg (1777), and later in Paris (1806), where the house of Durlacher was active from the 19th century. In England, where Hebrew had been printed — in London and Oxford — in earlier centuries, London had a Hebrew press in the 19th century as did Edinburgh in Scotland. In Italy, Venice continued to decline, with Leghorn becoming from 1740 the center of liturgical work for the Mediterranean area. First Sadun and then Solomon Belforte were the leading printers in Leghorn. Venice printers branched out to Pisa in 1779, printing for the oriental market, and in Constantinople (so it was stated) books exclusively printed by Jews were preferred. Reggio Emilia had a small press from 1805 to 1820. Salonika and Smyrna continued in this period to turn out large amounts of rabbinical literature but no copies of the Talmud.

UNITED STATES. Hebrew printing in the United States at first took the form of Christian printers inserting isolated Hebrew words or phrases into their English publications, for which the type was brought over from England. Thus, in the first book printed in

Title page of a Passover *Haggadah* entitled *Arba'ah Ammudei Kesef* which includes the commentaries of Moses Alshekh, Isaac Abrabanel and Ephraim Luntschitz. Its format is similar to that of the *Haggadah* printed in Amsterdam in 1781. This *Haggadah* was printed in Mezhorov, Podolia, 1794. The title page includes the words "Printed in Mezhorov as in Amsterdam," the last word in large letters so as to give the impression that it was actually printed in Amsterdam.

the American colonies, an English version of Psalms (Cambridge, Massachusetts, 1640), the Hebrew alphabet accompanied Psalm 119 and Hebrew words were used six times in the preface. In the two centuries following, many works containing some Hebrew were printed in Cambridge, Andover, Boston, New Haven, New York and Philadelphia, comprising mainly Hebrew lexica, grammars, primers, and single books of the Bible. Hebrew was also used in printed rules and regulations of Jewish communities and religious societies, or in special orders of services. From the middle of the 18th century onward complete prayer books (*maḥzorim* with English translations) began to appear. In the 19th century Hebrew printing of sorts is found also in Baltimore (1843), Charleston, South Carolina (1842), Cincinnati (1824), New Orleans (1850), San Francisco (1850), and Kingston, Jamaica (1842). Jewish printers began to be active from 1825 (Solomon Henry Jackson, Henry Frank, both in New York). With rising immigration from Eastern Europe, Hebrew and Yiddish newspapers began to appear from 1874 onward.

NEW TRENDS. While no new trends developed in Hebrew printing up to World War I and even World War II, the Russian Revolution and the debacle of European Jewry in the Holocaust terminated almost all Hebrew printing in Central and Eastern Europe. With the establishment of the Jewish National Home in Palestine (1918–47) and the State of Israel (1948), Jerusalem and Tel Aviv became the centers of Hebrew printing and publishing. New York too, as well as other cities in the U.S.A., produced a good deal of Hebrew, particularly rabbinic literature. England, France, and Switzerland made a minor contribution. The invention of new processes of photomechanical printing have been applied to a great number of the best editions of the 19th century as well as to incunabula and rare early prints to satisfy – if not the bibliophiles – the growing demand for rabbinic and other scholarly literature. On the other hand, the phenomenal growth of modern Hebrew (and Yiddish) literature was reflected in the work of the Hebrew printers and publishers in Israel, some of whom began their activities in Russia, Poland or Germany before or after 1900. Yiddish literature too was being printed in the U.S.A. and to a very small extent in Soviet Russia.

IN EREẒ ISRAEL.

Safed. For the early period, see above pages. In 1831, a fresh start was made in Safed by Israel Bak, who had brought with him from Berdichev, Russia, type-

פאת השלחן
והוא סוף וסיום לארבע שלחן ערוך
פה גליל העליון
עה״ק צפת תובב״א
בשנת שאלו שלום ירושלים לפ״ק

Title page of *Pe'at ha-Shulḥan* by Israel of Shklov, leader of the non-ḥasidic community in Safed. It was printed at the Bak press in Safed between 1833 and 1837, and is a definitive code of the laws relating to the agricultural produce of Ereẓ Israel, supplementing the responsa of Joseph Caro. The author was a disciple of Elijah the Gaon of Vilna, and the book was written many years before its printing since he did not want to have it printed outside of Ereẓ Israel. In 1834 Bedouin peasants attacked the Jewish quarter in Safed, and the damage they caused brought the press to a standstill for three years. Most of *Pe'at ha-Shulḥan* was printed before this but it was completed only in 1837 when Bak rebuilt his press and resumed his activity. Printing in Safed ceased finally in 1837, this time because of a serious earthquake.

founding equipment and two wooden presses. His printing house was destroyed by the earthquake that struck the town in 1837, after he had printed only six books.

Jerusalem. Hebrew printing in Jerusalem began in 1840 with Israel Bak who, in 1840 received a license to print in Jerusalem and for 22 years was the only Hebrew printer there. During those years he printed

The printing press of the partners Brill and Salomon, which appeared on their edition of *Goralot,* 1863. From Shoshanah Halevi, *Ha-Defus ha-Ivri bi-Yrushalayim.*

more than 60 books and pamphlets. In 1843 Moses Montefiore sent him a gift of a press, and from that time on the gift is mentioned in every item Bak printed and its likeness was often reproduced on the title page or at the end of the books printed on it.

In 1863, Michel Cohen and Joel Moses Salomon, in partnership, brought a lithographic printing press to Jerusalem. They had learned the art in Koenigsberg. As competitors they became involved in an acrimonious dispute with Bak but the latter regained his position as Jerusalem's only Hebrew printer after Salomon's license was revoked in 1865. However, Salomon's father-in-law, Abraham Rothenberg, received a license to print in 1866 and re-opened the press.

Israel Bak died in 1875; in all he had produced some 130 books in Jerusalem. His son, Nisan, took over the business and maintained it until 1883. In 1868 Salomon succeeded in renewing his license in his own name and from that time on, no further mention is made on the title pages of his father-in-law, Rothenberg. The Salomon press, operated by his descendents, still exists in Jerusalem.

In 1872 Isaac Gushzini and his partners established an important printing shop, and several other printers established themselves in Jerusalem by 1890: the brothers, Elijah and Moses Sassoon (1874–1883); the Gaguin family (1876–1855); and Zuckerman and son (1886–1915). In 1883, the scholar Isaac Hirshenson began a press and printed for a few years.

In the 20th century several large printing plants have been established in Jerusalem. These are equipped with the most modern setting and printing machines and can produce the entire range of printing.

After World War I Zionist and communal institutions began to give out considerable printing orders, and the first process engraving works were established in Jerusalem to facilitate the printing of Jewish National Fund stamps, pictures and illustrated publicity material for public bodies. Non-Jewish printing houses were to be found mainly in monasteries; there was one in the Schneller orphanage, which specialized in printing school exercise books. In the 1920s, the new town of Tel Aviv began to replace Jerusalem as the printing and publishing center.

Tel Aviv. The first Jewish printing works in the area was opened in Jaffa in 1906, where most printing houses were to be found in that area until the 1920s. Saadia Shoshani, nephew of the owner, Aaron Eitan, was a pioneer in the organization of the industry and became president of the Organization of Printing Presses in Israel. Many printing workers arrived from Poland in the 1920s with the Third and Fourth Aliyah. Some of them established the Ha-Po'el ha-Ẓair cooperative; others joined the Aḥdut cooperative, which had been set up in Jerusalem in 1909 and subsequently transferred to Tel Aviv. The daily press that grew up in Tel Aviv was an important factor in the industrialization of printing and modern equipment was purchased to meet its needs. When the canning industry started in the 1930s, Eliezer Lewin-Epstein, of the famous Warsaw printing family, set up a printing enterprise to cater for it which became the first offset press in the country and was particularly noted for the printing of postage stamps and posters. Other offset presses were soon established and supplied Israel industry with advertising material and printed packing materials.

In the State of Israel. The establishment of the Government Printer – at first in Tel Aviv and soon with a branch in Jerusalem – gave an impetus to the development of printing. It did photogravure work, which had previously been sent to the United Kingdom, and printed postage stamps and banknotes for various African and Asian countries. In 1966 it was transferred to Jerusalem. It was the largest printing establishment in the country, with some 300 workers, and was also a channel through which government orders are distributed to other printers in Jerusalem and elsewhere.

After 1966 modern machinery for cold type composition, including IBM, Monophoto, and Photon equipment, was installed by several firms, including Isratypeset and Keter Press Enterprises in Jerusalem, enabling high-quality bookwork to be done for local and foreign publishers. Offset notary presses for

Plate 25 (right). A page from a Passover *Haggadah* written and illuminated in Altona-Hamburg in 1740 by Joseph bar David Leipnick of Moravia, ostensibly illustrating the labors of the Israelites in ancient Egypt. In fact, it shows contemporary Jews at work in a German town. The British Library Board, London.

Plate 26 (below). A page from an anonymous travelog known as the *Casale Pilgrim,* from Casale Monferrato, Italy, dated 1758. The sketches seen here are stylized representations of the tombs of certain named Galilean scholars of the mishnaic period – the first and second centuries. Cecil Roth Collection.

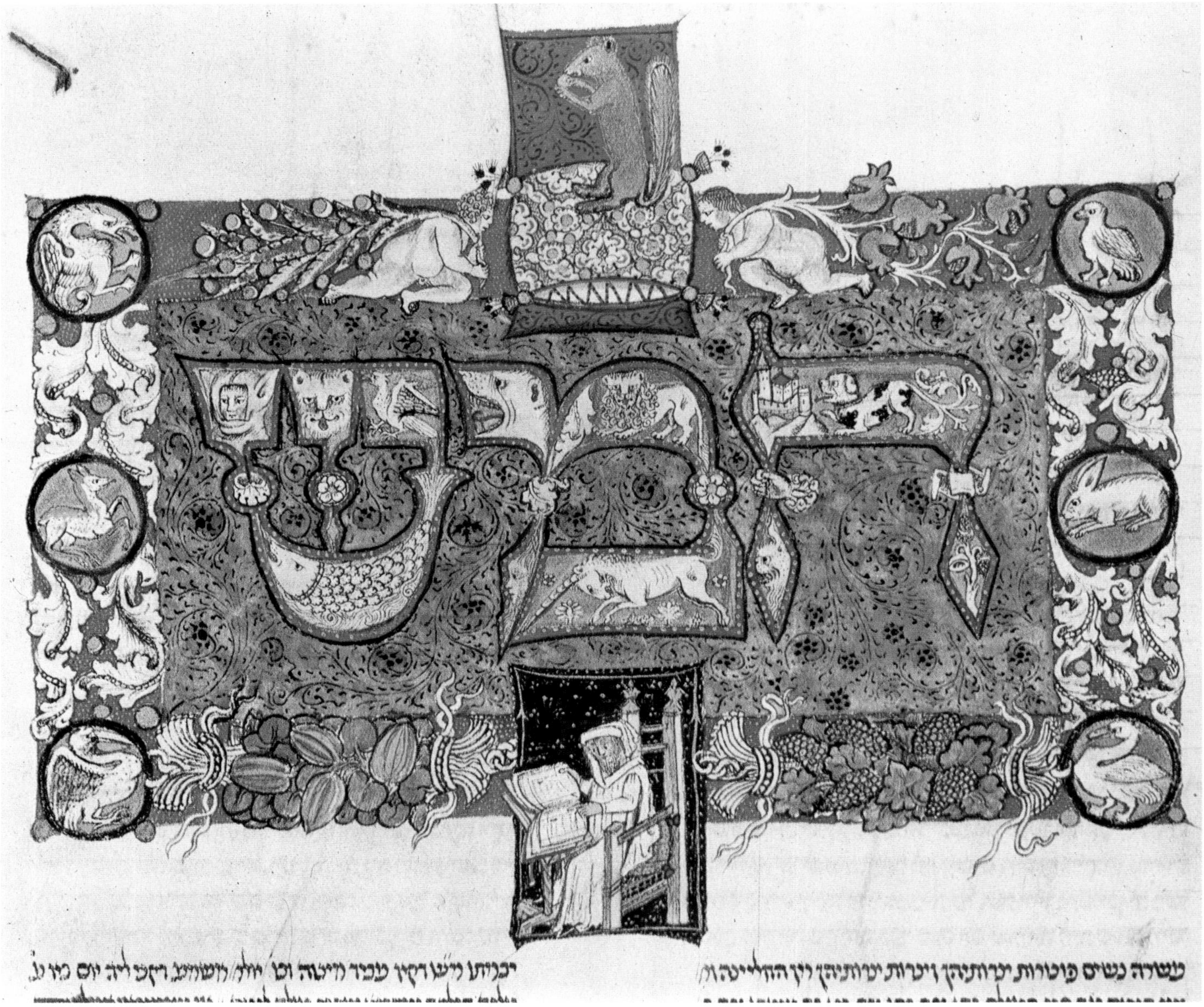

Plate 27. A page from Asher ben Jehiel's commentary on the Talmud, Germany, 14th century. Paris, Bibliothèque Nationale, Ms. Heb. 418, fol. 198.

Plate 28. A full-page miniature from the *Regensburg Pentateuch,* Bavaria, c. 1300, showing Moses receiving the Tablets of the Law and passing them on to the Israelites. Jerusalem, Israel Museum, Ms. 180/52, fol. 154v.

Plate 29. Page from the *Rothschild Miscellany,* Italy, c. 1470. The page contains an illuminated panel of the word *"Hoshana."* Israel Museum, Jerusalem.

printing illustrated weeklies were also imported; in 1970 there were over 30 offset presses in Israel that were capable, inter alia, of producing good-quality color work. Printing presses were also opened in Haifa, in many development towns, and in three kibbutzim. There were three Arabic presses in Nazareth and several in Jerusalem.

In 1969 there were some 900 printing and publishing enterprises in Israel, with 9,500 persons employed (about two-thirds of the employees working in Tel Aviv). Aggregate output was IL 262,000,000 (about $75,000,000) and exports totaled about $5,000,000 (about half of which went to the U.S.A.), compared with $2,900,000 in 1966 and $400,000 in 1956. About 80% of the enterprises employed a little more than a quarter of the workers, while two-fifths of the personnel were employed by 3.5% of the enterprises.

Right: A roll of tape used in the computerized printing of Hebrew text in the Photon equipment of Keter Enterprises, Jerusalem. Photo: David Harris, Jerusalem. Below: Proofs are inspected as they come off the offset printing press at Keter. The unfolded signatures are checked with a densitometer for correct ink density.

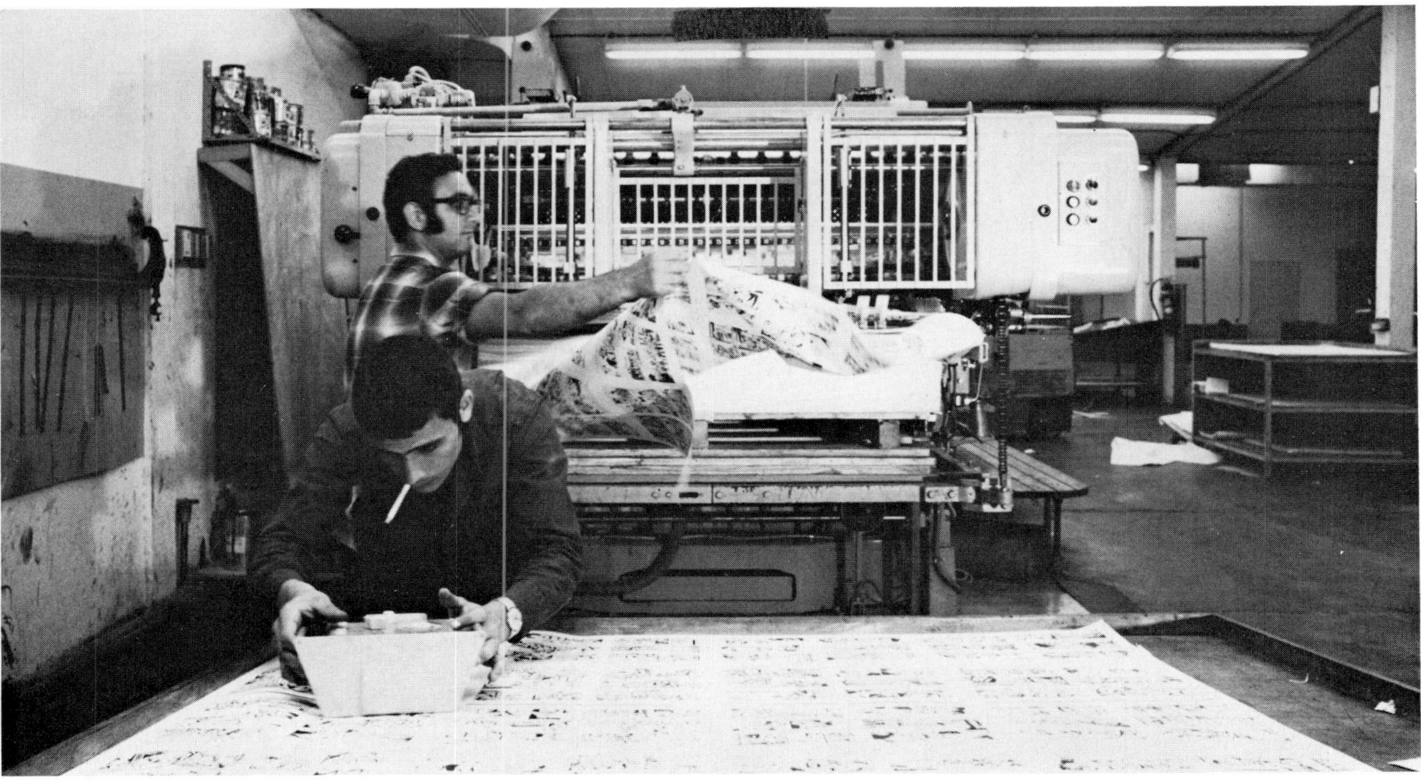

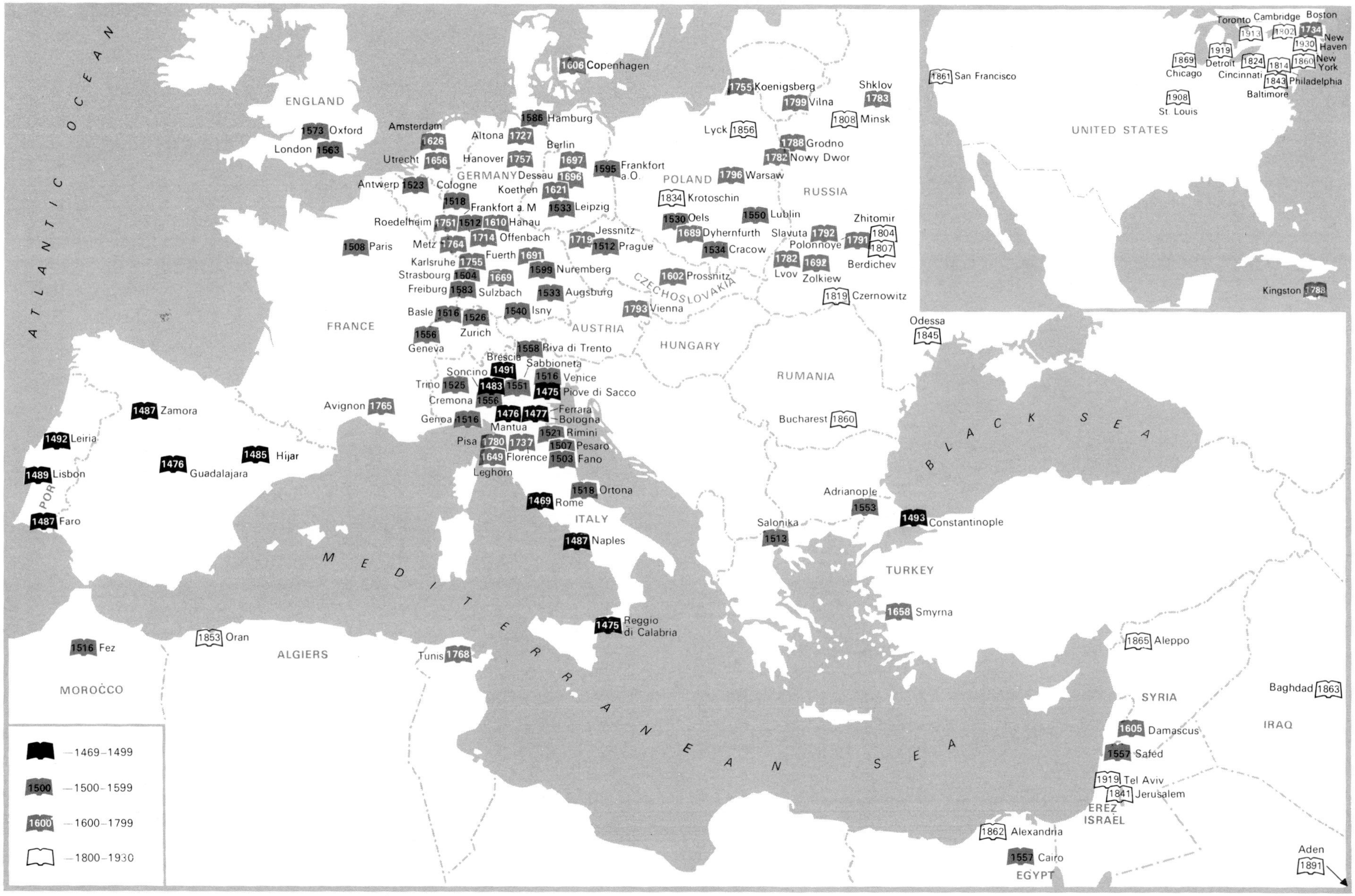

MAIN LOCATIONS OF HEBREW PRINTING, 15th-20th CENTURIES

6. major centers*

ADEN. A Hebrew printing house was founded in Aden in 1891 by Menaḥem 'Awwād and his four partners. Until 1925 some 15 books were printed at this press. The "Caxton Press," established in 1929, also published four Hebrew works. All the books printed in Aden are collections of prayers, religious law, etc.

ALEPPO. In 1865 Abraham Sasson and his sons set up a printing house, one of the sons having learned the craft in Leghorn. In 1887 Isaiah Dayyan established another printing press with the help of H.P. Kohen from Jerusalem. Two years later they had to cease operation, not being able to obtain a government license. The license was obtained in 1896 and printing was resumed and continued until World War I. From 1910 to 1933 Ezra Ḥayyim Jouejati of Damascus operated a press, having learned the craft with Eliezer Ben-Yehuda in Jerusalem. Another printing press was founded by Ezra Bijo in 1924 and continued until 1925. Altogether, approximately 70 books were printed in Aleppo, mostly works by local scholars, ancient manuscripts found locally, and prayer books of the local rite.

ALTONA. In 1727 Samuel S. Popert of Koblenz established a printing press in Altona, having learned the craft in nearby Hamburg where he had published a few books. He did the printing himself, assisted by the wandering typesetter Moses Maarsen of Amster-

*Excluding purely incunabula centers and the large centers discussed in Chapter 5.

בס״ד
הופת חתנים
הנקרא
שירה וזמרה
כולל
שירות ותשבחות · לאל המהלל בתשבחות ·
אימרות ה׳ אמרות טהורות · זכות
וברות · ורובם ממ״ור שלום
שבזי זיע״א · והמה בנוים
ע״ד הסוד · לשמחת
חתן וכלה · ולכבוד שבת ומילה · וכו׳
נדפס
בתוספת לשבח · ונייר משבח ·
פה עדן יע״א
שנת עד אשר תפ״רה ונחלת את הארץ לפ״ק
ע״י מנחם עוזן ושותפיו ס״ט

Sha'ar of *Ḥuppat Ḥatanim,* Aden, 1925, including laudatory poems for festive occasions: The Sabbath, circumcision, marriage, etc. Most of the poems are by Shalom Shabazi, the foremost Yemenite poet. A previous edition of the book, printed in 1902, has been lost.

dam. Until 1739 Popert published various works in Hebrew and Yiddish. In 1732 the wealthy Ephraim Heckscher set up a printing house which a year later passed into the hands of his assistant Aaron ben Elijah ha-Kohen, who was called Aaron Setzer ("setter"). He continued printing until 1743, when he became the manager of the press set up by Rabbi Jacob Emden, where later many of Emden's polemical writings were printed. In 1752 they separated, as Aaron had sided with Emden's pet hate Jonathan Eybeschuetz. Another assistant in Emden's printing works, Moses Bonn, set out on his own in 1765, and this business was operated for many years by his sons and grandsons as Brothers Bonn.

ANHALT. Hebrew printing presses were established in Koethen in 1621. Moses Benjamin Wolff, the court Jew, set up a Hebrew press in 1695 in Dessau (which was active till 1704) as well as in Jessnitz and Koethen. In Koethen, Israel ben Abraham, a proselyte, was active for many years. He printed Maimonides' *Yad* with commentaries (1739–42), and his *Guide for the Perplexed* with the standard commentaries in 1742. In 1742 also, Benjamin Moses Wolff's son Elijah restored his father's press for one year, producing the *Sifra* and *Seder Mo'ed* of the Palestinian Talmud. In the period of the Haskalah Moses Philipson (1774–1815) established a Hebrew press in Dessau; David (ben Moses) Fraenkel printed there the first Judeo-German monthly *Sulamith* (1806–33).

Title page of *Shirah Ḥadashah,* printed in Aleppo in 1888. It includes poems by Raphael Isaac Entebi, whose purpose was to encourage divine worship and a lifestyle conducted in a spirit of joy. He emphasizes that his poems were intended to counteract the widespread custom of reciting lewd poems at celebrations and festivities.

ספר
שירה חדשה
המה שירות ותשבחות מאשר
חנני ה׳ אלהי לשורר בקול
נעים ואלקים יודע כי לש״ש
נתכונתי בכדי שלא יותן
לפושעים יד לשורר שירי
עגבים כי השלוות של חשק
ונבול פה מפריד הנשמה
מצרור החיים ח״ו ויי משמים
ישלח משיחנו בענ׳ וב׳ק כ״ד
ש׳ תר מח

ALEXANDRIA. The first Hebrew press of Alexandria was founded in 1862 by Solomon Ottolenghi from Leghorn. In its first year, it printed three books. A second attempt to found a Hebrew press in Alexandria was made in 1865. Nathan Amram, chief rabbi of Alexandria, brought two printers from Jerusalem, Michal Ha-Cohen and Joel Moses Salomon, to print his own works. However, these printers only produced two books, returning to Jerusalem when the second was only half-finished. A more successful Hebrew press was established in 1873 by Faraj Ḥayyim Mizraḥi, who came from Persia; he operated his press until his death in 1913, and his sons maintained the press until 1916. Altogether, over 40 books were printed. In 1907 Jacob ben Attar from Meknès, Morocco, founded another press, which produced several dozen books. Apart from these main printing houses, from 1920 on the city had several small presses, each producing one or two books. A total of over one hundred books for Jews were printed in Alexandria, most of them in Hebrew, the others in Judeo-Arabic and Ladino. Most of them were works by eminent Egyptian rabbis, prayer books, and textbooks.

Title page of *Sha'arei Dura* by Isaac ben Meir of Dueren, a 13th-century Ashkenazi scholar, printed in Jessnitz by Israel ben Abraham the proselyte, 1724. Among the basic collections of halakhic rulings of forbidden foods, this book, with additions by various scholars, has been printed in about ten editions, with many variations. The Jessnitz edition is the best among them. Its title page is reminiscent of Manuel Benveniste's of Amsterdam, 1655. On this title page appears the signature of Solomon Jedidiah Sinigaglia, the famous rabbi of Modena, Italy, in the first half of the 18th century.

ספר
שערי דורא
הנקרא איסור והיתר
נדפס פה ק"ק יעסניץ
CUM LICENTIA SERENISSIMI

BAGHDAD. The first Hebrew (lithographic) printing press in Baghdad was founded by Moses Baruch Mizraḥi in 1863. The press printed a Hebrew newspaper named *Ha-Dover* ("The Speaker") or *Dover Mesharim* ("Upright Speaker") until 1870 and three small books. A second printing press with movable characters was founded in Baghdad in 1866 by Raḥamim ben Reuben, a resident of Baghdad, who had previously gained printing experience in Bombay. The brothers Moses and Aaron Fetay later formed a partnership with Raḥamim, and after his death they continued his work until 1882. Fifty-five books were printed on this printing press.

In 1888 a new press was founded in Baghdad by Solomon Bekhor Ḥuzin (1843–1892), a scholar, poet, author, journalist, bookseller and communal worker. He brought his printing letters from Leghorn, Italy. Besides prayer books, he also printed many books which he considered useful to the members of his community. These included tales and works by Baghdad scholars which had only been in manuscript until then. After his death, the printing press was taken over by his son, Joshua Ḥuzin, and operated until 1913. Seventy-five books were printed on it.

In 1904 another press was founded in Baghdad by Rabbi Ezra Reuben Dangoor (1848–1930), who was also the chief rabbi of Baghdad. This printing press was in existence until 1921 and over 100 books were printed on it. For the greater part they were books of prayers and *piyyutim* according to the custom of the Baghdad Jews, but there were also some popular books in the Judeo-Arabic dialect and a Hebrew weekly, *Yeshurun,* of which five issues were published in 1920. This was a second and last attempt at Hebrew journalism in Baghdad. During the British Mandate in Iraq, two small Hebrew printing presses were founded in Baghdad: the al-Wataniyya al-Isra'ilyya (The Israel Homeland) press, which printed about 20 books between 1922 and 1927; and the Elisha Shoḥet press, which printed more than 40 books between 1924 and 1937. When the British Mandate ended in 1948, these printing presses declined and finally ceased operation altogether.

BASLE. At the end of the 16th century Basle became a center for Hebrew printing. The printing houses were owned by Christians, but they needed Jewish proofreaders for whom they obtained residence permits. Johannes Froben published the Psalms in 1516. In 1536 his son Jerome published a Bible in Hebrew. In 1578–80 Ambrosius Froben was permitted to print a duly censored edition of the Talmud, which had been banned under Pope Julius III in 1553 and placed on the Catholic Index of proscribed books in 1559. Also printed there were the works of Johannes Buxtorf (father and son) who both taught Hebrew at Basle University (1591–1664). About 200 Hebrew books (excluding Bibles, Hebrew grammars for and by Christian Hebraists, etc.) were printed there up to the mid-19th century, among them not a few in Yiddish.

BERDICHEV. In 1807 Samuel ben Isachar Ber, who had printing presses in several towns, set up a press in Berdichev, initially as a branch of his Ostraha house. Samuel and, after 1817, his son Jacob Funkelmann, operated there until 1820, when the business was transferred to Sudilkov. Altogether they printed over 30 works on Ḥasidism, Kabbalah, and *halakhah* in addition to prayer books and popular books in Yiddish. Another printing house was established by Israel Bak in 1815–21. Before his emigration to Ereẓ Israel in 1831 he produced 26 works on roughly the same subjects, most of them set in a new typeface designed and cut by Bak himself, with his own illustrations. Other Berdichev printers were M.H. Rothenberg (1834–36) and H.J. Sheftel (1885–1910); the latter published a great number of scholarly works, including a popular edition of the Babylonian Talmud (with Rashi's commentary) in one volume (1894).

BERLIN. The first Hebrew printer in Berlin was the court preacher and professor, Daniel E. Jablonski, as Jews could not obtain the necessary license; nevertheless, the manager J.L. Neumark, and most of the setters and proofreaders were Jews. The first book published by them was the Book of Psalms (1697), followed by the complete Bible (1699), and other scholarly and liturgical works. An application by Rabbi Mirels for permission to print the Talmud in Berlin was refused by Frederick I, king of Prussia; and permission to publish Maimonides' *Yad* was not acted on as the code was being printed in Amsterdam by J. Athias at this time. But a Talmud edition was issued by Gottschalk and Jablonski, in partnership with a Frankfort on the Oder printer, 1715–22. Among other printers to be mentioned are Baruch Buchbinder (Radoner) of Vilna (1708–17), who printed a number of important works such as the *Ẓe'ena u-Re'enah* and works by the Shabbatean Neḥemiah Ḥayon (1713), a Mishnah with Rashi and Jacob Ḥagiz's commentary (1716–17), and a *Ḥoshen Mishpat* (1717). Nathan, son of J.L. Neumark, was active 1719–27, while his son-in-law Aaron ben Moses Rofe of Lissa built up an important press, (1733–62), publishing a series of well-known rabbinic works, above all the second Berlin Talmud edition, 1734–39. Aaron's press was continued for a while by his grandson Moses ben Mordecai. An annual *Lu'aḥ* began to appear probably from 1725 but not later than 1738. Of some importance was the press of Isaac ben Jacob Speyer (1764–70), a son-in-law of the Berlin rabbi David Fraenkel, who printed notable rabbinic works – Steinschneider calls it "the highlight of Hebrew printing in Berlin"; and that of Mordecai Landsberg, also from 1764. The prolific writer and editor Isaac Satanow took over Landsberg's press in 1772 and issued a considerable number of books, particularly his own (until 1804). In 1784 David Friedlaender and his friends founded the Verlag der juedischen Freischule, managed by A. Wolfsohn-Halle who bought the Landsberg press and obtained a license to print and sell books. Pupils of the society were taught the craft of printing and a number of books were published from 1796 with the imprint "Orientalische Druckerei." During these years Berlin became the center for the printing of Enlightenment literature, notably the writings of M. Mendelssohn, N.H. Wessely and D. Friedlaender. Mendelssohn's edition of the Pentateuch appeared here in 1783.

In 1830 the Landsberg press was bought by Isaac Levent. In that year the printer Trevitsch and son moved to Berlin from Frankfort on the Oder. In 1834, the year of his death, David Friedlaender founded his own press and published a number of important books; the scholar D. Cassel worked there as a proofreader. In 1836 the apostate Julius Sittenfeld set up a printing house which published the complete Talmud (1862–68), Maimonides' *Yad* (1862), and other works. In the late 19th and early 20th century H. Itzkowski, Siegfried, Arthur and Erich Scholem were active as general Jewish, and also

ספר
תקון תפלה
והוא תיקונים ונסחאות אמיתיות וסדרים ומנהגים יקרים בדברים העומדים ברומו של עולם מלוקטים ומקובצים מספר הכוונות של רבינו הגדול האר"י זצ"ל אשר קיבל מפי אליהו זכור לטוב ואת לברכה עוד מסידור רבינו הרש"ש זצ"ל אשר כל דבריו בנויים על פי קבלה האמיתית של רבינו האר"י זצ"ל דוקא יה"ר זכותם יגן בעדינו תמיד אכי"ר:
פה בבל יע"א
שנת
כה תברכו את בני ישראל
לפ"ק

The title page of *Tikkun Tefillah*, Baghdad, 1870. The book contains special mystical "intentions" for prayers and the performance of *mitzvot* according to the Lurianic system.

Hebrew publishers and printers in Berlin. In 1930 a Pentateuch was printed for the Soncino-Gesellschaft by the "Officina Serpentis" with a new Hebrew type cut for this occasion.

BOMBAY. Hebrew printing began in Bombay with the arrival of Yemenite Jews in the middle of the 19th century. They took an interest in the religious welfare of the Bene Israel (the Jewish community in India), and for them as well as for themselves, they printed various liturgies from 1841 onward, some with translations into Marathi, the vernacular of the Bene Israel. Apart from a shortlived attempt to print with movable type, all this printing was by lithography. In 1882, the Press of the Bombay Educational Society was established (followed in 1884 by the Anglo-Jewish and Vernacular Press, in 1887 by the Hebrew and English Press, and in 1900 by the Lebanon Printing Press), which sponsored the publication of over 100 Judeo-Arabic books to meet their liturgical and literary needs, and also printed books for the Bene Israel.

BRATISLAVA. Some 340 Hebrew and Yiddish books were printed in Bratislava between 1831 and 1930, the first being *Torat ha-Emunah,* an ethical treatise in Yiddish. But two smaller items had been issued here earlier in 1789 and 1790. In 1833 the well-known Vienna printer Anton Edler von Schmidt bought the press of K. Schniskes, and Schmidt's son printed Hebrew books until 1849. He was succeeded by Heinrich Sieber, and he and his heirs were active to 1872, and their successors F. and S. Nirschi to 1878. O. Ketterisch, later K. Ketterisch and Zimmermann, set up a Hebrew press in 1876. The first Jewish

The *sha'ar* of *Shivḥei ha-Ari*, Berdichev, 1817. This edition has not been listed and is extremely rare.

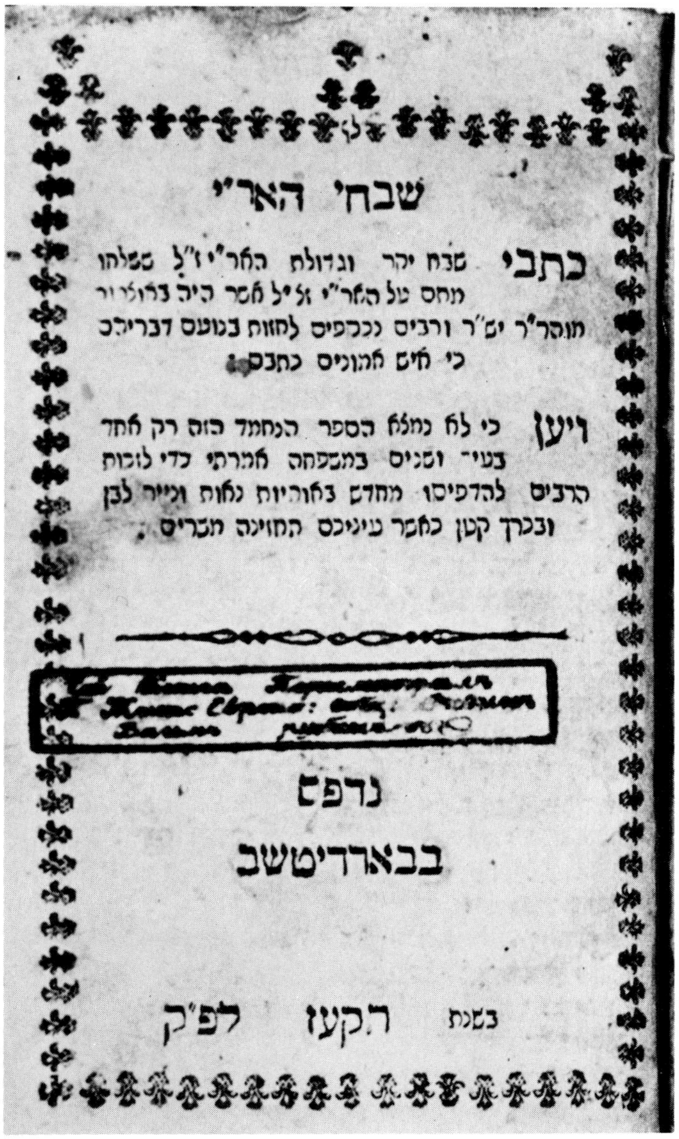
שבחי האר"י
נדפס
בבארדיטשב
בשנת הקעז לפ"ק

printers were Lewy and Alkalay, later A. Alkalay only, whose firm printed from 1877 to 1920.

BRESLAU. Some 190 Hebrew books were printed in Breslau between 1719 and the end of the 19th century. Toward the end of the 18th century the Grassche Stadt-Buchdruckerei was active in face of fierce opposition from the privileged Dyhernfurth printers. When the Dyhernfurth monopolies lapsed, Loebel Katzenellenbogen-Sulzbach, who had served his apprenticeship in Dyhernfurth, set up a press in 1814, with his son Hirsch as partner from 1825 and sole owner from 1836 to 1877, when it was sold to T. Schatzky.

Tosefot Yeshenim on several talmudic tractates, intended to be an appendix to the edition of the Talmud published, in a joint venture, in Berlin – Frankfort-on-Oder, 1734–1739. The book was printed in 1736 and the title page claims that it was based on an ancient manuscript. This, however, is not so. The text was taken in toto from the first edition which appeared as an appendix to the Talmud of Amsterdam, 1714–1717, and Frankfort-on-Main, 1720–1722.

תוספות ישנים
על

CAIRO. The first Hebrew printing press in Cairo, which was also the first one in the whole Middle East outside of Palestine, was founded in 1557 by Gershom ben Eliezer Soncino. He was the last of a famous family of printers, and previously worked in his father's press in Constantinople. Two of his books printed in this first year are known: *Refu'ot ha-Talmud,* a book of remedies, and *Pitron Ḥalomot* ("Interpretation of Dreams"), attributed to Rav Hai Gaon. A second printing press was founded in Cairo in 1740 by Abraham ben Moses Yatom, who had also previously worked as a printer in Constantinople. He printed only one book, the first edition of *Ḥok le-Yisrael,* edited by Rabbi Isaac Baruch of Cairo. This work was later reprinted in many editions. The renewal of Hebrew printing in Cairo took place in 1905, and after that year there were six Hebrew printing presses. They were principally used for

Title page of a Passover *Haggadah* with a Yiddish translation and commentary printed in Hebrew letters, Bombay, 1865, lithographic printing.

הגדה של פסח לשון ושרה
נדפסה ההגדה זו עם לשון ושרה עם הדינים
ואמרורבותינו וברכת המזון :
פה עיר במבי יע״א
בשנת התרכה לפ״ק

אגודת פרחים
כוללת
הגדה של פסח . פרקי אבות
אזהרות . פתגמים
בעברית וערבית
מאת דר' הלל יעקב פרחי
שנת בעבור זה עשה יהוה לי בצאתי ממצרים לפ״ק

مجموعة فارحي
تحتوي على
رواية الفصح . حكم الاقدمين . الوصايا
وحكم بالعبري والعربي
جمع وتعريب
الدكتور فارحي
سنة ١٩٢٢
طبع بمطبعة الخواجه روبرتو موسكوفيتش - بمصر

Agudat Peraḥim ("a Bunch of Flowers"; Cairo, 1922) which contains the Passover *Haggadah,* tractate *Avot* and various aphorisms, in Hebrew with an Arabic translation on each facing page. This edition (including the translation) is the work of Dr. Hillel Parḥi ("the flower man," thus the title), a physician and scholar who was one of the central figures in the Egyptian Jewish community at the beginning of the 20th century. His prayer book, *Siddur Parḥi* (1917) was exceedingly popular. In *Agudat Peraḥim* he also translated the *azharot* (a kind of liturgical poem) of Solomon ibn Gabirol.

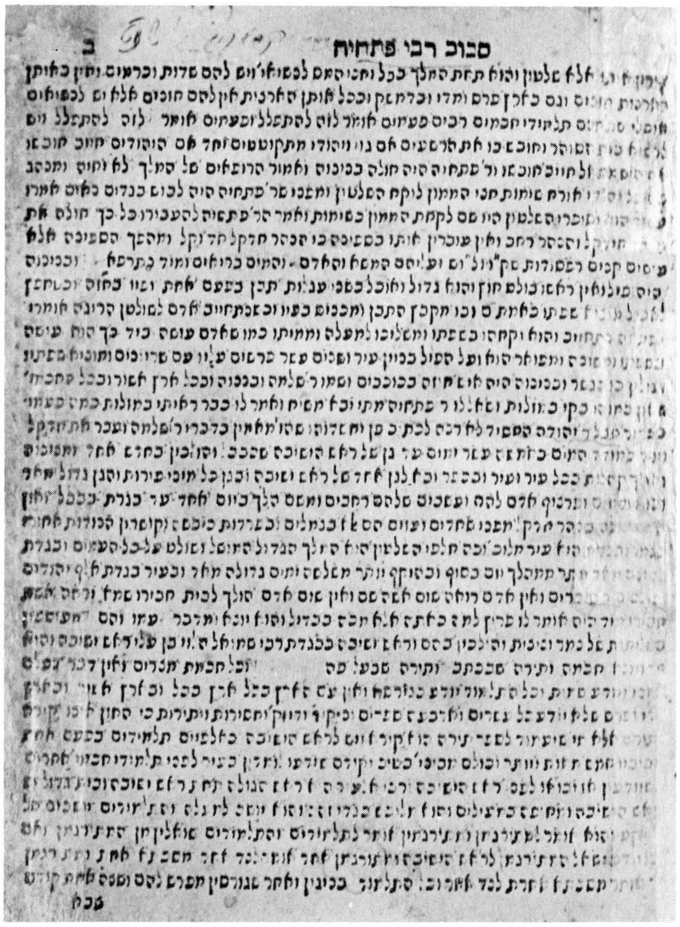

סבוב רבי פתחיה ב

A page from *Sibbuv Rabbi Pethahiah,* second printing, Cracow, 1599. This is a unicum. Israel Mehlman, Jerusalem.

commercial purposes and for other languages, with the printing of Hebrew books as a secondary activity. Up to World War II, they printed over 40 books, most of which served the needs of the Egyptian communities or were the works of authors living in Egypt.

CALCUTTA. The first Hebrew printing press in Calcutta was founded in 1840 by a native of Cochin, Eleazar ben Aaron Saadiah 'Iraqi ha-Cohen and was in existence until 1856, producing 25 books. A scholar and poet, 'Iraqi was an expert printer who probably cast his own type. The products of his press, some of them his own writings, are comparable with the best European productions of the time. Another press operated by Ezekiel ben Saliman Hanin from 1871–93, printed the Judeo-Arabic weekly in Hebrew type, *Mevasser,* from 1873–78. This paper was followed by *Peraḥ* (1878–88), printed from 1881 by Elijah ben Moses Duwayk ha-Cohen. Two further weeklies, *Maggid Meisharim* (1889–1900) and *Shoshannah* (1901), were edited and printed by Rabbi Solomon Twena, author of almost 70 works published by his own press, (1889–1901).

CHERNOVTSY. Hebrew works were printed in Chernovtsy for over a century, from 1835 to 1939, and nearly 320 items were issued by nine publishers and printers. Of these the most important was the house of Eckhardt (Peter, Johann, and Rudolf, 1835–92), where, with the help of Jewish experts, there were printed a complete Babylonian Talmud (1839–48), a Bible with standard commentaries (1839–42), the Mishnah with commentaries (1840–46), and other important rabbinic and kabbalistic-ḥasidic works; at a later stage some Haskalah literature was also printed there, and some Hebrew and Yiddish periodicals.

CONSTANTINOPLE. (The 19th and 20th centuries – for earlier periods see page 99). Using the remnants of the Ashkenazi press, Elijah Pardo produced six books between 1799 and 1808, among them Rashi's *Pardes* (1802) and the *Zohar* on Genesis (in instalments, 1807–08). Isaac ben Abraham Castro, his sons and his grandsons printed intermittently from 1808 to 1848, beginning with *Tikkunei Zohar,* rabbinical works, Ladino translations, and polemics against the Christian missions. The Castro press remained active until 1925. The Christian printer Arap Oglu Bogos, commissioned by Jews, printed at least 18 books in Hebrew and Ladino from 1822 to 1823. In the 20th century, with the gradual decline of the Hebrew presses, Ladino literature came to be published by Christian missionaries; French and English literature in Ladino was published by Greek and Armenian printers. From 1860 to 1940 the Ladino newspaper press, as well as some Jewish printers and publishers, printed mainly Ladino literature.

CRACOW. Hebrew printing was first introduced in Cracow in 1534 by the brothers Samuel, Asher, and Eliakim Halicz, who had learned the craft with Gershom Kohen in Prague, and whose style their productions betray. They printed the first edition of Isaac of Dueren's *Sha'arei Dura* – in Rashi type and with a beautifully decorated title page – in 1534, the year in which they received a license from King Sigismund I of Poland. A few other works followed, until in 1537 the three brothers converted to Christianity, which did not prevent them from continuing to print Hebrew books (a *maḥzor* and the first two parts of the *Tur*), but their products were boycotted by the Jewish community. Eventually the king forced the Jewish communities of Cracow, Poznan, and Lvov to buy the Haliczs' entire stock. Great success was attained by the Hebrew press set up in 1569 by Isaac ben Aaron of Prostitz (Prossnitz), who was trained in Italy and received a 50 year license from Sigismund II Augustus. He acquired his equipment from the Venetian printers Cavalli and Grypho and also brought with him from Italy the scholarly proofreader Samuel Boehm. In the next 60 years Isaac and his successors (sons and nephews) produced some 200 books, of which 73 were in Yiddish. The Babylonian Talmud was printed twice (1602–08; 1616–20); a fine edition of the Jerusalem Talmud in 1609; Alfasi's *Halakhot* together with *Mordekhai* in 1598; and several editions of the *Shulḥan Arukh* with Isserles' annotations. Among kabbalistic literature was a *Zohar* (1603), and some of Moses Cordovero's writings. Other works included a Pentateuch and *haftarot* with the classical commentaries (1587), *Yalkut Shimoni* (1596), and *Ein Ya'akov* (1587, 1614, 1619). In his title-page decoration Isaac copied the Italian style. His printer's mark was first a hart, but from 1590, fishes. For the next four decades (1630–70), prominent Hebrew printers in Cracow were Menaḥem Naḥum Meisels, his daughter Czerna, and his son-in-law Judah Meisels, a grandson of Moses Isserles. Menaḥem Naḥum took over Isaac ben Aaron's equipment which he enlarged and improved, but he returned to the Prague style of printing, with Judah ha-Kohen of Prague as his manager. There was no Hebrew press active in Cracow in the 18th century. Between 1802 and 1822 Naphtali Herz Shapiro and his son Aaron Solomon issued such works as the *Midrash Tanḥuma* (1803) and *Midrash Rabbah* (1805). Some "modernist" literature was also printed by Shapiro's son. Karl Budweiser printed various books between 1867 and 1874, before moving on to Lvov. Joseph Fischer, at first in partnership with B. Weindling, printed a good deal of Haskalah literature from 1878 until 1914, including a number of Hebrew periodicals such as *Ha-Tor, Ha-Zeman,* and *Ha-Maggid.* S.N. Deitscher and son were active as Hebrew printers from 1890 to 1940 and A. Lenkowitch from 1897.

CREMONA. The Christian Vencenzo Conti printed about 40 Hebrew books in Cremona between 1556 and 1567, the best known being the *Zohar* in 1559. The first production was Isaac ben Joseph of Corbeil's *Ammudei Golah* for which Conti had as his associates Samuel Boehm and Zanvil Pescarol. From 1558 until 1567 Conti continued to print Hebrew books whose contents had been sanctioned by the Inquisition. Until 1559 Conti used almost exclusively "Rashi" (cursive) type, as in his first edition of *Ẓiyyoni* by Menahem ben Meir, of which the Inquisition destroyed 1,000 copies. From then onward he used square type, as in the *Zohar* and the second edition of *Ẓiyyoni.* In Cremona Conti finished the Ashkenazi *Maḥzor* begun in Sabbionetta in 1557, while books printed there for Conti by Zifroni in 1567 (*Pirkei de-Rabbi Eliezer, Halikhot Olam, Ẓeidah la-Derekh,* and an Ashkenazi *siddur*) are continuations of Cremona work. Conti used a variety of title page decorations: in 1556, faun and nymph with the coat of arms of Cremona; 1557–67, the typical Cremona tailpiece inscribed SPQR; 1565–66, portals with turkey cocks; and, for folios, portals with *Akedah* illustration. In 1576 another Christian printer, Cristoforo Draconi, printed (with the help of Solomon Bueno) Eliezer Ashkenazi's *Yosef Lekah.*

DJERBA. David Idan established a Hebrew printing press in Djerba in 1904, and many books, mainly Passover *Hagaddot* and other liturgical items, were printed there until 1960. During the 20th century, Djerba was the printing center for most of the countries of North Africa, and the printing industry there was an important source of employment for the local inhabitants.

DYHERNFURTH, BRESLAU. Its Jewish community dates from 1688, when Shabbetai Bass, founder of modern Hebrew bibliography, leased printing privileges from the local magnate who, in turn, held them from the emperor. The first work he printed in Dyhernfurth was Samuel ben Uri Shraga Phoebus' *Beit Shemu'el,* a commentary on *Shulḥan Arukh Even ha-Ezer* (1689). A community was formed by

A Passover *Haggadah* with a commentary by Ẓemaḥ ha-Kohen of Djerba, printed in 1919. Some of the pages, including the title page, were printed in Susa, North Africa, at the press of Makhluf Najar and Partners.

13 families, all employed in Bass's printing works. Both Bass and his son Joseph had to contend with the hostility of the Jesuits, but printing continued until 1762, from 1717 under Berel Nathan, husband of Bass's granddaughter Esther, and later under Esther herself. Other printing houses were established by Samuel ben Abraham Katz (until 1767), Abraham Lewin (until 1771), Solomon Koenigsberg (1774–75), M.L. May (until 1819), H. Warschauer & Co. and lastly D. Sklower, whose press closed in 1834 when he moved to Breslau. The Dyhernfurth productions, which included a complete Talmud and Maimonides' *Mishneh Torah,* were very popular at the time, but business declined because of outside competition. A Yiddish newspaper, serving the Breslau community, was printed there in 1770.

DUBNO. The first Hebrew printing press was set up in Dubno in 1794 by Jonathan ben Jacob of Wielowies, Silesia. Jonathan's partner was M. Piotrowsky, a non-Jew, and the business was under the patronage of Prince Lubomirski, the ruler of the town, whose escutcheon and initials appeared on the title pages. The press was active for nine years and produced 22 books. Another press was founded in 1804 by the printer Aaron ben Jonah, who owned a similar business in Ostraha, in partnership with Joseph ben Judah Leib. During the four years Aaron was in Dubno ten books were published. Dubno's rabbi, Ḥayyim Mordecai Margolioth, established a press in 1819, printing works by his brother Ephraim Zalman of Brody, and a *Shulḥan Arukh* with his own commentaries (*Sha'arei Teshuvah*) and those of his brother (*Yad Ephraim*). The press was closed after a fire.

FANO. Between 1502 and 1517 Gershom Soncino set up his press in Fano, printing books in Hebrew as well as in other languages. Altogether 15 Hebrew books came from his press here, the earliest being the *Me'ah Berakhot* after the Roman rite (1503), and possibly Ibn Sahula's *Meshal ha-Kadmoni* (second edition with illustrations) which Soncino may have begun before 1500 while still in Brescia. Later appeared the *Rokeah,* a *maḥzor* according to the Roman rite, a *siddur* in Judeo-Italian, the *Kuzari,* and Albo's *Sefer ha-Ikkarim.* After his return from Pesaro in 1516, he printed during that year and the next the *Arba'ah Turim* of Jacob ben Asher. However Fano now belonged to the Papal States, and when the Jews were expelled from this area, they had to leave Fano.

FERRARA. Under the enlightened rule of the House of Este, Hebrew printing flourished twice for short

Engraved title page of the *Sifrei* with the *Zera Avraham* commentary by Abraham Jekutiel Lichtenstein who was the head of the rabbinical court in Plonsk, near Warsaw; Dyhernfurth, 1811. This magnificent *sha'ar* is an exact copy of the proselyte Abram ben Jacob's engraving for the *Shenei Luḥot ha-Berit,* Amsterdam 1698, but is not as delicate. It is signed by a non-Jewish artist.

periods in Ferrara in the 15th and 16th centuries. In 1477 Abraham ben Ḥayyim the Dyer of Pesaro, using Abraham Conat's type, printed here Levi ben Gerson's commentary on Job, and finished printing the edition of *Tur*, *Yoreh De'ah* which Conat had begun in Mantua. The second longer period extended from 1551 to 1558, when first Samuel ibn Askara Ẓarefati of Pesaro and then Abraham Usque, partly with the former's assistance, printed well over 30 books in Ferrara. Among the first was Isaac Abrabanel's *Ma'yenei ha-Yeshu'ah* and Jedaiah ha-Penini's *Beḥinat Olam.* Under Usque, halakhic, theological and liturgical items were printed, among them the first editions of Menaḥem ibn Zeraḥ's *Ẓedah la-Derekh* (1554), Hasdai Crescas' *Or Adonai* (1556), Jonah Ashkenazi's *Issur ve-Hetter* and Jacob Fano's *Shiltei ha-Gibborim* (including an elegy on the Marrano martyrs of Ancona), 1556. Apparently complaints by the Church about this publication led to the closing of the press. Usque also printed a number of works mainly, but not exclusively, of Jewish significance in Spanish and Portuguese, including the Ferrara Bible (1553) and the "Consolation for the Tribulations of

Title page of *Sefer ha-Zikkaron* by Ishmael ha-Kohen of Tunis, printed at the Usque press in Ferrara, 1555. The book is a short description of the laws which apply after the destruction of the Temple for the lesser educated who are unable to use the famous complete halakhic works. The order of the presentation follows the Talmud in an extremely brief fashion so that a few pages can be studied daily.

Israel" by Samuel Usque (1553). Toward the end of the 17th century an attempt at reviving Hebrew printing at Ferrara was made by the non-Jewish printer Girolamo Filoni, who printed in 1693 a handsome small prayer book (*Siddur mi-Berakhah*), compiled by J. Nisim and Abraham Ḥayyim da Fano, printers from Mantua. Filoni also issued a broadsheet primer with the Hebrew alphabet and some basic prayers. Shortly afterwards, Filoni melted down his Hebrew type and converted it into a Latin font. The *takkanot* of the Ferrara community of 1767 provided for less gifted pupils of the Jewish school (*Talmud Torah*) to attend the workshop of the printer Salvador Serri to learn the craft of Hebrew printing, both for their own information and for the preservation of this important craft.

FRANKFORT-ON-MAIN. The book fairs of Frankfort were visited by Jewish printers and booksellers as early as 1535. Some Hebrew printing was carried on in Frankfort as early as the 16th century; in 1512 the brothers Murner published "Grace after Meals." Hebrew printing seriously developed in Frankfort in the 17th century. The earliest work, *Megillat Vinẓenz* (Fettmilch) was published by Isaac Langenbuch after the Fettmilch riots. From 1657 to 1707 Balthasar Christian Wust and later his son (?) Johann issued a great number of Hebrew books. For this part of their work they employed Jewish printers and other Jewish personnel, and found Jewish financial backing. (As Jews could not obtain printing licenses, they used Christian firms as a front.) They printed mainly liturgical items, but also a Pentateuch with a German glossary (1662), bibles (1677, 1694) and Wallich's Yiddish *Kuhbuch* (1672). Several other Hebrew printers published books in the late 17th and early 18th centuries. An important publisher was Johann Koellner, who in 20 years of printing, was responsible for about half of the books issued in Frankfort. Among his more important publications were the *Arba'ah Turim* (5 volumes, 1712–16), and an excellent Talmud edition (1770–73). Soon after the completion of the latter, the whole edition was confiscated and not released until 30 years later. In the first half of the 19th century the names of seven non-Jewish printing houses are known. Subsequently Jewish printers emerged for the first time. Among them were J.H. Golda (1881–1920), E. Slobotzki (from 1855), and the bookseller J. Kauffmann, who took over the Roedelheim press of M. Lehrberger in 1899. Hebrew printers were active in places like Homberg, Offenbach, Sulzbach, Roedelheim, and others in the neighborhood of Frankfort, because Jewish printers were unable to establish themselves in Frankfort.

FRANKFORT-ON-ODER. The earliest Hebrew book printed in Frankfort-on-Oder was a Pentateuch which was printed by J. and F. Hartman in 1595. Eighty years later J.C. Beckman, professor of theology at the local university, obtained a license to extend the privilege to print in Hebrew, and a Pentateuch with *haftarot* and the Five Scrolls, as well as other books, were published in 1677. The most important work published there was a new edition of the Talmud (1697–99). The Court Jew Berend Lehmann of Halberstadt invested in it and presented a large number of the 2,000 sets printed to various communities, *battei midrash,* and yeshivot. Further editions were printed in 1715–22 and 1736–39. Michael Gottschalk succeeded Beckmann as manager and before 1740 Pro-

Tokfo Kohen by Shabbetai ha-Kohen, author of the *Siftei Kohen* commentary on the *Shulḥan Arukh* and one of the three greatest Ashkenazi halakhic authorities of the past 400 years. This was the first printing of the book, Frankfort-on-Oder, 1677, which is entirely devoted to a section of the talmudic tractate *Bava Meẓi'a* with the same title, dealing with laws of possession.

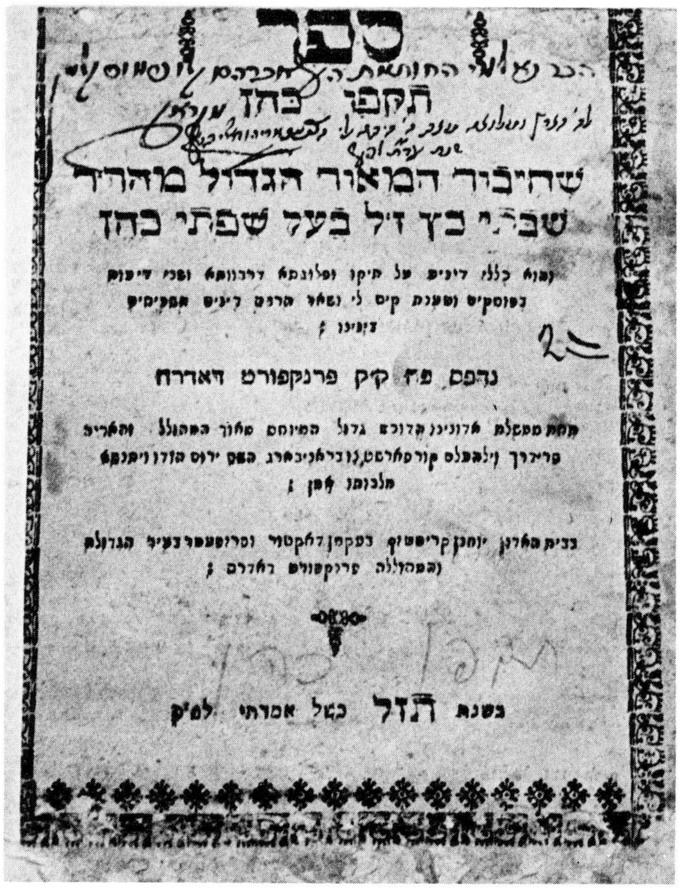
ספר
תקפו כהן
שחיבר המאור הגדול מוהר״ר
שבתי כץ ז״ל בעל שפתי כהן
נדפס פה ק״ק פרנקפורט דאודרה

fessor Grillo bought Gottschalk's press. It continued in his family until the end of the century, and in the hands of his successor, C.F. Elsner, until 1813. Grillo's turnover in trade of Hebrew books reached 80,000 Reichsthaler annually – a measure of the importance of the press for Germany and Eastern Europe. The main midrashim, *Yalkut Shimoni,* the *Zohar,* and other important rabbinic works were printed in Frankfort-on-Oder. As the result of the Prussian legislation of 1812, it was possible in 1813 for Hirsch Baschwitz, a Jew, to acquire the Hebrew printing press from Elsner. In turn, he sold the business in 1826 to Trebitsch & Son of Berlin.

FREIBURG. Some Hebrew works were printed in Freiburg in the 16th century as the result of difficulties with Hebrew printing in Basle. Israel Ẓifroni printed a number of Hebrew books for Ambrosius Froben, among them Benjamin of Tudela's *Massa'ot* (1583), Jacob ben Samuel Koppelman's *Ohel Ya'akov*, and the first edition of Aaron of Pesaro's *Toledot Aharon* (1583–84). In 1503 and 1504, editions were issued of Gregorius Reisch's *Margarita Philosophica* including a page with the Hebrew alphabet in woodcut.

FUERTH. Hebrew printing was begun in Fuerth in 1691 by S.S. Schneur and his sons Joseph and Abraham and son-in-law Isaac Bing. From 1691 to 1698 they issued 35 works, including *Sifra* with commentaries. Hirsch Frankfurter opened a press which issued nine books, between 1691 and 1701. Confiscations of Hebrew books from 1702 onward account for a pause in printing until it was resumed by the Shneur family from 1722 to 1730. Between 1737 and 1774, Ḥayyim ben Hirsch of Wilhermsdorf published 80 works and his press continued in the family until 1868; their non-Jewish successor issued a Pentateuch with *haftarot* as late as 1876. Between 1760 and 1792 Isaac ben Loeb Buchbinder printed 73 Hebrew books. Joseph Petschau and his son Mendel Beer printed 17 books between 1762 and 1769. S.B. Gunsdorfer was active as a printer from 1852 to 1867.

HALBERSTADT. In the 1850s and 1860s some Hebrew works were printed in Halberstadt. A beautiful *maḥzor* was issued by H. Meyer; J.Z. Jolles' *Melo ha-Ro'im* was edited by Y.F. Hirsch and printed at the press of J. Hoerling's widow (1859); B.H. Auerbach's controversial *Sefer ha-Eshkol* appeared in 1867–79; and Elijah of Vilna's *Adderet Eliyahu* was published there.

HALLE. About 1708 a Hebrew printing press was set up in Halle by J.H. Michaelis, for whom the wandering proselyte printer Moses ben Abraham and his son Israel (of Amsterdam) printed a Hebrew Bible (1720). With the help of generous patrons, in 1709 Moses himself began to print some Talmud tractates.

HANAU. In the 17th and 18th centuries Hanau developed into an important center of Hebrew printing. From Hans Jacob Hena's press, which was established in 1610, issued such important works as responsa by Jacob Weil, Solomon ben Abraham Adret, and Judah Minz as well as Jacob ben Asher's *Arba'ah Turim.* Employing both Jews and gentiles, this press produced a great number of rabbinic, kabbalistic and liturgical items within about 20 years. A hundred years later Hebrew printing was resumed in the city by H.J. Bashuysen, who published Isaac Abrabanel's Pentateuch commentary (1709). In 1714 Bashuysen's

Ornate copper engraving printed as the title page of *Yalkut Shimoni,* Frankfort-on-Main, 1687. This lavish edition was printed by Isaac and Seligman, sons of the late Herz Reis. The bottom section depicts David and Goliath and the top the traditional images of Moses and Aaron, with Cherubs above.

זה ספר הרוקח
אלהים ואנשים משפחה · הקדיש

The title page of *Sefer ha-Roke'aḥ* by Eleazar of Worms who was active in Germany in the 12th–13th centuries. The book was printed in a small format (12 x 16 cm.) in 1630 in Hanau during the Swedish War, because of which it was produced in such an economical way – to all intents and purposes, a pocket book. At the bottom of the decorated title page, Venus rises naked from the waters on a seashell – a common pagan motif. The book was printed at a non-Jewish press and so no attention was paid to the decoration at the time. Afterwards, many Jewish purchasers tore out the offending page which is today quite rare.

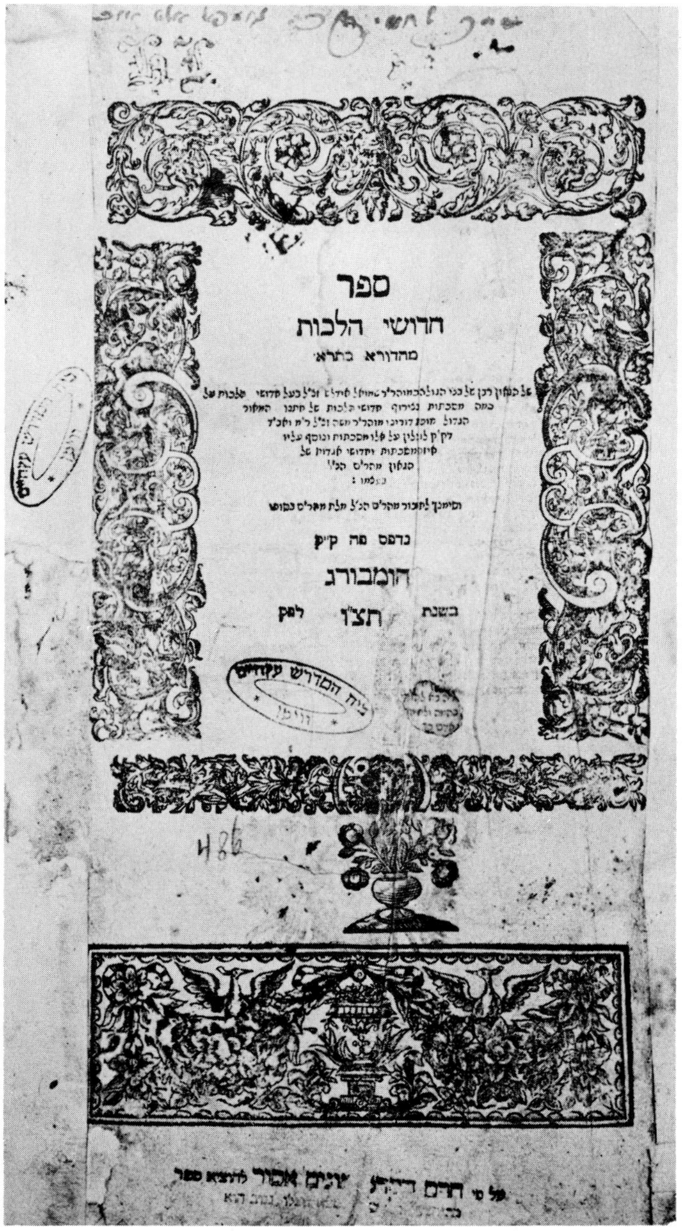
ספר
חדושי הלכות
מהדורא בתרא
הומבורג
בשנת תצ"ו לפק

Sha'ar of *Ḥiddushei Halakhot – Mahadura Batra* by Samuel Edels (the Maharsha). Today this work is included in all large editions of the Talmud, following the regular novellae of the Maharsha. The novellae of his son-in-law Moses, head of the religious court of Lublin, also included in this edition, are usually printed in the Talmud. This work was printed in Hamburg, 1736; the name of the printer is not mentioned.

press was taken over by J.J. Beausang and was active until 1797.

HOMBURG. A Hebrew printing house was run in Homburg by Seligmann ben Hirz Reis from 1710 for three years until he moved to Offenbach. Among other items, he published Jacob ibn Ḥabib's *Ein Ya'akov* (1712). Hebrew printing was resumed there in 1724 by Samson ben Salman Hanau but lack of capital limited his output. The press was acquired in 1736 by Aaron ben Ẓevi Dessau whose publications included the *Shulḥan Arukh Ḥoshen Mishpat* with commentary (1742). The press was sold in 1748 and transferred in 1749 to Roedelheim.

IZMIR. Izmir was one of the three printing centers in the Ottoman empire, following Constantinople and Salonika. The first Jewish printer in Izmir was Abraham ben Jedidiah Gabbai (1657–75). His first book was J. Escapa's *Rosh Yosef* (1657). Besides

וזאת ליהודא
העוסק במלאכת שמים הנקיה
והחמורה: כלילות יופי כוליה
נאה וחסודה: הפועל המסדר
אותיות ספיר גזרתם על
מאורות שפתיי טמוני יהו
הרה: ומבורך על המוגמר
בשבח ותודה: להבורא יתיש
המסייע והפורה: גדול
ביהודא שמו ובישראל
נודע: הקטן ליב בן
כמר משה ווערמייש
זעצר בק"ק
קארלסרוא
נתם ונשל' שבח לאל בורא
עולם בנר"ך ואע'

A back title page, appearing at the end of the book of *Over Ore'ah* by Simeon ben Meir of Karlsruhe, containing selections of laws, greatly abbreviated, for use by travelers who have no books with them. There are also certain laws which apply specifically to travelers. For this reason the book's size is very small (8 x 12 cm.). It was printed in Karlsruhe in 1763. The back title page is a kind of colophon; in it the setter, Moses Wermeis, reports having completed his work — a very rare phenomenon.

several Hebrew works, Gabbai also printed two in Spanish, in Latin characters; a second edition of *Mikveh Yisrael (Esperanza de Israel)* by Manasseh ben Israel; and *Apologia por la noble nación de los Judios, por Eduardo Nicholas,* translated from English into Spanish by Rabbi Manasseh. Hebrew books continued to be issued in Izmir until 1922, the last printer there being Ben Senior (1913–22). Some 12 major printers produced more than 400 books, ranging over the entire field of biblical, talmudic and rabbinic literature, besides a large amount of liturgy and Kabbalah. Many of the authors were local scholars. From 1838, 117 books were printed entirely, or partially, in Ladino. These were at first religious works only, but toward the end of the 19th century stories, novels and poetry were also published. Additionally, from 1842, Jewish newspapers such as *La Buena Esperanza* (1871–1910), *El Novelista* (1889–1922) and *El Messerret* (1897–1922) were printed in Ladino.

JASSY. Hebrew books were published in Jassy from 1842 onward, among them Eliezer ben Reuben Kahana's commentary on the Five Scrolls, *Si'ah Sefunim*; two editions (one with Yiddish translation) of Nathan Hannover's *Sha'arei Ziyyon* (1843); and the *Likkutei Amarim* of Shneour Zalman (of Lubavich; published 1843). Hebrew printing continued into the 1880s. Some Hebrew and Yiddish periodicals

Tiv Gittin by Ephraim Zalman Margolioth, Korets, 1819, among the last books printed there and very rare. It was printed in sections at the end of *Penei Moshe,* responsa on *Even ha-Ezer Shulhan Arukh,* by Moses Pinehas, also printed in sections and also very rare. The illustration depicts a boy sitting in the shade of a tree playing a harp. It is not a Jewish theme and almost never appears on Hebrew books. Most of the books printed in Koretz were by the non-Jewish printer, Anton Krieger.

ספר
טיב גיטין
שחבר הגאון הגדול מהורר אפרים זלמן מרגליות מבראד בעל
המחבר ספר בית אפרים על יורה דעה ושאלות ותשובות על
ארבעה שולחן ערוך
בקארעץ

were also published in Jassy. A Yiddish biweekly *Korot ha-Ittim* was published from 1855 to 1871. For a year in 1872 the first Jewish all-Rumanian newspaper *Vocea aparatorului* ("Voice of the Defender") was published. The weekly *Rasaritul* ("The East") was published from 1899 to 1901 by the Zionists, who also issued two annuals. In 1914 four numbers of a literary review, *Likht* ("Light"), were published in Yiddish, with the collaboration of Jacob Groper, Abraham L. Zissu, Motty Rabinovici and Jacob Botoshansky. The illustrations were the work of the painter Reuven Rubin.

JERUSALEM. See page 117.

KARLSRUHE. Nethanel Weil's commentary on *Asheri, Korban Netanel* (on tractates *Mo'ed* and *Nashim*), was printed in 1755 in Karlsruhe by L.J. Held, a successor to old and well-known Augsburg printers. His successors F.W. Lotter and M. Macklott continued publishing Hebrew works, including some by Jonathan Eybeschuetz (printed 1762–82) and the *Torat Shabbat* of Jacob Weil (1839). The firm continued printing until 1899, mainly liturgical items, Judeo-German circulars, and popular stories. D.R. Marx, licensed in 1814, printed in 1836 a Hebrew Bible (1845^2), edited on behalf of the Jewish authorities (*Oberrat*) by a group of rabbis, among them Jacob Ettlinger. Altogether some 60 Hebrew books were printed in Karlsruhe.

KORETS. Between 1766 and 1819 there were four Hebrew printing presses in Korets, some of them associated with those in Shklov, Nowy Dwor, and Ostraha. They printed nearly 100 books, mostly works of Kabbalah and Ḥasidism, which contributed considerably to the spread of Ḥasidism in Poland and adjoining countries. Works by Jacob Joseph of Polonnoye and Dov Baer of Mezhirech were first printed there. Korets was a center of Ḥasidism, and Dov Baer the Maggid of Mezhirech and Phineḥas Shapiro were active there.

KROTOSZYN. In 1833 Dov Baer (Baer Loeb) Monash (1801–1876) set up a press in Krotoszyn which was active from 1834 until 1901. Monash had learned the trade (and obtained the Hebrew type) from Dyhernfurth. He was the father-in-law of Heinrich Graetz, the historian. The most important books printed by him were: a five-volume Pentateuch with Onkelos, Rashi, *haftarot,* and German translation by Johlson (1837); a 12-volume Bible with Onkelos, Rashi, and German translation (1839–43); a *maḥzor* (*Minḥah Ḥadashah,* 1838). The Hebrew press in Krotoszyn was known through its edition of the Jerusalem Talmud which became the standard (1866–67). The most beautiful production of this press was Isaac Aboab's *Menorat ha-Ma'or,* with German translation by Fuerstenthal and Behrend (1845–48).

LEGHORN. The first Hebrew press was set up by Jedidiah Gabbai (1650). Some 80 years later, Abraham ben Raphael Meldola, followed by his son Raphael, both with various partners, were active as Hebrew printers (1740–57). Sixteen other printers set up in Leghorn between 1763 and 1870, the most important being the house of Solomon Belforte (established in 1838) which supplied the North

אורים ותומים

קינטרים זה נקרא כן ע"ש אורים שמאירין את הדברים ותומים
שמשלימין את דברי אורי פייבש החו' פה ק"ק לונדריש קרתא
רבתא באינגלטירא ומתוכו יתבארו כמה דינין בגרון החרם
דתורא מרבינו יעקב תם ז"ל והגדולים הגאונים שהיו בימיו.
ולה"ה נגד המוציאים לעז על הגיטין:

ואלה הדברים נתנו להכתב ולערוך אותם על מכבש
הדפוס על גט אחד שסדרתי פה ביום שביעי
לחודש אלול שנת טמע בין אחים
ושפטתם צדק:

בין איש ובין אחיו לפ"ק והוא התס"ו:

נדפס בלונדרין תחת ממשלת גדולת אדונתנו
החסידה המוצלחת המלכה
אנא יר"ה:

בסיב מרחשון שנת משפט אחד יהיה ליצירה
היא התס"ו:

Urim ve-Tumim of Uri Phoebus (better known as Aaron Hart), London, 1706. This is the first all-Hebrew book printed in London and it deals with a controversy over a bill of divorce issued in the community. Its appearance is connected with the division of the Ashkenazi community of London as a result of which two separate synagogues were established: the Great Synagogue and the Hambro synagogue. In the same year a book called *A Great Happening Here in the Holy Congregation of London* appeared, which presents the other side of the dispute, by Johanan Halishoy (?).

African and Levantine market with liturgical books until the outbreak of World War II.

LEIPZIG. Some Hebrew lettering (from wood-blocks) appears in books printed in Leipzig even before 1500 and in the two decades following, as in Novenianus' *Elementale Hebraicum,* 1520. In 1533 appeared a Hebrew psalter, prepared by Anthonius Margarita (like Novenianus, a lecturer in Hebrew) and printed by his father-in-law, Melchior Lotther. Hebrew printing was resumed in the last quarter of the 17th century through the effort of the apostate F.A. Christiani, and among these productions was a beautiful edition of Isaac Abrabanel's commentary on the Latter Prophets (1685). Numerous books were printed, again by non-Jewish presses, in the 19th century, among them Maimonides' responsa and letters (1859). At the end of the 19th and early 20th century the leading oriental printing house in Europe, W. Drugulin, produced, among other works, S. Mandelkern's famous Bible Concordance (for Veit and Co., 1896) and *Antologia Hebraica* for the Insel Verlag. By that time Leipzig had become the most important printing and publishing center in Germany. Drugulin designed a new type, taking early printing type as his model. Another new type was designed by Raphael Frank, cantor in Leipzig, in 1910, for the Berthold'sche Schriftgiesserei in Berlin.

LONDON. Some Hebrew printing on wood blocks appeared in works printed in London from 1524, when a few isolated words and phrases figured in R. Wakefield's *Oratio de utilitate . . . trium linguarum.* Movable Hebrew type was apparently first used in 1563 in W. Musculus' *Common Places of Christian Religion,* and consecutive Hebrew printing (a 14-line "sonnet") appeared in 1588 in a single-sheet broadside of poems in various languages by Theodore Beza celebrating the defeat of the Spanish Armada. In the 17th century a few books mainly or partly in Hebrew were published by Christian Hebraists, such as a Hebrew text of Psalms (1643), a vocalized text of *Avot* (1651), and Bryan Walton's Polyglot Bible (1653–57). Communal controversies in the early 18th century produced the first Hebrew publications printed for (though not by) Jews, particularly the dispute that raged around Ḥakham David Nieto's disputed Orthodoxy (1705) and a dispute concerning a divorce two years later (Aaron Hart's crudely produced *Urim ve-Tummim,* 1707. In 1714-15, some works by Moses Hagiz and Joseph Ergas aimed against the Shabbateans appeared in London, presumably because of the unfavorable atmosphere in Amster-

Illustrated title page of a Passover *Haggadah* printed at the Barnett press, London, 1836. Many illustrations were inserted on separate pages which were glued in and this title page was originally of a *maḥzor* for the whole year printed by Barnett some years earlier. For this title page Barnett printed only the text in the middle and stuck it on the previous text, which can still be seen underneath. The title page was engraved by R. Gaveyir, probably a non-Jew, and depicts symbolic representations for four restivals – Rosh Ha-Shanah, Yom Kippur, Sukkot and Pesaḥ. Moses and Aaron appear on the sides.

dam; and in the same year Nieto's classical *Matteh Dan* was brought out by Thomas Ilive's printing house, in three editions – in Spanish alone, Spanish and Hebrew, and Hebrew alone. Thereafter there was a long hiatus in London Hebrew printing, though Ephraim Luzzatto's poems *Elleh Benei ha-Ne'urim*

Sha'ar of *Shulḥan Arukh Ha-Ari* – laws, customs, and intentions to which one should direct oneself in prayer, selected from the writings of the disciples of Isaac Luria (Ari), printed by Judah Solomon Herz, Lvov, 1788. The book had been printed by the same printer three years earlier, together with Abraham Ibn Ezra's *Iggeret Shabbat* and *Nevu'at ha-Yeled,* the first printing of the latter works.

appeared there in 1766 with a reprint in 1768. In 1770, printing by and for Jews at last began, possibly in consequence of the removal of some trade restriction. A consortium of Jewish printers from Amsterdam (who, however, failed after a few years) set up a printing house which produced ambitious editions of the Jewish liturgy (three volumes 1770; other editions 1771, 1785) and many other works. Simultaneously, A. Alexander began his printing activity which was continued by his son Levi (mainly liturgical works) well into the 19th century. Other printers, Jewish and non-Jewish, appeared in the following years. In 1820 J. Wertheimer set up his Hebrew press, which was active for over a century, subsequently under the name of Williams, Lea and Company. With the increase in the London Jewish population, especially after the immigration from Eastern Europe from the 1880s onward, Jewish printers and printing in London proliferated, though learned works were mainly produced at the presses of the universities of Oxford and Cambridge.

LUBLIN. The wandering printer Ḥayyim Schwartz (Shaḥor), his son, and son-in-law, went to Lublin around 1547, where they began printing, with periodically renewed privileges (1550, 1559, 1578). Their first productions were liturgical items, notably the *maḥzor* of 1550. With the help of Eliezer ben Isaac (Ashkenazi) of Prague they brought out a fine Pentateuch in 1557, and a (complete?) Talmud edition (1559–77), partly printed in nearby Konska Wolwie when the plague broke out in Lublin in 1559. With a fresh outbreak of the plague in 1592, the printers moved temporarily to Bistrowitz. Kalonymus ben Mordecai Jaffe, who had married Ḥayyim Schwartz's granddaughter and whose name appears in the Pentateuch mentioned above, took over when Eliezer ben Isaac and his son left for Constantinople around 1573. Kalonymus managed the printing house till his death in about 1603, and it was continued (with interruptions) under his descendants to the end of the century and possibly beyond. A fire destroyed the plant and most of the books in 1647, but printing was resumed soon after. A great variety of works – liturgical, homiletical, and rabbinical – was issued there, among them Mordecai Jaffe's *Levushim* (1591–1595), a Mishnah (1594–96), the Talmud (1611–39), the first editions of Samuel Edels' *Novellae* (1617), and the *Zohar* (1623–24). Jacob Hirschenhorn and Moses Schneidermesser opened a Hebrew printing press in 1875 (from 1910 Hirschenhorn and Streisenberg); Feder and Setzer were active from 1894; and M. Schneidermesser in the 1920s.

LVOV. After the first partition of Poland (1772), which brought Galicia under Austro-Hungarian rule, the government forced Jewish printers to transfer their presses from Zolkiew to the Galician capital of Lvov in order to facilitate their censorship. The first to move were W. Letteris and H.D. Madfes, the latter producing Elijah Levita's *Pirkei Eliyahu* in 1783. The house of Madfes brought out a new edition of the Talmud (1859-68) and a seven-volume *Shulḥan Arukh* with standard commentaries (1858-61), which remained one of the best editions (a similar one was printed by J.L. Balaban and his son, who began printing in 1839). In 1785 J.S. Herz set up his press, which produced a good edition of Maimonides' *Mishneh Torah* (1805–11). Madfes' granddaughter, Judith Mann-Rozanes, also moved from Zolkiew, while her son, M.H. Grossmann, continued printing until 1858. About 20 other printers were active in Lvov in the century and a half before the outbreak of World War II, making the city one of the main centers for the production of Hebrew books, not only for Eastern Europe but for the Balkans as well.

LYCK. Eliezer Lipmann Silbermann founded the Hebrew weekly *Ha-Maggid* which was printed in Lyck from 1856 to 1891. The Mekiẓei Nirdamim Society was also founded by Silbermann and, between 1864 and 1874, 15 of its publications were printed in Lyck. Among them were S.D. Luzzatto's 1864-edition of Judah Halevi's *Diwan,* S. Buber's edition of the *Pesikta de Rav Kahana* (1868), and parts of I. Lampronti's *Paḥad Yiẓḥak* (1864–74). In the second half of the 19th century many Hebrew books were printed in the town and smuggled across the border to Russian Jewry.

METZ. In 1764 Moses May set up a Hebrew printing press in Metz, and issued in association with the royal printer Joseph Antoine a Yiddish translation of Daniel Defoe's *Robinson Crusoe* (1764) and the first edition of Bezalel Ashkenazi's *Asefat Zekenim* (*Shitah Mekubbeẓet,* to tractate *Beẓah,* 1765). These were followed by a great number of rabbinic and liturgical works, some by the outstanding rabbis of Metz, such as Aryeh Leib ben Asher's novellae *Turei Even* (1781). May's venture in publishing a small-scale edition of various talmudic tractates from 1768 onward brought about his financial ruin. His son-in-law and successor Godechau-Spire printed some "enlightened" literature in Hebrew, such as a volume of riddles by Moses Ensheim (1787). May and his successors were active until 1793. Other Hebrew printers in Metz were Ephraim Hadamar and Seligmann Wiedersheim and successors, who continued until 1870, when the German annexation of Alsace-Lorraine led to the closure of this press.

MINSK. In 1808 Simḥah Zimel set up in Minsk a Hebrew printing press which he had brought from Grodno. Up to 1823, he had printed at least 12 books, mostly liturgical. Another press was established in 1820 by Gerson Blaustein, who by 1837 had also printed 12 books, again mostly liturgical, though including one volume of Hebrew poetry by M. Letteris (1832). In the 20th century a Hebrew press once more operated in Minsk, printing books and newspapers mainly for local use. After the Russian Revolution, the studies in the history of Russian Jewry and Yiddish literature which were published in Yiddish by the Jewish section of the Institute of Belorussian Culture were printed in Minsk.

אסיפת זקנים
חדושים על מסכת ביצה
שיטה מקובצת
נדפס פה ק"ק מיץ
תחת ממשלת אדונינו המלך האדיר לואי ט"ו מלך
צרפת ונאוואר השם ירום הודו ינשא מלכותו ויאריך ימין
על ממלכתו הוא ובניו
שנת תקכ"ה לפק
A METZ,
Chez JOSEPH ANTOINE, Imprimeur ordinaire du Roi,
& de l'Académie royale des Sciences & des Arts, &c.

Title page of *Shitah Mekubbeẓet,* novellae on the talmudic tractate *Beẓah,* the first book printed in Metz. The title page mentions "the great king Louis XV, king of France and Navarre." It was first printed in Constantinople, 1731, together with *Naḥalah li-Yhoshua,* responsa by Joshua Soncino. It is not absolutely certain that the author of this work was indeed Bezalel Ashkenazi, author of the rest of the *Shitah Mekubbeẓet* series.

NAPLES. See Chapter 5.

NOWY DWOR. A German editor, J.A. Krieger, had taken over a Hebrew printing privilege from the Warsaw printer and bookseller Du Four, so that between 1781 and 1816 Nowy Dwor had one of the most active Hebrew presses in Eastern Europe, issuing well over 100 works. The driving powers behind the business were Eliezer ben Isaac of Krotoszyn and his son-in-law, Jonathan ben Moses Jacob of Wielowicz, who had also acted as proofreader and later as manager of Krieger's bookshop in Warsaw. An ambitious project of a Talmud edition did not proceed beyond the publication of the first two volumes in 1784, and subsequently the Napoleonic wars put an end to Krieger's enterprise.

OFFENBACH. The Frankfort bookseller Seligmann Reiss and his son Herz set up a Hebrew press in Offenbach, and issued a variety of Hebrew and Judeo-German books between 1714 and 1721, among them *Beit Yisrael* by Alexander ben Moses Ethausen (1719); *Historie vom Kitter Siegmund* (1714); and similar medieval tales. Israel ben Moses Halle printed Hebrew books in Offenbach with interruptions from 1718 to at least 1738. In 1767 Hirsch Spitz of Pressburg (Bratislava) set up a Hebrew printing press in Offenbach; the press continued to operate until 1832, when competition from Roedelheim became too

Tohorat Aharon by Aaron Perles of Prague, printed in Offenbach, 1722, by Israel ben Moses at the press of the non-Jew Bonaventura della Nay. The book deals with the laws of porging and is part of a popular "professional" literature written by expert porgers to aid their colleagues; therefore there is a summary of the laws in Yiddish at the end of the book. This is one of the earliest works on the subject, causing, like similar works, great literary opposition on the part of rabbinic authorities whose views often differed from the professional traditions of the porgers.

ספר
טהרת אהרן
פה קק אופי באך
ע"י המדפיס הה"ר ישראל בן הה"ר משה

Title page of *Derashot ha-Torah* by Shem Tov ibn Shem Tov, Padua, 1567. Only two books were printed in Padua in the 16th century. In this book the author, who wrote one of the better-known commentaries on Maimonides' *Moreh Nevukhim,* makes use of philosophical ideas for support. The book was printed for the first time in Salonika in 1525 and this is the second edition. Shem Tov ibn Shem Tov the Elder, the grandfather of the author, was one of the sharpest opponents of Maimonides and composed a book, *Sefer ha-Emunot* (Ferrara, 1555) which is in fact one of the strongest polemics against Maimonides.

טוב שם משמן טוב
ספר
דרשות התורה
להחכם הכולל

strong. The Amsterdam printer Abraham Proops published Nathan Maz's *Binyan Shelomo* in Offenbach in 1784.

PADUA. In 1563 Meir ben Ezekiel ben Gabbai's *Derekh Emunah* was printed by Lorenzo Pasquato of Padua, with Samuel Boehm serving as proofreader. This was followed by Shem Tov ibn Shem Tov's *Derashot ha-Torah* in 1567. A conference of Italian communities convened at Padua in 1585 to consider a new approach to Pope Sixtus V on the question of printing the Talmud, then available only in a censored and emasculated edition. In 1622 Hebrew printing was continued in Padua by Gaspare (later Giulio) Crivellari, who printed Jacob Heilprin's *Naḥalat Ya'akov,* followed in the same year by the printing of *Kinot Eikhah,* printed by Abraham Catalono, and Leon de Modena's Hebrew-Italian dictionary, *Galut Yehudah* (1640–42). In the 19th century Antonio Bianchi printed S.D. Luzzatto's *Isaiah* (1885) and other works, between 1834 and 1879. Francesco Sacchetto printed Luzzatto's Pentateuch commentary in 1872.

PESARO. Pesaro occupies an important position in the history of Hebrew publishing. Abraham ben Ḥayyim the Dyer left there in 1477 to open one of the first Hebrew presses in Ferrara. In 1507 Gershom Soncino opened a printing house in Pesaro and worked there with interruptions until 1520, producing, besides books in Italian and Latin, an impressive range of classical Hebrew texts; some 20 Talmud treatises, a complete Bible (1511–17), Pentateuch or Bible commentaries by Baḥya – the first Hebrew work issued in Pesaro and four times reprinted there – by Moses ben Naḥman (Naḥmanides), Levi ben Gershom, David Kimḥi, Isaac Abrabanel, as well as an edition of Nathan ben Jeḥiel's *Arukh* (1517). Some of these works appear as issued by the "Sons of Soncino."

POLONNOYE. Hebrew printers were active in Polonnoye between 1780 and 1820. Among them was Samuel ben Issachar Ber, who also printed in Korets and Shklov, and who transferred the press to Ostraha in 1794. Another was Joseph ben Ẓevi ha-Kohen, active from 1800 to 1820, who founded another press in Medzibozh, in 1815. Altogether some 90 works, mostly kabbalistic, ḥasidic, and ethical, were issued, some of the latter in Yiddish.

PRAGUE. Prague was the first city north of the Alps where Hebrew books were printed. The earliest, printed in 1512, was a book of miscellaneous prayers. Of the early printers Gershom Kohen emerged as the leading figure; from 1526 he and his sons carried on the printing business which for several generations remained one of the outstanding Hebrew presses in Europe. Gershom Kohen, with his brother Gronim (Jerome), produced independently in 1526 the famous illustrated Passover *Haggadah* (facsimile edition, 1926). In the following year (under the name of Herman) he obtained from King Ferdinand of Bohemia a printing privilege, which at his death in 1545 was reissued to his son Moses, and in 1598 to his great-grandson Gershom ben Bezalel. He and his brother Moses after him were active until the middle of the 17th century. The Gersonides printed mainly liturgical items in this period, but also such important works as Jacob ben Asher's *Turim* (1540) and Moses Isserles' *Torat ha-Olah* (1569). Another printing press was founded by Jacob Bak who was printing in Prague by 1605. Jacob died in 1618, and after him eight generations of Baks printed Hebrew books in Prague up to the threshold of the 19th century. Their productions were mostly liturgical and for local use,

ספר
הר אדני
והוא זהר על מגילת רות המיוחס להתנא
הגדול רשבי
נדפס פה קק פולנאי
בעיר הדש

Sha'ar of *Har Adonai,* part of the *Zohar* treating the Book of Ruth, printed in Polonnoye, 1791, by Samuel ben Issachar Ber. A Commentary to the *Zohar* on Ruth, *Ẓaddik Yesod Olam,* attributed on its title page to Solomon Luria, was printed together with this book.

The title page of *Shulḥan Arba* of Baḥya ben Asher which is a work of *halakhah* and etiquette relating to meals. The book was printed in Prague in 1596 by the typesetter Moses ben Katriel Weiswasser, apparently at the press of the Kohen family. The printers' mark is a poor imitation of the mark of Giustiniani of Venice about 50 years earlier.

A *Haggadah* with a commentary by Isaac Abrabanel entitled *Zevaḥ Pesaḥ* printed in Riva di Trento, 1561.

and they, like other Hebrew printers, suffered much under the Jesuit censorship (from 1528) and occasional book burnings (1715, 1731). Jonathan Eybeschuetz obtained permission to print the Talmud at Bak's (1728–41). Besides Kohen and Bak, other Hebrew printers of note in Prague included Abraham Heide-Lemberger and his sons (1610–41). From 1828 Moses Landau printed independently, in particular a Talmud edition (1830–35).

RIVA DI TRENTO. The press in Riva di Trento owed its success to the cooperation of three men: Cardinal Cristoforo Madruzzo, bishop of Trent, who had jurisdiction over the town and whose coat-of-arms appears on many of the Riva publications; Joseph ben Nathan Ottolenghi, rabbi and *rosh yeshivah* at Cremona; and Jacob Marcaria, *dayyan* and physician, also of Cremona, who was the printer and contributed brief prefaces to his productions. The first work issued was Isaac Alfasi's *Halakhot* (1558), followed by other halakhic works, including two editions of Jacob ben Asher's *Turim* (1560 and 1561). With the Talmud banned in Italy, there was a need for these substitutes. The press also produced philosophic works, notably the first printing of Levi ben Gershom's *Milḥamot Adonai* (1560), and ethical literature. The illiberal attitude of Cardinal Madruzzo's nephew and successor must have led to the abrupt end of Marcaria's venture. For about another year he continued to print non-Hebrew books, including some concerned with the Council of Trent (1545–64), though only one of them carried the printer's name. Joseph ben Jacob Shalit of Padua, who had been Marcaria's proofreader, took some of the unfinished works to Venice and had them printed there. In all, some 25 books were printed in Riva.

ROEDELHEIM. About 1750 the Hebrew printer,

Karl Reich, transferred his press from Homburg to Roedelheim. In 1799 Wolf Heidenheim established what was called an "oriental and occidental printing house," where he published, among other things, classical editions of liturgical texts. After his death in 1832 his partner M. Lehrberger printed S. Baer's famous *siddur, Avodat Yisrael* (1868) and other liturgical works. The clear Roedelheim texts were still being reproduced over a hundred years later.

ROME. It is the opinion of a majority of scholars that nine or ten incunabula printed in square type without date or place-name, (but probably before 1480), should be ascribed to Rome. Only one Hebrew press was licensed in Rome in the 16th century, and few Hebrew books were brought out by non-Jewish printing houses. The one Jewish press was run by Elijah Levita who, with the help of the three sons of his kinsman, Avigdor Ashkenazi Kaẓav, and under a papal privilege, printed here in 1518 three of his grammatical works. Around 1508 a prayer book was produced by J. Mazzochi and perhaps a Hebrew grammar a few years later. Between 1540 and 1547 Samual Sarfati, Isaac ben Immanuel de Lattes in partnership with Benjamin ben Joseph d'Arignano, and Solomon ben Isaac of Lisbon printed a number of works with Antonio Bladao. Among them were Hebrew grammars by David ibn Yaḥya, then rabbi in Naples, and David Kimḥi; the *Mahalakh*; responsa by Nissim ben Reuben Gerondi, and smaller works. Between 1578 and 1581, Francesco Zanetti, with the help of Levita's baptized grandson Giovanni Battista Eliano, printed editions of Genesis, the Five Scrolls, and Psalms. Owing to the reactionary atmosphere which prevailed in Rome in the 17th century, only some missionary tracts in Hebrew were printed in Rome, and in 1773 a psalter for non-Jewish use with an Italian translation by Ceruti.

Title page of the code of Isaac Alfasi (Rif), Sabbioneta, 1554, printed at the Foa press, where Zerachiah ha-Levi's *Sefer ha-Ma'or* and Naḥmanides' *Milḥamot Ha-Shem* were first printed.

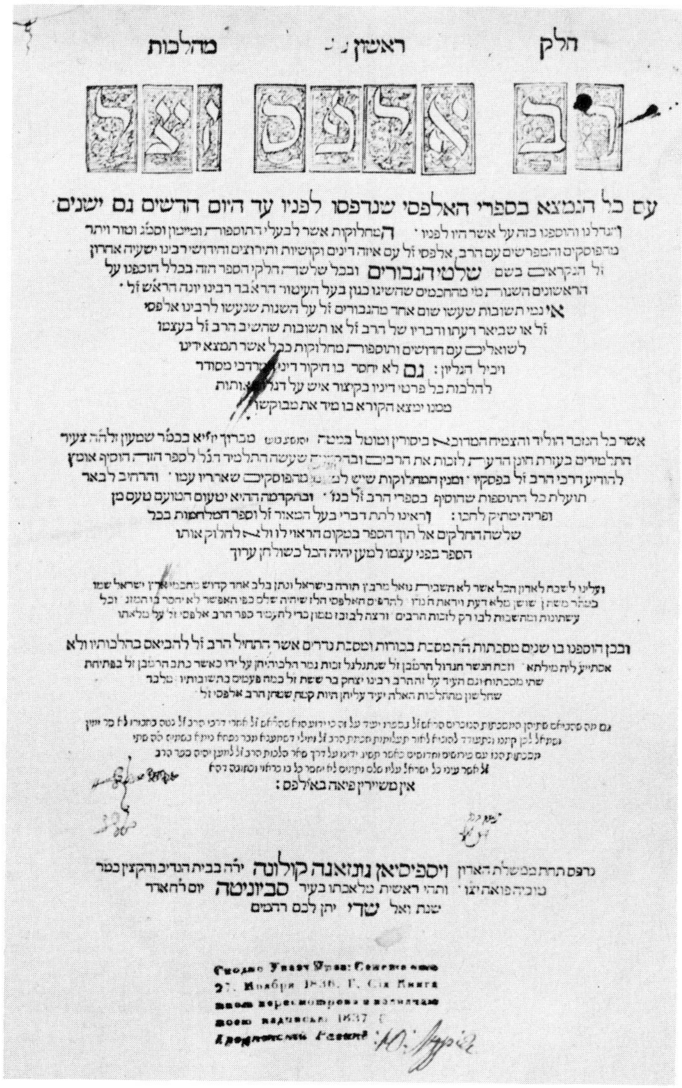
הלק ראשון מהלכות

רב אלפס זצל

עם כל הנמצא בספרי האלפסי שנדפסו לפניו עד היום חדשים גם ישנים

אין משירין פיאה באלפס :

נדפס תחת ממשלת הארון ויספיסיאן גונזאגה קולונה

סביוניטה

שנת ואל שדי יתן לכם רחמים

SABBIONETA. Sabbioneta is known for its Hebrew press, which was founded in 1551 by Joseph ben Jacob Shalit of Padua and Jacob ben Naphtali of Gazzuala, in the house of Tobias ben Eliezer Foa. In 1553 Foa became sole owner of the press with Cornelio Adelkind as the printing expert, and Joshua Boaz Baruch as corrector and setter. After Adelkind converted to Christianity, Foa's sons, Eliezer and Mordecai, took his place; 26 books were issued, including the first printed edition of Isaac Abrabanel's *Mirkevet ha-Mishneh* (1551), before the press was compelled to close down in 1559. A proposed edition of the Talmud did not go beyond one tractate (*Kiddushin,* 1553), and a Mishnah edition with Maimonides' and Bertinoro's commentaries was not printed beyond the order *Zera'im* and part of *Mo'ed* (1558); the rest appeared in Mantua.

In 1567 Vicenzo Conti, the gentile printer of Cremona who had served his apprenticeship with Foá at Sabbioneta, left Cremona and in that year printed a number of works at Sabbioneta.

SAFED. In 1832 the printer Israel Bak of Berdichev settled in Safed and issued four books up to 1834, the year the community was pillaged by Arab villagers. In 1836 printing was resumed with the publication of *Pe'at ha-Shulḥan* by Israel of Shklov. As a result of the earthquake of 1837 Bak went on to Jerusalem. Between 1863 and 1866 Dober ben Samuel Kara of Skole (Galicia) printed some eight books in Safed. Ten years later Abraham Ẓevi Spiegel-

ספר
מפעלות אלקים
בשקלאוו

Mifalot Elohim, poplar remedies selected from the writings of famous contemporary kabbalists and physicians, Shklov, 1823. Like other similar works, it is very rare.

mann and his partners began printing, but only three works are known to have appeared up to 1885. In 1913 Barukh Barzel and his partners opened a Hebrew press called "Defus ha-Galil," and some 20 books were printed there before 1926. This press served Hebrew writers who found refuge in Safed during World War I. Later, A. Friedmann took over the press, which printed the Haganah paper *Kol Ẓefat* during the War of Independence.

SEINI. The Seini community was important in the history of Transylvanian Jewry because of the Hebrew printing press established there by Jacob Wieder. The first Hebrew work was printed in 1904 and the last in 1943. Between the two world wars the press was among the most important in Transylvania. It printed religious works, religious periodicals, and several works in Yiddish. A member of this family of printers, the son of the founder, Judah Wieder, settled in Haifa in 1932 and established a press there.

SHKLOV. Shklov was a center of Jewish culture where disciples of Elijah ben Solomon, the Gaon of Vilna, were influential. Between 1783 and 1835 several printing presses operated in Shklov, and about 150 books were published. It was in Shklov that Haskalah first actively emerged in the Pale of Settlement. Baruch Schick, Nathan (Note) Notkin, and Joshua Zeitlin were active in the town. The Hebrew version of *Kol Shavat Bat Yehudah* (1804) by Y.L. Nevakhovich, which called on the Russian government to grant Jews equal rights, was published in Skhkov.

SLAVUTA. During the late 18th and first half of the 19th centuries, the Slavuta community became known for its printing press, founded in 1791 by Rabbi Moses Shapira, son of the *ẓaddik* Rabbi Phinehas ben Abraham of Korets. Later Moses' two sons, Samuel Abba and Phinehas, took over the administration of the press. Three editions of the Babylonian Talmud, an edition of the Bible (with commentaries), the *Zohar,* and many other religious works, especially ḥasidic literature, were all produced handsomely and with great care. In 1835 the press was closed down when the owners were arrested for the alleged murder of a worker who had supposedly denounced them for printing books without permission from the censor.

SULZBACH. The inclination of Duke Christian-August toward mysticism and Kabbalah aroused his interest in the Hebrew language and led him to grant an authorization in 1669 for the founding of a Hebrew press in his town. As a result Sulzbach became renowned in the Jewish world. The first of the Jewish printers was Isaac ben Judah Loeb Yuedels of Prague. In 1684 the ownership of his press passed to the Bloch family, and from 1699 until 1851, the year the press shut down, it was held by the Frankl-Arnstein family. The Sulzbach press printed 700 works, which consisted mostly of *siddurim, maḥzorim,* Bibles, three editions of the Talmud, and popular *musar* (ethical) literature in Judeo-German. The press first achieved fame as a result of its excellent edition of the *Zohar,* printed in 1684. The half-folio edition of the *maḥzor* enjoyed a wide circulation ever since 1699 when it first appeared; there was hardly a community in southern Germany ("Ashkenazi ritual") where it was not employed as *maḥzor-kahal* (community *maḥzor*) by the *ḥazzan.* The publication of the Talmud in Sulzbach was the cause of a serious dispute with the Proops brothers of Amsterdam. The demise of the press was due partly to the prohibition on importing Hebrew books into the Austrian Empire as well as to the excellent quality of work produced by the Wolf Heidenheim press in Roedelheim, with which the Sulzbach press could not compete.

TARNOPOL. About 1813 a Hebrew printing press was set up in Tarnopol by Naḥman Pineles and Jacob Auerbach, the type as well as some of the personnel coming from Zbarazh. In all, some 25 works were printed in Tarnopol. This printing venture came to an end about 1817, due apparently to the boycott by the Orthodox of a press supporting Haskalah.

VENICE. See page 100.

VERONA. A few books in Hebrew type were printed in Verona at the press of Francesco delle Donne between 1592 and 1595, one of them in Judeo-German (*Pariz un Viena,* 1594). Most important of the Hebrew books was the *Tanḥuma* of 1595, produced by Jacob ben Gershon Bak, of Prague, and Abraham ben Shabbetai Bath-Sheba. Fifty years later Hebrew printing was resumed at the press of Francesco de' Rossi (1645–52), on the initiative of the Verona rabbis Samuel Aboab (and his sons Jacob and Joseph) and Jacob Ḥagiz, the first part of Ḥagiz's edition of the Mishnah with his commentary *Ez Ḥayyim* appeared in 1649 (the rest was printed in Leghorn in 1650). Abraham Ortona was employed as typesetter. Two other printers were active in Verona late in the 18th and early in the 19th century, printing mainly liturgical items.

COMPENDIUM
ORATIONUM
סדר
הגדה של פסח
כפי מנהג
אשכנזים
נדפס לתשוקת הנערים
ישר״א ואחיו אשכנזים נכדי הגביר שלמה
אהרן הכהן נ״ר
וירונה .
VERONAE
EX TYPOGRAPHIA LIBANTEA
EDITORIS SUMPTU
MDCCCXXVIII.

Passover *Haggadah,* printed in Verona, 1828. The Coliseum in Rome is depicted on this title page.

VIENNA. In the 16th century a number of books were published in Vienna which had some rough Hebrew lettering (from wood-blocks?): Andreas Planeus' *Institutiones Grammatices Ebreae,* printed by Egyd Adler, 1552; J.S. Pannonicis' *De bello tureis in ferendo,* printed by Hanns Singriener, 1554; and Paul Weidner's *Loca praecipuo Fidei Christianae,* printed by Raphael Hofhalter, 1559. Towards the end of the 18th century extensive Hebrew printing in Vienna began with the court printer Joseph Edler von Kurzbeck, who used the font of Joseph Proops in Amsterdam. He employed Anton (later, von) Schmid (1775–1855), who chose printing instead of the priesthood. Their first production was the Mishnah (1793). In 1800 the government placed an embargo on Hebrew books printed abroad and thus gave him a near monopoly. His correctors were Joseph della Torre and the poet Samuel Romanelli (to 1799), who with Schmid printed his *Alot ha-Minḥah* for Charlotte Arnstein's fashionable marriage (1793). Among the works they printed were a Bible with Mendelssohn's *Biur* (1794–95) and David Franco-Mendes' *Gemul Atalyah* (1800). Schmid also issued the 24th Talmud edition (1806–11) and the *Turim* (1810–13) with J.L. Ben-Zeev's notes on *Ḥoshen Mishpat.* Besides Kurzbeck and Schmid there were other rivals and smaller firms: Joseph Hraszansky, using a Frankfort on the Main font, opened a Hebrew department in Vienna. Among his great achievements is an edition of the Talmud (1791–97). In 1851 "J.P. Sollinger's widow" began to print Hebrew texts including a Talmud, with I.H. Weiss as corrector (1860–73). Hebrew journals printed in Vienna at this time included *Bikkurei ha-Ittim* (1820/21–31), *Kerem Ḥemed* (1833–56), *Ozar Neḥmad* (1856–63),

Copper engraving printed opposite the title page of *Sekhiyot ha-Ḥemdah,* printed by George Hranszansky, Vienna, 1811. It contains prayers and sayings for the month of Nisan, including *Amirat ha-Nesi'im,* i.e., the sections on the special sacrifices offered by the tribal leaders during the dedication of the altar (Numbers 7). For this reason the engraving depicts the leaders, holding the tribal flags, standing near the altar. The engraving was made by Israel ben Ḥayyim, whose signature appears at the bottom left.

ראשית חכמה
חבר הגאון החסיד המקובל איש האלהי כמוהר"ר אליה
בן מוה"ר משה די וידאש זלה"ה
תלמידי האשל הגדול עמוד התורה ויסוד הקבלה כמוהר"ר
משה קורדואירו ז"ל
חברו בארמת הקדש צפת תו"בב
נדפס פק"ק
זיטאמיר
פאולאוויטש
Ж. Т. ТЫПОГРАФІЯ Е. Г. Ш.

Sha'ar of *Reshit Ḥokhmah* by Elijah de Vidas, printed in Zhitomir, 1804. The author lived in Safed during the second half of the 16th century, during the golden age of its rabbis and kabbalists, and this is the classic kabbalistic *musar* book even today. It was first printed in Venice in 1579, and since then has gone through some 40 reprintings, in addition to summaries and other editions.

Kokhevei Yizhak (1845–73), and *Ha-Shaḥar* (1868–84/5).

VILNA. Hebrew printing in Vilna began in 1799 with three ethical books: a short version of Kalonymus ben Kalonymus' *Even Boḥan* by Phinehas ben Judah Polotsk; Abraham Lichtstein's *Hin Ẓedek* on Maimonides' *Shemonah Perakim* (1 and 2), by the press of Aryeh Loeb, Gershom Luria and Moses ben Menaḥem; and Gershon ben Benjamin's *Shemirat ha-Mitzvot.* The former two were printed by the Canonicus Joseph Mirski (died 1812) and the third in the printing house. Jan Jasienskie Luria's firm produced various small books and a Bible (1806). The firm still existed in 1823. The Drukarnia Djecezjalna (Mirski) and Vilna University had their own Hebrew press.

Hebrew printing in Vilna, however, owes its fame chiefly to the house of Romm. Baruch ben Joseph (died 1803), after some years in Grodno, set himself up in Vilna in the last years of the 18th century. Baruch's son Menaḥem Man Romm (died 1842) and Simḥah Zimel ben Menaḥem Naḥum of Grodno printed some liturgical items, 1815-17. Menaḥem Man's three sons – David (died 1860), assisted by his second wife Deborah, née Harkavy; Ḥayyim Jacob; and Menaḥem Man Gabriel – greatly developed the firm. Due to censorship, by 1845 the firm enjoyed a virtual monopoly in Russia and Poland.

Trouble arose over the printing of the Talmud, and this eventually led to the closing of all Jewish printing-presses in Lithuania and Volhynia, excepting one in Vilna and another in Zhitomir (until 1862). In 1835 Man Romm, in association with Simḥah Zimel, began printing the Talmud against the protest of the

Slavuta printers; as a result, Slavuta's second printing (their first dates from 1815/16–1822/23) was never finished. Romm completed their edition in 1854. It was their masterpiece: in 1846 even Sir Moses Montefiore came to visit their establishment. From 1871 it was known as the firm of "the widow and the brothers Romm" (i.e., Deborah, Ḥayyim Jacob, and Menaḥem Man). The 1866 edition was produced by 100 devoted workers and 14 correctors. Many standard texts, among them the Mishnah, the *Turim,* Maimonides' *Mishneh Torah,* the Jerusalem Talmud, and S. Buber's Midrash editions, made Vilna printing famous for its beauty and accuracy.

There were also a number of small firms. Abraham Ẓevi Rosenkranz and his brother Menaḥem Schriftsetzer, originally typesetters with the Romms, established their own press in 1863. They also took over the 30 year old Samuel Joseph Fuenn press in 1893. In 1920 the firm was bought up by A.L. Shalkowitz (Ben Avigdor). Among smaller presses, that of Boris Kletzkin (died 1938) employed more than 50 workers and printed some newspapers.

WANDSBECK, GERMANY. A number of Hebrew books were printed in Wandsbeck between 1688 and 1722. When the proselyte printer, Israel ben Abraham Halle, arrived in the town in 1726 a serious printing venture began. It owed its inspiration to Moses Ḥagiz, who was the official censor. Between 1726 and 1733 40 items were issued here, many of them works of Ḥagiz himself.

WARSAW. The beginning of Hebrew printing in or near Warsaw arose from the government's wish to stem the outflow of capital abroad for the import of Hebrew books. In Warsaw the first Hebrew book (Ẓevi Hirsch ben Ḥayyim's notes on the Yalkut Shimoni *Ẓemaḥ le-Avraham*) was printed by Peter Zawadzki in 1796. After his death his widow continued printing – mainly anti-ḥasidic literature – until 1801. Another non-Jewish Hebrew printer was V. Dombrowsky (to 1808). The first Jewish-owned press was that of Ẓevi Hirsch Nossonowitz of Lutomirsk, who printed, with Krieger's Nowy Dwor type, from 1811, in partnership with Avigdor Lebensohn 1818-21. Later they separated, Nossonowitz now changing his name to Schriftgiesser ("typecaster"). He died in 1831, and was succeeded by his son Nathan; the firm continued for another century, printing a Talmud edition (1872). Lebensohn and his descendants were active to 1900. More than 30 additional presses were established in Warsaw during the 19th century, including that of S. Orgelbrand and sons, who printed Talmud editions as well as *Turim,* Maimonides' *Yad,* and *Shulḥan Arukh,* and a Mishnah edition.

Among the moving spirits of Hebrew printing in Warsaw was Isaac Goldmann (1812–1887), who ran his own press from 1867 producing more than 100 books, among them Talmud tractates. In 1890 the brothers Lewin-Epstein established a Hebrew printing house, still active in Israel in the 1970s. About a dozen more presses were set up in the first quarter of the 20th century. At the outbreak of World War II in 1939 more than 1,000 workers were engaged in the Hebrew printing works in Warsaw.

ZHITOMIR, UKRAINE. The first Hebrew printing press in Zhitomir was established in 1804 by the wandering printer Ẓevi Hirsch ben Simeon ha-Kohen, who came from Zolkiew, where he had worked as a typesetter. He had worked in the printing press in the town of Nowy Dwor, and had subsequently possessed his own press in 1796 in Kopel, and in 1803-04 in Brezitz (Beresty). Ẓevi Hirsch had his printing press in Zhitomir until 1806, and during the three years of its existence at least nine books were published, five of which were ḥasidic and kabbalistic works.

In 1847 a second printing press was established there by the three brothers Ḥanina Lipa, Aryeh Leib, and Joshua Heschel Shapira, sons of Samuel Abraham Abba Shapira, the printer in Slavuta. Until 1862 this was one of the only two Hebrew presses the Russian government permitted to operate in the whole of Russia, the other being in Vilna. This press had 18 hand presses and four additional large presses. In 1851 Aryeh Leib broke away and established his own printing press in Zhitomir. In these two establishments sacred books only of every kind were printed. During the years 1858-64 the press of the two brothers printed a beautiful edition of the Babylonian Talmud together with the *Halakhot* of Isaac Alfasi, while between 1860 and 1867 Aryeh Leib printed an edition of the Jerusalem Talmud.

In 1865 a Hebrew printing press was established by Abraham Shalom Shadov, and in 1870 another one by Isaac Moses Bakst. In 1888 the Hebrew press of Brodovitz was founded, and in 1891 this passed into the possession of his successors. In c. 1890 a printing press was founded by Joseph Kesselman and in c. 1902 it passed into the possession of his widow, Rachel, who entered into partnership with Elijah Feinberg. In these three presses all kinds of Hebrew and Yiddish books were printed.

ZOLKIEW, UKRAINE. The first Hebrew press in the

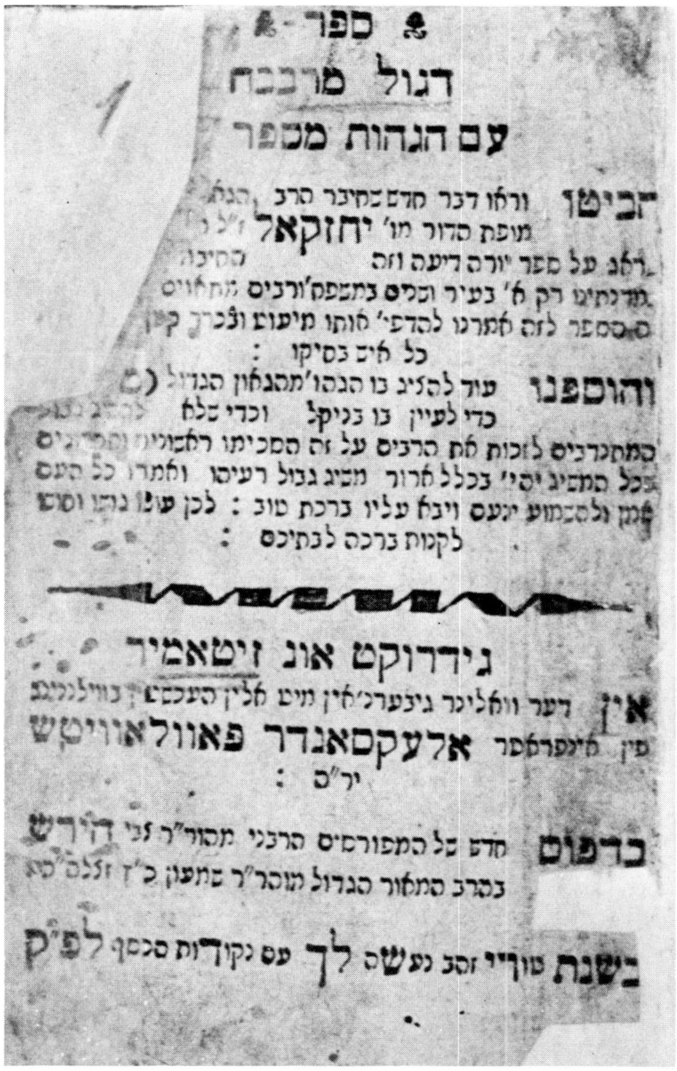
ספר
דגול מרבבה
עם הגהות מספר
גידרוקט אונ זיטאמיר
אלעקסאנדר פאוולאוויטש
בדפוס

Dagul mi-Revavah on *Yoreh De'ah* by Ezekiel Landau, author of *Noda bi-Yhudah,* printed in Zhitomir, 1804. Appended to it are David ha-Levi's emendations to his *Turei Zahav* on *Yoreh De'ah* which were made after the printing of the book. These emendations were first printed in Halle, 1716, on some loose pages, and were copied with this book. The original printing is very rare today. These emendations have been incorporated into the printed editions of *Turei Zahav* on *Yoreh De'ah* only in the past 50 years.

city was set up by the Amsterdam printer Uri ben Abraham Phoebus ha-Levi in 1692 under license to John Sobieski. The first production appears to have been novellae by Samuel Edeles. For eight decades Uri Phoebus, his sons, grandsons, and other members of the family, (Madfes, Grossmann, Rosanes), printed a great variety of books, covering all branches of Hebrew literature. Productions were generally of a high quality, with handsomely decorated title pages. The Letteris family, which was related to the Uri Phoebus clan, printed in the city from 1794 to 1828, moving their presses from Lvov. In 1793 A.J.L. Mayerhofer obtained a printing license from the Austrian government, and he and his sons were active till 1830. Originally he was in partnership with M. Rubinstein, but they separated in 1797, and Rubinstein and his son continued on their own until well into the 19th century. Other Hebrew printers of importance in the 19th century were S. P. Stiller, who began work in 1859 and produced a *Zohar* (1862–64), and J.Z. Balaban, who established a press in 1862.

ZURICH. During the 16th and 17th centuries a number of Christian printers in Zurich produced books containing Hebrew type; chief of these was the house of Froschauer (from 1528), which used the type of Fagius. In 1558 Eliezer ben Naphtali Herz Treves printed Psalms with a rhymed Yiddish translation by Elijah Baḥur Levita. In the same year Hebrew type was used in J. Reuchlin's *Clarorum Verorum Epistolae.* In the 17th and 18th centuries the presses of J.J. Bodmer and of J.H. Heidegger used Hebrew type, the former from 1635 to 1727, the latter from 1673 to 1766. A few Hebrew works were also produced in Zurich in the 19th century.

The title page of the second edition of Shabbetai Bass' *Siftei Yeshenim,* the first Hebrew bibliographical list. This edition was printed in Zolkiew in 1806 and includes at its end a list of the books which appeared since the first edition in 1680 "as far as the author knows." The author is, in fact, the publisher of the book, the noted printer Mordecai Rubenstein.

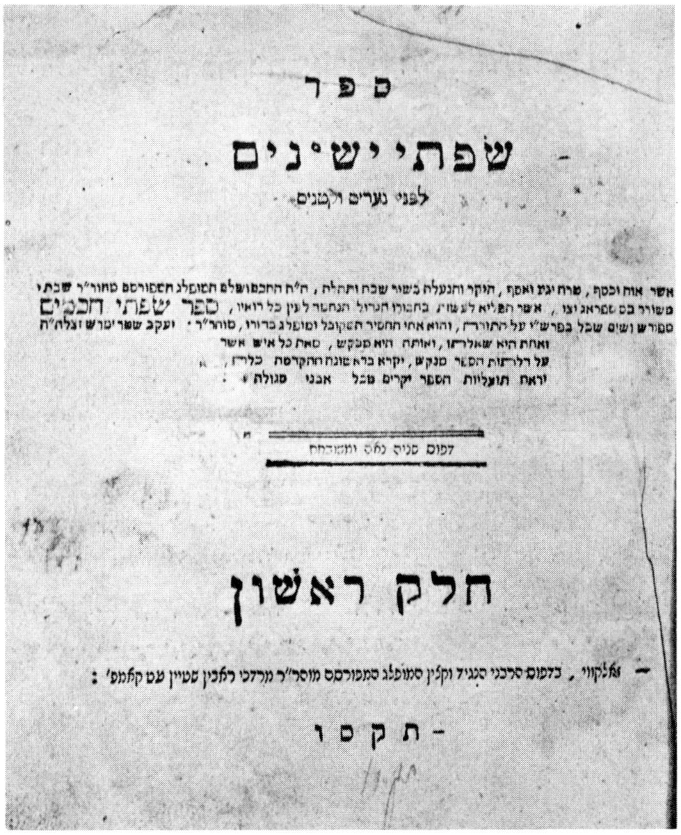
ספר
שפתי ישנים
חלק ראשון
תקסו

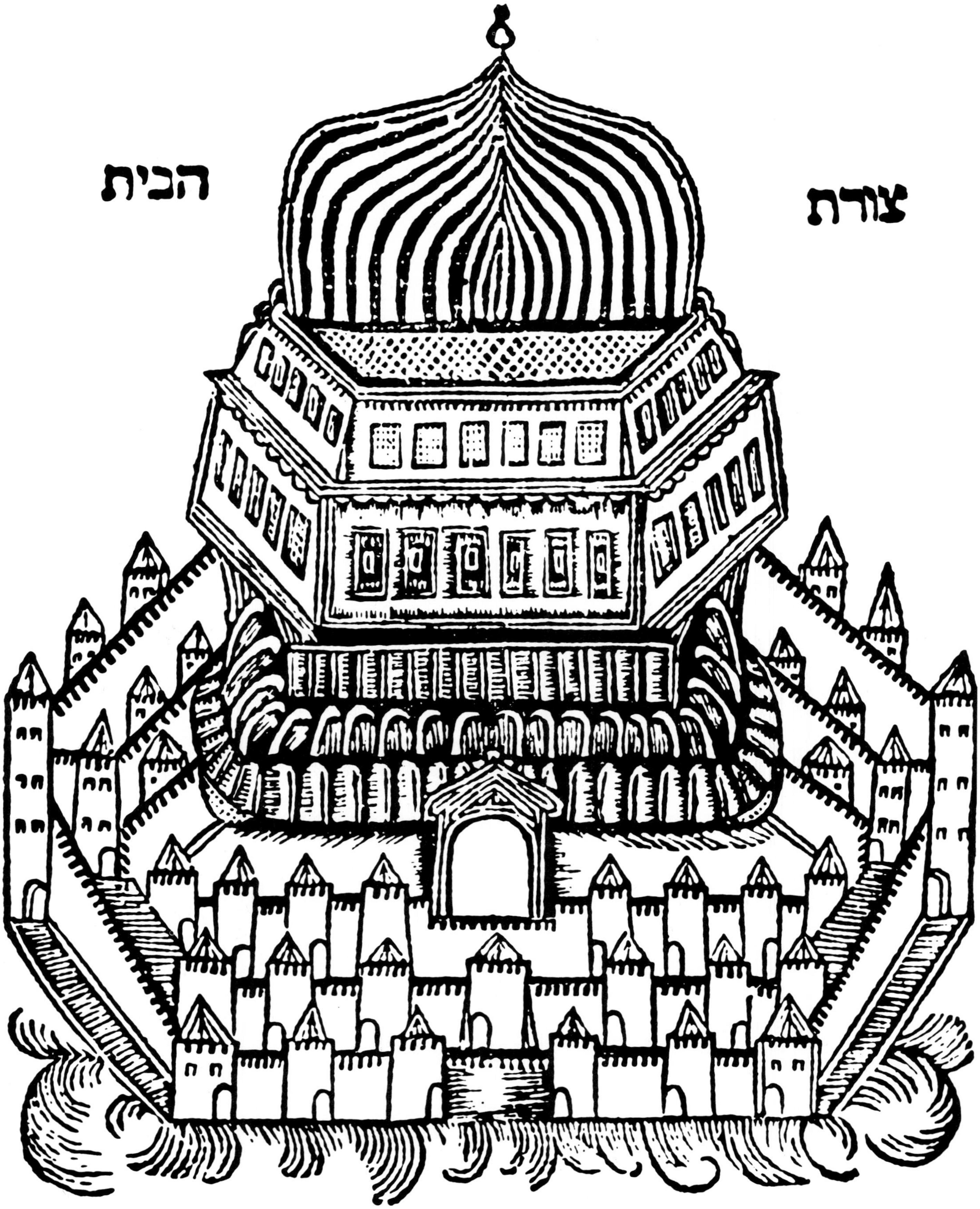

הבית
צורת

7. hebrew printers*

ADELKIND, ISRAEL CORNELIUS (16th century), Italian printer. Adelkind was the son of a German immigrant who settled in Padua. He worked in the publishing house of Daniel Bomberg in Venice from the time of its establishment, except for intervals at other Venetian publishers, such as Dei Farri (1544; where one of his brothers and later his son Daniel also worked) and Giustiniani (1549–52). Adelkind greatly admired the Bomberg family, adding the name of Daniel Bomberg's father, Cornelius, to his own, and named his son after Daniel himself.

Adelkind supervised the publication of the first editions of the two Talmuds (1520–23) which Bomberg printed, and the *Midrash Rabbah* (1544), printed jointly by Bomberg and Giustiniani. In 1553 the printer Tobias Foa invited Adelkind to manage a printing press in Sabbioneta and, in particular, to supervise the publication of the Talmud. However, a ban was imposed on the Talmud in 1553 after only a few tractates had appeared. Nevertheless, he remained with the firm until 1555 and took part in the publication of other works. He also printed books in Judeo-German, e.g. Elijah Levita's translation of the Psalms (1545). The statement of a Christian contemporary that Adelkind converted to Christianity is highly probable.

ASHKENAZI, JONAH BEN JACOB (died 1745),

Printers' mark of Reuben ben Jonah Ashkenazi. It portrays the Temple in Jerusalem.

*This is a selective listing which does not include the printers discussed in Chapter 5.

Hebrew printer in Turkey. Born in Zalosce (in the province of Lemberg) Poland, Ashkenazi emigrated to Turkey and settled in Constantinople. In 1710 he established a new printing press, using characters which he had engraved himself. Later he cast new ones, together with decorations for the title pages, and finally produced some beautiful books. During the first two years Ashkenazi was in partnership with another Polish emigrant, Naphtali ben Azriel of Vilna. He was compelled to leave Constantinople twice, continuing his work in the nearby village of Ortaköy. In 1720 a consignment of his books was lost at sea, and a dishonest agent of his fled to Poland. Ashkenazi followed him, and on his way back to Constantinople, stopped in Amsterdam. There, in 1721, he printed the *Shitah Mekubbeẓet* of Bezalel Ashkenazi on *Bava Meẓ'ia* according to a manuscript which he had brought with him from Constantinople. On his return to Constantinople, he printed mainly the works of local rabbis. In 1714 he traveled to Egypt where he received several works of Egyptian rabbis for printing. There he found a manuscript of the *Tikkunei Zohar,* which had been corrected by Ḥayyim Vital, and which he published. In 1728 he established a branch of his press in Smyrna in partnership with David Ḥazzan, who in 1739 emigrated to Palestine. The press then closed down.

During the 35 years of his activity in Constantinople and Smyrna, Ashkenazi printed 125 books. After his death in 1745, the press passed to his three sons: Reuben, Nissim, and Moses; later to his grandsons; and continued until 1778. In all 188 books were printed by the three Ashkenazi generations. He printed in Ladino the Bible, a *siddur, Josippon* and the first edition of *Me-Am Lo'ez,* among other works. Ashkenazi made Constantinople the center of Hebrew printing in the Orient.

ATHIAS, JOSEPH AND IMMANUEL (17th century), publishers and printers in Amsterdam. Joseph was a man of considerable learning and was a close friend of the Dutch poet Joost van den Vondel. According to tradition, Joseph sought his friend's opinion before publishing a manuscript.

He founded a combined Hebrew-Dutch printing house which proved successful. Christoffel van Dijk carved a beautiful set of type for the press. In 1681, after the death of Daniel Elsevier, Joseph also bought up the stock and equipment of the famous publishing house which he had founded.

Joseph's first book, a prayer book according to the Sephardi rite, was published in 1658, and in 1659 he published a commentary on the Pentateuch. The famous Bible he produced in 1661 was prepared under the editorial supervision of the distinguished scholar Johannes Leusden; a second edition appeared in 1667. He also published translations of the Bible, and in 1687 he announced that he had printed more than a million Bibles for England and Scotland. Athias' designs were widely copied. On Joseph's death in 1700 his son Immanuel, who had been a partner since 1685, took over the business. He completed the elegant four-volume edition of Maimonides' *Yad* which the elder Athias had begun. This edition, of 1,150 copies, was dedicated to Moses Machado, army purveyor for King William III of England, who had given economic support to Joseph and Immanuel when they had purchased the Elsevier type-casting foundry. After the completion of the *Yad,* Immanuel began the production of Abraham de Boton's commentary to it, the *Leḥem Mishneh*, of which three volumes were published before his death in 1709. The molds and letters of the Athias press later passed into the possession of the Proops printing house. It is not known whether Abraham ben Raphael Ḥezkia, who printed Hebrew books in Amsterdam from 1728 to 1743, was a member of the same family. Joseph Athias was accused of appropriating long-term copyright and reprint privileges which had been given by the Polish Jewish authorities in order to produce a Judeo-German translation of the Bible.

BAK, (also **PAK**), a family of Jewish printers of Ashkenazi origin, who lived first in Venice and later in Prague. According to Zunz, the name represents

The monogrammed printers' mark of Joseph and Immanuel Athias, MJA, in mirror-writing.

Plate 30 (above). Scroll of Esther, parchment and wood, Lisbon, 1816. Hechal Shlomo, Sir Isaac and Lady Wolfson Museum, Jerusalem.

Plate 31 (below). *Megillat ha-Melekh* ("King's Scroll"), Italy, 18th century, so designed that every column begins with "the king." In this example, the scenes from the Purim story are in Italian Renaissance style. Formerly New York, Michael Zagaysky Collection.

Plate 32. Full-page illumination as the opening to Genesis in the *Schocken Bible,* southern Germany, c. 1300. It is composed of 46 medallions arranged symmetrically around the initial-word panel. Within the roundels are biblical illustrations, the subjects of which are arranged chronologically from right to left and top to bottom, covering the entire Pentateuch, beginning with Adam and Eve and ending with Balaam and the angel. The decoration in the background of the panels is typical of German illumination around Lake Constance, c. 1300. Jerusalem, Schocken Library, Ms. 14840.

Plate 33. David playing the harp. An historicated initial-word panel to the Book of Ecclesiastes, from the *Duke of Sussex Pentateuch,* written by Ḥayyim the Scribe, South Germany, c. 1300. London, British Museum, Add. ms. 15282, fol. 302.

Plate 34. An illuminated Rosh Ha-Shanah *piyyut* showing the blowing of the *shofar* and an illustration of a ram caught in a thicket. *Leipzig Maḥzor,* South Germany, c. 1320. Leipzig University Library, Ms. V.1102, Vol. II, fol. 26v.

Plate 35. Illuminated opening panel of the Book of Ruth from the *Tripartite Maḥzor,* South Germany, c. 1320. The panel shows the corn harvest as related in the Book of Ruth. Of special interest in the illumination is the depiction of women with animal or birds' heads, whereas the men have human features. The reason for this may be the artist's misunderstanding of the biblical prohibition, "Thou shalt not make graven images." The British Museum, Ms. Add. 22413, fol. 71r.

the initials of *Benei Kedoshim* (Children of the Martyrs).

Gerson, the progenitor of the family, lived in Italy in the early 16th century, where his son Jacob was a printer. Jacob printed the *Midrash Tanḥuma* in Verona (1595) and in Venice *Tanna de-Vei Eliyahu* (1598), and *Tiferet Yisrael* by Judah Loew (the Maharal) of Prague in 1599. Apparently his connections with the latter brought him to Prague. From 1605 until his death in 1618 he printed numerous Hebrew and Judeo-German books. He was succeeded by his sons Joseph and Judah, who in 1623 set up a new printing house called "Jacob Bak's Sons." Their output was considerable, despite the temporary slowing down during the Thirty Years' War (1616–48) and the persecutions of 1648–49 and 1656. In about 1660 Joseph left the printing business, and Judah carried on alone. A libel action brought against the press led to its closure in 1669. Judah died in 1671, and two years later his sons, Jacob (1630–1688) and Joseph (died 1696), were authorized to resume printing books, as "Judah Bak's Sons," but a special permit was required for each book. In 1680 Joseph completed a *maḥzor* at nearby Weckelsdorf – the only Hebrew work ever printed there. Between 1680 and 1683 Joseph apparently continued alone in Prague, while Jacob worked under the name "Judah Bak's Sons" (1682–88). Joseph was joined by Jacob's son Moses (died 1712) in 1686. From 1697 Moses ran the firm with his cousin, Joseph's son (later "The Bak Press"). Moses' son Judah (died 1767 or 68), who was a compositor, managed the press from 1735 to 1756. In 1757 Judah's brother Yom Tov Lipmann joined as his partner, and the firm became "Moses Bak's Sons." Later it was "The Bak and Katz Press" (1784–89), and afterwards passed into other hands entirely. The Bak family were pioneers in the field of Jewish printing, and they also made an important contribution to the Jewish community of the time. Israel Bak, the printer of Safed and Jerusalem, does not seem to have had any connection with this Bak family.

BAK, printers and pioneers in Ereẓ Israel. Israel Bak (1797–1874) was born in Berdichev, Ukraine, into a family of printers. Later he owned a Jewish press in Berdichev, printing about 30 books between 1815 and 1821 when the press closed down. In 1831, after various unsuccessful efforts to reopen the works, he emigrated to Palestine and settled in Safed. There he renewed the tradition of printing Hebrew works, which had come to an end in the last third of the 17th century. During the peasant revolt against Muhammad Ali in 1834 his printing press was destroyed and he was injured. Later he reopened his press, and also began to work the land on Mount Yarmak (Meron), overlooking Safed. His was the first Jewish farm of modern times in Ereẓ Israel. After the Safed earthquake in 1837 and the Druze revolt in 1838, during which his farm was despoiled and his printing press again destroyed, he moved to Jerusalem. In 1841 he established the first – and for the next 22 years, the only Jewish printing press in Jerusalem. It was thus of great cultural importance to Jerusalem; 130 books were printed on it. Bak also published and edited the second Hebrew newspaper in Ereẓ Israel, *Havaẓẓelet* (1863). It was published for a short time only, but was revived in 1870 by his son-in-law, I.D. Frumkin and others. Israel Bak was a leader of the ḥasidic community; as a result of his efforts and those of his son Nisan, a central synagogue for the Ḥasidim, called Tiferet Israel (after Rabbi Israel of Ruzhin) came into being. In Jerusalem it was also known as "Nisan Bak's synagogue," and

Characteristic decoration by the Israel Bak press in Jerusalem. Pictured are blossoming branches and plants in a beautiful vessel, surrounded by the words, "It is a tree of life . . ."

was destroyed in 1948 during the War of Independence. After the death of Israel Bak, Nisan managed the printing press until 1883, when he sold the business.

BASEVI, Italian family of German origin, especially associated with Verona. In Hebrew, they called themselves Bath-Sheba and in abbreviation, Bash. The name Naphtali was common in the family, and therefore some of its members took a deer's head as their crest and became known as "Basevi Cervetto" (Italian: "little deer"), in accordance with the Blessing of Jacob (Genesis 49:21). Others chose a boat for their crest, in accordance with the Blessing of Moses (Deuteronomy 33:23), and became known as "Basevi della Gondola." It is not clear what relationship existed between this family and the Basevi family of Prague. The brothers Abraham and Joseph, sons of Sabbatai Mattathias Bath-Sheba, were printers in Salonika (1594–1605). Abraham subsequently became a printer in Damascus (1605–06), and his brother was a proofreader in the Verona press – a *Midrash Tanḥuma* appeared with his name (1595).

BASS (or BASSISTA), SHABBETAI BEN JOSEPH (1641–1718), the first Jewish bibliographer. Bass's parents were killed in a pogrom in Kalisz (Poland) by the Cossacks in 1655, but he and his elder brother were saved and fled to Prague. Possessing a pleasant voice, Bass was engaged as an assistant singer (hence his nickname Bass) to the cantor Loeb at the Altneu synagogue (Altneuschul) in Prague. In Prague he acquired a thorough knowledge of the Talmud, and also a general education which included Latin. His love of books and a critical spirit drew him to publication and printing. In 1669 in Prague he printed a revised edition of the Yiddish commentary on the Pentateuch and the Five Scrolls by Moses Saertels, *Be'er Moshe,* with an appendix on "grammatical rules." As there was no complete list in Hebrew of Jewish literature, he undertook to compile one. Between 1674 and 1679 Bass visited libraries in Poland, Germany, and the Netherlands. In Amsterdam he studied the art of printing and proofreading, and published *Massekhet Derekh Ereẓ,* a guide book for travelers (1680); the Pentateuch with a supercommentary on Rashi, *Siftei Ḥakhamim* (1680), a popular commentary often reprinted; and *Siftei Yeshenim* (1680), a list in Hebrew of some 2,200 Hebraica and Judaica titles. This was the first Jewish bibliography in Hebrew giving, apart from the names of the books, the name of the author, content, format, place and year of printing, and sometimes

Printers' mark of Shabbetai ben Joseph Bass. The figure holding musical notes and the arrangement of the Hebrew letters of the date are allusions to his name.

also the location of the book. He also listed manuscripts. In some copies a prayerbook was appended to the list. In 1688 Bass obtained a permit to set up a Hebrew printing press at Auras, and this was shortly afterward transferred to Dyhernfurth. The first book printed by Bass was Samuel ben Uri Sharga's commentary *Beit Shemu'el* (1689), on *Shulḥan Arukh Even ha-Ezer.* He also successfully engaged in bookselling. When the Jesuits accused Bass of spreading hatred against the Christians and the government, he at first succeeded in refuting the accusations; but in 1712 the Jesuits repeated their accusations and he was arrested. In the trial he successfully proved the ignorance of his accusers, and was released. His sons and grandsons continued to print books at Dyernfurth until the second half of the 18th century.

BELFORTE, SOLOMON (19th century), printer of Leghorn. Belforte was both a scholar and an able businessman. He established a new printing house in Leghorn in 1834. In addition to books for the religious needs of Italian Jewry, such as the Pentateuch, the Mishnah, *maḥzorim,* and other books in Hebrew and Italian, Belforte printed prayer books for the Jewish communities of North America and even for the Jews of Yemen. At the end of the 19th century he was also a partner in a bookselling business. In 1926 the printing house employed 100 workers and published several catalogs. After the establishment of the State of Israel, all the equipment of the printing house, including the many matrices, were transferred to Tel Aviv.

BOMBERG, DANIEL (died between 1549 and 1553),

one of the earliest and most prominent Christian printers of Hebrew books. Bomberg left his native Antwerp as a young man and settled in Venice. Rich and well educated, having studied even Hebrew, he developed a deep interest in books. He probably learned the art of printing from his father Cornelius. In all, nearly 200 Hebrew books were published (many for the first time) at Bomberg's printing house in Venice, which he set up on the advice of the apostate Felice da Prato (Felix Pratensis). He published editions of the Pentateuch and the Hebrew Bible, both with and without commentaries, and was the first to publish the rabbinic Bible *Mikra'ot Gedolot* (four volumes, 1517–18), with da Prato as editor, i.e., the text of the Hebrew Bible with Targum and the standard commentaries. In order to produce this work, he had to cast great quantities of type, and engage experts as editors and proofreaders. As a result of the success of his early work, Bomberg expanded his operations. He published the first complete editions of the two Talmuds (1520–23) with the approval of Pope Leo X (only individual tractates of the Babylonian Talmud having hitherto been published), as well as the Tosefta (appended to the second edition of Alfasi, 1522). The pagination of Bomberg's editions of the Talmud (with commentaries) has become standard universally. Similarly, his second edition of the rabbinic Bible (1524–25), edited by Jacob ben Ḥayyim ibn Adonijah, served as a model for all subsequent editions of the Bible. He is said to have invested more than 4,000,000 ducats in his printing plant. Bomberg spent several years trying to obtain a permit from the Council of Venice to establish a Hebrew publishing house. He also had to secure special dispensation for his Jewish typesetters and proofreaders from wearing the distinctive Jewish (yellow) hat. In 1515 the Venetain printer P. Liechtenstein printed, at Bomberg's expense, a Latin translation by Felice da Prato of the Psalms. Apparently, the first Hebrew book to come off his press was the Pentateuch (Venice, December 1516), though there is some evidence that his first work was printed in 1511. In 1516 he obtained a privilege to print Hebrew books for the Jews, and went on printing rabbinic books, midrashic-liturgical texts, etc. Among Bomberg's printers, editors and proofreaders whose names are known were: Israel (Cornelius) Adelkind and his brother and Jacob ben Ḥayyim ibn Adonijah (all of whom were later baptized); David Pizzighettone, Abraham de Balmes, Kalonymus ben David and Elijah Levita (Baḥur). It seems that Bomberg's fortunes declined as a result of competition from other publishers. In 1539 he returned to Antwerp, though his publishing house continued to operate until 1548. His distinctive type became popular, and his successors not only lauded his typography but went as far as to print on the title pages of their publications "with Bomberg type," or some similar reference. The name Bomberg which appears in the Plantin Bible published in Antwerp in 1566 almost certainly refers to his son, and from him Plantin obtained a manuscript of the Syriac New Testament on which he based the Polyglot Bible known as *Regia* (8 volumes, 1569–73).

DANGOOR, EZRA SASSON BEN REUBEN, (1848–1930), Iraqi rabbi. Dangoor studied in Baghdad and was a pupil of Abdullah Somekh. Although he devoted much of his time to religious activity, he obtained his livelihood from business. From 1880 to

A Passover *Haggadah,* with an Arabic translation written in Hebrew letters, printed by Ezra Dangoor, Baghdad, 1908.

הגדה של פסח
נדפסה
באותיות גדולות העברי׳ והערבי
בנקודות עם כמה הוספות ׳ דיני ביעור
חמץ ׳ וסדר הלילה בלשון ערבי
שיובן דבר אדם
ולדעת מה יעשה
ישראל :
פה בגדאד יע״א
בא סי׳
חד גדיא בתרי זוזי לפ״ק
בדפוס ה׳ עזרא דנגור נ״ט

1886 he was in charge of documents issued by the Baghdad *bet din*. In 1894 he was appointed rabbi of Rangoon, Burma, but ill-health compelled him to return a year later to Baghdad, where he was appointed chief of the *shoḥetim*. During 1923 to 1928 he served as chief rabbi of Baghdad but resigned office because of communal disputes. He established a Hebrew press in Baghdad in 1904, and many books were published there under his editorship, including festival prayer books according to the Baghdad rite; *Seder ha-Ibbur,* calendars for the years 5665–5683 (in other presses until 5691); *Birkhot Shamayim* (1905), on the blessings for precepts and for pleasures; *Sefer ha-Shirim*(1906), containing poems by different authors. There remain in manuscript in the Sassoon collection: responsa, a history of Baghdad from the years 1793 to 1928, homilies, commentaries on biblical books, laws, customs, poems, and *piyyutim.* After his death, his children published a memorial volume (1931).

FOA, TOBIAS BEN ELIEZER (16th century) set up a Hebrew printing press in his house in Sabbioneta in 1551. In its last years, Tobias' sons Eliezer and Mordecai headed this enterprise, which had to close after difficulties with the censor – the last works on the press were finished in Cremona and Mantua. Tobias started the fashion of printing special copies, often on parchment, for wealthy patrons. Nathanel ben Jehiel Foa began printing as a hobby in Amsterdam in 1702, prompted by his uncle and brother-in-law Joseph Ẓarefati. Most of the works he issued (12 up to 1715) were written by emissaries from Ereẓ Israel or were manuscripts which they had brought with them. Isaac ben Gad (born c. 1700), physician and one of the leaders of the Venice Jewish community, ventured into Hebrew printing about the time of the birth of his son Gad (1730–1811) and produced mainly liturgical items until 1739. From 1741 Isaac was in the book trade proper. In 1742 he entered into partnership with his kinsman Samuel, who also had a son called Gad, the two Gads later taking over the business. Gad ben Samuel appears as the sole printer between 1775 and 1778; he transferred to Pisa in 1796, producing 13 books at his own press or at that of David Cesna. His last major production, in association with Eliezer Saadun, was a handsome Hebrew Bible of 1803. Gad ben Isaac resumed printing in Venice in 1792 until 1809. Among the few major works produced by the Foas of Venice are the first four volumes of Isaac Lampronti's talmudic encyclopedia *Paḥad Yiẓḥak.*

GABBAI, family of Hebrew printers. Isaac ben Solomon (born second half of 16th century) lived in Leghorn and was the author of the Mishnah commentary *Kaf Naḥat* (appended to Mishnah, ed. Venice, 1614). Early in the 17th century he worked as a typesetter for Bragadini in Venice. His son Jedidiah acquired the Bragadini type and decorations and set up the first Hebrew press in Leghorn, which was active there from 1650 to 1660, issuing a number of important works. With part of the equipment and staff of this press, Jedidiah's son Abraham in 1657 established a printing house in Smyrna, which existed until 1675. Abraham himself moved to Constantinople in 1660, where he was a printer for a number of years. His corrector (proofreader) was Solomon ben David Gabbai – probably not of the same family – author of the kabbalistic work *Me'irat Einayim* (between 1660 and 1665) and a theological work *Ta'alumot Ḥokhmah.*

GEDALIAH, (DON) JUDAH (died c. 1526), Hebrew printer. Gedaliah was born in Lisbon and worked there at Eliezer Toledano's Hebrew press (1489–95) until the expulsion from Portugal (1497). He settled in Salonika, establishing the first Hebrew printing press there using fine typefonts he had brought from Lisbon. Between 1515 and 1535 he, his daughter, and his sons (who continued the firm after his death)

The family emblem of the Foa family employed as the printers' mark of Tobias Foa. The central feature is two lions against a palm tree supporting a shield of David.

carefully edited and printed about 30 Hebrew books including the first edition of *Ein Ya'akov* of Rabbi Jacob ibn Ḥabib (1516–22). The latter, in his introduction, highly praised Gedaliah for his efforts in spreading the knowledge of Torah among the other Iberian refugees in Salonika.

HALICZ, (HELICZ, HALIC, HELIC), family of printers in Cracow in the 16th century. Three brothers, Samuel, Asher, and Eliakim, sons of Ḥayyim Halicz, established Poland's first Jewish press there in about 1530. Their name indicates that the family originally came from the small town of Halicz on the Dniester in eastern Galicia. Their type and page arrangements show they learned their craft (and probably obtained type and equipment) in Prague. It is likely that they left Prague because a royal order of 1527 designated Gershom Kohen as Bohemia's sole Hebrew printer; all other Hebrew print shops closed, and the brothers probably could find no other work there. The decorative borders for their opening pages were certainly brought by them from Prague. Three works listed by Zunz as being from Cracow in 1530 were probably the earliest products of their press. These were a Pentateuch; *Tur Yoreh De'ah;* and a Passover *Haggadah* (all otherwise unknown). Their earliest surviving works, both dating from 1534, were *Issur ve-Hetter* by Rabbi Isaac Dueren and *Mirkevet ha-Mishnah,* a Hebrew-Yiddish Bible dictionary by a Robert Anshel. Yet evidently they did not prosper, and Asher left the business.

In 1553 Samuel and Eliakim produced Rabbi David Cohen's *Azharot Nashim* in Yiddish, a work dealing with religious laws for women. Then Eliakim alone issued a Yiddish version of Asher ben Jeḥiel's *Oraḥ Ḥayyim.* Samuel spent 1536 in Olesnica, Silesia, where he and his brother-in-law printed a book of *Tefillot mi-Kol ha-Shanah* ("Prayers for All Year") in large type. However, his books and equipment were destroyed in a fire and he returned to Cracow.

It was probably economic misery or possibly excessive pressure from the Polish church that made the three undergo baptism in 1537; they became Andreas (Samuel), Johannes (Eliakim) and Paul (Asher; or perhaps Asher became Andreas, and Samuel was Paul). Repelled by their act, the Jews boycotted them and would not even pay their debts. At the brothers' plea, King Sigismund I issued a decree dated March 28, 1537, commanding Poland's Jews to buy only their books; no one else was to print or sell Jewish works and no books might be brought in from other countries, on pain of a heavy fine. Yet, under tacit excommunication by the Jews, their plight only worsened. Believing, though, that the royal decree must improve matters, Johannes resumed printing in 1538–39, issuing books mainly for popular use.

Through their bishop, the desperate Halicz brothers sought and obtained a new royal decree on December 31, 1539, ordering the Jews of Cracow and Posen to buy their entire stock of some 3,350 volumes, valued at 1,600 florins. Pleading poverty, the two Jewish communities had their coreligionists in Lvov (Lemberg) included in the order. The complete stock of books was paid for in three years and destroyed. The Halicz firm went out of existence. In 1540 Johannes began printing Latin and Polish theological works. Paul, who became a Catholic missionary among the Polish Jews, printed a New Testament (Cracow, 1540–41), in a Judeo-German transcription of Luther's translation. He also produced *Elemental oder Lesebuechlein* (Hundsfeld, 1543), an instruction book in Hebrew for gentiles. Lukasz Halicz, a printer in Posen (1578–93), was apparently his son. Samuel returned to Judaism. After working as a bookbinder in Breslau, he went to Constantinople (c. 1550) and resumed Hebrew printing. He subsequently printed the Scriptures (1551–52), repenting of his conversion in the colophon; the "Story of Judith" (1552–53); and Rabbi Isaac Dueren's *Issur ve-Hetter,* retitled *Sha'arei Dura* (1553). In 1561–62, when Samuel was no longer living, the name of Ḥayyim ben Samuel Ashkenazi, apparently his son, appears as the printer of part two of the responsa of Rabbi Joseph ibn Lev.

'IRAQI, ELEAZAR BEN AARON HA-KOHEN (died 1864), Yemenite-Indian scholar and printer. 'Iraqi was born in Cochin, India, before 1816, but he was of Yemenite parentage. He spent most of his life in Calcutta where he served as teacher, *ḥazzan,* and *shoḥet* in the new Jewish community there. He opened a printing press in 1841, becoming the first Jewish printer in Calcutta and in all India; during the next 16 years he printed 25 ritual books for the use of the Jewish communities of India and the east. His particular interest was the printing of works of Yemenite scholars and poets. Some of his own poems are included in the *Sefer ha-Pizmonim* ("Book of Hymns") which he printed in 1842.

JABEZ, a 16th century family of scholars and Hebrew printers of Spanish origin. Solomon (died before 1593) and Joseph Jabez set up a Hebrew press in Salonika in 1546. They were the sons of Isaac Jabez (died before 1555) and grandsons of Joseph Jabez, called "the preacher." In 1494 in Mantua, Joseph, the

Shield-shaped printers' mark of Ẓevi Hirsch Jaffe. The deer, rising from a crown, symbolizes the name of the printer, Ẓevi, and the two fish represent either the zodiac sign Pisces for the printer's birthdate, or his assumed tribe of origin, Naphtali, who was allotted the area of the Sea of Galilee.

grandfather, wrote a homiletical work, *Ḥasdei ha-Shem,* which his son Isaac prepared for publication. An edition of Psalms with his commentary was published by his grandson Joseph in Salonika in 1571. From 1546 to 1551 Solomon and Joseph printed a number of Hebrew books there. After a short interval in Adrianople, where they printed two books (1554–55), Solomon went to Constantinople and Joseph returned to Salonika, where he was active in printing until about 1570.

A plan to print the Talmud, which had been burned and banned in Italy in 1553, was not fulfilled beyond a few tractates (1561–67). Meanwhile Solomon had begun printing in Constantinople in 1559, and his brother Joseph joined him there in 1570. Separately and together they printed about 40 important works, among them responsa by Elijah Mizraḥi (1559–61) and Joseph ibn Lev (3 parts, 1560? – 73), the first editions of Saadiah's *Emunot ve-De'ot* (1562), and A. Zacuto's *Yuḥasin* (1566). The brothers then tried once more to reissue the Talmud; the larger part of it appeared 1583-93. Solomon's son Isaac Jabez was the author of *Ḥasdei Avot* (Constantinople, 1583), a commentary on *Avot, Yafik Razon* (Belvedere, 1593), a commentary on *haftarot,* and *Torat Ḥesed* (Belvedere, after 1593), on Hagiographa; he was not a printer. The Jabez press in Constantinople was financed by patrons such as Solomon Abenaes. Ḥayyim Halicz worked at the press in about 1568.

JAFFE, a family of Hebrew printers in Lublin in the 16th and 17th centuries. In 1557 Kalonymus ben Mordecai Jaffe (died c. 1603) was associated with Eliezer ben Isaac and other printers in the production of a Pentateuch with *haftarot* and the Five Megillot. Kalonymus was a second cousin of Mordecai Jaffe, author of the *Levushim,* and married Hannah, the granddaughter of Ḥayyim Shaḥor, a well-known wandering printer. In 1559 she and her cousin Ḥayyim ben Isaac Shaḥor obtained a printing privilege from Sigismund II, king of Poland. Kalonymus published two *maḥzor* editions, one in the German rite (1563), the other in the Polish (1568), and a Talmud edition (1559–77). When Eliezer ben Isaac and his son left Lublin for Constantinople in 1574, Kalonymus bought most of his type – Prague-style borders and other decorations – and from then until his death he continued printing a great number and variety of works, simultaneously going ahead with the Talmud edition. He was soon assisted by his sons, Joseph, Ẓevi Hirsch, and Ḥayyim. In 1578 he obtained a new privilege from King Stephen Bathory; in 1590 he acquired new type borders and decorations. When plague broke out in Lublin in 1592, the family and staff took refuge in nearby Bistrowitz, where they printed a Passover *Haggadah* in 1593. Kalonymus' son Ẓevi Hirsch took up the family trade in 1604. He too issued a Talmud edition (1611–39), Samuel Edels' novellae (1617–36), and a number of other important rabbinic and non-rabbinic works. A great fire, the Chmielnicki persecutions (1648–49), and the Swedish War (1656) led to the suspension of printing activites, but in 1665 another Jaffe, Solomon Zalman (Kalmankes) of Turobin, a nephew of Kalonymus and husband of his daughter Sarah (who herself took an active part in the work), took over and continued printing, certainly until 1700 and possibly after that year. Solomon Zalman was in partnership with a certain Jacob ben Abraham and, after the latter's death, with his son Ẓevi.

KOHEN, first major family of Hebrew printers in

Prague and the whole of Central Europe. Hebrew printing began in Prague before anywhere else in Central or Eastern Europe. It was certainly established there by 1512, when four craftsmen and two backers produced a prayer book. By 1514 the group had been joined by Gershom ben Solomon Kohen (died 1544), a 16th century Hebrew printer, who was evidently a man of means, and two others. From then until 1552 they issued four prayer books and a handsome Pentateuch.

Kohen's dominant importance in the group is indicated by two facts: in all these works, the colophons list him first; and an ornamental border on the opening page of the Pentateuch, used again in the 1522 *maḥzor,* shows a pair of hands held in position for the priestly blessing – he was a *kohen* (priest). He was to use this as his printers' mark in later works also, with his name added.

After 1522 the group broke up in order to open several Hebrew printing shops in Prague. Together with his brother Gronem Kohen, Gershom produced a Passover *Haggadah* (1526). Set in large, handsome type and lavishly illustrated with over 60 woodcuts (mostly by Ḥayyim Shaḥor, a fellow printer), this earliest printed, illustrated *Haggadah* is a masterpiece. Each double page has a harmonious unity and balance of its own. A facsimile edition appeared in Berlin in 1926 (but by error the order of facing pages was not kept), and two others in the late 1960s – one (Shulsinger, New York) a faithful and splendid replica, the other (Universitas, Jerusalem) in colors. In 1526 Ferdinand I became king of Bohemia, and Kohen applied to him for a *privilegium* (royal decree), to make him the exclusive Hebrew printer in Bohemia. This was granted him in 1527 and his competitors had to close their shops. He engaged Meir Michtam, the typographer of the original group of printers of 1512, as his assistant to instruct his sons in the craft. With his sons Solomon and Mordecai (died 1592), Kohen produced a steady stream of prayer books and Pentateuchs, as well as learned and talmudic works. In time his sons Moses (died 1549) and Judah (died 1593) also joined the firm. Printing more volumes than the Prague community could absorb, the Kohen family appointed the Halicz brothers of Cracow as agents in Poland; in 1535 Mordecai, the most talented businessman among Kohen's sons, went to the Frankfort trade fair to arrange for distribution there.

Printers' marks of Gershom ben Solomon Kohen, using the symbol of the hands in the posture of the priestly blessing. This was the first use of the hands in a printer's mark.

The 1540s were unsettled years for Prague's Jews. An edict of expulsion left only 15 families in the city, until the decree was lifted in 1543. In 1544 the resulting economic difficulties forced Mordecai Kohen to travel in an attempt to sell some of the stock. Towards the end of the year Gershom Kohen died, and shortly afterwards his son Moses Kohen applied to Ferdinand I for the same *privilegium* that his father had enjoyed. In 1545 his request was granted. In the 1550s, however, life for all Prague Jewry was unusually difficult. Fire ravaged the ghetto and expulsion was threatened. Beset in any case by competition from Hebrew works imported from Italy, Mordecai Kohen left printing and devoted himself to the communal welfare, acting as *shtadlan.* His brother Moses Kohen died, and for years no volumes were issued from the Kohen family press, except for a small prayer book (afternoon and evening services) printed by Judah Kohen. In 1566, however, Mordecai Kohen resumed the craft with his five sons. But adverse conditions interrupted printing for another seven years (1571–77), after which Mordecai's sons continued, while he himself remained occupied with communal affairs until his death. The firm was then named in his memory. In 1589 Kohen's son Bezalel died. In 1590 his son Solomon requested, and received, yet another royal *privilegium,* enabling the Kohen firm to remain the sole Hebrew printers in Prague until the very early 1600s.

From 1592 the firm was managed by Solomon Kohen and his son Moses (died 1659). Afterwards, Moses

רב אלפס
חלק שני מסדר נשים עם כל הדברים אשר
היו על לוחות ספרי אלפסי הראשונים
כל אלה יגעתי ומצאתי לזכות בהם את הרבים
נאם מאיר בר יעקב איש פארינץ

Title page of *Rav Alfas,* the code of Isaac Alfasi (Rif), printed by Meir Parenzo, Venice, 1552, at the Bragadini press. The fine printing of this work attests to the very high professional and aesthetic standards achieved.

continued alone for over 50 years, personally supervising proofreading and corrections. The Thirty-Years' War (1618–48), however, brought the press to a standstill when Moses was already old; when he died, his grandsons Israel and Moses continued under the firm name of "the Grandsons of Moses Katz" (=*kohen zedek,* "the righteous *kohen*"). They were succeeded in time by this latter Kohen's son Aaron (died 1701), who managed the press until his death. After 1701 Aaron Kohen's son David carried on, until 1735, under the firm name of "the descendants of

Printers' mark of Asher Parenzo, showing a high mountain rising out of the sea. To the left is an eagle and above the mountain is a wreath. The Hebrew inscription around the oval frame is an adaptation of Isaiah 43:4 – "Since [*me-Asher*] you have been precious in My sight, I have been honored."

Moses Katz." The press continued sporadically thereafter, until economic conditions prompted the Kohen family printing firm to merge with the Bak firm in 1784, bringing its long course of independent printing to an end.

PARENZO, a 16th-17th century family of Hebrew printers in Venice. Jacob (died 1546) had come to Venice from Parenzo, on the Dalmatian coast of Italy (whence the family name), but in fact the family was probably of German origin. His son Meir (died 1575) probably learned the printing trade at the Bomberg press, where he worked together with Cornelio Adelkind in 1545, and his own productions compare favorably in beauty and elegance with those of his masters. Parenzo worked for some time as a typesetter and corrector at the press owned by Carlo Querini. During 1546–48 he worked on his own, publishing five works, and later he published for Querini an edition of the Mishnah with Bertinoro's commentary, although from about 1550 his main work was with Alvise Bragadini. The Parenzos used various printers' marks: Meir, a seven-branch *menorah,* and a rather daring design with Venus directing arrows at a seven-headed dragon; and his brother, Asher, a mountain rising from the sea, with a laurel wreath above and a flying eagle at the left. Meir's colophons abound in editions prepared by him. In 1547 the great French engraver and typecutter Guillaume Le Bé, and later Jacob of Mantua, produced Hebrew type for him. At Meir's death (1575), his brother Asher took over working for the Venetian printer Giovanni di Gara, as well as for Bragadini, until 1596. Gershon ben Moses, probably a nephew of Meir and Asher, descendants of Jacob Parenzo, worked for the Venetian printer Giovanni di Gara during 1599–1609, as did his son Moses in 1629.

PROOPS, family of Hebrew printers, publishers, and booksellers in Amsterdam. Solomon ben Joseph (died 1734), whose father may have been a Hebrew printer as well, was established as a bookseller in Amsterdam and associated with other printers from 1697 to 1703. In 1704 he set up his own Hebrew press, which produced mainly liturgical books but also a wider range of works in *halakhah, aggadah,* Kabbalah, ethics, and history. In 1714 Proops began to print a Talmud edition in competition with that planned by Samuel ben Solomon Marches and Raphael ben Joshua de Palasios, but was forced by them to discontinue in view of their prior rabbinic monopoly. From 1715 productions by Proops carried advertisements of books he had published, and in 1730 he issued a sales catalog *(Appiryon Shelomo),* the first such Hebrew publication.

After his death, appointed guardians continued to operate the press, and even when his sons Joseph (died 1786), Jacob (died 1779), and Abraham (died 1792) took over, they traded under the old name until 1751. Between 1752 and 1765 the sons – now working under their own name – printed a Talmud edition with interruptions, which were due in part to attempts to print a Talmud in Sulzbach, against which they successfully asserted their own rabbinical monoply. In 1761 they bought the typographical material of the Athias press, but business declined. In 1785 Joseph Proops sold most of his work to Kurzbeck of Vienna, and when he died a year later his widow and sons – for some time in partnership with Abraham Prins – continued printing on a small scale until 1812. From 1774 to his death Jacob Proops worked on his own; his widow and sons continued alone until 1793 and in partnership with Solomon (died 1833), son of Abraham Proops, until 1797; Solomon worked on alone until 1827. Abraham Proops had been active on his own in 1775–79; afterward he removed the business to Offenbach, but his son, who worked with him, returned to Amsterdam when his father died. David, a son of Jacob Proops, printed from 1810 to 1849 in partnership with H. van Emde and his widow, when the press was sold to Levisson who continued it until 1869; the Levisson brothers remained active until 1917.

PROSTITZ, ISAAC BEN AARON (died 1612), Hebrew printer. Isaac was born in Prossnitz, Moravia, and learned the printing trade in Italy, working with G. Cavalli and G. Grypho in Venice. There he met the proofreader Samuel Boehm (died 1588), who later joined Isaac in Cracow, where he printed from 1569. From Italy they had brought with them typographical material and decorations, and in the privilege issued in 1567 to Isaac by King Sigmund August II of Poland for 50 years he is called an "Italian" Jew. In spite of initial intrigues by the Jesuits, Isaac and later his sons – Aaron and Issachar – and grandsons were able to print for nearly 60 years some 200 works of which 73 were in Yiddish, using fish and a ram (symbol for the offering of Isaac) as printers'

Printers' marks of Joseph and Jacob Proops utilizing the symbol of the hands to depict their priestly descent, and two fish for the zodiac sign of the month Adar, Jacob's birth month.

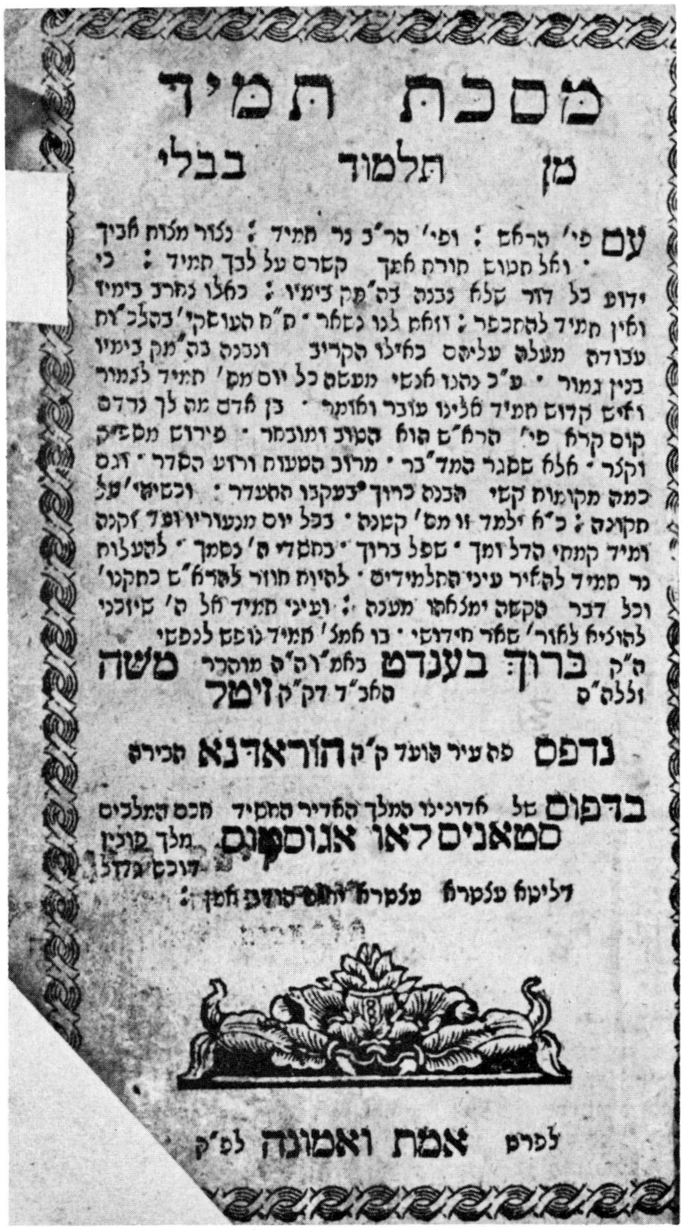

מסכת תמיד

מן תלמוד בבלי

נדפס פה עיר הוראדנא

בדפוס של אדונינו המלך האדיר החסיד חכם המלכים

סטאניסלאו אגוסטוס מלך פולין

לפרט אמת ואמונה לפ"ק

Title page of the talmudic tractate *Tamid* with commentaries by Asher ben Jehiel and Baruch Bendet, rabbi of Grodno. This book, printed in Grodno, 1789, was among the first printed there by the Romm family.

mark. The productions covered a wide field: rabbinics, Bible, Kabbalah, philosophy, history and even mathematics. The Babylonian Talmud was printed twice (1602–08; 1616–20); these were poor editions after an earlier and more auspicious beginning in 1579. The Jerusalem Talmud of 1609 became standard in the form in which it was reissued at Krotoschin in 1886. Isaac was printer to the great scholars of the time: Moses Isserles of Cracow, Solomon Luria of Lublin, and Mordecai Jaffe of Prague and Poznan. In 1602 he returned to his native Prossnitz, where he printed some works until 1605, while his son Aaron remained active in Cracow until 1628 printing (apart from the Talmuds) the *Zohar* (1603), and the *Shulḥan Arukh* (1607, 1618–20), *Turim* with Joseph Caro's commentary (1614–15), and *Ein Ya'akov* (1614, 1619). Isaac's descendants were working as printers' assistants almost until the end of the 17th century.

ROMM, a family of printers and publishers in Vilna. In 1789 Baruch ben Joseph (died 1803) received permission to establish a press in Grodno. He opened a second plant in Vilna in 1799. After his death his son, Menaḥem Mannes (died 1841), directed the operation and between 1835 and 1854 published an edition of the Babylonian Talmud. This caused a dispute with a press operated by the Shapira family of ḥasidic rabbis in Slavuta and more than a hundred rabbis were involved in the resulting litigation. In 1836 the Russian government closed all but two Jewish printing houses, the Romm plant being the only one left in all of Lithuania and Belorussia. In 1841 the plant burned down. Joseph Reuben and his son David headed the company from 1841 to 1862. After their deaths, David Romm's widow Deborah (died 1903) headed the company, together with her two brothers-in-law. This is the origin of the name of the company, which came to be known as "Defus ha-Almanah ve-ha-Aḥim Romm" (The Press of the Widow and Brothers Romm). The firm prospered from 1867 to 1888 under the leadership of its literary director, the Hebrew writer Samuel Shraga Feiginsohn. Modern presses were installed, rights to various manuscripts purchased, many reprints were published, and painstaking editorship prevailed. Most of the firm's income came from the publication of religious works in editions of tens of thousands of copies. Among the more important publications was the Babylonian Talmud with over a hundred commentaries and addenda ("The Vilna Shas," first edition 1880–86). Romm also published popular works in Yiddish, such as the books of I.M. Dick, and Shomer, and Haskalah works.

After the death of Deborah Romm the firm declined. The heirs were not interested in running it and Feiginsohn was reinstated as director. He remained with the firm even after it was sold to Baron D. Guenzburg in 1910 and resold several years later to the firm of Noah Gordon and Ḥaim Cohen. During this period, a complete edition of the Jerusalem Talmud was published. The Romm Press continued in Vilna until 1940. With the Soviet conquest, the plant was confiscated and turned into a Russian-Lithuanian printing house.

SHAḤOR (Czerny, Schwartz), family of pioneers in Hebrew printing in Central Europe. Ḥayyim joined the first printing group in Prague, the Kohen family, in or before 1514. After 1522, when the group disbanded, he joined Meir Michtam in issuing two works of prayer, in 1525 and 1526. During 1526 he evidently prepared almost all the woodcut illustrations for the Passover *Haggadah* of Gershom Kohen. Some have doubted that Shaḥor made the majority of the woodcuts for the *Haggadah* as he is not mentioned in the colophon; however, four illustrations contain a small letter *shin* and it was the practice of non-Jewish woodcut artists to mark their work with their initials. Moreover, one of the four represents King David, and David was also his father's name. The *shin* similarly appears near a lion in the *Haggadah's* third full border (ornamenting the verse *shefokh ḥamatekha*); Shaḥor could have considered the lion a suitable "family crest," for it is a royal symbol, and his father's personal name was synonymous with royalty in ancient Israel and in Jewish tradition. Furthermore, in his Pentateuch of Augsburg (1533) the first page of every book is ornamented with two small figures: one, a crab, is probably a zodiacal sign of his birth month; the other, a lion, was evidently retained as a "family crest." To adorn the opening page of his Pentateuch of Ichenhausen (1544), he copied on to a new woodcut the complete third border of Gershom Kohen's *Haggadah* with the lion (Kohen retained and reused the original), and he used it again for the opening page of his *seder seliḥot* of Heddernheim 1545. It might be noted, too, that in the 1518 Pentateuch of Prague's pioneer printers, Shaḥor is listed second (after Gershom Kohen) in the colophon to part I (end of Exodus), which part contains two full borders; in the colophon to part 2, which has no new woodcut ornamentation, he is listed last. This indicates that he made those two borders as well.

In April 1527 a royal privilege made Gershom Kohen the sole Hebrew printer in Bohemia and Shaḥor had to leave Prague. Taking with him a good amount of type and equipment, he became an itinerant printer, comparable only to Gershom Soncino (although his output was much smaller). About 1529 he settled in Olesnica, Silesia (near Breslau), where he with a partner printed a Pentateuch. A storm destroyed the printing shop, however, and Shaḥor left Silesia, whose Jews frequently suffered harsh edicts. In 1531 he reached Augsburg, a center of humanism, where he apparently used the press of August Wind, a Christian printer who issued some Hebrew texts for the clergy. By 1540 he had produced nine works of quality there (including a modest but handsome Passover *Haggadah* in 1534), evidently helped by his son Isaac and son-in-law Joseph ben Yakar, who were listed in the colophon of their edition of Jacob ben Asher's *Turim* (1540). In this period (1531–40) Shaḥor traveled about, too, in an attempt to sell his stock. Conditions worsened, though, and in the final years in Augsburg the family could not issue its planned volumes. At his request the influential apostate Paulus Emilius went to Ferrara, Italy, in 1541–42 to explore possibilities for the Shaḥor family to settle there, but nothing came of it. In 1543 the family moved to Ichenhausen, Bavaria, where they issued a prayer book with Judeo-German translation as well as a Pentateuch. Political unrest and local war made them move on, however, to Heddernheim, near Frankfort-on-Main, where they resumed printing in 1545.

Finally the family concluded that for them there was little hope for a stable future in Germany, and they left for Lublin, as early as 1547. An official permit for printing could not be obtained until 1550, by which time Shaḥor had died and his son-in-law Joseph ben Yakar had left Lublin to try his luck in Italy. With Giustiniani he produced a Pentateuch in Venice (1548), but then rejoined the family. Until 1554 he and Ḥayyim's son Isaac Shaḥor ran the press jointly, producing a notable Polish *maḥzor* in 1550. By 1557 Shaḥor had died, leaving a small son; his brother-in-law may also have died, as his name no longer appears in the press's output. The family craft was carried on by Kalonymus ben Mordecai Jaffe, the husband of Ḥayyim Shahor's granddaughter (i.e., Joseph ben Yakar's son-in-law), together with two partners, one of whom may have been an elder son of Ḥayyim Shaḥor's son Isaac. The family's printing privilege of 1550 was renewed in 1559, and under Kalonymus and his sons the press continued in Lublin for many years.

SONCINO, family of Hebrew printers active in Italy, Turkey and Egypt in the 15th and 16th centuries. The Soncino family originated in Germany and claimed among their ancestors Moses of Speyer, mentioned in the *tosafot* by Eliezer of Touques (13th century). Five generations later another Moses, resident at Fuerth, succeeded in driving the wandering Franciscan monk and rabble-rouser John of Capistrano (1386–1456) out of the town. His sons Samuel

Elaborate printers' mark used by Gershom Soncino in his earlier works. The tower is probably the badge of the city of Soncino in Lombardy.

and Simon left Fuerth for Italy, where in 1454 they obtained permission from Francesco Sforza, duke of town Milan, to settle near Cremona in Soncino, from which they took their surname. Samuel's son Israel Nathan (died 1492?), a physician, was renowned for his talmudic scholarship and piety; he died in Brescia. Printing had taken place in Italy from 1465, and it was, no doubt, under the influence of Israel Nathan and in partnership with him and his other sons (Benei Soncino) that his son Joshua Solomon (died 1493) set up a Hebrew printing press which in 1484 produced its first book, the Talmud tractate *Berakhot,* with commentaries, in an arrangement which became standard. This was followed by a complete, voweled Hebrew Bible (1488), the *Maḥzor Minhag Roma* (Soncino and Casalmaggiore, 1486) and 15 other works (to 1489). His were the first printed editions of the Hebrew Bible and Talmud tractates. From 1490 to 1492 Joshua Solomon printed at least nine works in Naples, and altogether more than 40 works are ascribed to his press.

His nephew Gershom ben Moses (died 1534), also called Menzlein – perhaps for having learned the art of printing in Mainz – became one of the most successful and prolific printers of his time – and one of the finest printers of all times. He printed from 1489 to 1534, not only in Hebrew (and Judeo-German?) but also in Latin, Greek and Italian; for non-Hebrew literature he used the names Hieronymus, Geronimo or Girolamo. During his extensive travels, to France in particular, he obtained valuable manuscripts for publication, e.g. the *tosafot* of Eliezer of Touques which he was the first to publish. He was also the first to use woodcut illustrations in a Hebrew work (Isaac ibn Sahula's *Meshal ha-Kadmoni,* Brescia, c. 1491), and to produce secular Hebrew literature (Immanuel of Rome's *Maḥberot,* Brescia, 1492). Soncino also printed in small, pocketsize format, assembling an expert staff of literary advisers, typesetters, and proofreaders. His letters were cut by Francesco Griffo da Bologna, who also worked for the humanist printer Aldo Manutius.

Apart from Soncino and Casalmaggiore, Soncino also printed in Brescia, Bacco, Fano, Pesaro, Ortona, Rimini, Ancona and Cesena; both his Hebrew and non-Hebrew productions exceeded 100 volumes each, of which about 20 were Hebrew incunabula. His constant wanderings were due as much to the chicaneries of the local overlords as to fierce and perhaps unfair competition, though in the decade 1494–1504 (with an interval from 1499 to 1502) he was the world's only Hebrew printer. Eventually

The Tower of Soncino in Gershom Soncino's simpler printers' mark, used in his books printed in Rimini, Salonika, and Constantinople. This symbol was subsequently adopted by the Soncino Gesellschaft in Germany and by the 20th-century Soncino Press in London.

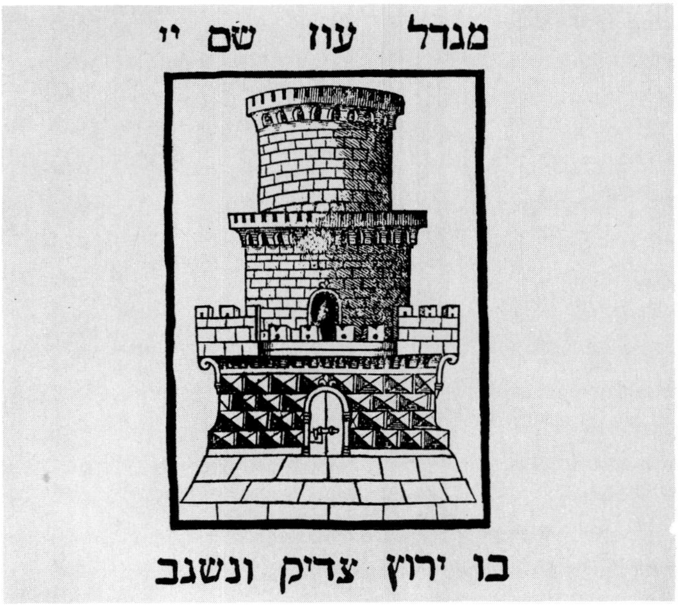

Soncino had to leave Italy for Turkey, where he continued to print in Salonika (1527) and Constantinople (from 1530, assisted by his son Eliezer who died 1547). Gershom Soncino did much to bring relief to the victims of the Spanish and Portuguese expulsions of 1492 and 1497.

His brother Solomon is mentioned as printer in only one work: Jacob ben Asher's *Arba'ah Turim* (1490?), though he belonged no doubt to the collective Benei Soncino. His son Moses printed a number of books in Salonika from 1521 to 1527. Eliezer ben Gershom Soncino continued printing after his father's death, and after he himself died the press was taken over by his partner, Moses ben Eliezar Parnas. His son Gershom printed in Cairo, Egypt, in 1557, being the last of the known Soncino printers. Joshua Soncino (died 1569) of Constantinople was the author of a volume of responsa and novellae (*Naḥalah li-Yhoshu'a,* 1531). It is believed that the Hebrew press in Prague, where printing began in 1512, was founded by the Soncino family.

URI (Phoebus) BEN AARON HA-LEVI (also called Uri Witzenhausen or Witmund; 1625-1715), Hebrew printer. Uri's father was *ḥazzan* of the Neveh Shalom congregation, Amsterdam, and his grandfather, Moses Uri ha-Levi, was rabbi of Emden and one of the founders of the Portuguese Jewish community in Amsterdam. Uri established his first press in Amsterdam in 1658 and was active there until 1689. He published numerous rabbinical and religious works, some of them in Yiddish, including the first Yiddish translation of the Bible by Jekuthiel Blitz (1679); the *Josippon* (1661), and the *Bava Bukh* (1661) by Elijah Baḥur Levita. Uri also published the first Yiddish newspaper; it appeared every Tuesday and Friday and was called *Dienstagische un Fraytagische Kurant* (1680–87). The bulk of the works he printed was for distribution among the Jews of Poland. In 1692 he moved to Zolkiew where he was reportedly invited by the Polish king John Sobieski to print Hebrew books, which previously had been imported from abroad. At the sessions of the Council of the Four Lands in Jaroslaw in 1697 and 1699 Uri obtained rabbinical backing against business competitors in Lublin and Cracow. His press was continued by his children and their descendants for some time after his death. His descendants include Gershom ha-Levi Letteris who was still printing in Zolkiew in 1828, and Gershom's son, the author and poet, Meir ha-Levi Letteris.

USQUE, ABRAHAM, Marrano printer. Born in Portugal and known there as Duarte Pinel (Pinhel), Usque fled from the Inquisition shortly after 1543, established himself at Ferrara, and became associated with the press established by the Spanish ex-Marrano, Yom-Tov ben Levi Athias (Jerónimo de Vargas). He followed Athias' plan of publishing Jewish liturgies in the vernacular, as well as other texts intended to facilitate the Marranos' return to Judaism. Usque's name first appears in connection with the famous Bible translation of 1553, the so-called Ferrara Bible. This Bible was published in two forms: one intended for a Jewish audience, bearing a Hebrew date (14 Adar 5313) and a dedication to Doña Gracia Nasi, and listing the Hebrew names of the printer and publisher (Usque and Athias); the other for the Christian world, dated March 1, 1553, with a dedication to Duke Ercole d'Este of Ferrara and the names of Duarte Pinel and Jerónimo de Vargas. Books published by Usque also include the enigmatic *Menina e Moça,* by Bernardim Ribeiro, Samuel Usque's *Consolaçam as tribulaçoens de Israel* (1553), and various works in Hebrew. The fury of the Counter-Reformation gradually halted Usque's printing activities. He published no books in Spanish or Portuguese after 1555 and continued the publication of Hebrew books only to 1558.

Solomon Usque may be identical with Usque's son and assistant Solomon, but his relationship to Samuel Usque is impossible to determine.

ZIFRONI, ISRAEL BEN DANIEL (16th century), Hebrew printer. Zifroni was a native of Guastalla, near Padua, Italy, and lived in Gazzuolo. In 1567 he worked as corrector in Sabbioneta for Vicenzo Conti, who produced three works, among them Menaḥem ben Zeraḥ's halakhic compendium *Ẓeidah la-Derekh.* The period of his finest achievements was 1578–83, when among other works he printed a fine edition of the Talmud (1578–80) for Ambrosius Froben in Basle, and a Pentateuch with *haftarot,* the Five Scrolls, etc. (1583) for Th. Guarin. Because of difficulties with the Basle city fathers, Froben and Zifroni printed some of their works in Freiburg-im-Breisgau, such as Aaron of Pesaro's *Toledot Aharon,* Benjamin of Tudela's *Massa'ot,* and a Judeo-German paraphrase of Berechiah ha-Nakdan's *Mishlei Shu'alim* (1584). Zifroni eventually returned to Italy, where he worked for Di Gara of Venice as corrector from 1588. Zifroni's son Moses Elishama also became a Hebrew printer and was active in Mantua for T. Ruffinelli and the brothers I. and S. Norzi (1593–97), after which time he joined his father in Venice.

למה

שהיתה ההצלחה האנושית נתלית בעיון ובמעשה כמו שבאר הפילוסוף בספר הנפש והיו הדעות האמתיות והמעשים המשובחים אי אפשר שיושגו על נכון מצד השכל האנושי להיות שכל האדם לואה מהשיג הדברים על אמתתם כמי שיהא מחויב בהכרח שימצא דבר הוא למעלה מהשכל האנושי על ידו יוגבלו המעשים המשובחים ויושכלו הדעות האמתיות בענין שלא יהיה בהם שום ספק כלל וזה לא יהיה אלא בהישרה אלהית וע״כ היה ראוי ומחוייב על כל האדם להכיר הדת האלהית המישרת לזה מזולתה מן הדתות וז׳ לא יתכן אלא בידיעת העקרים שאי אפשר שתמצא הדת האלהית זולתם והיא היתה כוונת החבור הז׳ לבאר העקרים ההכרחיים לדת האלהית כמה הם ובעבור זה נקר׳ שמו ספר העקרי׳ ויחלק להקדמ׳ וד׳ מאמרי׳ :

הקדמה היא להודיע ההכרח המביא לחבר הספר והחקירות שראוי שיפלו בו דרך כלל ויתבאר בה גודל מעלת החקירה הנופלת בזה הספר ויפרש בה פסוק ויהי נועם :

המאמר הראשון

יחקור מעיקרי הדתו׳ כמה הם ואי אלו הם וההבדל שיש בין הדתות האלהיות והנימוסיות ואי אלו הם עקרי הדת האלהי׳ ואי אלו הם עקרי הדת הנימוסית ויבאר שיש לדתות עיקרים כוללים ועקרים מיוחדי׳ ושהעקרים הכוללים לדתות האלהיות הם ג׳ שהם מציאות השם ותורה מן השמים ושכר ועונש ויבאר שיש תחת אלו עקרים אחרי׳ נתלים בהם ומסתעפי׳ מהם ויבאר במה תוכר הדת האלהית מן הדת המזוייפת המתדמה באלהית :

המאמר השני

בביאור העקר הראשו׳ שהוא מציאות השם והעקרים הנתלים בו ומסתעפים ממנו :

המאמר השלישי

בביאור עקר הב׳ שהוא תורה מן השמים והעקרים הנתלים בו ומסתעפים ממנו :

המאמר הרביעי

בביאור עיקר הג׳ שהוא שכר ועונש והעקרים המסתעפים ממנו והדברים הנתלים בו :

המאמר הראשון

בחקירה מעקרי הדתות כמה הם ויחלק אל שש ועשרים פרקים

פרק ראשון

יודיע בו הקושי שיש בחקירה על העקרים לדתות ויאמר שיש שם עקרים כוללים וחלקיים לכל דת ודת ויקשה על הרמב״ם ז״ל שמנה ביאת המשיח מעקרי תורת משה וכן יקשה על האומרים שחדוש העולם עקר לתורה משה :

פרק שני

יבאר בו מי הוא המכחיש דבר מן העקרים שיקרא

עיקרים א ב ו וו

8. love of the book

Opening page of the *hakdamah* of *Sefer ha-Ikkarim* by Joseph Albo (c.1380–1435), with the first word in woodcut. In the *hakdamah* the author presents the reader with a "table of contents," and this is clearly visible in the arrangement of this edition by Daniel Bomberg, Venice, 1521. J.N.U.L., Jerusalem.

There are two main aspects to bibliophilia: the relationship of the author to the book, and that of the reader. The love which the author bears towards his creation manifests itself in many ways, of which the most important are the book's physical beauty, the manner in which its value is made apparent, and the name which he gives his work. From a pyschological standpoint, this last matter can be compared to naming a child, and indeed often the author includes his own name or the names of close relatives in the title he gives his book, usually in some hidden form such as *gematria.* The feelings of the reader to the book are manifested in the way he treats the book, in how he has it bound, in how he sets about collecting books, and in the type of bookcase he keeps his books in. A third relationship towards the book is revealed in the way the book is printed and distributed, which functions are performed by people standing between the author and the reader, as it were.

Another type of relationship, albeit negative, is manifested in the matter of censorship which, although at first glance seems to suggest hatred of the book, is of course a clear indication of appreciation for the power of the book. A study of the history of censorship therefore provides a comprehensive lesson about the love for the Hebrew book.

The first real dissemination of an original, bound, Hebrew book is linked with the intensive exegetical activity devoted by the *geonim* to the Babylonian Talmud, written at the request of Diaspora Jews who had difficulty in understanding it. Their commentary was accompanied by a literature of responsa – at first brief, but later longer and more detailed – to practical questions of *Halakhah* and everyday life. The responsa of the *geonim* and their commentaries on the Talmud were put together by the questioners in *kontresim,* pamphlets, bound together according to a common topic, a common author, or any other feature they might have in common. These pamphlets, many of them quite large in scope and quantity, were the first Hebrew books – in the technical meaning of the term – to be widely distributed. Many copies were made in Babylon itself, at intermediate stations (especially Egypt) en route to the questioners (mainly in North Africa and Spain) and by the recipients, and many more copies were made of these copies. To each of these pamphlets was generally appended a table-of-contents and sometimes all that has survived is that table, with whose aid we can reconstruct the original composition of the ancient pamphlets by comparison with surviving copies found in the Cairo *Genizah* and printed literature. The distribution of this geonic material brought in its wake a wider distribution of the Mishnah and the Talmud throughout all the countries of the Diaspora.

The first to write a full-scale book, with a plan and structure determined in advance, a book in the modern meaning of the word, was Saadiah Gaon. He wrote scores of books on a wide range of topics. He was also the first to write on Jewish topics in Arabic. Saadiah Gaon gave literary expression to the revolution he introduced in the development of the Hebrew book in the forewords he wrote to all his books. He was the first to write a foreword to a Hebrew book. Other books prior to Saadiah Gaon should be noted, but they are not books in the full sense of the word as they are with him: the *She'iltot de-Rav Aḥa* and the two books *Halakhot Gedolot* and *Halakhot Pesukot.* The first prayerbook, accompanied by laws, was also put together in the time of the *geonim* by Amram Gaon, in response to a request by the inhabitants of Lucena in Spain. From then on the Hebrew book spread throughout the Diaspora, and for hundreds of years after the time of Saadiah Gaon, hundreds and thousands of books were written on every topic and in every country. Many of the books from these periods have come down to us only in fragments, in quotations or merely in references. Many lists of books have been preserved in the *Genizah,* compiled by book owners, copyists and booksellers, and from these we learn of many books that have perished, of the distribution of different Hebrew books and of their binding, preservation, price etc. These book lists are of immense historical and literary importance.

The main cultural phenomenon connected with the development of the Hebrew book in these periods is the application of the rules of sanctity – originally applied to the Bible – to any Hebrew book written in Hebrew characters which are sacred. There are many rules and customs which show respect for books: they must not be thrown or left upside down, one may not sit on a chair on which a book is lying, a book must not be used for any purpose except reading, and many more. A book which is worn out is stored in the synagogue and after a time all the worn

A page of *Seder Rav Amram,* by Amram ben Sheshna (died 875), *gaon* of Sura. The *Seder* is the first known order of prayers ever compiled, and was undertaken by Rav Amram in response to a query addressed to him by Jews who had newly settled in Spain. The page shows the *Aleinu* prayer with a censored portion. The manuscript is of Spanish origin, written in the 13th or 14th century. British Museum, Ms. Or. 1067.

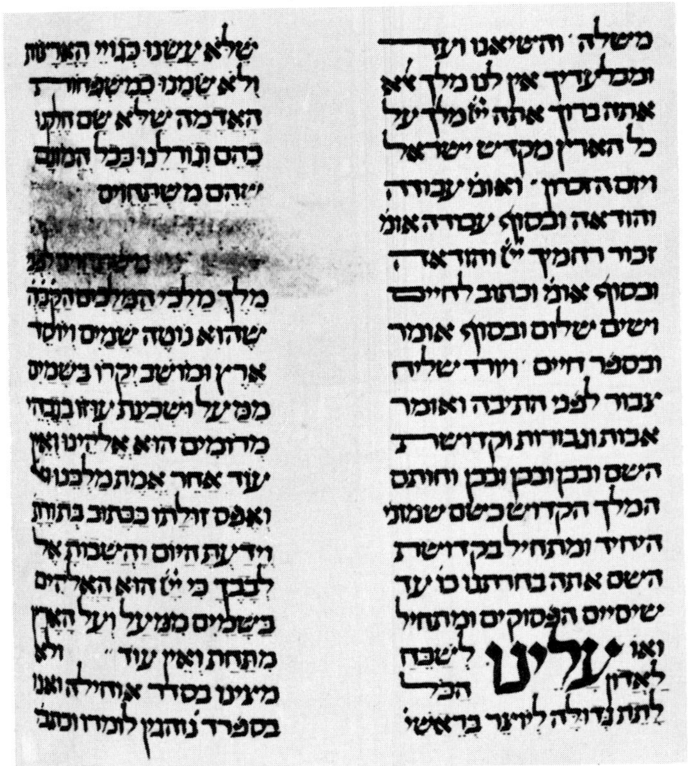

books in store are buried in the ground. The sages were quick to see that the binding of books should be beautiful and strong, that there should be rules for borrowing books – which were very expensive – and laid down various regulations for public benefit such as the prohibition (from the 11th century) which forbade the seizure of a book on account of any manner of debt whatever (with the exception of a school teacher who was permitted to seize the text-books from which he taught). On other questions the sages were divided, such as whether the borrower of a book was permitted to copy from it; this was a sort of "infringement of copyright" and reduced the financial value of the book, though there was profit in the wider dissemination of knowledge. The obligation to lend books played an important role among Ḥasidei Ashkenaz, the medieval sect of pietists, who almost completely denied absolute ownership of books and regarded the owner as someone who merely held the book in trust, a part owner of the book – which really belonged to whoever was studying from it – who shared with the student the reward for fulfilling the commandment of studying Torah. In every generation there were rich men, great Jews who spent huge sums on the purchase of books for their private libraries, and paid copyists to sit and copy these books, and sent them free of charge to academies and distant communities who had no books. Famous among these in the 11th century in Spain were Ḥisdai ibn Shaprut, Samuel ha-Nagid, and many other scholars.

The "publication" of a book in the Middle Ages generally meant in effect the handing over of a book by its author to his students for copying and dissemination, and since they were his students, the copies were reliable. After this stage it became impossible to make any corrections, since the copies had already been distributed in all directions; this problem has disturbed authors at all times. Isaac Alfasi, the great Talmud commentator and codifier of the 11th century "gave orders for corrections" in his books, and his students carried them out and tried to pass on the corrections along the chain of copies which had been made from the beginning. In later times the practice took root of publishing a "second or further edition" of a book, and sometimes the different versions have survived side by side in their entirety, each one a different book compared with its predecessor, as happened with the work of Isaiah di Trani. Very often the versions have been combined, especially when both are short and the differences between them few but sharp, and "our" text is a blend of the original and the corrections which can no longer be distinguished.

Until the establishment of the great Hebrew printing houses in Poland in the first third of the 19th century, Hebrew publishing was in the hands of the authors or the printers, depending on the book, the copyright and the terms of its financing. A fundamental difference existed at all times between new books and sacred classics – the prayerbook, the Talmud, the Bible, and the works of the great rabbinic interpreters of the Law, Alfasi, Jacob ben Asher, Maimonides – which were not bound by copyright. These holy books constituted the majority of Hebrew books printed during the first 70 years of printing, and the initiative for the work came exclusively from the printers themselves. The printing, which was expensive, was free and subject to commercial competition. The first printer-publishers to become famous in this field were Bomberg and Giustiniani from Venice (who were not Jewish) and the Soncino family at the beginning of the same century, who worked in Italy and Eastern Europe.

With the development and improvement of the art of printing grew the conviction that the printers – who had invested money, time and effort in establishing a new format (of typography and pagination) for the great sacred books – were entitled to copyright on the format they had created; however, printers did not obtain genuine legal approval of copyright in the eyes of *Halakhah* (and/or the civil authorities), until the 19th century. Against this background there took place the great quarrels between the different printer-publishers, who maintained that they had been robbed of the rights accruing to them from their "format" (especially with respect to the Talmud). Many authors had their books printed at their own expense, either with what money they had at their disposal or by collecting contributions for the purpose before printing, and sometimes the book was printed, and even sold, section by section, as the money became available. Another method was to get subscribers to guarantee payment in advance. The names of these subscribers were usually printed in later times, especially in Poland and Eastern Europe, in a special list at the end of the book, a tribute both to the subscribers and the book. Many books were printed with the aid of rich local benefactors, who are praised for their action by the authors in their forewords. The printing-house of the Nasi family, near Constantinople, acted as a Maecenas and at its own

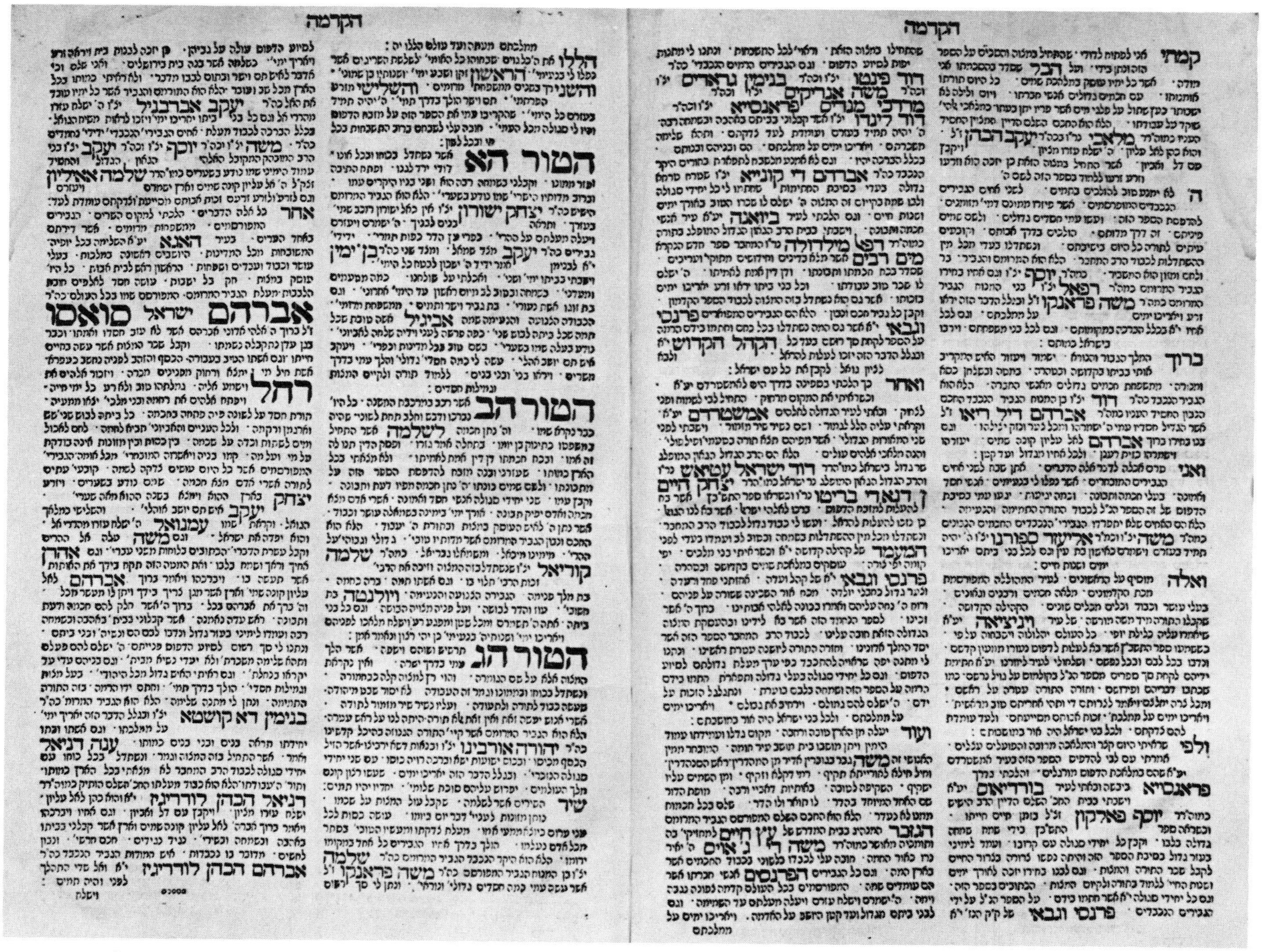
הקדמה

הקדמה

Two pages from the *hakdamah* by Meir Crescas, who brought to the press Simeon ben Ẓemah Duran's *Tashbeẓ*, Amsterdam, 1741. In this lengthy foreword, the editor lists all the people who had helped him with funds and effort, in the various countries in which he had sought financial backing for printing this large book. The names of the backers are printed in large letters, and about 30 names can be counted on these two pages — only part of the list.

expense printed important books by scholars of that period and place. Manasseh ben Israel, who wrote many books, established a commercial press to print them, and also printed many other books. A publisher's catalog (the earliest of its kind that has survived) has come down to us from this press, and from it we can learn both the prices of the books and the methods of distribution. We can also learn the prices of books from various early lists in the *Genizah*. The number of copies printed in an "edition" did not usually exceed 1,000. There was no such thing as organized distribution until the 19th century. Many important books were not known, sometimes for many years, outside the town (or country) where they were printed. In the correspondence which took place between Jewish scholars in different countries we find repeated requests for assistance with information concerning books that had been printed and ways to acquire them. This state of affairs continued into the period of the Haskalah, and even later.

The first organized distribution in the world of the Jewish book was perhaps that established by the Ḥevrat Mekiẓei Nirdamim ("the Company of Wakers of the Sleeping") which functioned by means of subscribing members who undertook to acquire the books that would be published, in exchange for annual subscriptions. A similar method of advance subscription was practiced by the Romm family for the publication of their great edition of the Talmud in Vilna, 1880–1884.

HEBREW BOOK TITLES

THE BIBLE. There is no single designation common to all Jews and employed in all periods by which the Jewish Scriptures have been known. The earliest and most diffused Hebrew term was *Ha-Sefarim* ("The Books"). Its antiquity is supported by its use in Daniel in references to the prophets (Daniel 9:2). This is how the sacred writings are frequently referred to in tannaitic literature (*Megillah* 1:8; *Mo'ed Katan* 3:4; *Gittin* 4:6; *Kelim* 15:6; et al.). The Greek-speaking Jews adopted this usage and translated it into their vernacular as τὰ βιβλία. The earliest record of such is the Letter of Aristeas (mid-second century b.c.e.) which uses the singular form (v. 316, ἐν τῇ βίβλῳ) for the Pentateuch. The translator of The Wisdom of Ben Sira into Greek (c. 132 b.c.e.) similarly employs "The Books" to designate the entire Scriptures (Ecclesiasticus, prologue v. 25: καὶ τὰ λοιπὰ τῶν βιβλίων). It is from this Hellenistic Jewish usage, which entered European languages through its Latin form, that the English "Bible" is derived.

The term *Sifrei ha-Kodesh* ("Holy Books"), although not found in Hebrew literature before the Middle Ages, seems to have been used occasionally by Jews even in pre-Christian times. The author of I Maccabees (12:9), who certainly wrote in Hebrew (c. 136–135 b.c.e.), speaks of "the Holy Books" (τὰ βιβλία τὰ ἅγια). In the early first century c.e., the Greek writer of II Maccabees 8:23 mentions "the Holy Book" (τὴν ιἐρὰν βίβλον) and toward the end of that century, both Josephus (Antiquities 20:261) and Pope Clement I (*First Epistle*, 43:1) refer to "the Holy Books." The appelation is rare, however, since the increasing restriction of *sefer* in rabbinic Hebrew to sacred literature rendered superfluous any further description. On the other hand, *Kitvei ha-Kodesh* ("Holy Writings"), is fairly common in tannaitic sources as a designation for the Scriptures (Shabbat 16:1; Eravin 10:3; Yadaim 3:2, 5; 4:6; Bava Batra 1:6; Parah 10:3). Here the definition "Holy" is required since the Hebrew root *ktv* ("write") did not develop a specialized meaning and was equally employed for secular writing (cf. Tosefta, *Yom Tov* 4:4). The title "Holy Writings" was also current in Jewish Hellenistic and in Christian circles, appearing in Greek as αἱ ἱεραὶ γραφαί (Philo, *De Fuga et Inventione* 1:4; Clement's *First Epistle* 45:2; 53:1), as τὰ ἱερὰ δράμματα (Philo,*De Vita Mosis* 2:290, 292; Josephus, Antiquities, 1:13; 10: 210; et al; and as γραφαί ἅγαι (Romans 1:2). Closely allied to the preceding is the title *Ha-Katuv* ("The Scripture"; *Pe'ah* 8:9; *Ta'anit,* 3:8; *Sanhedrin* 4:5; *Avot* 3:7,8, et al.) and the plural *Ha-Ketuvim* ("The Scriptures"; Yadayin 3:5 et al.). These, too, were taken over by the Jews of Alexandria in the Greek equivalent, probably the earliest such example being the Letter of Aristeas (vv. 155, 168). This term was borrowed by the early Christians (η γραφὴ John 2:22; Acts 8:32: II Timothy 3:16 et al.; αἱ γραφαί Mark 12:24; I Corinthians 15:34 et al.; τὰ γράμματα John 5:47).

These uses of the Hebrew root *ktv* ("to write") to specify the Scriptures have special significance, for they lay emphasis on the written nature of the text in contradistinction to the oral form in which the rabbinic teachings were transmitted. In the same way, *Mikra* (literally "reading"), another term for the Bible current among the rabbis, serves to underline both the vocal manner of study and the central role that the public reading of the Scriptures played in the liturgy of the Jews. The designation is found in tannaitic sources (*Nedarim* 4:3; *Avot* 5:21; TJ, *Ta'anit,* 4:2), but it may be much older, as Nehemiah 8:8 suggests. It is of interest that *Mikra* as the Hebrew for "Bible" achieved wide popularity among Jews in the Middle Ages. The acronym תַּנַ"ךְ (*TaNaKh*),

Miniature in an opening to a Byzantine Octateuch, 11th century, illustrating the Letter of Aristeas, in which is found the first recorded use of the term "Bible." King Ptolemy is shown ordering his scribe to write a letter to Eleazar the high priest to instigate the translation of the Bible into Greek. Vatican Library, Ms. Gr. 747, fol. 2v.

derived from the initial letters of the names of the three divisions of the Bible (*Torah, Nevi'im, Ketuvim*), became similarly popular.

Still another expression for the Scriptures is Torah, used in the widest sense of the term as the revelation of religion. While it is only occasionally so employed for the Bible in rabbinic literature (cf. *Moed Katan* 5a with respect to Ezekiel 39:15; *Sanhedrin* 91b citing Psalms 84:5; *Pesikta Rabbati* 3:9, in reference to Ecclesiastes 12:12), the fact that *νόμος*, the Greek rendering of Torah, is found in the New Testament in the same way (John 10:34, quoting Psalms 82:6) indicates that it may once have been in more common use among Jews.

Thoroughly Christian is the characterization "Old Testament" (i.e. Covenant; II Corinthians 3:14; cf. Hebrew 9:15–18). This term is used to distinguish the Jewish Bible from the "New Testament" (i.e. Covenant; I Corinthians 11:25; II Corinthians 3:6; Christian interpretation of Jeremiah 31:30–32). At the same time, it is possible that the designation "Testament" (i.e. "Covenant," Gr.: *διαθήκη*) may have been a reflection of an extended use among Jews of the Hebrew *berit* ("covenant") or *Sefer ha-Berit* ("Book of the Covenant"; Exodus 24:7; II Kings 23:2, 21). Jeremiah (31:30–32) himself uses "covenant" and "Torah" synonymously, and the "Book of the Torah" found in the Temple (II Kings 22:8,10) is alternatively styled the "Book of the Covenant" (*ibid.* 23:2,21). The Wisdom of Ben Sira (24:23) actually uses the latter term *βιβλως διαθήκης* parallel with Torah (*νόμος*) and a similar usage is found in I Maccabees 1:56–57.

TALMUDIC LITERATURE. In the Mishnah and Talmud the names of orders and tractates reflect contents rather than authorship, but the unwieldy size of tractate *Nezikin,* homonymous with the entire order, led to its being divided into *Bava Kamma, Bava Meẓia,* and *Bava Batra*("the first, middle, and last gate"). Chapters, which were not numbered, are quoted by one or several initial words. Alternatives to the title Talmud ("study") are *Gemara* ("learning"), or the abbreviation ש״ס *(shas),* for *Shishah Sedarim,* the six orders of the Mishnah and Talmud. The oldest Midrashim on the books of the Pentateuch, take their titles either from these books (e.g., *Torat Kohanim* "priestly law" but later *Sifra,* "a book"), from their use as textbooks (e.g., *Sifrei de-vei-Rav,* "school-books"), or from their hermeneutic character (*Mekhilta,* "canons"). Aggadic Midrashim bear either the generic name of Midrash added to that of the biblical book (e.g., *Midrash Shemu'el* or *Midrash Tehillim*) – sometimes with the word *Rabbah* ("great") added, or that of a talmudic teacher reputed to be its compiler (e.g. *Midrash Tanḥuma,* which is also called *Yelammedenu* from a characteristic opening phrase, and the *Pesikta de-Rav Kahana*). Later Midrashim have more fanciful titles such as *Lekaḥ Tov* ("Good Teaching," Proverbs 4:2), *Shoḥer Tov* ("Seeker of Good," Proverbs 11:27) etc. Midrash אַבְכִּיר *(Avkir)* derived its name from the initials of the concluding peroration אָמֵן, בְּיָמֵינוּ כֵּן יְהִי רָצוֹן ("Amen, in our days, may it be [His] will").

In geonic literature titles express the general nature of their compilations, such as *Halakhot Gedolot* or *Halakhot Pesukot* ("Great Rules" and "Clear Decisions") or these together with the author's name (e.g. *She'iltot* – ritual questions – and answers – of Aḥai Gaon; the *seder* of Rav Amram, or of Saadiah Gaon).

THE MIDDLE AGES. In the Middle Ages, with the great increase in Hebrew literature of all sorts, there was a proliferation of titles, which may be roughly classified as follows:

Names as Titles. The names or abbreviations of names of the leading exegetic or halakhic authors are now used to describe their works, such as Rashi (whose Talmud commentary was also called by the generic name *Kunteres,* from *commentarius*) RaSHBA (Rabbi Solomon ben Abraham Adret), RoSH (Rabbi Asher ben Jehiel), Mordecai (ben Hillel) etc. Often the particular nature of the work (*tosafot,* "glosses"; *ḥiddushim,* "novellae"; *she'elot u-teshuvot,* "responsa") precedes the name. Later the names of authors appear as part of titles taken from a biblical phrase such as the *Ein Ya'akov* (Deuteronomy 33:28) by Jacob ibn Habib; *Kaftor va-Feraḥ* (Exodus 25:33) by Estori Farhi; *Paḥad Yiẓḥak* (Genesis 31:53) by Isaac Lampronti or *Magen Avraham* by Abraham Gombiner. Combinations of names with the word *beit* ("house of"), *sha'ar* or *sha'arei* ("gate" or "gates of"), *minḥat* and *korban* ("offering of"), *derekh* ("way of"), *even* ("stone of"), *yad* ("hand of") etc. are very frequent. While almost all titles in medieval (and post-medieval) religious literature began with the word *sefer* ("book of"), in some cases the word *maḥberet* or *maḥbarot* ("composition of") was used in combination with the author's name, e.g. *Maḥbarot Menaḥem* (ben Saruk, a dictionary); *Maḥbarot Immanuel* (of Rome, poems). The author's desire for anonymity, stemming from a genuine or assumed modesty, was in constant conflict with that of per-

ספר
בר ששת

Bar Sheshet, responsa by Isaac ben Sheshet (Ribash), called by the name of the author's father. On the title page appear the words "written by his son Isaac." Isaac ben Sheshet was the foremost halakhic authority of 14th-century North African Jewry. The book was printed in Riva di Trento, 1559.

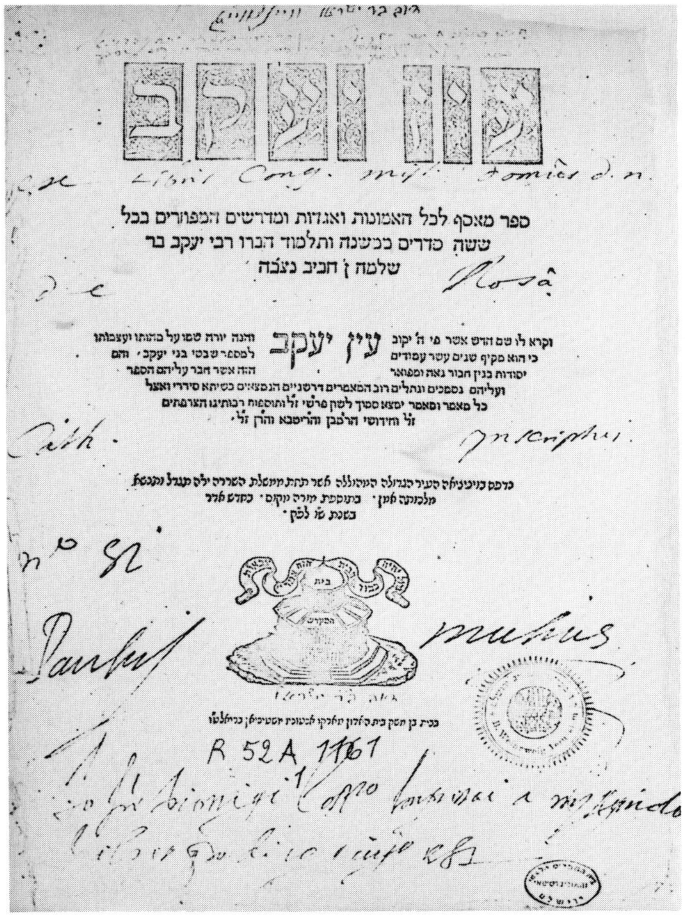
עין יעקב
R 52A 1161

Title page of *Ein Ya'akov* by Jacob ben Solomon ibn Habib (c. 1460–1516), printed by Marco Antonio Giustiniani in Rialto, Venice, 1546. The book is a collation of all the *midrashim* and *aggadot* found in the Talmud, and its title illustrates the common practice of naming a book by choosing a biblical phrase containing at least one of the author's names. J.N.U.L., Jerusalem.

petuating his or his father's name; the result was devious titles, both concealing and revealing. Thus Joseph ibn Kaspi (of L'Argentiere, "silver"; 13th–14th centuries) incorporated this byname in all his works; *Adnei Kesef* ("Sockets of Silver," Exodus 26:19), *Ḥaẓoẓerot Kesef* ("Silver Trumpets," Numbers 10:2), *Kesef Sigim* ("Silver Drops," Proverbs 26:23), etc.

Titles Reflecting Contents. In the Middle Ages this way of titling books was widely adopted. Saadiah Gaon called his treatise the *Book of Beliefs and Opinions,* and the title of Judah Halevi's philosophic dialogues, *Kuzari* ("The Khazars") reflects their imaginary framework. Similarly, titles such as Ibn Gabirol's *Mekor Ḥayyim* ("Source of Life"), Maimonides' *Guide of the Perplexed,* and Albo's *Ikkarim* ("Principles") express the basic idea or purpose of the works in question. In the same vein Maimonides called his code *Mishneh Torah* ("Repetition of the Torah" alluding both to Deuteronomy 17:18 and to Judah ha-Nasi's Mishnah), though it was also called the *Yad ha-Ḥazakah* ("The Strong Hand," Deuteronomy 34:12), since the numerical value of *yad* is 14, the number of books into which the code is divided. There are several works called "Book of Precepts," *(Sefer Mitzvot),* one by Maimonides (originally in Arabic), one by Moses of Coucy, and the *Sefer Mitzvot Katan* of Isaac ben Joseph of Corbeil. Israel Najara wrote a short manual of *sheḥitah* for youngsters, to which he gave the equivocal title of *Shoḥatei ha-Yeladim* ("Slaughterers of Children").

Metaphorical Titles. These occasionally overlap with the previous categories, as can be seen from examples mentioned above. However, most of these fanciful appellations do not provide the uninformed reader with any clue to the true contents of the work. Jacob ben Asher called his code *Arba'ah Turim* ("Four Rows") from the four rows of precious stones on the high priest's breastplate (Exodus 28:17); Joseph Caro named his code *Shulḥan Arukh* ("Prepared Table"; Ezekiel 23:41); and Moses Isserles entitled his annotations to it *Mappah* ("Tablecloth"). Early halakhic compendia bore such titles as *Eshkol* ("Cluster of Grapes"), and *Shibbolei ha-Leket* ("Gleanings of Corn"). In his work *Levushim* ("Garments"), Mordecai Jaffe named each of the ten sections with one of the epithets of the biblical Mordecai's attire (Esther 8:15). Solomon ibn Gabirol called his philosophic treatise *Keter Malkhut* "Royal Crown"; the kabbalistic classic is known as the *Sefer ha-Zohar* ("Book of Splendor") and kabbalistic literature in general indulged in euphuistic titles which usually expressed some mystical idea as well; e.g. *Eẓ ha-Ḥayyim* ("Tree of Life") by Hayyim Vital and *Tomer Devorah* ("Palm Tree of Deborah") by Moses Cordovero.

The *gematria* system of using the numerical value of letters and words also played a great part. Thus the responsa of Simeon ben Ẓemaḥ Duran were named *Tashbeẓ* – this was not only the abbreviation of *Teshuvot Shimon ben Ẓemaḥ* and the biblical term "chequer-work" (Exodus 28:4), but also its numerical value was 792, the number of responsa included in the work. In the responsa and homeletic literature of the last 200 years, a common phenomenon has been the creation of a *gematria* relating to the name of the book and the name of the author, his parents or his children etc. The first known book of which the name is explicitly created by a *gematria* is the *Sefer ha-Rokeaḥ* of Eleazar of Worms; the author points to this fact in his introduction. Apparently he was the first to be guided by the principle that "every man should include his name in his book," and in the literature of Ḥasidei Ashkenaz this was done by hinting at the name of the author through *gematria*.

In some cases an abbreviation based on initials displaced the title in common parlance: a typical example (apart from the classical case of Rashi) is *Shelah* (for *Shenei Luḥot ha-Berit*). The author, Isaiah Horowitz, became generally known as Ba'al ha-Shelah ("the author of the Shelah"), and sometimes by paradoxical rebound the book was popularly called by this latter title. Similarly the Pentateuch commentary ascribed to Jacob ben Asher, author of the *Arba'ah Turim*, is known as the *Ba'al ha-Turim*.

The importance the Jews attached to a man's literary or scholarly work caused authors like those mentioned above to be known almost exclusively by the titles or abbreviation of titles of their books, such as the Shelah just mentioned, or the Ḥatam Sofer (title of Moses Sofer's works: responsa, novellae etc.), the Ḥafeẓ Ḥayyim (Israel ha-Kohen of Radun, after his ethical treatise of that name), the Ḥazon Ish (Abraham Isaiah Karelitz, after the title of his novellae).

Some titles seemingly chosen simply from biblical personal or place names – e.g., *Avi'ezer* (by Eliezer ben Joel ha-Levi); *Taḥkemoni* (by Judah Al-Ḥarizi); *Tishbi* (by Elijah Levita) – usually contained an allusion to the author's name.

Initial Words as Titles. As with biblical and midrashic literature, medieval works were also occasionally called by their initial word or words, e.g. *Tanya*, the

Title page of *Tomer Devorah* by Moses Cordovero (1522–1570), printed in Mantua, 1623. This is a good example of an obscure, metaphoric book title which does not provide the uninformed reader with any clue to its contents. *Tomer Devorah* ("The Palm Tree of Deborah") is a book of religious ethics in kabbalistic terms. J.N.U.L., Jerusalem.

ספר
תומר דבורה
והוא מאמר נכבד מהרב המקובל האלהי
כמהר"ר
משה קורדואירו ז"ל
פה מנטובה
Con licenza de' Superiori. 1623.

ספר
שני לוחות הברית
אמרות טהורות · מפנינים יקרות · חבור על שתי תורות · בכתב
ובפה מסיני מסורות · ערוכות וסדורות · מהגבור בגבורות ·
איש אלהי בוצינא קדישא מרא דארעא דישראל · החכם
השלם בכל מדות וחכמות גלויות וסתומות · הגאון
אשר שפעת יפעת אור תורתו · זרח בכל
התפוצה · מקצה אל קצה · כבוד מה״ר
ישעיה במהור״ר אברהם הלוי זצ״ל
ממשפחת הורוויץ · הספון וטמון
במנוחתו בארעא קדישא
ונשמתו בגנזי מרומים תחות כורסיה דעתיקא קדישא:
וברכה לראש משביר · נאור וכביר · בן דמתבר · ענף עץ אבות העשר הגדול בעל כנפים הפורש
כנפיו לתיכון שם החכמה והמדע ותבונה אבן ראשה אבן פנה החסיד ועניו הגאון הגדול
מופת דורנו כמה״רר שעפטל סג״ל נר״ו · אב״ד ור״מ דק״ק פוזנא והגליל
יצ״ו · אשר נתן לבו ונפשו להביא ספר הנכבד הזה לדפוס להאיר
עיני חכמים באור יקר · המזהיר ומזהיר כזוהר
ספר הקדש הזה כאשר יחזו עיני מישרים ·
כישאל איש בתומים ואורים :
באמשטרדם
בדפוס ומשובח של
הבחור והחשוב עמנואל בן חישיש הנכבר יוסף עטיאש יצ״ו
בשנת בשובה ונחת הרשטן לפ״ק

Shenei Luḥot ha-Berit by Isaiah ha-Levi Horowitz, Amsterdam, 1698. This book is popularly known as *Ha-Shelah ha-Kaddosh* (the Holy Shelah – the acronym of the title), or simply the *Shelah*, but never by its full title. There is a popular tradition that it was never called by its proper name because of the audacity of the title, since the "Two Tablets of the Law" were given only once, and it is not fitting to call something else by this name. Therefore the description "The Holy" was added. Similarly, Moses Alshekh's biblical commentary, that he had entitled *Torat Moshe* ("The Law of Moses"; Belvedere, 1597; Venice, 1601) was also popularly known as "The Holy Alshekh." J.N.U.L., Jerusalem.

title of a 14th-century ritual and one popularly given to Shneur Zalman's *Likkutei Amarim*.

"Follow-up" Titles. These were often used for commentaries, like the previously mentioned *Mappah* for the *Shulḥan Arukh*. Shem Tov Falaquera gave his commentary to Maimonides' *Moreh Nevukhim* the title *Moreh ha-Moreh* ("Guide to the Guide"), and Naḥman Krochmal wrote a *Moreh Nevukhei ha-Zeman* ("Guide for the Perplexed of the Time"), Solomon ben Abraham Adret's *Torat ha-Bayit* ("Law of the House," Isaiah 30:9) was criticized by Aaron ha-Levi in his *Bedek ha-Bayit* ("Repair of the House," II Kings 12:6) and this was countered by Adret by his *Mishmeret ha-Bayit* ("Guard of the House," *ibid.*, 11:6). Samuel ben David ha-Levi's *Turei Zahav* ("Circlets of Gold") prompted Shabbetai Kohen to write *Nekuddot ha-Kesef* ("Studs of Silver," cf. Song of Songs 1:11). Further classifications and subclassifications can and have been made. For translators the older Hebrew book titles sometimes present a problem.

MODERN TIMES. While the medieval manner of entitling rabbinic books has continued into modern times, as exemplified by Rabbi A.I. (Ha-Kohen) Kook's responsa *(Da'at Kohen, Ezrat Kohen, Mishpat Kohen)* and other writings *(Iggerot Re'iyyah, Olat*

The *Tanya*, Shklov, 1814, the only edition with the name *Iggeret ha-Kodesh* on its title page. Its first printing, Slavuta, 1796/7, is entitled *Likkutei Amarim*, while most editions are called *Tanya*. Another common title is *Sifran shel Beinonim*, according to the author's own definition of the purpose of this book, but this title has never been printed on title pages.

אגרת הקודש
מאמו״ר ג״ע אשר כתב בכ״י הקדושה ולשונו
הטהור ומחמת שבכמ׳ מקומות הציב לו
ציונים בס׳ לקוטי אמרים שלו וד״ת עניים במ״א ועשירי׳
במ״א ומה שקיצר כזה גילה בזה ומה גם בשביל דבר
שנתחד׳ בו קונטרס אחרון על איזה פרקים לכן הדפסנו נ״כ
הספ׳ לקוטי אמרים עם אגרת התשוב׳
כל אלה חוברו יחדיו תמים מלמעלה עיר וקדיש
משמי׳ נחית הוא ניהו כ״ק ארמו״ר הגדול
הגאון האלקי אור עולם מופת הדור נזר ישראל ותפארתו
קדוש ה׳ מכובד מרנא ורבנא שניאור זלמן נבג״מ
לפ״ט צדקת ה׳ עשה ומשפטיו עם ישראל
נדפס
בשקלאוו
תחת ממשלת ארונינו הקיסר האדיר אוסי׳ פריסלוויטש
דיערזשאוויישע וויליקי האטודאר ימפעראטאר
אלכסנדר פאוולאוויץ סאמא דיערזיטש
אווסיא ראסיסקאי האסידאר אוסיע מילאסטווישיע יר״ה
לרשיון הצענזור אשר באקדעמיא דווילנא

Re'iyyah, etc. – *Re'iyyah* being an abbreviation and a translation of his name), modern writers in Hebrew follow the prevailing standards in Western literature and scholarship, without abandoning recourse to the former Hebrew tradition. Examples are the titles of some of S.Y. Agnon's novels and short stories (such as *A Guest for the Night,* Jeremiah 14:18) and M. Shamir's *King of Flesh and Blood,* a frequent midrashic phrase.

THE FOREWORD

The first known *hakdamah* is the introduction to the *Halakhot Gedolot.* In effect it is a sermon in praise of the Torah which its author saw fit to place at the beginning of his book as a preface. In medieval literature the *hakdamah* served as a literary genre and halakhic authors regarded themselves duty bound to attach a *hakdamah* to their works. Generally speaking the author in his *hakdamah* gives his motives for writing the book, and says something about its contents, but very often the *hakdamah* has important literary value of its own. Spanish and Italian authors also gave their *hakdamot* an aesthetic form by means of rhyme, meter, and even verses and complete poems, and some of them are literary gems. Especially noteworthy are those of Naḥmanides who wrote many fine *hakdamot,* of especial merit being those to his *Milḥamot ha-Shem* and his *Torat ha-Adam.* Some *hakdamot* are complete works, both in scope and in quality, and of these the introduction of Menaḥem ben Solomon Meiri to his commentary *Beit ha-Beḥirah* on *Avot* is especially noteworthy. Occasionally the contents, purpose and scope of the book cannot be fathomed without the *hakdamah.* Because the ordinary reader usually omits the reading of the *hakdamah,* and because copying (on parchment) was usually a very expensive enterprise, some authors literally adjured copyists not to copy their works without the introduction, as did, for example, the anonymous author of *Ha-Ḥinukh.* So important was the *hakdamah* regarded that a popular proverb has it that "a book without a *hakdamah* is like a body without a *neshamah*" ("soul").

The *hakdamah* attained full development with Saadiah Gaon, in the tenth century. A systematic thinker, he found it necessary to explain what had motivated him to treat the particular subject he had chosen, thus laying the foundation of his thesis as well as apprising the reader of the content of the book he was presenting. He followed this pattern in his *siddur* and particularly in his philosophical work, the *Sefer ha-Emunot ve-ha-De'ot.* In his rather lengthy introduction he states that he wrote this book in order to resolve the doubts and confusions of his contemporaries concerning their traditional faith. The method followed by Saadiah Gaon was further developed and perfected by Moses Maimonides. He used his prefaces to certain orders, tractates, chapters of the Mishnah and sections of his great code, the *Mishneh Torah,* to expound his own philosophical ideas, in addition to elucidating such recondite subjects as the various degrees of ritual inpurity dealt with in the order of *Tohorot.* Thus, in the "Eight Chapters" prefacing his commentary on the tractate *Avot,* he unfolds a complete system of ethics while in his introduction to the tenth chapter of the tractate *Sanhedrin,* where the afterlife is mentioned, he discusses resurrection, listing what he regards as the fundamentals of Jewish belief, the 13 "principles" of Judaism. Maimonides' philosophical magnum opus, the *Guide of the Perplexed,* has both a short dedicatory preface addressed to his favorite pupil for whom it was written, as well as a fairly extensive general introduction, outlining his understanding of the text of Scripture which, according to him, cannot always be taken literally. He also cautions the reader not to judge the merit of his book by a few isolated statements but to consider it in its totality and with the same seriousness with which it was written. Among the medieval Jewish scholars whose prefaces to their works are worthy of note, Abraham ibn Ezra stands high on the list. In a rhymed introduction to his commentary on the Pentateuch, after dismissing as worthless four other methods of interpretation, he summarizes his own approach, namely that of a critical understanding of the biblical text, making use of all the aids of philology available, regardless of the conclusions to which such an approach may lead.

The prefaces of books by medieval Jewish authors started out, like those of the Muslim writers of the time, with praise of God. With the introduction of printing it became customary for publishers, editors, and even proofreaders to write prefaces asking the indulgence of the readers for typographical errors and mistakes due to other causes.

THE RECOMMENDATION

Although the Hebrew term *haskamah* (literally "agreement") has several different usages, it most

הקדמה לרבי לוי בן גרשון ב

אמר

החלק הראשון

והחלק

Opening page of the *hakdamah* of Levi ben Gershom (Gersonides) of Avignon (1288–1344) to his commentary on the Pentateuch. Among the foremost of the later medieval philosophers, Gersonides used his *hakdamah* to present an analytical classification of the concept *Torah*. From the edition printed in the house of Daniel Bomberg, Venice, 1546. J.N.U.L., Jerusalem.

commonly refers to the recommendation given by a scholar or a rabbi to a book or a treatise.

ORIGINS AND HISTORY. Various opinions have been offered on the origin or development of the *haskamah* for books. Some see the influence of the *approbatio* of the Church, others see it as resulting from the papal action of 1553 in the dispute between the publishing houses of Bragadani and Giustiniani which resulted in the burning of the Talmud. The first *haskamah* appeared in the 15th century, in the *Agur* by Jacob Landau (Naples, c. 1490), the first Hebrew book printed during its author's lifetime; it was signed by seven rabbis. The *haskamah* for Elijah Levita's *Sefer ha-Baḥur* (Rome, 1519) signed by the rabbi of Rome, threatens excommunication for republication within ten years. Thus the *haskamah* fulfilled the function of a copyright, the period of protection extending from five to 25 years. The *haskamah* in Joseph Caro's *Bedek ha-Bayit* (Venice, 1606) is signed by three rabbis (the number of *haskamot* varied from book to book); and it concluded with a declaration by the sexton that he has read it in all the synagogues of Venice. With the introduction of title pages in the 16th century, *haskamot* came to be printed at the beginning rather than at the end of a book.

Thus, the *haskamah* developed from a recommendation to an expression of approval to a method of protecting the author's rights and finally to a form of self-censorship to protect the Jewish community against the church censorship and later to counteract kabbalistic, pseudo-messianic, and Haskalah tendencies. Thus, at the Rabbinical Synod of Ferrara of 1554, it was enacted that no book should receive its first printing without prior approbation of three rabbis of the particular region. Similar *takkanot* were issued in Poland in 1594 and 1682. Such restrictions were used to prevent the spread of the heretical Shabbatean doctrines, or to protect the printers of the expensive Talmud editions. This led to many disputes and litigations. The majority of *haskamot* issued in the 17th and 18th centuries originated in the centers of Hebrew printing, such as Venice, Amsterdam and Constantinople. *Haskamot* were usually written in a combination of Hebrew and Aramaic, frequently using the florid style of rabbinic writings. They sometimes contain bibliographic, biographic, and geographic data, which are an important source for historians and scholars. The *haskamot* are particularly useful for reconstruction of the history of their authors themselves, because generally each *haskamah* is signed with the exact date on which it was given, including the year, month and day of the week. Many of the great ḥasidic leaders were persecuted and driven from place to place and their biographies are not exactly clear. The *haskamah* thus serves as an important primary source.

Haskamot have been much abused. Often their place and date were intentionally altered. Some writers, eager to have *haskamot* appended to their works, forged signatures and *haskamot,* as was the case in Neḥemiah Hayon's *Ha-Kolot Yeḥdalun* (Amsterdam, 1725). Earlier *maskilim* used forged approbations to

Two closely-packed pages of *haskamot* to *Lev Aryeh* by Judah ben Joshua Ashkenazi, rabbi of *Busk*, Poland. This collection of homilies on the Bible was printed in Wilhermsdorf, 1674.

their works in order to deceive the pious reader. In Poland and Russia between 1760 and 1837 different *haskamot* were frequently used on different copies of the same book. This was done in order to help the sales of the book; in areas under ḥasidic influence *haskamot* of great ḥasidic leaders were printed in the book whereas for the purpose of selling the same book in "anti-ḥasidic" locations, *haskamot* of great scholars who were famous for their anti-ḥasidic attitude would be printed instead. These instances were not cases of forgery since the author actually had both *haskamot;* they were, however, cases of manipulation. Others printed only part of the book which had received the *haskamah,* and some authors published their books on inferior paper with unclear type. As a result some *haskamot* included such specifications as "the condition of this *haskamah* that the printing of this book should be completed within two years" or "on condition that the printer should print the book on white paper with black ink." These factors, and others as well, made many rabbis reluctant to write *haskamot.* Samson Wertheimer was ready to approve only the works of relatives or scholars who were poor. Some writers of approbations made no secret of the fact that they had been given to help the author financially (see Abraham ha-Kohen's *Beit Ya'akov,* Leghorn, 1792). Some rabbis denied *haskamot* to any book which dealt with Jewish law; others were ready to add their names only if a well-known rabbi had already given his *haskamah.* Still others protested that they had no time to read the entire book, or that they were not sufficiently acquainted with the subject; which did not prevent some from granting their approbation merely on the reputation of the author. Some authors were not eager to obtain the *haskamah* of rabbis who could not read the work; thus Moses Mendelssohn did not request *haskamot* for his books, nor did Raphael ha-Kohen for his *Torat Yekuti'el* (Berlin, 1772); other authorities disapproved of them altogether (Responsa *Ḥatam Sofer, Ḥoshem Mishpat,* 41).

Haskamah of Abraham Abele ben Abraham Solomon (1764–1836) to the work *Te'udah be-Yisrael* by Isaac Dov (Baer) Levinsohn. The *haskamah* is unusual in that it was written by a devout rabbi for one of the best-known and most active Russian *maskilim.* From the first edition printed in Vilna in 1828. J.N.U.L., Jerusalem.

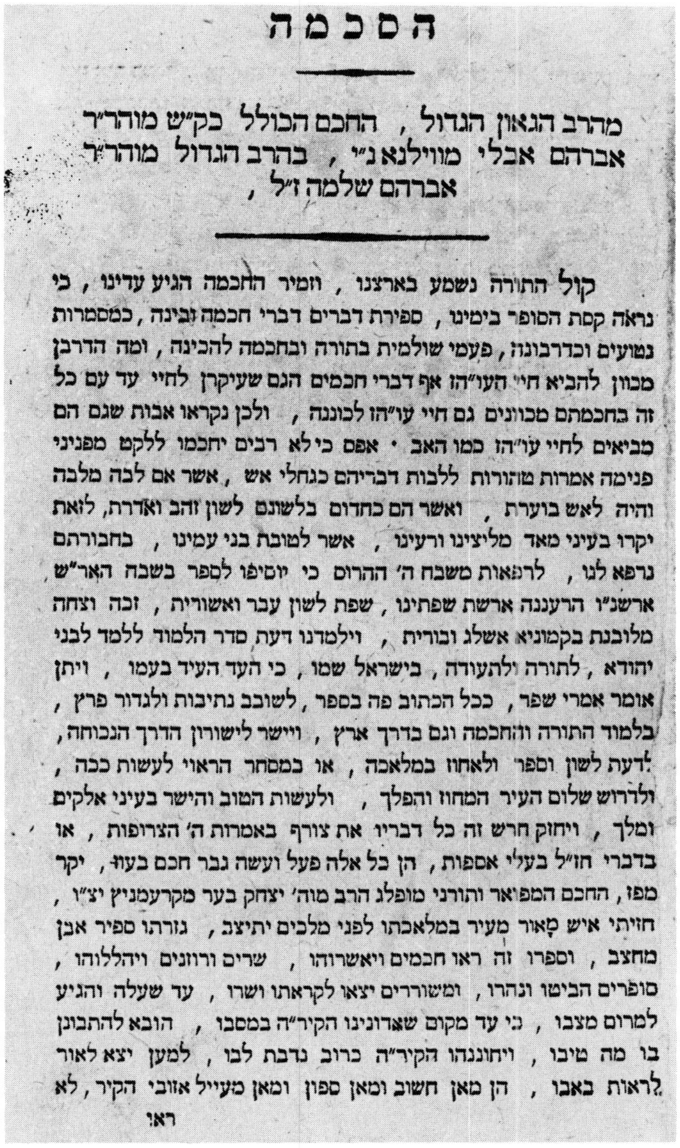
הסכמה

מהרב הגאון הגדול , החכם הכולל כק"ש מוהר"ר
אברהם אבלי מווילנא נ"י , בהרב הגדול מוהר"ר
אברהם שלמה ז"ל ,

קול התורה נשמע בארצנו , וזמיר החכמה הגיע עדינו , כי
נראה קסת הסופר בימינו , ספירת דברים דברי חכמה ובינה , כמסמרות
נטועים וכדרבונה , פעמי שולמית בתורה ובחכמה להכינה , ומה הדרבן
מכוון להביא חיי העו"הז אף דברי חכמים הגם שעיקרן לחיי עד עם כל
זה בחכמתם מכוונים גם חיי עו"הז לכוננה , ולכן נקראו אבות שגם הם
מביאים לחיי עו"הז כמו האב · אפס כי לא רבים יחכמו ללקט מפניני
פנימה אמרות טהורות ללבות דבריהם כגחלי אש , אשר אם לבה מלבה
והיה לאש בוערת , ואשר הם כחדום בלשונם לשון זהב ואדרת, לזאת
יקרו בעיני מאד מליצינו ורעינו , אשר לטובת בני עמינו , בחבורתם
נרפא לנו , לרפאות משבח ה' ההרוס כי יוסיפו לספר בשבח האר"ש
ארשנ"ו הרעננה ארשת שפתינו , שפת לשון עבר ואשוריה , זכה וצחה
מלובנת בקמוניא אשלג ובורית , וילמדנו דעת סדר הלמוד ללמד לבני
יהודא , לתורה ולתעודה , בישראל שמו , כי העד העיד בעמו , ויתן
אומר אמרי שפר , ככל הכתוב פה בספר , לשובב נתיבות ולגדור פרץ ,
בלמוד התורה והחכמה וגם בדרך ארץ , ויישר לישורון הדרך הנכוחה ,
לדעת לשון וספר ולאחוז במלאכה , או במסחר הראוי לעשות ככה ,
ולדרוש שלום העיר המחוז והפלך , ולעשות הטוב והישר בעיני אלקים
ומלך , ויחזק חרש זה כל דבריו את צורף באמרות ה' הצרופות , או
בדברי חז"ל בעלי אספות , הן כל אלה פעל ועשה גבר חכם בעוז , יקר
מפז , החכם המפואר והורני מופלג הרב מוה' יצחק בער מקרעמניץ יצ"ו ,
חזיתי איש מאור מעיר במלאכתו לפני מלכים יתיצב , גזרתו ספיר אבן
מחצב , וספרו זה ראו חכמים ויאשרוהו , שרים ורוזנים ויהללוהו ,
סופרים הביטו ונהרו , ומשוררים יצאו לקראתו ושרו , עד שעלה והגיע
למרום מצבו , כי עד מקום שאדונינו הקיר"ה במסבו , הובא להתבונן
בו מה טיבו , ויחוננהו הקיר"ה כרוב נדבת לבו , למען יצא לאור
לראות באבו , הן מאן חשוב ומאן ספון ומאן מעייל אזובי הקיר , לא
ראו

Ezekiel Landau used his *haskamah* to the Prague Pentateuch of 1785, to express his disapproval of Mendelssohn's Pentateuch edition. Between 1499 and 1850, approximately 4,000 *haskamot* were issued, the majority in Eastern Europe. Authors of religious books are still anxious to print a *haskamah* by a prominent rabbi or authority. In secular works the worldwide custom of using a preface or an introduction by a well-known authority fulfills the same role.

COPYRIGHT. The first hints at recognition in Jewish law of the ownership of incorporeal property were given as early as talmudic times. Thus it was stated, "a person who eavesdrops on his neighbor to reproduce his teachings, even though he is called a thief, acquires for himself" (Tosefta, *Bava Kama,* 7:13), and support for the prohibition against interchanging one scholar's statements with another's was found (Sifra Deuteronomy 188) in the passage, "Thou shalt not remove thy neighbor's landmark." At the end of the 12th century the same passage was quoted by Judah he-Ḥasid in warning an heir against complying with a direction in the will of his deceased father to inscribe the latter's name as the author of a book, even though it was known to have been written by someone else (*Sefer ha-Ḥasidim,* ed. Mekiẓe Nirdamim, nos. 17–32). It was nevertheless only from the 16th century onward that copyright became a defined legal right, protected by sanctions and partially based on the extended doctrine of *hassagat gevul.* As in other legal systems, this development arose from the spread of printing and a need for the protection of printers' rights. We have already referred to the *haskamah* to the *Sefer ha-Bahur* of Elijah Levita which contained a warning, on pain of ban, against anyone reprinting the book within the following ten years. In the mid-15th century, when Meir Katzenellenbogen complained to Moses Isserles about the appearance of a rival edition of Maimonides' *Mishneh Torah* (shortly after this work had been printed by Katzenellenbogen), Isserles responded by imposing a ban on anyone purchasing the *Mishneh Torah* from Katzenellenbogen's competitor. Thereafter it became customary to preface books with approbations containing a warning against trespass in the form of any unauthorized reprint of the particular book within a specified period. Halakhic literature contains detailed discussions on various aspects of encroachment on printers' rights. Thus Isserles imposed his above mentioned ban on anyone purchasing the *Mishneh Torah,* because in that instance the

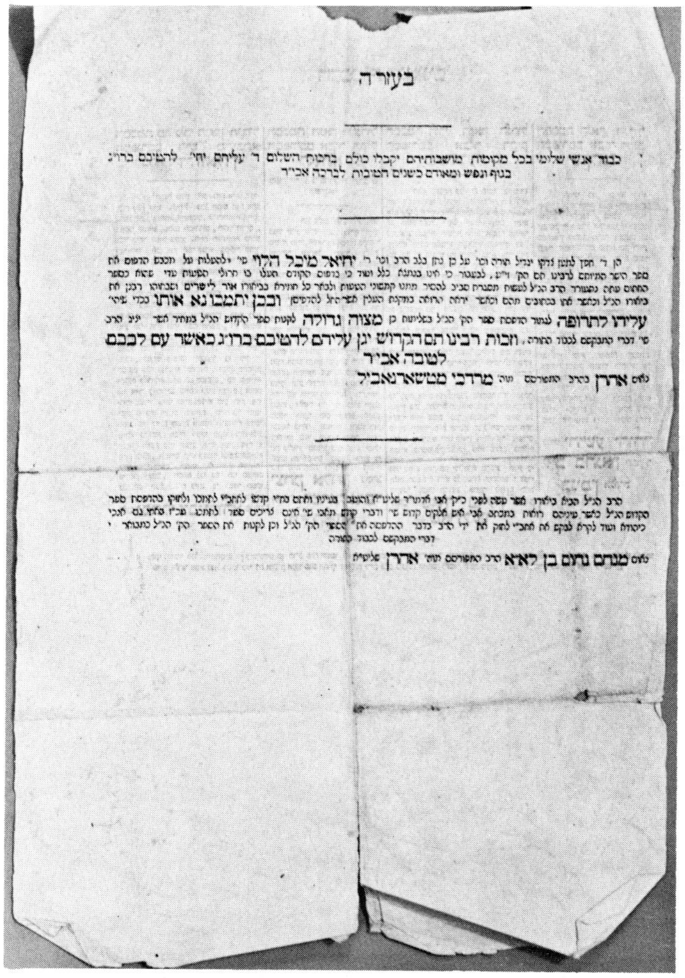

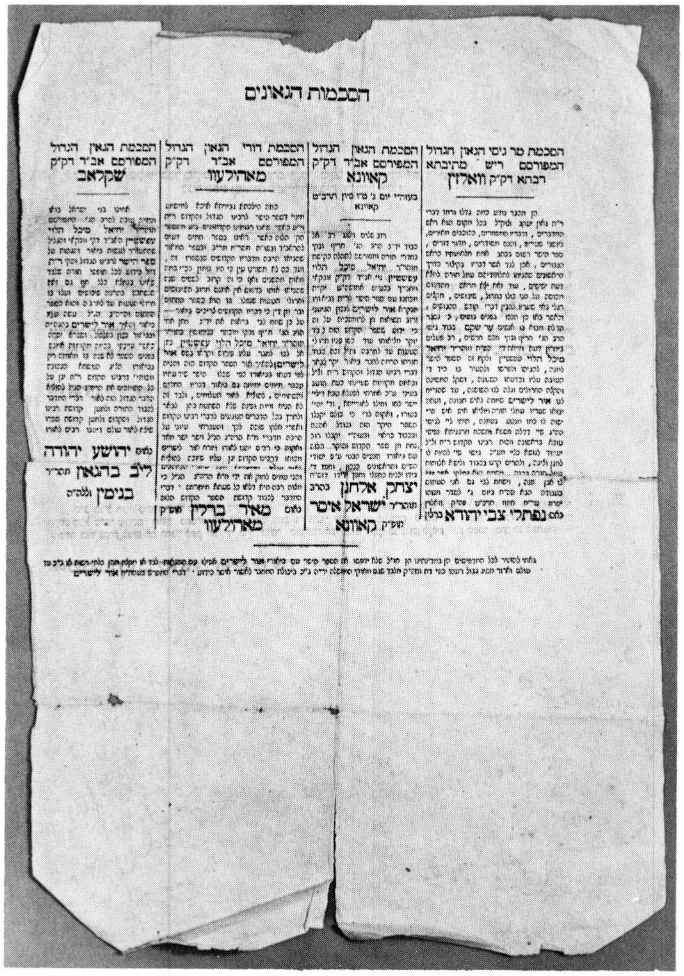

The two sides of the page of *haskamot* for Jehiel Michal Epstein's *Or li-Ysharim,* a commentary on Jacob Tam's *Sefer ha-Yashar.* The book was printed in Zhitomir in 1870. The author was one of the best-known rabbis of his time who wrote what has since become a classic in Jewish law, *Arukh ha-Shulḥan.* He wrote *Or li-Ysharim* in his youth and before it was printed he obtained *haskamot* from the ḥasidic leader of Tzernobyl, Aaron ben Mordecai and his son Menahem Nahum. He needed these ḥasidic approbations in order to distribute the book in the district around the town where he served as rabbi, since it was entirely hasidic. These approbations were printed on one side of the page; on the other were printed approbations from some of the most famous heads of the Lithuanian yeshovot, Naftali Ẓevi Judah Berlin (the head of Volozhyn yeshivah), Isaac Elḥanan Spektor (the rabbi of Kovno), Meir Berlin, and Joshua Leib Diskin. In c. 1874 Rabbi Epstein was appointed rabbi of Novogrod, a community known for its opposition to Hasidism. He took with him the remaining copies of his book and the extremists in the congregation, who could not countenance the fact that the approbations from the ḥasidic rabbis preceded that of their master, the *rosh yeshivah* of Volozhyn, tore the page out of all the copies. This page is therefore very rare.

ban would not have made an impression on the other printer who was a non-Jew. Other scholars held the opinion that the ban should be imposed, not on the purchasers of the book – as this would adversely affect the study of Torah – but on the printer instead, except if he be a non-Jew. Unlike Isserles, who confined the operation of his ban to purchasers within the country concerned only, other scholars extended operation of the ban to printers everywhere (Responsa *Ḥatam Sofer, Ḥoshen Mishpat* 41 and 79).

In most cases the period of the prohibition varied from three to 15 years, but was sometimes imposed for as long as 25 years. Some of the scholars held that a prohibition imposed against trespass on a printing right takes effect from the date of the approbation in which it has been formulated, but other scholars held the prohibition to come into effect upon commencement of the printing.

The above prohibition was mainly justified on grounds of the printer's need for an opportunity to recover his heavy outlay through the subsequent sale of the printed product, since reluctance to undertake any printing in the absence of such protection was likely to send up the price of books and cause study of the Torah to be neglected by the public. In this regard there was a fundamental difference of opinion among scholars concerning the fate of the prohibition once the printer had sold the whole of his edition, i.e., prior to expiry of the period of his protection. According to some scholars the prohibition remained fully effective against all other printers, but others held that continuation of the printer's protection, after he had already obtained his remuneration, was itself likely to cause the price of books to rise and to contribute to the neglect of study. This was the central halakhic issue in the dispute, at the beginning of the 19th century, between the respective printers of the Slavuta edition of the Talmud (the Shapiro Brothers) and the Vilna-Grodno edition (the Widow and Brothers Romm).

Out of this discussion grew the recognition given, in later generations, of the existence in Jewish law of a full legal right in respect of one's own spiritual creation. Thus Joseph Saul Nathanson, rabbi of Lvov, distinguished between printing the work of others, e.g., the Talmud, and printing one's own work, stating that in the latter event "it is clear that he has the right thereto for all time . . . for with regard to his own [work] a person is entitled to decree that it shall never be printed without his permission or authority . . . and this right avails him against the world at large" (*Sho'el u-Meshiv,* part 1, no. 44). In support of this opinion, Nathanson made an analogy to the copyright offered the patent-holder of an invention under general Polish law, and added his own formulation, i.e., that the effect of an author's restriction against any reprint of his work within a specified period was not to prohibit what would otherwise be permissible, but, on the contrary, to authorize others to reprint his work upon expiry of the period specified because "even if no express restriction is imposed . . . this remains prohibited as *hassagat gevul* by the law of the Torah" *(ibid.).* A similar view was expressed by Naphtali Ẓevi Judah Berlin concerning the individual's right in respect of his own teachings; he held that the individual might treat these as he would his own property – save for its total destruction, because it was a *mitzvah* to study and to teach others (*Meshiv Davar,* part 1, no. 24).

This view was not, however, generally accepted by the halakhic scholars. Thus Isaac Schmelkes saw no reason why others might not reprint a book – even if first printed by the author himself – once the original edition had been completely sold: "Everyone retains the right to study and to teach . . . why should another not be able to benefit his fellow men and print and sell cheaply?" (*Beit Yiẓḥak, Yoreh De'ah,* part 2, no. 75). In his opinion Nathanson's analogy of a patent-right offered no real support for the correctness of his view, since in that case the perpetuity of the right derived from royal charter, without which others might freely copy the inventor's model, and furthermore, a work relating to the Torah was to be distinguished from any other work of the spirit inasmuch as "the Torah was given to all free of charge . . . not to be used with a view to gaining

Colophon containing the printer's prayer of thanksgiving to God for having completed the printing of the 13th-century scientific encyclopaedia, *Sha'ar ha-Shamayim,* by Gershom ben Solomon of Arles. Printed by Meir ben Jacob of Florence in Venice, 1546. J.N.U.L., Jerusalem.

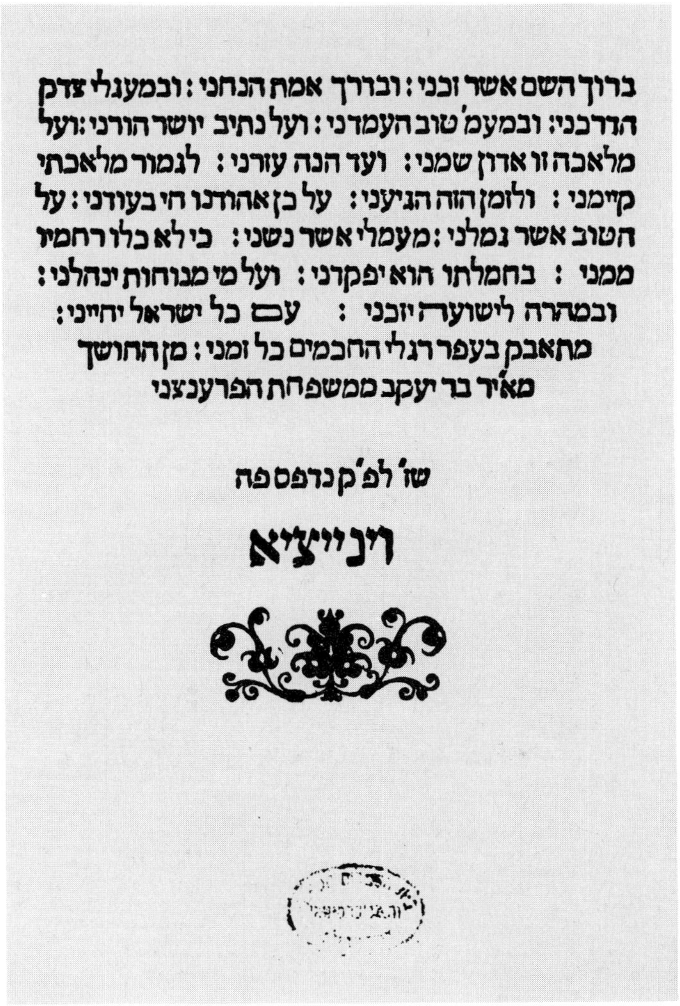
ברוך השם אשר זכני : ובדרך אמת הנחני : ובמעגלי צדק
הדרכני: ובמעמ׳ טוב העמדני : ועל נתיב יושר הורני :ועל
מלאכה זו אדון שמני : ועד הנה עזרני : לגמור מלאכתי
קיימני : ולזמן הזה הגיעני : על כן אהודנו חי בעודני : על
הטוב אשר גמלני : מעמלי אשר נשני : כי לא כלו רחמיו
ממני : בחמלתו הוא יפקדני : ועל מי מנוחות ינהלני :
ובמהרה לישועה יזכני : עם כל ישראל יחייני :
מתאבק בעפר רגלי החכמים כל זמני : מן החושך
מאיר בר יעקב ממשפחת הפרענצני

שו׳ לפ׳ק נדפס פה

ויניציא

remuneration" *(ibid.)*. At the same time Schmelkes conceded the validity of a restriction imposed against reprint of a book within a specified period, not as a matter of *halakhah,* but in pursuance of the general law of the land, by virtue of the rule of *dina de-malkhuta dina* ("the law of the land is law").

COLOPHONS

When books were first printed, the colophon was used by the printer to convey information about himself and his assistants and about the date of the beginning and/or finishing of printing, as was the practice of manuscript copyists. It often contained apologies for mistakes or self-praise for their absence and sometimes, paeans in honor of the new and wonderful art of printing. One also finds in colophons the name of the ruler under whose protection the production took place, thanks to financial backers of the venture, the number of copies printed, and so on. The Jewish printer also used the colophon to give thanks to God for permitting him to accomplish his holy task and to pray that he might be enabled to continue his work and witness the restoration of the Temple. Warnings to respect the printers' copyright for a stated number of years, with references to the sanctions of rabbinic law, such as excommunication, were also inserted in the colophon. These appeared later in the *haskamot* (see page 174). The formulae were much the same as those used in manuscripts. For the date, the Jewish era was normally used, the year being given in general by complicated chronograms, which lead to much confusion in determining the exact dates.

The colophon in printed books is a source not only of bibliography but of the history of printing and Jewish genealogy in general, e.g. the colophon of Judah Halevi's *Kuzari* (Fano, 1506), which provides important data on the Yaḥya family. Colophons varied in size: in Rashi's commentary on the Pentateuch published by Soncino (Rimini, c. 1525) the colophon occupies a whole page. The length and shape was influenced by the space available, the idea being that, as in the Scroll of the Law (*Soferim* 1:12), no blank space must be left at the end. In works appearing in several volumes one occasionally finds a different colophon at the end of each volume, e.g. Meshullam Cusi's *Turim* (Pieve di Sacco, 1475 and after). Colophons were sometimes rhymed verse with an acrostic giving the name of the printer or even the proofreader.

PROOFREADERS

During the age of printing the influence of proofreaders and printers on the texts of books became increasingly important, and today it is occasionally possible to trace the methods of different proofreaders. After it had been established beyond doubt that the Leiden manuscript of the Jerusalem Talmud is the one from which the first edition was published in Venice (1523, by Bomberg), Saul Lieberman showed us in his essay on the tractate *Horayot* in the Jerusalem Talmud how great a share the proofreader Cornelius Adelkind had in establishing the text. The research of R.N.N. Rabbinovicz on the text of

Colophon of *Sefer Torat Ḥakham*, a volume of sermons by Ḥayyim ben Abraham ha-Kohen (c. 1585–1655), a kabbalist from Aleppo. The page shows the author's concluding prayer of thanksgiving and that of the printer Giovanni Vendramini, Venice, 1654. J.N.U.L., Jerusalem.

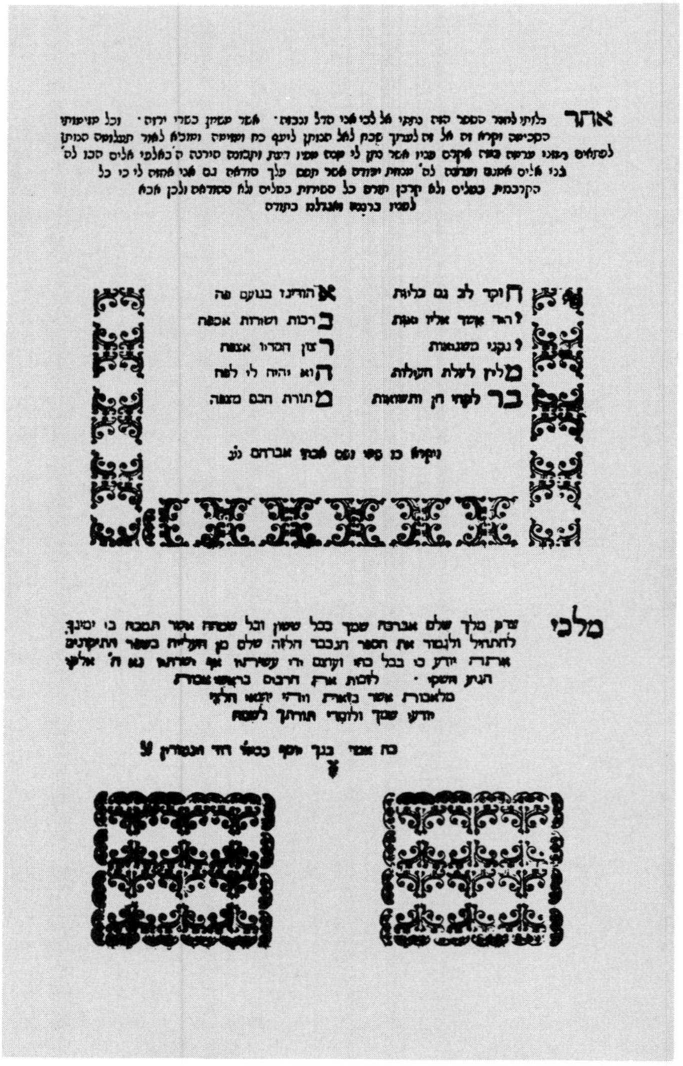

the Babylonian Talmud provides a great deal of information on the activities of its first proofreaders. The most prominent of them was Ḥiyya Meir ben David, one of the rabbis of Venice, who was given the responsibility of correcting the whole Talmud edition by Bomberg in the course of three years (1520–23), as well as the commentary of Asher ben Jehiel. The proofreader of the first tractates of the Soncino Talmud (1484) was Gabriel ben Aaron Strasburg, and Rabbinovicz shows that his work is very faulty. Often proofreading was divided into two separate sections: proofreading the manuscript before it was given for setting, and proofreading the printed galleys against the manuscript. In all periods and places the proofreaders used to add a short or long apology at the end of the book in which they made the reader aware of the great difficulty of their work, including the difficulty of deciphering the manuscript from which the book was printed, and the human impossibility of ever arriving at perfection. All proofreaders signed their names.

Some of the proofreaders became very famous as expert craftsmen and some authors employed special proofreaders for their books, such as Rabbi Joseph

Colophon page of *Sefer Orḥot Ẓaddikim,* an anonymous ethical work. This last page shows the concluding portion of text and the signatures of the Cracow printers Mordecai ben Gershom Katz and his sons Bezalel and Solomon. Printed in Prague, 1581. J.N.U.L., Jerusalem.

שער יראת שמים

ברוך

אלה דברי הישישו הקצין כ״מר מרדכי ב״ר גרשם כ״ץ מחוקק זצ״ל ׳ ובנוו

Hitnazzelut ha-Maggiha, proofreader's statement to *Shitah lo Noda le-Mi,* an early anonymous commentary to the talmudic tractate *Kiddushin,* first printed from an ancient manuscript in Constantinople, 1755. The proofreader, Shalom Joseph Mizraḥi, describes the condition of the manuscript, then 190 years old, on which the writing was very faint. Furthermore, many of the lines in the manuscript had often been inserted incorrectly, and there were other inaccuracies which made it impossible for the typesetters to work without intensive aid by the proofreader. He also informs us that the manuscript had first been copied by Halafta ben Moses Adjiman, one of the most important Jewish families in Constantinople at the beginning of the 18th century.

הסכמת רבני גאוני קושטאנדינה

התנצלות המגיה

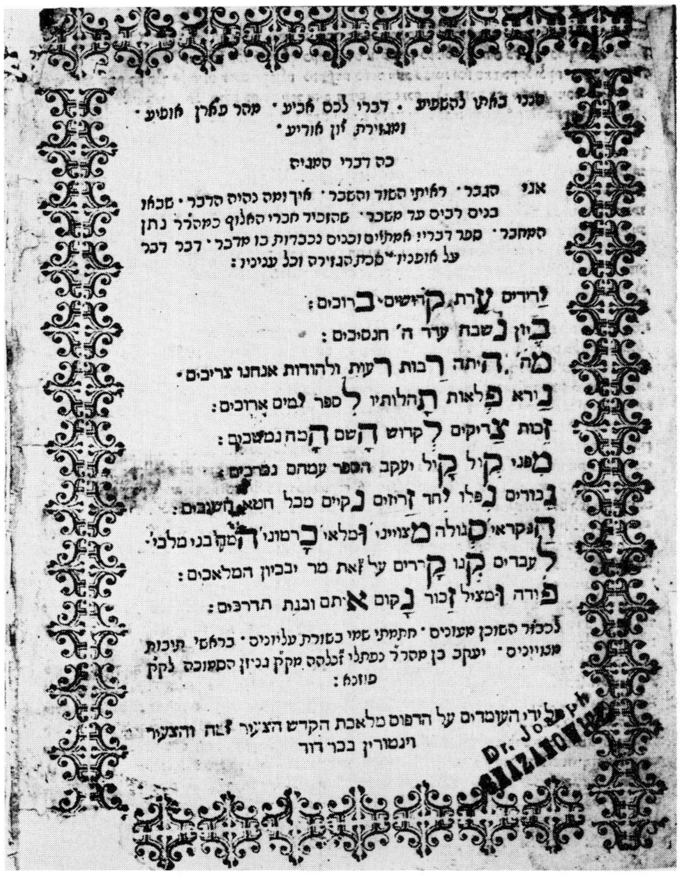
כה דברי המגיה

ידידים עדת קדושים ברוכים:
ביון נשבת עיר ה' חנסיכים:
מה היתה רבות רעות ולהודות אנחנו צריכים.
נורא פלאות תהלותיו לספר ימים ארוכים:
זכות צדיקים לקדוש השם הכה נמשכים:
מפני קול קול יעקב הספר עמהם נערכים:
גבורים נפלו יחד זריזים נקיים מכל חטא ועונים:
הנקראי סגולה מצוייני ומלאי כרמוני ה' בני מלכי'
לעבדים קנו קרים על זאת מר יבכיון המלאכים:
פודה ומציל זכור נקום איתם ובנת תרדכים:

Last page from the first edition of *Sefer Yeven Meẓulah,* a chronicle of the destruction of Polish Jewry during the Chmielnicki massacres of 1648–52, written by Nathan Nata Hannover (d. 1653). The page contains comments and a poem of the proofreader, Jacob ben Naftali of Gniezno, in which he adds his expressions of woe to those of the author. Printed in Venice at the press of Vendramina, 1653. J.N.U.L., Jerusalem.

Caro. Some books were also proofread at later, even final stages of printing, and the mistakes which were discovered were printed in a special errata list which was added to the end of the book after it had been completely printed. This was done in order to make it easier for the reader, and in some cases the mistakes were corrected in subsequent editions of the book.

TRADE IN BOOKS

When books began to be printed from the end of the 15th century onward and were available in greater quantities and at considerably cheaper prices, it became possible to speak of a proper trade in Hebrew or Jewish books. Once more the printers themselves or their agents – as well as the authors – were the principal booksellers. The famous Gershom Soncino sold his books while travelling from place to place, while his great competitor Daniel Bomberg handed the Swiss scholar Conrad Gesner a list with prices of 75 Hebrew books, printed by himself and others, and Gesner printed the list in Latin in his *Pandectae* (1548). Two Jewish bookdealers on a large scale, David Bono and Graziadio (-Judah?) are mentioned in Naples in 1491, being exempted from tolls and duties like other bookdealers who followed the same calling. The former is recorded as exporting 16 cases of printed books in one consignment. Whether they were in Hebrew is not specifically stated, but is probable. Rabbi Benjamin Zeev of Arta (c. 1500) refers in his responsa to the useful function of the itinerant booksellers of his day. The will of Rabbi Aaron ben David Cohen of Ragusa (1656) gives some interesting details on how books were diffused: he left money for the publication of his *Zekan Aharon,* of which 800 copies were to be printed: 200 were to be sent to Constantinople, 100 to Salonika, 50 to Venice, 20 to Sofia, 10 to Ancona, 20 to Rome, 50 to Central and Eastern Europe, 50 to Holland, to various places in Italy and to Ereẓ Israel; the last were to be distributed without charge. Issuing works in "installments" was not uncommon in early Jewish publishing, particularly by the Constantinople presses. Thus the responsa of Isaac ben Sheshet (Constantinople, 1547) were printed in sections and sold in this form by the printer to subscribers week by week.

CATALOGS. From the 17th century onward the book fairs of Frankfort on the Main became centers for the diffusion of Hebrew books also. Two Jewish booksellers of Frankfort, Gabriel Luria and Jacob Hamel, were in correspondence with the famous Christian Hebraists, the Buxtorfs with reference to the sale of books. The Buxtorfs were also in contact with Judah Romano of Constantinople, who, whether a professional bookdealer or not, was active in the Hebrew book trade. Manasseh Ben Israel is known to have attended the Frankfort fair in 1634 – the only Jew among 159 Christians – but his application for membership of the Amsterdam booksellers' guild in 1648 was refused. The catalog (in Spanish) published by his son Samuel (1652) includes some books which were apparently printed by other firms. Some years before, Samuel had also distributed a list of secondhand books which he had for sale, copies of which even reached England. Isaac Fundam (Fundao) of Amsterdam produced a printed catalog of books and manuscripts in Spanish and Portuguese (1726), and works purchased from him are occasionally recorded.

Plate 36 (right). *Ketubbah* from Rome, 1795. The shape is typical of Roman *ketubbot* and the decorative frames are composed of micrographic texts from the Book of Esther. Israel Museum, Jerusalem.
Plate 37 (below). Parchment *ketubbah* from Leghorn, 1679. Mishkan le-Omanut, Kibbutz Ein Harod.

Plate 38. *Ketubbah* from Rotterdam, Holland, 1648. The ornamented cartouches framing the text depict scenes relating to the husband, Issac (Pereira), and wife, Rachel (bat Abraham da Pinto). The work is signed by the engraver, Shalom Italia. Israel Museum, Jerusalem.

Plate 39. The Dead Sea Scrolls, the oldest Hebrew (or Aramaic) manuscripts in existence, are housed in the Shrine of the Book, Israel Museum, Jerusalem. The focal point of the Shrine is the raised platform on which the Scroll of Isaiah is displayed, fully opened, around a drum. Above it is a representation of a scroll handle. Photo: David Harris.

Plate 40. Title page of *Or li-Ysharim,* the sermons of Rabbi Zerah Eidlitz, the well-known preacher, and one of the most famous rabbis in Prague during the time of Rabbi Ezekiel Landau, author of *Noda bi-Yhudah.* The book was first printed in Prague in 1785. This lavish and beautifully embellished edition was printed in Budapest, in the Katzburg press, at the end of 1942. Several of the greatest Hungarian rabbis of the time wrote numerous and lengthy *haskamot* to the book. Courtesy I. Ta-Shema, Jeruslaem.

Plate 41. Simeon ben Ẓemaḥ Duran's book of responsa, *Tashbez,* printed in Amsterdam in 1741, shown here in its original colored fish-skin binding. According to popular tradition, Duran's great love for books was rewarded by his responsa being beautifully printed and magnificently bound, preserving the book as a whole and its pages. Courtesy I. Ta-Shema, Jerusalem.

At the end of the 17th century, the Proops firm of Amsterdam styled themselves in their publications "Printers and Booksellers": their first catalog *(Appiryon Shelomo)* appeared in 1730; they had already been admitted to the booksellers' guild in 1677.

At the end of the 18th century Johanan Levi Rofe ("the physician") was also active in the book trade in Amsterdam. In the 18th century, especially in England, Jewish and Hebrew works were frequently published by subscription, a wealthy person sometimes purchasing several copies. The lists of subscribers printed with the works in question are often important historical sources. The business of distributing books in bulk by the publishers could be complicated. They were not infrequently disposed of by barter, in some instances in exchange for wine. In Eastern Europe the great fairs were the centers for bookdealing, and cheap chapbooks were sold all over the country by itinerant dealers. The Council of Lithuanian Jewry in 1679 ordered that each community should appoint a person to purchase tractates of the Talmud at the fairs of Stolowicze and Kopyl so as to stimulate study. James Levi, who conducted book auctions in London from about 1711 to 1733, presumably dealt solely in non-Jewish books. On the other hand, Moses Benjamin Foa (1729–1822), book purveyor to the court of Modena and a dealer on a grand scale, was deeply interested in Jewish literature also, though more as a collector than a merchant. In 1784 D. Friedlaender and his friends obtained a royal license for their *Orientalische Buchdruckerei und Buchhandlung*. Heirs to collections of Hebrew books who wished to dispose of them produced sale-catalogs, such as those published by the heirs of David Oppenheim; two separate catalogs of this famous and outstanding collection were printed: *Reshimah Tammah* (Hamburg, 1782); and *Kehillat David* (Hamburg, 1826, with Latin translation).

MODERN TIMES. In the 19th century, in Hebrew as in general books, there was a division between printers on the one hand and publishers and booksellers on the other. In Eastern Europe, however, the three functions remained united in the activities of such firms as Romm in Vilna, who published catalogs as well. In the 20th century, the center of the Jewish secondhand book trade was first Berlin, with the firm of Asher, and then Frankfort with Joseph Baer, Bamberger and Wahrmann (later of Jerusalem), A. J. Hoffmann, J. Kauffmann, and Leipzig with M. W. Kaufmann. The firms of Schwager and Fraenkel (of Husiatyn, later Vienna, Tel Aviv, and New York), F. Muller (Amsterdam), and B. M. Rabinowitz (Munich) made contributions to scholarship through their diffusion of rare books, and sometimes through their learned catalogs, as did Ephraim Deinard in the United States. The journeys undertaken by some of these booksellers in search of rarities place them almost in the category of explorers. In London Vallentine (later Shapiro, Vallentine) was active from at least the beginning of the 19th century, followed by the firms of R. Mazin, M. Cailingold and Rosenthal, while in Paris the firm of Lipschutz was eminent for many years; in the United States the Bloch Publishing Company has been in existence for over a century and the Hebrew Publishing Company since the 1890s. Important Jewish booksellers in Switzerland were T. Gewuerz and V. Goldschmidt of Basle; in Holland J. L. Joachimsthal and M. Packter of Amsterdam; in Berlin M. Poppelauer and L. Lamm;

תמו ונשלמו הקינות שבח לשוכן מעונות

A Yiddish notice appearing at the end of *kinot* (the lamentations for the Ninth of Av), Fuerth, 1767, with a Yiddish translation by the printer Joseph Petschau and his son, Mendel. In it the printers announce that this book and other useful books, new and used, may be purchased at their home and that they also accept material for printing at their home in the Fuerth market, which they will undertake at a cheap price, in courteous and honest fashion.

שטר מכירה

מודה אני הח"ת וח"י דלמטה

בדבר הסכמת על הדפסו' ס"ל על וו"ג

יצחק ... אשר ... אברהם

משה ז"ל

יצחק

עה"ת יום א' י"ב אלול תקפ"ד לפ"ק פ"ק בארדיטשב

הקטן נחשון יוסף יחיאל בהרב מוה' יעקב פנחס

נחשון יוסף יחיאל ... יעקב

פנחס

סימנים של הספר

שער א

שער ב

שער ג

שער ד

A bill of sale according to which Nahshon Joseph Jehiel ben Jacob Pinehas sold the *haskamah* in his possession, which had been given in esteem of his father by the ḥasidic leader, Abraham Joshua Heschel of Apta, for printing *Sha'arei Ẓiyyon* in a particular format. This approbation, given in the middle of 1823, was sold by Nahshon at the end of 1824 to the partners Isaac ben Asher and Abraham ben Moses, to grant them sole copyright to print the book. The two buyers, who operated in Berdichev, had bought other *haskamot* to obtain the printing rights. A *haskamah* is usually sold by its owners after bankruptcy or the death of one of the partners, and is not the subject of a speculative venture.

in Vienna and Budapest J. Schlesinger. Some non-Jewish booksellers, such as O. Harrassowitz (Leipzig, then Wiestbaden) and Spirgates (Leipzig); Mags Brothers and Sothebys (London), have also played a role in the sale of Hebraica and Judaica.

CENSORSHIP

CHURCH CENSORSHIP. The theory of the Catholic Church that it had a duty to protect man from endangering his eternal salvation through exposure to heretical books and ideas made its form of censorship the most intolerant, and the power of the church enabled it to become all pervasive. Although the church had denounced and burned books early in its history, the first instance of Jews being forced to eliminate supposed blasphemies against Christianity is dated from the mid-13th century. After the disputation of Barcelona in 1263, James, the king of Aragon, ordered that the Jews must within three months eliminate all the passages in their writings which were found objectionable. Non-compliance with this order was to result in heavy penalties and the destruction of the works concerned. The official intrusion of the Church into Jewish life came to a head with its persecution of the Talmud. Listed in 1559 in the *Index auctorum et librorum prohibitorum* issued by Pope Paul IV, the Talmud was subjected to innumerable disputations, attacks, and burnings. In March 1589 Sixtus V extended the ban in his *Index* to "Books of the Jews" containing anything which might be construed as being against the Catholic Church. In 1595 the *Index Expurgatorius (Sefer ha-Zikkuk)* of Hebrew books was established. This *Index* listed books which could not be read without having individual passages revised or deleted before publication. Official revisers, who often were apostate Jews, were appointed to effect this revision according to the rules laid down in *De correctione librorum,* which appeared with the *Index* of Clement VIII in 1596. Objectionable passages in Hebrew books and even expressions such as "Talmud" and "*goi*" were deleted, altered, and at times torn out. Four hundred and twenty Hebrew books, beginning with *Ẓeror ha-Mor* by Abraham Saba (Constantinople, 1514) and ending with *Sefer Seliḥot ke-Minhag Ashkenazim* (Venice, no date) are listed in a manuscript of the *Sefer ha-Zikkuk* (published by N. Porges, in *Festschrift . . . A. Berliner* (1903), 273–95). There are thousands of Hebrew books with signs of the censor's work, words or whole passages blacked out with ink, and censors' signatures at the end of the volumes. Quite a number of textual errors in the standard editions of Hebrew texts owe their origin to such censorial activity. The last edition of the papal *Index librorum prohibitorum* in 1948 still included works written by Jews, converted Jews, and non-Jews dealing with Jewish subjects. Among the Hebrew books still on the list were: *Ein Yisrael (Ein Ya'akov)* by Jacob ibn Habib, published with *Sefer Beit Leḥem Yehudah* by Leone Modena and banned in 1693 and

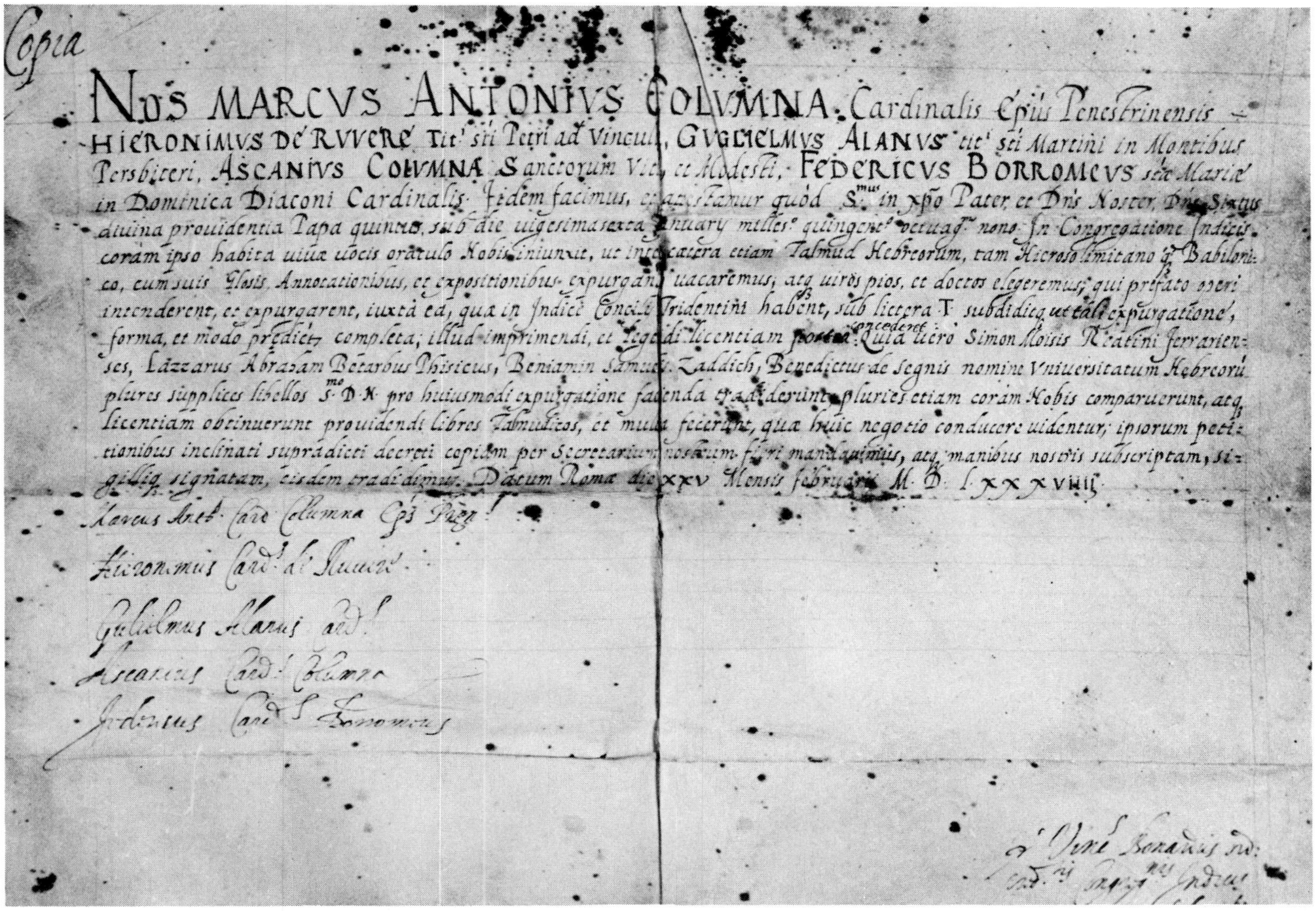

Copia

Nos Marcus Antonius Columna Cardinalis Epus Penestrinensis
Hieronimus de Ruuere Tit. sti Petri ad Vincula, Guglielmus Alanus tit. sti Martini in Montibus
Persbiteri, Ascanius Columna Sanctorum Viti, et Modesti, Federicus Borromeus scte Mariae
in Dominica Diaconi Cardinalis fidem facimus, et attestamur quòd S.mus in xpo Pater et Dns Noster Dns Sixtus
diuina prouidentia Papa quintus, sub die uigesimasexta January milles.o quingent.o octuag.mo nono In Congregatione Indicis
coram ipso habita uiuae uocis oraculo Nobis iniunxit, ut inter caetera etiam Talmud Hebreorum, tam Hierosolimitano quam Babiloni-
co, cum suis Glosis, Annotationibus, et expositionibus expurgandi uacaremus, atq uiros pios, et doctos elegeremus, qui prefato operi
intenderent, et expurgarent, iuxta ea, quae in Indice Concilii Tridentini habent, sub littera T subdiditq ut tali expurgatione,
forma, et modo predict. completa, illud imprimendi, et legendi licentiam concederet. Quia uero Simon Moisis Reatini Ferrarien-
ses, Lazzarus Abraham Betarbus Phisicus, Beniamin Samuel Zaddich, Benedictus de Segnis nomine Vniuersitatum Hebreoru
plures supplices libellos S.mo D.N. pro huiusmodi expurgatione facienda dederunt, pluries etiam coram Nobis comparuerunt, atq
licentiam obtinuerunt prouidendi libros Talmudicos, et multa fecerunt, quae huic negotio conducere uidentur; ipsorum peti-
tionibus inclinati supradicti decreti copiam per Secretarium nostrum fieri mandauimus, atq manibus nostris subscriptam, si-
gilloq signatam, eisdem tradi iussimus. Datum Romae die XXV Mensis februarij M.D.LXXXVIIII

Marcus Ant. Card. Columna Eps Praen.
Hieronimus Card. de Ruuere
Gulielmus Alanus Card.
Ascanius Card. Columna
Federicus Card. Borromeus

Censhorship of the Talmud and other "books of the Jews" ordered by Pope Sixtus V in this *Index* of 1589. Jerusalem, C.A.H.J.P.

again in 1694; *Sha'arei Ẓiyyon* (1662) by Nathan Neta Hannover, the publication of which resulted in the trial of its publisher Shabbetai Bass of Dyhernfurth, banned in 1675; the kabbalistic work *Eshel Avraham* (1701) by Mordecai ben Judah Leib Ashkenazi, forbidden by the Church authorities in 1702; and the aggadic collections *Yalkut Shimoni* and *Yalkut Re'uveni* which have various kabbalistic interpretations of the Bible. Christian censors deleted the entire tractate *Avodah Zarah* from the Basle edition of the Talmud (1578–80). The Latin translation of *Hilkhot Avodah Zarah* of Maimonides (*De Idolatria liber cum interpretatione latina et notis Dionysii Vosii,* Amsterdam, 1641) was placed on the *Index* in 1717. Among other well-known books placed on the *Index* were Manasseh Ben Israel's *De resurrectione mortuorum* (Amsterdam, 1636); Baruch Spinoza's *Tractatus Theologico-Politicus,* published anonymously in 1670; Spinoza's other work, banned under the heading *Opera Posthuma,* as was the German translation of the *Tractatus* (*Theologisch-Politische Abhandlungen von Spinoza,* 1826) by J. A. Kalb; and the works of Spinoza's followers. Among historical books found unacceptable by the Church is an excerpt from Josephus prepared by Johann Baptist Otte, *Spicilegium sive excerpta ex Flavio Josepho* (Amsterdam, Leyden, 1726), which was placed on the *Index* in 1743. Some of the most famous names in philosophy and literature figure in the prohibited lists, among them Jews such as Edmond Fleg, whose *L'Enfant prophète* (1926) and *Jésus, raconte par le juif errant* (1933) were placed on the *Index* in 1940.

GOVERNMENT CENSORSHIP. The 19th century saw the introduction of severe censorship of Hebrew and Yiddish literature in Russia and Poland. Ḥasidic literature in particular was burned and destroyed. The Polish censors prevented the importing of Hebrew books not printed in Poland, and examiners visited

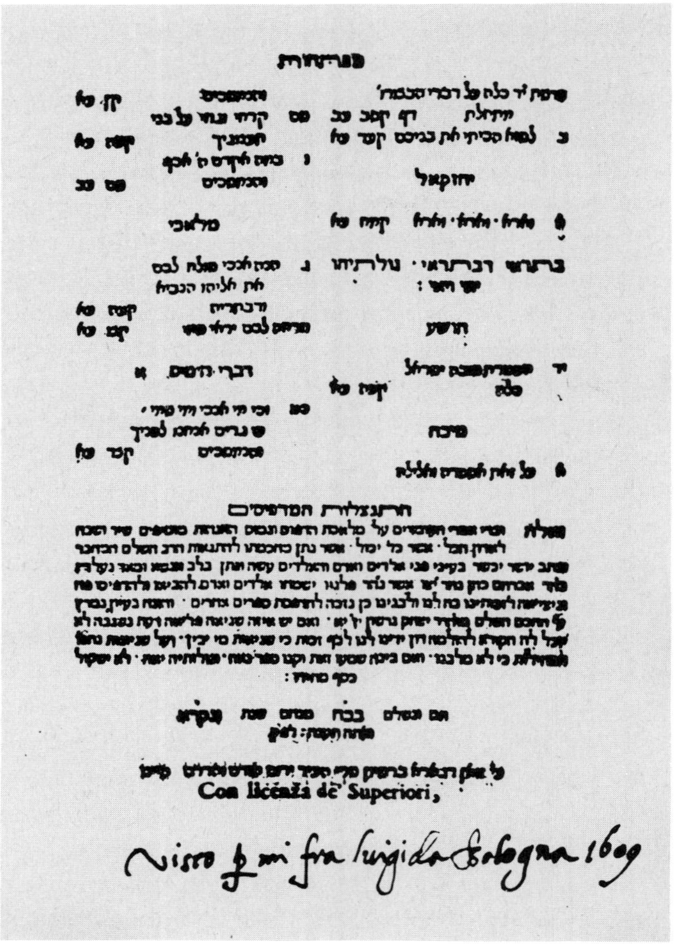
Con licenza de' Superiori,

The signature of the censor, Brother Luigi da Bologna, appears at the bottom of this colophon page of *Lehem Shelomo*, a commentary on the Talmud, Midrash, and *Zohar*, by Solomon ben Isaac Levi, printed in Venice, 1597. Cecil Roth Collection.

Polish cities to make sure that this regulation was obeyed. In Prague, Jesuits had controlled the censorship of Hebrew books by means of a *Commissio inquisitionis Judaicae pravitatis.* Only with permission given by the consistorium appointed by the archbishop could Hebrew books be printed. The power of censorship was in the hands of the consistorium until the end of the 18th century when the Landesgubernium took it over. The Nazi and fascist persecutions were directed not only at the Jews but at their literary and scientific work as well, which was confiscated, banned, and burned en masse. In Germany the confiscation of thousands of books, which began with the order signed by Hindenburg on February 28, 1933, "for the protection of the nation and the state," ended with the Gestapo's list of forbidden books containing 12,400 titles and 149 authors. On May 10, 1933, the works of Jewish authors were burned in many cities of Germany; among the many authors whose works were burned were Alfred Adler, Shalom Asch, Max Brod, Ilya Ehrenburg, Sigmund Freud, Lion Leuchtwanger, Heinrich Heine, Franz Kafka, Else Lasker-Schueler, Emil Ludwig, Jakob Wasserman, Franz Werfel, and Arnold and Stefan Zweig. In Hungary, books dealing with anti-Semitism in Hungary and with the *numerus clausus,* the law limiting the number of Jewish students enrolled in universities, were confiscated in September 1919, following the counterrevolution. In 1940 a general censorship was introduced in Hungary, and everything unacceptable to fascism was banned, including the works of Jewish writers. In June 1944, when 600,000 Jews were deported from Hungary to the extermination camps of Poland, 500,000 Hebrew and Jewish books and the works of Jewish writers composed in different European languages were destroyed.

JEWISH CENSORSHIP. Censorship in the proportion

Sefer Abudarham, a commentary on the prayers, by David Abudarham, Prague, 1784. In the penultimate line is the signature of Leopold Tirsch who, in his capacity as supervisor and Hebrew translator in the service of the czar, affirms that he has seen the contents of the book and approves it for publication.

ספר משה
אבודרהם
נדפס פה פראג
· Vidi Leop. Tirsch Cæsar. Reg. Revis. transl. & in hebr.

יורה דעה

A page from the section dealing with idolatry in Jacob ben Asher's *Tur Yoreh Deah,* which treats what articles it is forbidden to sell to non-Jews and the question of neighborly relations with them. A great deal of the censored passages contain completely innocuous material, and words were crossed out without reason. In one passage the word *min,* which can mean heretic but which in this context means "kind" or "sort" was crossed out. In the last section of the second column none of the censorship makes sense at all.

of the Christian world was unknown to Judaism. Even the restrictions against the Apocrypha *(Sefarim Ḥizoniyyim)* referred to its use in public study only. The Talmud quotes the Wisdom of Ben Sira, although the reading of it is forbidden by rabbinic authorities. Opposition to Greek culture was expressed because of a fear of Hellenization. The Aramaic translation of Job, the first book described in the Talmud, was suppressed (*Shabbat* 115a). The "books of the *Minim*" (probably referring to the books of the early Christians) were also considered objectionable (Tosefta, *Shabbat* 13 (14): 5). On June 21, 1554, a rabbinic ordinance was adopted by a synod in Ferrara, Italy, establishing a system of internal control over the printing of Hebrew books. Fourteen rabbis representing the Italian Jews resolved that no Hebrew book be printed without the authorization of three recognized rabbis and the lay leaders of the nearest large community. The action in Ferrara was repeated in Padua in 1585; similar steps were taken by the Council of the Four Lands in Poland and the Jewish community of Frankfort in 1603 and by the Sephardi community in Amsterdam in 1639. In the past 400 years there have been a number of reasons for censorship within the Jewish community. Salacious and trivial publications were banned by rabbis. A classic example of a distinct prohibition is Joseph Caro's interdiction in his *Shulḥan Arukh* (*Oraḥ Ḥayyim* 307:16) of Immanuel of Rome's erotic *Maḥbarot.* Books that contained what were considered incorrect halakhic decisions and explications; books written or published by apostates; books printed on the Sabbath; and prayer books in which changes opposed by the rabbis were made by the editor or publisher were banned. The banning of books was used as a weapon in ideological struggles. Books on philosophy and Kabbalah were banned because it was felt that the study of those subjects might mislead the masses. Banning books was also used as a weapon in the fight against various movements that the traditional authorities saw as heretical, such as the Shabbateans, the Frankists, Ḥasidism, Haskalah and Reform. The later two ideologies were working for political and cultural emancipation and raised the fear that the achievement of those aims would lead to assimilation and apostasy. Some rabbis also viewed Zionism as a dangerous and heretical ideology and made efforts to control its publications.

BIBLIOPHILES

Little is known about private book collectors in antiquity and in the early Middle Ages. It might be assumed, however, that patrons of learning, such as Ḥisdai ibn Shaprut, collected important Hebrew and other books. Historical sources refer to the library of Samuel ha-Nagid. Judah ibn Tibbon's advice on how to care for a library is well-known, but unfortunately, little is known about the titles of the books making up his collection. Several book lists, some compiled for auctions after the owner's death, were found in the Cairo *Genizah.* It appears that the most remarkable of known medieval Jewish book collectors was the world traveler and physician Judah

Leon Mosconi of Majorca. His library included Hebrew and Arabic books in many branches of learning. Two catalogs have been preserved, one of them drawn up for the auction after his death in 1377. The king of Aragon ultimately canceled the sale and seized the library for himself. In Renaissance Italy there were many enthusiastic book collectors, such as Menaḥem ben Aaron of Volterra (15th century) whose library is now in the Vatican. The library of Solomon Finzi, son of the Mantuan scientist Mordecai (Angelo) Finzi, contained 200 volumes, at that time a number considered worthy of a great humanist. Elijah Capsali, a Cretan scholar of the 16th century, possessed a famous collection of Hebrew manuscripts, now at the Vatican. The largest Jewish library in the Renaissance period was that built up in successive generations by the family of Da Pisa. They were outdone in the 17th century by Abraham Joseph Solomon Graziano, rabbi of Modena, who wrote the initials of his name, reading *ish ger,* in vast numbers of books now scattered in Jewish libraries throughout the world. His contemporary Joseph Solomon Delmedigo, a physician who traveled widely, boasted that he collected no fewer than 4,000 volumes, on which he had expended the vast sum of 10,000 (florins?). Doubtless, many of these were in languages other than Hebrew.

The first printed sale catalogs of private Hebrew libraries emerged in Holland in the 17th century, for example, the one printed for the disposal of the collections of Moses Raphael d'Aguilar, the earliest such publication known to Jewish booklore, and that of Isaac Aboab da Fonseca's collection, comprising about 500 volumes, many in Spanish, French, and even Greek and Latin, including some classics and the writings of the Church Fathers. Other book collectors of that period in Amsterdam were Manasseh Ben Israel and Samuel Abbas. One of the greatest Jewish book collectors of any period was David Oppenheim, rabbi of Prague, who in 1788 compiled the first catalog of his collection, comprising the 480 books he owned at the time. Ultimately, he acquired 4,500 printed works in addition to 780 manuscripts, possibly the most important Jewish library in private ownership that has ever been assembled. It was purchased in 1829 by the Bodleian Library in Oxford. The Italian Catholic abbé Giovanni Bernardo de'Rossi, a Hebrew scholar of repute and a book collector of genius, had opportunities in Italy that were unequaled elsewhere. His great collection of Hebrew manuscripts, which he himself cataloged and which included several superb illuminated codices, is now housed at the Palatine Library in Parma, having been acquired after his death by the ruler of that petty principality. What the printed book collection includes is still barely known, but one example of its treasures is the only known copy of the earliest of dated Hebrew printed books – Rashi's Commentary printed at Reggio di Calabria in 1475. The next century produced a large number of more self-conscious collectors, such as Heimann Joseph Michael, a Hamburg businessman, not very affluent but a considerable scholar. The learned catalog he composed, still a standard work of reference, describes 860 manuscripts and 5,400 printed books, which in due course joined the Oppenheim collection in Oxford. At about the same time Solomon Dubno of Russia and Holland assembled some 2,000 printed books and about 100 manuscripts, which were sold by auction in Amsterdam in 1814. Another scholarly collector was Solomon Halberstam of Poland. Business reverses compelled him to dispose of his

Portrait of Joseph Solomon Delmedigo (1591–1655), rabbi, philosopher, mathematician and bibliophile who boasted of having amassed a library of 4,000 volumes. The portrait was engraved in the Netherlands in 1628.

manuscript collection, part going to the Montefiore Library (now in the library of Jews' College, London), and part to the library of the Jewish Theological Seminary of America, New York. The most valuable part of his collection of printed books was sold to the library of the Vienna Jewish community but the bulk was acquired by Mayer Sulzberger and presented to the Jewish Theological Seminary in New York. Eliakim Carmoly, rabbi in Brussels, who destroyed the value of everything he owned by embellishing it with ingenious, but sometimes transparent, forgeries possessed some 1,200 printed volumes and 290 manuscripts. His manuscripts can be found in Oxford, the British Museum, and the Guenzburg Library in Moscow.

In Russia David Guenzburg of St. Petersburg built up a magnificent manuscript collection, which is now in the Lenin State Library, Moscow. In the United States Mayer Sulzberger, assisted by the dealer Ephraim Deinard, built up an important collection. In 1903 Sulzberger gave his collection of 3,000 rare books to the Jewish Theological Seminary. Moritz Steinschneider's library in Berlin, comprising some 4,500 books and manuscripts, was important both for the caliber of its contents and for the copious scholarly annotations that Steinschneider added to his books. His collection passed into the ownership of the Jewish Theological Seminary of America; much of it was destroyed by fire in 1966. Judaica was only part of the great library which Salman Schocken assembled in Germany, but in that field he concentrated on Hebrew poetry and rare printed books. This collection is now housed in the Schocken Library, Jerusalem, and in recent years has been enriched by some remarkable illuminated manuscripts. A specialized library of another sort was that of David Montezinos of Amsterdam, who created a unique collection of works, largely in Spanish and Portuguese, illustrating the history of that community. He gave it to the Sephardi synagogue, where he then became librarian. This library worked in friendly competition with the Bibliotheca Rosenthaliana in that city for many years. The latter, the library of Leiser Rosenthal, a rabbi, was given by his son George to the city of Amsterdam; it is now a constituent of the University Library. Another outstanding rabbinical bibliophile was the Hungarian scholar David Kaufmann whose remarkable collection, largely of Italian provenance, including some splendid illuminated manuscripts, was presented by his widow to the Hungarian Academy of Sciences. Elkan Nathan Adler, an English lawyer, who traveled around the world in the course of his business affairs, built up a library of incunabula, rare printed works, and manuscripts which for bulk, if not for quality, was perhaps the greatest collection assembled by a private person. Just after World War I in order to make good the defalcations of a business associate, he was compelled to sell his library to the Jewish Theological Seminary of America, thus elevating it to a foremost position among the Jewish libraries of the world. Adler's collection also contained some 30,000 fragments from the Cairo *genizah,* which he had visited even before it achieved fame. Moses Gaster, *ḥakham* (chief rabbi)of the English Sephardi community, also built up a great collection of manuscripts reflecting every side of his versatile interests. Towards the end of his life he sold the bulk to the British Museum. Some of the remainder was ruined during the German

David ben Abraham Oppenheimer (1664–1736), rabbi of Prague, who collected an immense library of Hebrew books and manuscripts. Cecil Roth Collection.

David Solomon Sassoon (1792–1864), one of the best-known bibliophiles of the last century. Courtesy Rabbi Solomon David Sassoon, Jerusalem.

air raids on London in World War II; what remained, including the Samaritan manuscripts, was acquired by the John Rylands Library in Manchester to add to its already remarkable Hebrew collection. David Solomon Sassoon of London had the advantage of great wealth, close connections with the Orient, and a family tradition of book collecting. He assembled his collection of manuscripts with scholarly discrimination and described it in an elaborate catalog, perhaps the most exhaustive work of its type that has appeared in print. This collection went into the possession of his son Solomon David Sassoon now in Jerusalem. The important collection of Berthold Strauss of London (1901–1962), cataloged in part in his *Ohel Barukh* (1959), was acquired after his death for Yeshiva University, New York. The 20th-century scholars whose private collections have become part of established libraries include Israel Davidson (Jewish Theological Seminary, where it was destroyed by fire), Hyman Enelow (Jewish Theological Seminary), Lazarus Goldschmidt (second collection, Royal Library, Copenhagen), Mordecai Margolioth (Bar Ilan University), and Alexander Marx (Jewish Theological Seminary, partly destroyed). Other large private collections were assembled by Saul Lieberman, Cecil Roth, and Gershom Scholem. Significant private collections were also built up by ḥasidic dynasties, e.g. Gerer, Sadogerer, and Lubavicher. Other important private collections belonged to Abraham Merzbacher (now in Frankfort City and University Library), Nathan Porges, Israel Solomons (Jewish Theological Seminary and Hebrew Union College libraries), Mathias Straschun (part in YIVO Institute, New York), and Michael Zagayski. Among other collectors, mention should be made of Fritz Bamberger (New York), Ludwig Jesselson (New York), Jacob Lowy (Montreal), and Israel Melman (Jerusalem), and Rabbi Judah Leib ha-Kohen Maimon (Fishman). The last two had between 40,000 and 50,000 Judaica books each, mostly printed books including many incunabulae and thousands of the most rare books in Judaica. Part of Maimon's library is now incorporated in Mosad ha-Rav Kook Library (Jerusalem), and the main part of Mehlman's library was divided between the Hebrew University Library (Jerusalem) and the Tel Aviv University Library. A very important collection of early Yiddish literature was that of Judah A. Joffee (Jewish Theological Seminary).

Christian scholars and collectors who owned many important Hebrew books included Johannes Buxtorf, Bishop Huntington, Bishop Kennicott, Sir Thomas Phillips, Edward Pococke, the Duke of Sussex, and Aldis Wright.

BOOKPLATES

Most people who own books put their name in them. Because the purchaser of a book usually sees it as a thing of beauty, it became customary for the owner to have a specially designed label to paste onto the inside of the front cover. The labels, known as bookplates, commonly contained a quotation, either from the Bible or some other classical Jewish source, which made some reference to knowledge or books and the owner's name. Often the quotation contained some allusion to the owner's name. Many collectors had special designs or engravings made for their bookplates which, in the course of time, became an art vehicle expressing both the owner's and the artist's love of the book.

The earliest *ex libris* with Hebrew wording were made for non-Jews. One of the first bookplates was made by Albrecht Duerer for Willibald Pirkheimer (c. 1504) with an inscription in Hebrew, Greek and Latin of Psalms 111:10. Hector Pomer of Nuremberg had a woodcut *ex libris* (1525) that is attributed to Duerer or his disciple Hans Sebald Beham, with the Hebrew translation of "Unto the pure all things are pure" (New Testament, Titus 1:15). "A time for everything" (Ecclesiastes 3:1) in Hebrew is found on the bookplate (1530) by Barthel Beham, of Hieronymus Baumgartner of Nuremberg. Among the Jewish artists

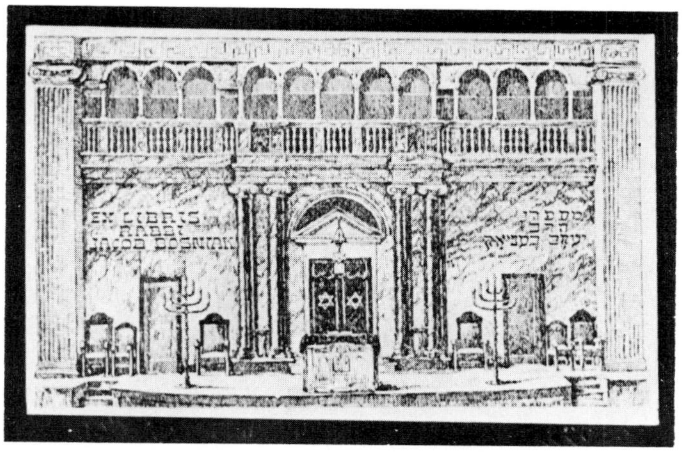

Ex libris of Rabbi Jacob Bosniak. The scene might be the almemar in his synagogue.

in England who engraved bookplates in the 18th century were Benjamin Levi of Portsmouth, Isaac Levi of Portsea, Moses Mordecai of London, Samuel Yates of Liverpool, and Mordecai Moses and Abraham Ezekiel Ezekiel of Exeter. However, they only made a few bookplates for Jews. The first known *ex libris* of a Jew was made by Benjamin Levi for Isaac Mendes of London in 1746. A number of British Jews in the 18th and 19th centuries had armorial bookplates bearing the family coat of arms, although some of them were spurious. Sir Moses Montefiore had several *ex libris* which bore his distinctively Jewish coat of arms. Among the few Jewish *ex libris* made in the latter half of the 18th century in Germany were those for David Friedlaender, engraved by Daniel N. Chodowiecki in 1774; and Bernhardt Friedlaender, by Johann M. S. Lowe in 1790. In the 18th century Dutch members of the Polack (Polak) family were among the early bookplate artists. A. S. Polak engraved an heraldic *ex libris* for the Jewish baron Aerssen van Sommelsdyk. Isaac de Pinto, a Dutch Sephardi Jew, had a bookplate featuring a huge flower vase with his monogram. The modern Russian-Jewish artist S. Yudovim engraved a number of exquisite woodcut bookplates which are among the relatively few with Yiddish inscriptions. Among other European Jewish artists who have used various graphic media to execute *ex libris* are Uriel Birnbaum, Lodewijk Lopes Cardozo, Fré Cohen, Michel Fingesten, Alice Garman-Horodisch, Georg Jilovsky, Emil Orlik, and Hugo Steiner-Prag. Marco Birnholz (1885–1965) of Vienna, a foremost collector, had over 300 different ones for his own use that were made by many of the European Jewish graphic artists. Bookplates of three Jews are considered to be among the earliest American *ex libris,* dating from the first half of the 19th century. The pictorial bookplate of Barrak (Baruch) Hays of New York incorporated a family coat of arms. Benjamin S. Judah had two armorial bookplates, although there is no evidence that he was entitled to bear a coat of arms. Dr. Benjamin I. Raphael also had two *ex libris* – one showing a hand grasping a surgeon's knife and the other a skull and bones, symbols frequently found on medical *ex libris.* Among the early American college bookplates that have Hebrew words are those of Yale University, inscribed with *Urim ve-Thumim,* Columbia with *Ori El* ("God is my light" alluding to Psalms 27:1) and Dartmouth with *El Shaddai* ("God Almighty"). Many of the major universities in the United States have a variety of bookplates for their Judaica collections. American Jewish artists of bookplates include Joseph B. Abrahams, Joanne Bauer-Mayer, Todros Geller, A. Raymond Katz, Reuben Leaf, Solomon S. Levadi, Isaac Lichtenstein, Saul Raskin, and Ilya Schor. Ephraim Moses Lilien, the "father of Jewish bookplates," designed many for early Zionist leaders which revealed national suffering and hopes. He gave the Hebrew rendering of the Latin term *ex libris* – *mi-sifrei* ("from the books of") for the numerous *ex libris,* which he created with definitive Jewish significance, and inaugurated a new era in this field that was pursued by other Jewish artists. Hermann Struck drew inspiration from the monuments and landscape of Ereẓ Israel for the *ex libris* he made. Joseph Budko created more than 50 bookplates in aquatints, woodcuts, etchings, and drawings, mostly in a purely ornamental style, leaning heavily on the decorative value of Hebrew script. His artistic *ex libris* are considered among the finest Jewish examples. Jakob Steinhardt also executed a number of bookplates. Among the other modern Israel artists who produced *ex libris* are Aryeh Allweil, David Davidowicz, Ze'ev Raban, J. Ross, Jacob Stark, and Shelomo Yedidiah. Synagogues, Jewish community centers, and institutions of Jewish learning have their own bookplates on which are imprinted names of the donors of books or names of deceased persons who are thus memorialized. Important collections of *ex libris* are at Hebrew Union College, Cincinnati, consisting mainly of the private collections of Israel Solomons and Philip Goodman, and at the Museum of the Printing Arts, Safed, based mainly on the private collection of Abraham Weiss of Tel Aviv.

9. the artistry of the book

TYPOGRAPHY

Hebrew printing began about 1475, in Italy at Reggio di Calabria and at Piove de Sacco, near Venice. In the short span of the following few years new Hebrew presses were established in Mantua, Bologna, Ferrara (Italy), and Hijar (Spain). Thus, within a short space of time Hebrew printing spread to relatively distant places. Since printers at that time had to provide each of his own letter founts, a remarkable variety of alphabets and styles appeared at the inception of Hebrew typography.

The books printed in Spain and Reggio de Calabria display the reed born alphabets (square and cursive, a short of italics) customary in the manuscripts of the Jews centered on Spain (Sephardi). These alphabets are distinguished by a great elegance in their curves and in the modeling of their strokes; the artist who cut the ones used in Guadalajara was mentioned by name, Piedro de Guadalajara, and was ostensibly a gentile. It is remarkable that the cursive Sephardi letter is already used as text letter in the first book printed in Reggio di Calabria, Rashi's commentary on the Pentateuch (hence its later name "Rashi-letter"), 26 years before a non-Hebrew cursive letter was used for the first time by the Venetian printer Aldus Manutius in 1501. In Piove di Sacco, where the printer was of German origin – as most of the early Hebrew printers in Italy – the alphabets used were

Printers' mark of the Basevi family, Verona, 1594–1605.

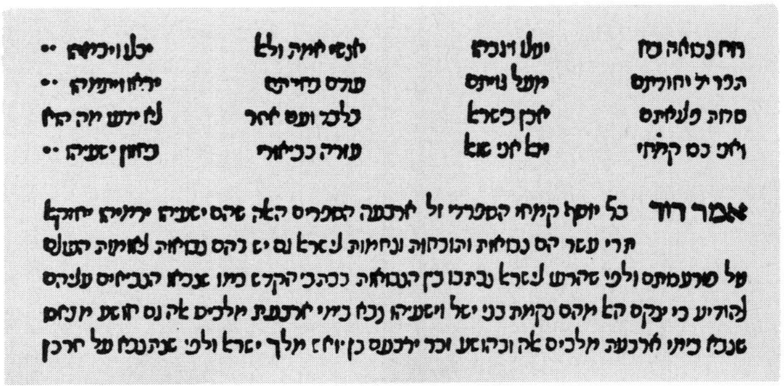

A page printed at Guadalajara (no. 148 on the incunabula list).

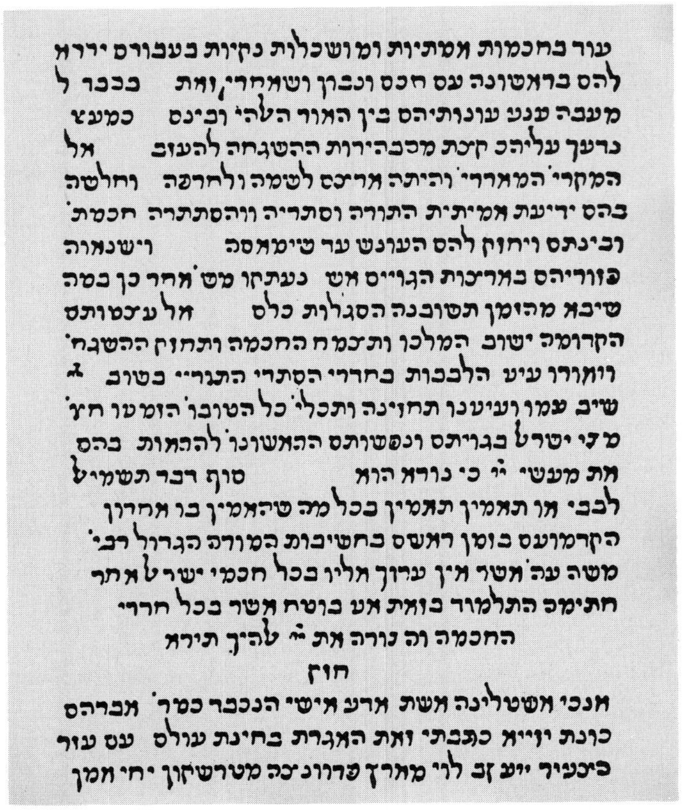

Conat's alphabet (no. 138 on the incunabula list).

developments of the quill-shaped Ashkenazi (German) manuscript letter, angular and based on heavy contrast between bold and fine strokes. The edition of *seliḥot,* undated and probably the first book by that printer, displays a distinguished page set in quite large letters and long lines with wide margins in 4° size.

The founder of the press in Mantua, Abraham Conat, who was a physician and scribe by profession, had an alphabet cut for himself, for which his own Italian-German cursive hand served as a model. His square letter was of the Ashkenazi type and similar to that used in Piove di Sacco. In 1477 the Book of Psalms with the commentary of David Kimḥi appeared in Bologna, the letters being of a similar type to those used in Mantua. In the same year Abraham ben Ḥayyim The Dyer of Pesaro started a short-lived press in Ferrara, buying the equipment from Abraham Conat. In 1482 he printed in Bologna an edition of the Pentateuch with Rashi's commentary; the text is set in a pleasantly large and elegantly light Sephardi new square letter and the commentary in a much smaller cursive letter of the Italian type. This edition fixed the layout for biblical texts with commentaries for all following editions.

The decisive turn in Hebrew typography after these initial trials was instituted with the activity of the Soncino family. This family, hailing from Germany, printed Hebrew books through five generations, starting in 1484 in Soncino and later publishing works in Casalmaggiore. Pesaro, Brescia, Naples, Rimini, Salonika, Constantinople and Cairo until 1557. The Soncinos, the most prolific and most creative Jewish Hebrew printer-publishers of all times, stabilized the style of letters used in Hebrew printing, employing an alphabet based on the Sephardi type and well adapted to the mechanical exigencies of printing, and which served as a base for later printers. They put out works of basic Hebrew literature in editions which became classical, as well as non-Hebrew books. The non-Hebrew books printed by Gershom Soncino typographically take a place of honor among the book productions of this time. He employed as a letter cutter the most accomplished letter artist of his time, and possibly of all times, Francesco Griffo, a friar of Bologna who had also worked for the famous Venetian printer Aldus Manutius, the first to print books in cursive letters (cancellaresca), which were cut by Griffo, in pocket size.

In the meantime Venice became a new center of Hebrew printing. A rich gentile humanist from Antwerp, Daniel Bomberg, assembled an impressive team of scholars – Jewish and baptized – as editors and proofreaders, as well as competent craftsmen, had excellent letters cut, and established a Hebrew press in Venice which was to excel in quantity and quality all those that had preceded him in this field. All of the products of Bomberg's press were distinguished by faultless composition and layout, improved typefaces, and high-quality paper. His products constituted the high mark of achievement of the first decades of Hebrew typography. Based on the shapes pioneered by the Soncinos, Bomberg's typefaces became dominant and greatly influenced the further development of Hebrew typography.

While the Spanish-Italian branch of Hebrew printing developed — after some initial wavering — a square and cursive typeface based on the Sephardi tradition of lettering, another Hebrew printing center came into being in the second decade of the 16th century in Prague (and somewhat later in Basle) whose lettering was based decidedly on the Ashkenazi letter shapes. From the start the Prague printers achieved high typographical excellence and their influence spread to various parts of Germany and to Poland. Hebrew printing in Prague started in 1512; in 1514 the printers' company was joined by new partners, among them Gershom Kohen, and from then on he was the central figure in the enterprise. His family continued his work well into the 17th century. In 1526 the Kohen press published an outstanding typographical work, a Passover *Haggadah* in large 4° with many woodcuts, the text being set in a superb large-size Ashkenazi typeface, which was probably

A page printed by Abraham ben Ḥayyim at Pesaro (no. 152 on the incunabula list).

איש

cut in wood and displays to the best advantage all the beauty in this late Gothic style of Hebrew lettering. The many initial words are of exceptional beauty and are set in a still larger size, or, more probably, cut as whole words in wood. Four of the woodcut illustrations have a letter *Shin*, ש unobtrusively incorporated, probably the signature of one of the partners, Ḥayyim Shaḥor (he had already left the partnership when the *Haggadah* was published but seems to have been responsible for the woodcuts or at least some of them). The *Haggadah* was reprinted in the same year with slight alterations by the original printers and was closely copied in 1560 in Mantua, with altered woodcuts and initial words; parts of the text were printed in smaller type.

Shaḥor set up a press in Olesnica, near Breslau, moving from there to Augsburg, Ichenhausen, Heddernheim (all in Germany), and finally to Lublin, Poland. He took typefaces from Prague and continued to use the skill he gained there. The Halicz brothers set up a press in Cracow about 1530, using mostly Prague type and style. The Hebrew Bible (c. 1551–52) with Rashi's commentary, printed by Samuel Halicz in Constantinople — of which only the Pentateuch with the Five Scrolls and Haftarot is known (in a unique copy) — is in good typographical tradition; the letters which were used show a strange mixture of Ashkenazi and Sephardi style.

In the 16th century the interest of Christian humanists in Hebrew printing became of the utmost importance. Apart from Daniel Bomberg in Venice, there was Johannes Froben of Basle, who used the Ashkenazi type of letters to great advantage, including the Ashkenazi cursive (chiefly for texts in Judeo-German). Froben printed quite a number of Hebrew and Judeo-German books in cooperation with the Christian Hebraists Sebastian Muenster and the two Buxtorfs, among them a Hebrew grammar written in Latin by Sebastian Muenster, 1534, in which the cantillation signs of the Bible were rendered in musical notes. Paulus Fagius in Isny and Paulus Aemilius in Augsburg carefully produced books in Ashkenazi Hebrew type. At the same time in France Robertus Stephanus (Etienne), who was responsible for the edition of many Latin and almost all Greek texts, printed the Hebrew Bible twice, once in a small format and once in 8° in beautiful letters of the Sephardi type, cut specially for these editions. Guillaume Le Bé, the man who influenced the further development of the Hebrew printed alphabet possibly more than any other single figure, emerged from

Stephanus' printing house. A native of Troyes, France, he was a letter designer and punch cutter who in 1545 was employed on Stephanus' recommendation by the Venetian humanist M. A. Giustiniani, the founder in that year of a Hebrew press in Venice. Le Bé, 21 years old when he came to Venice, mainly specialized from then onward in designing and cutting Hebrew letters (until 1550 in Venice and later again in Paris). He carefully studied the Hebrew letter shapes, collected what he considered the best samples from everywhere, and continued cutting Hebrew founts to the end of his long life. Almost 20 Hebrew founts are credited to him. Not only did Giustiniani and the Italian-Jewish printer Meir Parenzo depend on his typefaces but they were also later copied in Italy until the 19th century. The press of Belforte in Leghorn (closed in 1939) used a derivative of his letters, and the Nebiolo type foundry in Turin still produced them in 1970 in a later rendering.

More important still, Le Bé provided Christopher Plantin, the great printer of Antwerp, with Hebrew letters which the latter used in his Polyglot Bible (Antwerp, 1569–72), a superb piece of printing. Le Bé's letter style (and in part probably even the original letters) was passed on from Plantin on one hand to Christian printers in Germany and on the other to Holland, which took the lead in Hebrew printing in the 17th and 18th centuries, and from where Hebrew printing in Germany, England, Eastern Europe, and even the Near East was decisively influenced. The first Hebrew printer in Holland was Manasseh Ben Israel, who had his letters cut from models prepared by the chief Hebrew scribe of Amsterdam, Michael Judah. His first publication, a prayer book of the Sephardi rite, appeared in 1627. Further Hebrew presses were set up soon after in Amsterdam. The Jewish printers there, who were learned and cultured men, ordered their letters from the most accomplished punch cutters of their time, among them Christopher van Dyck and Johann Michael Fleischmann of Nuremburg. Since Hebrew books became an important export item in the economy of Amsterdam, all the important type foundries there produced Hebrew founts. These were used everywhere, and printers mentioned the use of "Amsterdam type" at different places on their title pages rather than the place and name of the actual printers. Typographically outstanding among the Amsterdam Hebrew presses was that of the Athias family, which produced, among others, the famous Hebrew Bible (1661) and the beautiful edition of Maimonides' *Mishneh Torah* (1702/03). Another Hebrew press in Amsterdam of high standing was that of the Proops family, which published a very large quantity of Hebrew books and continued their work into the late 19th century.

In the 17th and 18th centuries Hebrew printing spread widely to Germany, Poland, and some oriental countries, and continued at some presses in Italy. The centers all derived from Amsterdam, Prague, and Venice and continued their respective typographical traditions, mostly with loss of quality. Some Hebrew type was also used in the first book printed on the North American continent, the Bay Psalm Book (Cambridge, Massachusetts, 1640). The 19th century brought further innovations. In Roedelheim (near Frankfort) W. Heidenheim and B. Baschwitz published a new *maḥzor* in 1800 in nine volumes, using newly cut letters – square and cursive Sephardi for the commentary, and cursive Ashkenazi for the German translations – with a great deal of skill. This press continued printing in the same style and with the same letters throughout the 19th century, and its products were reprinted from stereotypes until the Holocaust, being reproduced in Basle even after World War II. In Eastern Europe the most important typographical production was the superb edition of the Babylonian Talmud by the house of Romm in Vilna (1880–86). In England Z. H. Filipowski printed Hebrew text editions in a pleasant small type. The 19th century, with its deep changes in Jewish life, made new claims on Hebrew typography. A secular literature arose, with newspapers and periodicals not only in Hebrew but also in Yiddish and Ladino which are written in Hebrew letters. By the end of the century changes in typographical techniques had taken place. The large European type founderies produced new Hebrew letters on traditional lines which were used in the printing of Bibles by the British and Foreign Bible Society and the Wuerttemberg Bible Institute, as well as in other scholarly editions. The most successful Hebrew type innovation was created through the cooperation of the Leipzig cantor and scribe Raphael Frank and the graphic artist Ruehl who worked for the Berthold type foundry. The Frank-Ruehl letter spread quickly, and after it was incorporated in the program of all the chief typesetting machines (Linotype, Monotype – under the name of Peninim – and Intertype) it held a near monopoly for quite a long period, in spite of its being an expression of the Art Nouveau style.

The rapid expansion of the press and of art and litera-

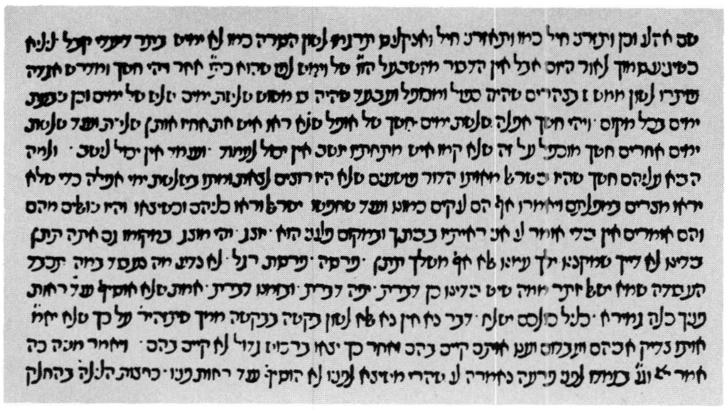

The cursive Sephardi letter used in an incunabulum of Rashi's commentary on the Pentateuch printed by Abraham ben Garton in Reggio di Calabria, 1475. Incunabula list, no. 171. From A. Freimann (ed.), *Thesaurus Typographiae Hebraicae,* 1924.

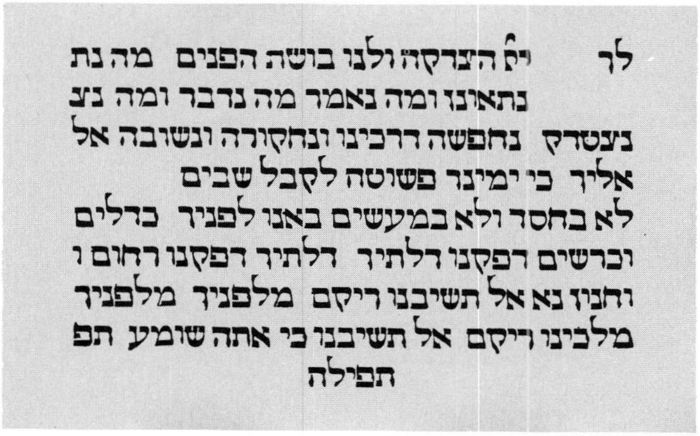

לך ייי הצדקה ולנו בושת הפנים מה נת
נתאונן ומה נאמר מה נדבר ומה נצ
נצטדק נחפשה דרכינו ונחקורה ונשובה אל
אליך כי ימינך פשוטה לקבל שבים
לא בחסד ולא במעשים באנו לפניך כדלים
וברשים דפקנו דלתיך דלתיך דפקנו רחום ו
וחנון נא אל תשיבנו ריקם מלפניך מלפניך
מלכינו ריקם אל תשיבנו כי אתה שומע תפ
תפילה

Example of quill-shaped Ashkenazi manuscript letter from an edition of *Seliḥot* printed by Meshullam Cusi's sons in Piove di Sacco, Italy, 1475. Incunabula list, no. 98. From A. Freimann, *ibid.*

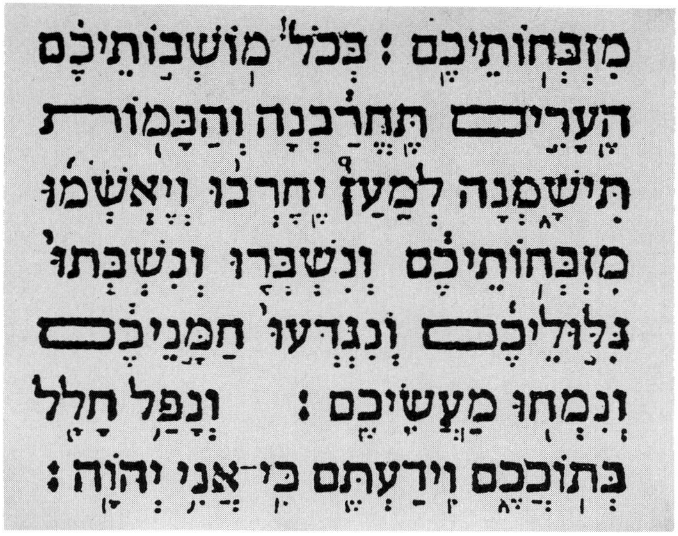

מִזְבְּחוֹתֵיכֶם׃ בְּכֹל מוֹשְׁבוֹתֵיכֶם
הֶעָרִים תֶּחֱרַבְנָה וְהַבָּמוֹת
תִּישָׁמְנָה לְמַעַן יֶחֶרְבוּ וְיֶאְשְׁמוּ
מִזְבְּחוֹתֵיכֶם וְנִשְׁבְּרוּ וְנִשְׁבְּתוּ
גִּלּוּלֵיכֶם וְנִגְדְּעוּ חַמָּנֵיכֶם
וְנִמְחוּ מַעֲשֵׂיכֶם׃ וְנָפַל חָלָל
בְּתוֹכְכֶם וִידַעְתֶּם כִּי־אֲנִי יְהוָה׃

Passage from Ezekiel in a small Bible printed by Stephanus' printing house, Paris, 1544-46.

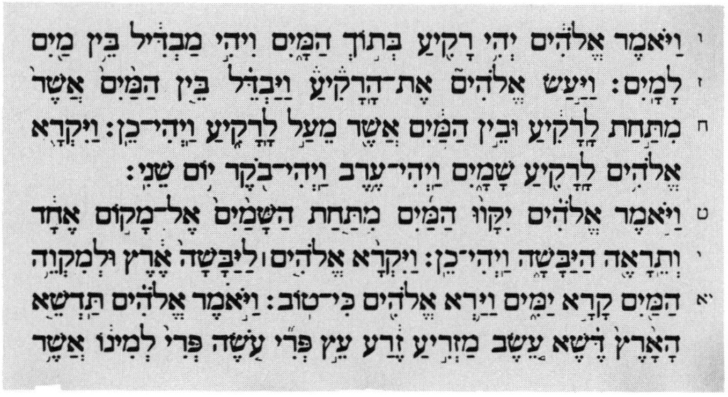

ו וַיֹּאמֶר אֱלֹהִים יְהִי רָקִיעַ בְּתוֹךְ הַמָּיִם וִיהִי מַבְדִּיל בֵּין מַיִם
ז לָמָיִם׃ וַיַּעַשׂ אֱלֹהִים אֶת־הָרָקִיעַ וַיַּבְדֵּל בֵּין הַמַּיִם אֲשֶׁר
ח מִתַּחַת לָרָקִיעַ וּבֵין הַמַּיִם אֲשֶׁר מֵעַל לָרָקִיעַ וַיְהִי־כֵן׃ וַיִּקְרָא
אֱלֹהִים לָרָקִיעַ שָׁמָיִם וַיְהִי־עֶרֶב וַיְהִי־בֹקֶר יוֹם שֵׁנִי׃
ט וַיֹּאמֶר אֱלֹהִים יִקָּווּ הַמַּיִם מִתַּחַת הַשָּׁמַיִם אֶל־מָקוֹם אֶחָד
י וְתֵרָאֶה הַיַּבָּשָׁה וַיְהִי־כֵן׃ וַיִּקְרָא אֱלֹהִים לַיַּבָּשָׁה אֶרֶץ וּלְמִקְוֵה
יא הַמַּיִם קָרָא יַמִּים וַיַּרְא אֱלֹהִים כִּי־טוֹב׃ וַיֹּאמֶר אֱלֹהִים תַּדְשֵׁא
הָאָרֶץ דֶּשֶׁא עֵשֶׂב מַזְרִיעַ זֶרַע עֵץ פְּרִי עֹשֶׂה פְּרִי לְמִינוֹ אֲשֶׁר

From the Koren Bible, set in the "Koren" typeface, Jerusalem, 1958.

From Henri Friedlaender's textbook on printing, *Melekhet ha-Sefer,* using the author's typeface, "Hadassah," and produced by the Hadassah Apprentice School of Printing, Jerusalem, 1962.

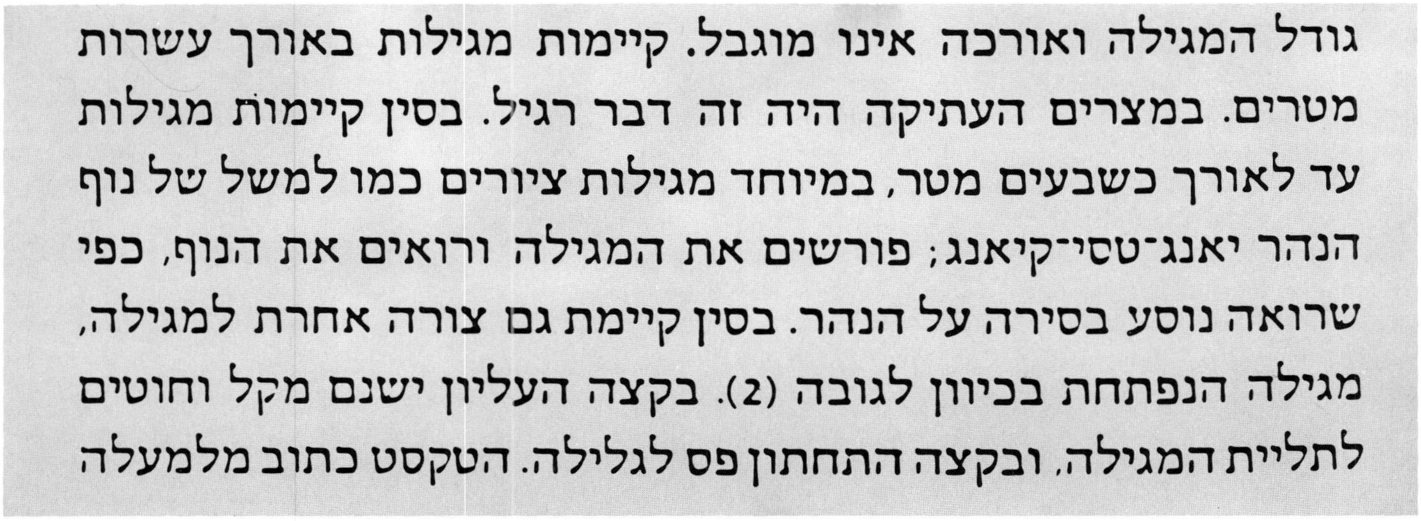

גודל המגילה ואורכה אינו מוגבל. קיימות מגילות באורך עשרות
מטרים. במצרים העתיקה היה זה דבר רגיל. בסין קיימות מגילות
עד לאורך כשבעים מטר, במיוחד מגילות ציורים כמו למשל של נוף
הנהר יאנג־טסי־קיאנג; פורשים את המגילה ורואים את הנוף, כפי
שרואה נוסע בסירה על הנהר. בסין קיימת גם צורה אחרת למגילה,
מגילה הנפתחת בכיוון לגובה (2). בקצה העליון ישנם מקל וחוטים
לתליית המגילה, ובקצה התחתון פס לגלילה. הטקסט כתוב מלמעלה

ture publications in Hebrew and Yiddish after World War I and the growing influence, first of the German expressionism and then of the New Typography promoted by the Bauhaus, were a new challenge to Hebrew typography. The existing letters were of little use in shaping the new typographical images. New Hebrew letters of the sanserif type were therefore created, at least for display, the first a letter called "Haim" by Jacob Levit (in Warsaw) and the second by the Tel Aviv graphic artist Aharoni which was published under his name in Germany. Both these typefaces were widely used for display and gave Hebrew printing an entirely new look. At the same time the cursive (Rashi) alphabet was totally abandoned in secular literature – a fact which resulted in a deplorable impoverishment of typographical possibilities.

The renascence of Hebrew literature, its concentration in Israel, and the tremendous growth of the production of books and periodicals, as well as of commercial printing, necessitated swift developments in Hebrew typography. They took shape chiefly from the end of World War II onward, and from the foundation of the State of Israel with accelerated energy. Between the two world wars new Hebrew types were still intended chiefly for what could be called ceremonial printing: This is true of the Ashkenazi square letter called "Stam," which was cut by the Berthold foundry and was dependant on a design by Franziska Baruch, and of the type designed by Marcus Behmer and ordered by the Soncino Society for their monumental Bible, of which only the Pentateuch was printed before the Nazis put an end to the project. From this time a different sort of typeface was needed. Serious attempts began in the period between the two world wars, such as those of Eric Gill and L. A. Meyer, together with Franziska Baruch, but were not successful in providing new letters for general use; others, such as those of the German letter designer E. R. Weiss (whose drawings were lost), the American F. W. Goudy, and the Englishman H. G. Carter, were abortive. A radical step forward was made in the Ha-Ẓevi family of typefaces (Jerusalem Type Foundry), which were designed by Ẓevi Hausmann in collaboration with M. Spitzer. Based on a quasi-sanserif style, it went back to old letter shapes and reduced the over decoration which had crept into Hebrew letter design in the course of centuries. In this way it achieved a modern appearance, but since it was available for hand composition only, it could not be used for book work. The David Hebrew, a letter built on somewhat similar principles but more cursive, was designed by Ismar David with some help from M. Spitzer, and is available on Intertype; it is used in book work and allows for a very light look of the page in contrast to the heavy look traditional in Hebrew printing. Other new types are a modern renewal of the Ashkenazi letter by Henry Friedlaender, "Hadassah" (Amsterdam Type Foundry), also available on Intertype; Franziska Baruch's "Schocken-Hebrew" (Monotype); Z. Korngold's "Koren" (Deberny et Peignot, Paris), a traditional letter useful for traditional literature; and Zvi Narkis' "Narkis" Hebrew on Linotype. As a result of the process of photo setting new faces are likely to be created. The general appearance of Hebrew typographical work – which in the present-day covers the whole range of printing from belles-lettres through scholarly and technical literature to art books, periodicals of all sorts, and a very wide range of commercial printing – will go on changing. Some substantial advances in bibliophile book production have also taken place.

METHODS AND TECHNIQUES

The proto-printers were not interested in creating anything looking different from the style and form of the manuscript codices. Books from Conat's presses have often been taken for manuscripts with popular appeal. The early incunabula, therefore, have no title pages, open spaces are left for the illuminators and illustrators, and only at the end of the text, in the so-called colophon, some information is given on the printer(s), their scholarly or technical staff, the place of work, and the date at which the printing was completed.

Hebrew incunabula were printed by the same methods and with the same utensils as those used by the non-Jewish presses. A letterpress was composed from types, the lead block supporting each of them being 27mm. long and 6mm. wide, the same measurements as of the Latin types of the same body. Types were arranged into lines by putting them into a composing stick; they were then transferred into the wooden galleys, and impressions of – mostly – two corresponding pages were made in the manually operated printing presses. Each copy had to be printed separately, the press each time to be opened, the letterpress to be blacked with printer's ink, and a new sheet of moistened paper to be inserted. When Conat claimed that the daily output of his printing shop was only 125 copies he may be taking also into account typesetting and correcting. The printers were keen to economize, to lease typographical material from other printers, or to buy it second-hand. In order to make the fullest use of the labor invested in typesetting, the printer of the Bible in Brescia in 1493 broke some of the columns of the letter-press composed for this edition into two parts, thus producing every time two pages of a handy pocket edition published by him in the same year.

The early book productions had no signature, a device which was introduced by Joshua Soncino in 1483 as a guide for the bookbinders' work of putting the book together from single sheets. Usually, the signature is found on the left side of the bottom of the page in Hebrew alphabetical numbers, but some Augsburg, Constantinople, and Salonika issues of the early 16th century have them on the top left or bottom right corner. Up to about 1515 only Hebrew letters were used, but Daniel Bomberg introduced Arabic figures as well. In rare cases the alphabet took the place of numbers (*Kol Bo,* Rimini, 1525; Rome, 1545). Pagination was introduced later than the signature. No incunabulum appears to have had it. The first to have had numbered folios, though not very consistently so, is Maimonides' *Mishneh Torah,* printed in Constantinople in 1509. Soncino did not number his pages to the end. Of Bomberg's productions those prepared by Adelkind – with the exception of Bibles and prayer books – have numbered folios; from 1525 this is the case with all Bomberg's works and most other Italian printers followed his example. The Hebrew number appears on the upper left of the first page in Bomberg's works; other printers added Arabic numerals. One work printed in Sabbioneta and one in Cremona repeat the number on the upper right of the second page of the leaf. Pagination of pages is rather rare at first, exceptions being the works of Stephanus at Paris, Plantin at Antwerp, and Zanetti at Rome in the 16th century. The Cremona *Zohar* of 1599 has two columns to each page and numbers opposite every tenth line.

The first Hebrew text with vowels was printed in the *Maḥzor Roma,* 1485; signatures were first used by Joshua Soncino, and the earliest attempt of a Hebrew title page was made by Gershom Soncino in his edition of *Tur Oraḥ Ḥayyim.* Eliezer Alantansi is the only Jew known to have used a printers' mark during the 15th century.

Joshua Soncino was also the first to introduce ornamented initials. He fitted such letters into frames of similarly engraved woodcut borders, marking in this way the beginning of a book. Such headings appeared for the first time in his edition of the Talmud tractate *Berakhot,* 1483. Four years later he began to use a beautifully ornamented woodcut frame previously used by Francesco del Tuppo in his edition of the Fables by Aesop, published at Naples, Italy, on February 13, 1485. Joshua used this border several times for framing the first pages of his editions before he passed it on to other printing shops. Other Hebrew printers who used ornamented initial letters and borders were the Gunzenhausers of Naples who printed with Soncino's woodcuts. The frame in Baḥya ben Asher's Pentateuch commentary was printed a month earlier in Leonardo Aretino's *L'Aquila* finished on June 27, 1492 by Aiolfo de Cantone. It may be assumed that this woodcut and all the other ornaments used by the Gunzenhausers were the work of Moses ben Isaac, a Jewish woodcut artist, the brother-in-law of Azriel Gunzenhauser.

The initials and frames used by the two Eliezers at Hijar and Lisbon are produced from metal-cuts executed by the silversmith Alfonso Fernandes de Cordoba, a printer in Valencia.

A Hebrew printer was able to acquire everything needed for his work by purchase, loan or exchange, the only exception being the Hebrew type which could not be obtained at the typefoundries or from other commercial sources. Every Hebrew printer therefore had to make his own set of matrices in order to case the typographical material required. The ductus to these types differs, of course, according to the style and taste of the scribes whose work was used as copy for the cutter of the punches.

Hebrew incunabula were printed on excellent, locally made paper which stood the test of centuries and sometimes helps to locate books whose place of printing is not established by the colophon. Copies of the same edition are known to have been printed on normal-size and on large-size paper, indicating that even then "deluxe editions" were produced. Thirty-six Hebrew incunabula survived in copies printed on parchment, thirty of them originating from Italian presses and six from Spain or Portugal. All these incunabula have also been published on ordinary paper.

PRINTERS' MARKS

The first known printers' mark (device or badge used

by early printers to distinguish their productions) in Hebrew printing is the lion rampant within a red shield, which was used by Eliezer Alantansi at Hijar in and after 1485. The Soncino family of printers, both in Italy and in other countries, used a tower, probably the badge of the city of Soncino in Lombardy; this was subsequently adopted by the Soncino Gesellschaft in Germany and by the 20th century Soncino Press in London. Later, various printers of the Kohen family, especially the Proops' of Amsterdam, used a printer's mark of the hands spread in priestly benediction. The Giustiniani Press in Venice employed a conventional representation of the Temple in Jerusalem – subsequently much copied – and the Bragadini used three crowns symbolizing the diadem of royalty, priesthood and Torah (cf. *Avot* 4:13).

At a later time Italian printers often employed their family badges as printers' marks. Thus, the productions of the Foa family, from the middle of the 16th century down to the 18th, were distinguished by a badge showing two lions rampant against a palm tree supporting the shield of David, with various permutations. Abraham Usque of Ferrara adopted the Portuguese royal badge of a sphere, losing the significance of the punning motto *spera in domimum* by translating it back into the Hebrew original *kavveh el Adonai* (Psalms 27:14). The Basevi brothers of Verona used their family badge, subsequently incorporated into their coat of arms, of a white lion back to back with a black eagle, both crowned. The badge of Manasseh Ben Israel was memorable, with the words *emet me-ereẓ tiẓmaḥ* ("Truth springeth out of the earth," Psalms 85:12) shown as a rebus, or in his non-Hebrew productions, a pilgrim with the motto *Apercebido como hu romeiro.* The Benveniste family of Amsterdam used a lion rampant against a tower, surmounted by a star, which presumably was their coat of arms. The symbols of fertility, fish, were common throughout the 17th and 18th centuries in various countries. Monograms in Latin characters were sometimes used. The Eastern European printers' marks were for the most part unoriginal and often poorly printed and designed. Among the Christian printers of Hebrew books, Froben used intertwined serpents, and Fagius, a leafy tree. From the 18th century, the use of printers' marks became less common and their designs less distinctive.

An illustration from *Ma'aseh ha-Ofanim,* a Hebrew translation of *Tractatus de Sphaera Mundi* by the French astronomer, John de Sacrobosco, which was made by Solomon ben Avigdor of Montpelier at the beginning of the 15th century. The book was printed in Offenbach in 1720. The picture is meant to illustrate the spherity of the earth by using a line of vision from different heights, from a boat at sea. The commentary, in Rashi script in the outer column, is by Jewish scholars of the 16th and 17th centuries.

ILLUSTRATIONS

In the early days of printing the illustrations were far inferior to those in contemporary illuminated manuscripts. European printing as a whole was preceded by block books, in which the text was subordinate to the illustrations. Hence, the illustrated book existed from the very beginning of printing. In early Hebrew printing nothing of the sort is known; but the very nature of the illustrated book subjected it to more wear than ordinary volumes, and it may well be that some early illustrated works have been thumbed out of existence. There are indeed some surviving woodblocks showing Passover scenes which were probably printed as early as c. 1480. These may have been prepared for the illustration of a Hebrew work. The earliest Hebrew printed books, however, while – like other books – leaving a space for illuminated words or letters to be inserted by hand, relied for their decorative effect entirely on the disposition of the type, which was sometimes ornamented. Such is the case with the *Turim* of Pieve di Sacco (1475), the second (dated) Hebrew book to be completed in type.

DECORATIVE BORDERS. It was only at a slightly later period that, in imitation of the more sophisticated (but not fully illuminated) manuscripts of the period, decorative borders began to be used for the opening – there were no title pages yet – and occasionally also for some of the more significant later pages.

The first Hebrew book to make use of a border was the Pentateuch printed at Hijar in Spain about 1486. The border, however, designed by Alonso Fernandez de Cordoba, was not on the opening page but appeared as a decoration to the Song of Moses (Exodus 15), as in some Spanish Hebrew Bible manuscripts. This border is outstanding with its beautiful traceries and charming animal figures. It appeared later in the *Manuale Saragossanum,* one of the great monuments of early Spanish printing, in which Cordoba and the Jewish printer Solomon Zalmati had collaborated. The border around the first page of the *Turim,* printed by Samuel d'Ortas at Leiria in Portugal in 1495, is of particular interest. This, presumably cut by a Jewish artist and incorporating Hebrew letters, elaborates on the similies in the opening passage of the work. About the same time, the Soncino family in Italy were making use of elegant black-and-white borders borrowed from non-Jewish sources. In some cases, in order to comply with the requirements of a Hebrew book, where the opening page needed to have the wider margin on the right rather than on the left, they sometimes broke up the border and in rare cases even had it recut to adjust to the requirements of Hebrew printing. The border used in Baḥya's commentary on the Bible (Azriel Gunzenhausen, Naples, 1492) appears to have been designed and cut by the Hebrew printer's brother-in-law, Moses ben Isaac. This border also appears in the Italian work *L'Aquila Volante,* produced there at about the same time by Aiolfo de Cantoni. Many of these borders were transferred from press to press or taken by the refugees from country to country. Thus the Hijar border referred to above appears in Lisbon in 1489, and later, increasingly worn and indistinct, in various works produced in Turkey between 1505 and 1509. The Naples border was used in Constantinople in 1531/32. There are some superbly designed borders around some pages of the Prague *Haggadah* of 1526. For the Mantua editions of 1550 and 1560 these were entirely recut, as framework around the identical text. With the development of the engraved title page in the 16th century, the use of borders became an exceptional luxury, as in some of the royal publications of the Mantuan press in the 18th century.

ENGRAVED TITLE PAGES. It is only in 1505 that the first title page appears in a Hebrew book. Thereafter, these also received special care, later being enclosed within an engraved border in the form of a gate (hence the common Hebrew term for title page, *sha'ar,* "gate"), often flanked by twisted columns and later and not infrequently by figures of Moses and Aaron. In due course, specially executed vignettes of biblical scenes of Jewish ritual observances were incorporated in these title pages.

ILLUSTRATED WORKS. Illustrations in the conventional sense first figure in a Hebrew book, so far as is known, in 1491, when the Brescia edition of the fable-book *Meshal ha-Kadmoni* by Isaac ibn Sahula contained a number of cuts illustrating the various fables (repeated in the Barco edition of 1497/98). After this, it was customary to add illustrations to most books of fables, for example the Yiddish *Kuhbuch* (Frankfort, 1687). The prayers for rain and dew recited on the feasts of Tabernacles and Passover were often accompanied in Ashkenazi prayer books with the signs of the Zodiac, which, however, first appear in a far from religious work, the frivolous *Maḥberot Immanuel* by Immanuel of Rome (Brescia, 1491).

Minhagim Books were usually arranged according to the order of the religious year and it was customary to add to their interest by the inclusion of illustrations. The anti-Semitic publications of the apostate J. Pfefferkorn (Judenbeichte, 1508) contain illustrations of Jewish observances which may be based on an authentic prototype.

The Prague *Birkat ha-Mazon* ("Grace after Meals"), of which one copy has survived, is the first Hebrew work

Woodcut from the *Venice Minhagim Book,* 1601, showing the baking of *mazzah.* J.N.U.L., Jeruslaem.

of the type known to contain such illustrations. The earliest published illustrated *minhagim* book is that of Venice of 1593. Its text was based on a similar work edited by one Simeon Ashkenazi in 1590. The 1593 edition, though printed in Italy, is in Yiddish. It was no doubt published partly for export and partly for the use of the Ashkenazi Jews then living in the north of Italy. It was accomplished by a series of woodcuts illustrating various observances and customs of Jewish religious life throughout the year, the participants dressed in the unmistakable German style. These illustrations became very popular. They were repeated but with growing indistinction in all manner of editions produced in Amsterdam and northern Europe from the second half of the 17th century onward. The same woodcut sometimes serves to illustrate two different subjects in different editions. Thus the Sabbath before Passover and the Day of Atonement is illustrated by a scene showing the delivery of the special sermon on that occasion. They are still reproduced to illustrate Dutch Jewish social life of the 17th–18th centuries, whereas they in fact belong to a much earlier period and in great part to another environment. In 1601 another *minhagim* book appeared in Venice with a series of remarkable woodcuts, far superior to the earlier edition and clearly illustrating the Italian Jewish environment.

A *minhagim* book produced in 1693 for the Sephardi community of Amsterdam but with illustrations in some cases showing typical Ashkenazi costume has some independent interest and attraction. Unfortunately this one was not imitated later. The imitative editions of Prague of 1665, of Frankfort c. 1674, and of Hamburg 1729, deserve cursory mention. That of Dyhernfurth of 1692, edited by S. Bass, has certain independent elements but like the earlier ones is poorly executed. The Frankfort edition of 1717 has half a dozen badly executed cuts (most of them repeated in the 1729 edition) reflecting tenth-century German Jewish customs and usages. The *minhagim* books as a whole, but particularly the hitherto neglected Venice edition of 1601, are of considerable importance for the study of Jewish social life. Of particular significance are the female costumes, the ritual details (e.g., the form of the Sabbath lamp and the *Havdalah* appurtenances), the interior of the synagogue and the separation of the sexes, the wedding ceremony, the Purim mummers, and even the barber's shop included to illustrate Lag ba-Omer.

Passover Haggadot. The most popular subject for illumination among Hebrew manuscripts was the

Circumcision ceremony illustrated in a woodcut from the *Amsterdam Minhagim Book*, 1662. J.N.U.L., Jerusalem.

Passover *Haggadah*, and this tradition naturally continued in the age of printing. The earliest known example of this is in some fragments conjecturally ascribed to Turkey (but obviously printed by Spanish exiles) c. 1515. But the oldest dated illustrated *Haggadah* now extant is that of Prague of 1526, published by Gershom Kohen and his brother Gronem and apparently illustrated in part by their brother-in-law Ḥayyim Shaḥor. This lovely production is one of the most memorable specimens of the 16th-century Hebrew press, the three fully decorated pages being especially noteworthy. It was exactly copied so far as the text was concerned but with fresh borders in the Mantua *Haggadah* of 1560, much improved in the subsequent edition of 1568. After some further experiments, an entirely fresh and more amply illustrated edition of the work was published by Israel Zifroni in Venice in 1609. This continued to be republished with few changes until late in the 18th century and served as the model for the *haggadot* produced in the Mediterranean basin (e.g., at Leghorn) down to recent times. In 1695, the Venetian *Haggadah* served as the model for the edition published in Amsterdam with copper-plate illustrations by the convert to Judaism who called himself Abraham ben Jacob. Though the general arrangement of the work and the choice of subjects was strongly influenced by the Venetian edition, the artist based his art to a great extent on illustrations to the Bible and other imaginative details gathered from the publications of Matthew Merian of Basle. The work reappeared with minor changes a few years later (Amsterdam, 1699) and served as the model for a large number of editions produced in central Europe throughout the 18th century and after. The actual illustrations, much deteriorated, continue to be reprinted or copied in popular editions down to the present day. Over 300 *haggadot* are illustrated. In recent years, artists of great reputation such as Arthus Szyk and Ben Shahn, have collaborated in or produced illustrated editions of this favorite work.

Other Works. Other Hebrew works which were traditionally enriched with illustrations – in most cases very crude – included the Yiddish pseudo-Josephus *(Josippon)*, from the Zurich edition of 1547 onward; and the women's compendium of biblical history, *Ẓe'enah u-Re'enah,* in numerous Dutch and German editions of the 17th and 18th centuries. On the other hand, for obvious reasons, the Hebrew Bible was never illustrated until a few experiments appeared in the second half of the 19th century.

Portraits. Portraits of an author occasionally appear in Hebrew books printed in Holland and Italy in the 17th and 18th centuries; for example, Joseph Solomon del Medigo in his *Sefer Elim* (Amsterdam, 1629) and Moses Hefez (Gentili) in his *Melekhet Maḥashevet* (Venice, 1701). The *Kehunnat Avraham* by Abraham Cohen of Zante (Venice, 1719) has, after the elaborately engraved title page, a portrait which seems to be by the author himself. A portrait of the rabbi Solomon Hirschell surprisingly accompanied the London prayer book edition of 1809, Judah Leon Templo's works on the Tabernacle of Moses and the Temple of Solomon (1650 etc.) included fine illustrative engravings.

Silver binder for a prayer book, Italy, 1790. Israel Museum, Jerusalem.

BINDING

With the invention of printing and the proliferation of books, Jewish bookbinders are found all over Europe. In Poland, during the reign of Sigismund III (1587–1632), Jewish craftsmen were employed by church and state. In Italy, in the 17th and 18th centuries, Bibles or prayer books were bound in silver, lavishly decorated, to serve as bridal presents *(sivlonot)*, sometimes bearing a representation of a biblical scene relating to the bride's or bridegroom's name, or the coats-of-arms of the two families. The art of filigree binding arose in Italy and France in the 17th century and spread to other European countries. At the same time embroidered or tortoiseshell bindings, though not characteristically Jewish, made their appearance in Holland and Germany, from where they spread eastward. Jews bound their ritualia, particularly bridal prayer books, in these beautiful materials. On these bindings, metal, usually silver, is used for clasps and corners, and both are often finely engraved and decorated with emblems, monograms, or animal figures representing certain Jewish virtues. These ornately bound books are sometimes inlaid with precious stones and even miniature drawings of the woman to whom they were presented. Similarly bound and decorated books figured as presentations by communities, societies, or wealthy individuals to Jewish or non-Jewish notables on special occasions: a rabbi or communal leader's jubilee, a sovereign's visit, or as a sign of appreciation for favors bestowed or assistance given.

From the 19th century onward, with growing prosperity particularly among Western Jewry, the art of binding Hebrew or Jewish books developed even further. In Ereẓ Israel, the establishment of the Bezalel School of Arts and Crafts in Jerusalem in 1906 included a deliberate effort to develop a specifically Jewish style in bookbinding. This produced olive-wood covers for a variety of books. Yemenite artisans too brought with them a tradition of bindings made from leather, silver, and gold filigree, and their styles have retained their popularity. There is, however, a more artistic and less traditional trend which has produced some magnificant bindings, such as that of the Golden Book and the Barmitzvah Book at the head office of the Jewish National Fund, in Jerusalem.

תלמוד ירושלמי

Der Jerusalemitische Talmud

1920 · 5680

VERLEGT BEI LOUIS LAMM IN BERLIN

10. some basic books

THE BIBLE

The story of the printing of the Hebrew Bible begins with the 1477 edition of the Psalms, most probably produced at Bologna. Each verse is followed by the appropriate passage from David Kimḥi's commentary, an arrangement which did not appear again in Hebrew Bibles. Since the first printers had considerable difficulty with the vowel-points, they abandoned them after Psalm 4:4, excepting only three consecutive verses, 5:12–6:1. Many words are printed *plene* (with vowel letters), including even *yod* for *segol.* There are frequent errors – whole verses (108), half verses (3), and odd words (43) are omitted, and there are dittographs both of letters and of words.

In 1479 Joseph ben Abraham Caravita invited from Ferrara to Bologna Abraham ben Hayyim di Tintori, a master craftsman who had largely solved the problems of both vowel-points and accents. The result of this move was the Bologna Pentateuch of 1482, which set the pattern for many future editions, culminating in the Bomberg rabbinic Bibles of the next century. The folios consist of Rashi's commentary across the page, top and bottom, with the Hebrew text in the inner and wider column and Targum Onkelos in the outer column. The type is

Title page of the Jerusalem Talmud, Berlin, 1920, decorated with a Shield of David, a *menorah,* and symbols of the Twelve Tribes of Israel. J.N.U.L., Jerusalem.

larger than that of the 1477 psalter, but, as in some Ashkenazi manuscripts, the final letters *kaf, nun,* and *pe* do not extend below the base-line of other consonants, so that it is virtually impossible to distinguish between *dalet* and *kaf.*

Joshua Solomon Soncino and his nephews, Moses and Gershom, after attracting Abraham ben Ḥayyim from Bologna, produced the first complete Bible, the Soncino Bible of 1488, with vowels and accents, but without a commentary (as was the custom of the Soncinos). The Soncino brothers also were responsible for the 1491–93 Naples Bible, in which the vowel-points and accents are better placed than before. Gershom Soncino also produced the 1495 Brescia Bible, an improved edition of the 1488 Soncino Bible but, more important, in small octavo format, making it a pocket edition specifically produced for the persecuted Jews who, perpetually moving from place to place, found it difficult to carry the huge and costly folio Bibles. It was this edition which Martin Luther used when he translated the Bible into German.

In Spain a Hebrew Pentateuch with Targum and Rashi was printed by Solomon Salmati ben Maimon in 1490 at Hijar. In 1487 the Faro (Portugal) Pentateuch was produced. In this edition the printer was unable to solve the problem of placing a dot in the middle of a consonant, so there is no *dagesh.* This was followed in 1491 by the Lisbon Pentateuch in two volumes with the Targum and Rashi's commentary, and in the next year by Isaiah and Jeremiah at Lisbon and Proverbs at Leiria. The expulsion of the Jews from Spain (1492) put an end to the printing of new editions of the Bible, both in Portugal and Italy, for wealthy Jews needed all their means to help the refugees, over a quarter of a million of them. The Portuguese tradition was revived in Salonika 23 years later in an edition of Psalms, Proverbs, Job, and Daniel with Don Judah Gedaliah as patron and Joseph Golphon as printer.

By the year 1511 the Soncinos, now at Pesaro, were able to make a new start and, in stages, they completed a fourth edition of the complete Bible. Gershom had used the interval to perfect his technique and this edition is the best produced by Ashkenazi Jews in Italy. Around this time Daniel Bomberg arrived in Venice and established his printing office there. In 1516–17 he published the first Great Rabbinic Bible, edited by Felix Pratensis, who was born a Jew but was baptized in 1506. The work is in four volumes, with Targums and commentaries. For the first time the *keri* is given, but in the variants in the margin. The last volume contains additional material, notably Maimonides' "Thirteen Articles of Faith" and the treatise on accents entitled *Dikdukei ha-Te'amim* said to be by the Masorete, Aaron Ben Asher, and here printed for the first time. Here, also for the first time in Hebrew, Samuel and Kings were each divided into two books in imitation of the Vulgate. The strangest thing thing about this edition is the statement made to the pope when his *imprimatur* was sought: it claimed that the many previously printed Bibles "contain as many errors as words" and that "no one had attempted it before." Daniel Bomberg and Felix Pratensis duly received the pope's blessing, though it proved more of a hindrance than an asset. Even before this four-volume Bible was published, Bomberg realized that he had made two bad mistakes: employing an apostate Jew as his

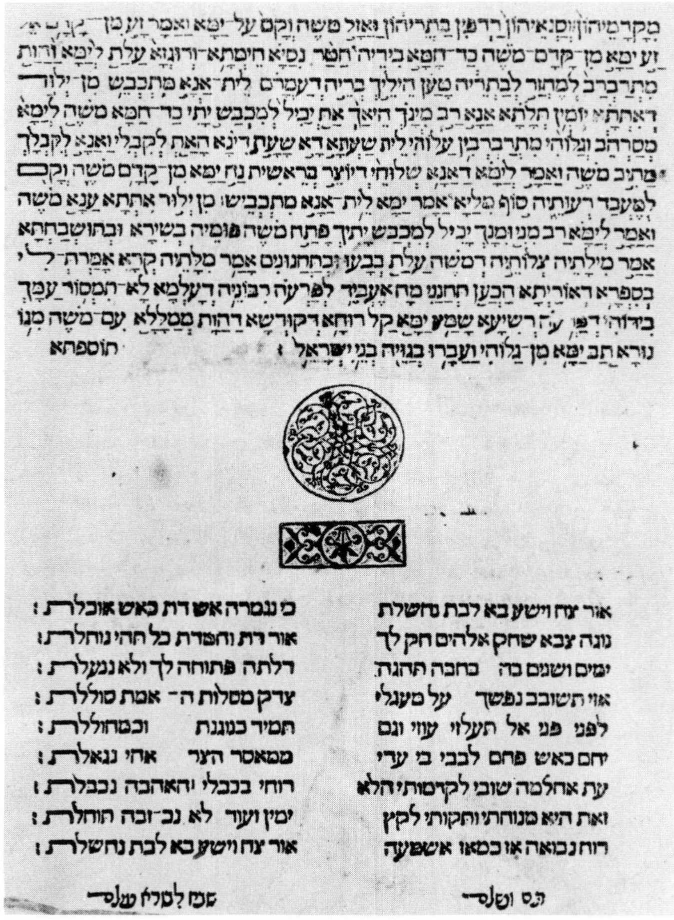

Colophon page from the 1491 Lisbon Pentateuch with the Targum and Rashi's commentary. The last section of the Targum Onkelos to Deuteronomy is shown at the top of the page; a circular and oblong design separates it from the colophon at the bottom of the page. This is a unicum. J.N.U.L., Jerusalem.

editor, and requesting the pope's *imprimatur.* He therefore remade the columns as soon as the folios of the large Bible had been run off and issued a quarto edition at the same time, this time without any mention of either editor or pope. A second edition was called for within four years, when the whole was reset; on this occasion the two sons of Baruch Adelkind were mentioned as printers, and great emphasis was laid on the fact that they were Jews, thoroughly Orthodox, and already engaged in printing the whole of the Talmud. An opportunity to produce a new Great Rabbinic Bible which would be acceptable to Jews arose when Jacob ben Ḥayyim ibn Adonijah arrived in Venice after his family had been driven out of Spain and again out of Tunis. After seven penurious years of wandering Jacob ben Ḥayyim found work with Bomberg in Venice. The chief fruit of the partnership was the second Great Rabbinic Bible of 1524–25, the text of which became the standard masoretic text, and continued as such for 400 years. Jacob ben Ḥayyim was very conscious of the importance of the Masorah as the guarantee of the correct text, and he went to great pains and undertook several journeys to secure as many codices with a Masorah as possible. Thus, for the first time, there was a printed Hebrew Bible with a marginal Masorah. As the editor discovered that "the Masorah did not harmonize with the majority of the codices," he had to exercise his discretion. The edition was in four volumes, with Targums, and with commentaries by Rashi, Ibn Ezra, David and Moses Kimḥi, and Levi ben Gershom. A third Bomberg quarto edition appeared in 1525–28, the text being a combination of that of Felix Pratensis and that of Jacob ben Ḥayyim.

Daniel Bomberg's tribulations were not over, for soon after 1525, Jacob ben Ḥayyim became a Christian. In 1527 Elijah Levita, a refugee originally from Neustadt near Nuremberg, came to Venice and found employment with Bomberg. No more is heard of Jacob ben Ḥayyim, Elijah Levita being henceforth chief adviser to the Bomberg firm. In subsequent reprints of the 1524–25 Bible, there is no mention of the editor. Bibles printed after 1525 all follow substantially the text of Jacob ben Ḥayyim ibn Adonijah until Buxtorf's small-format Bible of 1611 and his four-volume rabbinic Bible of 1618–19, printed at Basle, in which the text was influenced by Sephardi traditions, and not dominated by the Ashkenazi ones as were all previous editions printed under Jewish auspices. The text was edited by Jablonski in 1699, but the most important edition based on the Buxtorf text is that of

Wood engraving illustrating the beginning of the Book of Numbers from a Pentateuch commentary by Isaac Arama (c. 1420–1494), Venice, 1521. J.N.U.L., Jerusalem.

Psalms including excerpts in Latin from rabbinical commentaries edited by the Dutch Calvinist theologian and Hebraist, Heinrich Jakob van Bashuysen, Hanover, 1712. J.N.U.L., Jerusalem.

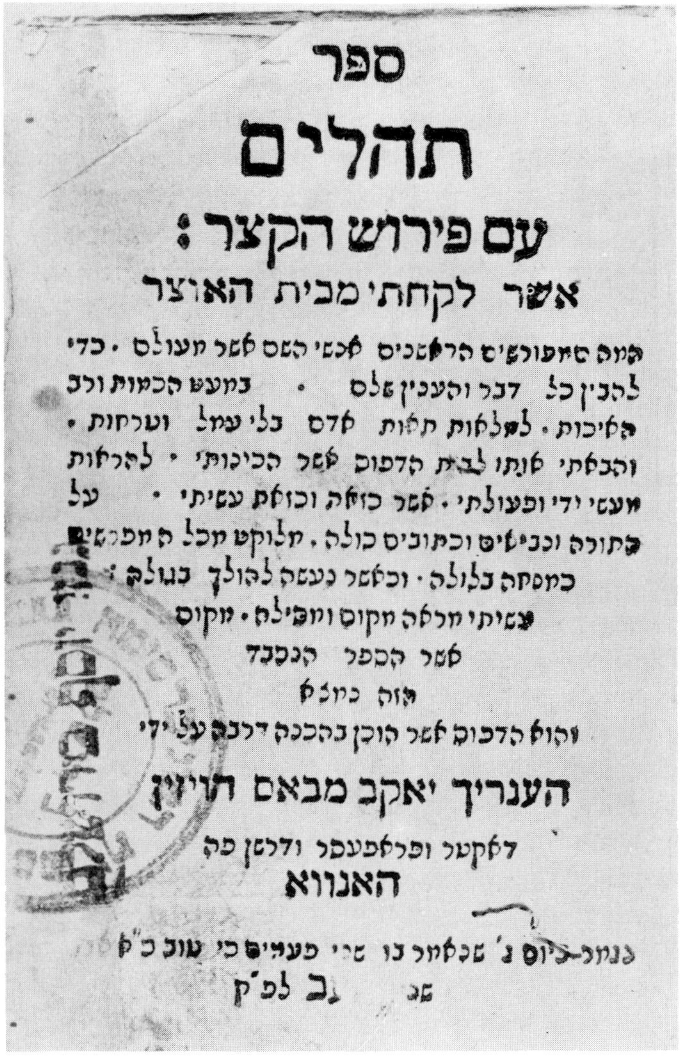
ספר
תהלים
עם פירוש הקצר:
אשר לקחתי מבית האוצר
האנווא

J.H. Michaelis in 1720. It is a critical edition, quoting 19 printed editions and five Erfurt manuscripts, especially the very important Erfurt 3 with its Masorah, and containing also *Okhlah ve-Okhlah,* an 11th century masoretic work of great importance, then printed for the first time. The critical notes and the variants provided by Michaelis indicate a masoretic tradition different from that of the 1524–25 Bible of Jacob ben Ḥayyim. They form a pattern, already discernible in Jablonski's 1699 edition, but more clearly in the two Bible commentaries largely devoted to Masorah, Lonzano's *Or Torah* and Norzi's *Minḥat Shai.*

The story of modern times begins with Seligmann Baer, who published the Hebrew Bible in single volumes with notes, except for Exodus to Deuteronomy (for which see the Roedelheim Pentateuch, a popular edition without notes). The dates of these volumes are 1869–1895. Baer believed that the Masorah is supreme, that firm rules can be established, and that these must be rigidly followed, whatever the manuscripts may say. In this he is the literary descendant of Elijah Levita and his *Masoret ha-Masoret.* Baer regularly followed a Masorah or a rule against the codices and frequently "corrects an error." Baer was supported by the Bible scholar Franz Delitzsch, whose authority was immense. In contrast, C.D. Ginsburg (British and Foreign Bible Society edition, 1911–26) followed Jacob ben Ḥayyim; where the various Masorah traditions disagreed either with the text or with each other, he exercised his judgment, with the result that he paid more attention to the manuscripts than to either Masorah or to Jacob ben Ḥayyim. With the third edition of R. Kittel's *Biblia Hebraica* (1936), a new signpost was erected. P. Kahle was responsible for the text, based on the Leningrad codex (Firkovich collection B 19a) which Kahle claimed was a true, accurate, and genuine Ben Asher codex. Ever since Maimonides supported the Ben Asher tradition against Saadiah ben Joseph Gaon, who favored the Ben Naphtali tradition, it had been agreed that a true masoretic Bible must follow Ben Asher.

MISHNAH AND TALMUD

The Mishnah was first printed in Spain in about 1485. But since only individual pages of this edition have been preserved, that printed at Naples in 1492 and comprising the entire Mishnah as well as Maimonides' commentary is generally regarded as the first edition. It inclines mainly to the text used in the Jerusalem Talmud, although several of its passages were emended in accordance with that of the Babylonian, as were most of the later printed versions of the Mishnah from that of Venice 1546–7 onward. Particularly important is the edition of Yom Tov Lipmann Heller, who, availing himself of manuscripts, produced a corrected version of the Mishnah. First published with his commentary *Tosafot Yom Tov* in Prague, 1614–17, it became the basis of all subsequent editions. As yet there is no critical edition of the Mishnah which includes all the variant readings contained in manuscripts, *genizah* fragments and quotations of the Mishnah found in the Talmuds and in the works of the early authorities and their commentaries. Basic research and preparatory work for such an edition are incorporated in J.N. Epstein's *Mavo le-Nusaḥ ha-Mishnah.*

The Talmud began to be published soon after the introduction of printing. Before the appearance of the entire Talmud, individual tractates of it were printed, especially in Portugal toward the end of the

Page from the Mishnah tractate *Kilayim,* with explanatory diagrams, in an incunabulum edition believed to be the first complete printing of the Mishnah. It was printed by Soncino in Naples, 1492. J.N.U.L., Jerusalem.

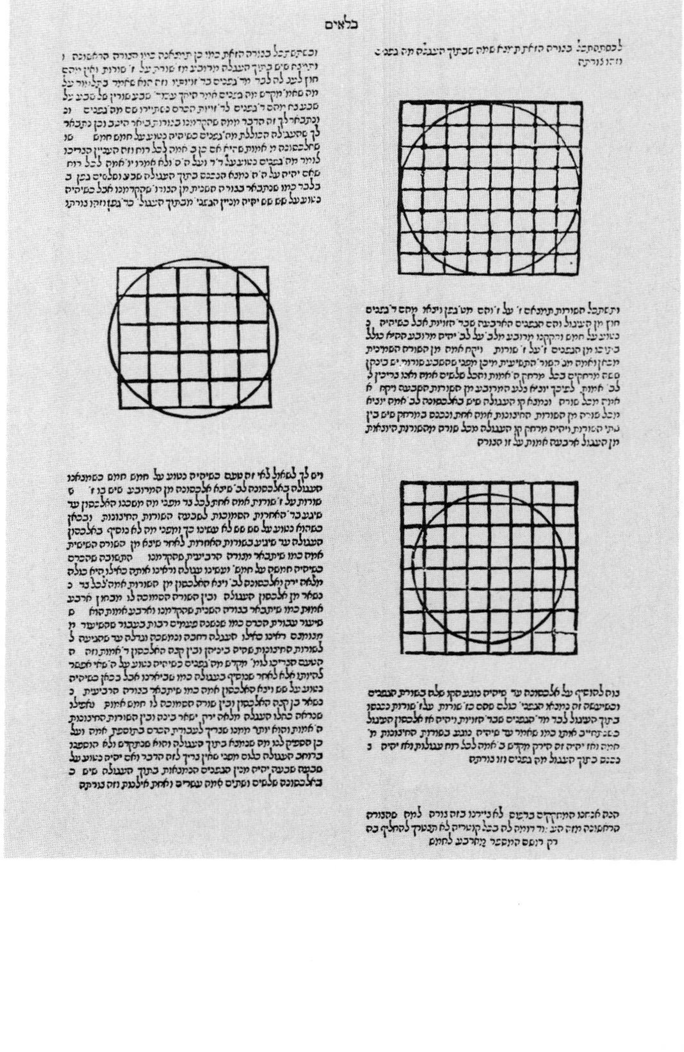
כלאים

15th century. Most famous were the volumes printed by Joshua Solomon, and his nephew Gershom, of Soncino, from 1484 to 1519. They brought out numerous single tractates, but not the entire Talmud. The first complete Talmud was printed by a Christian, Daniel Bomberg at Venice (1520–23). This *editio princeps* determined the external form of the Talmud for all time, including the pagination, the inclusion of Rashi's commentary in the inner margin and of the *tosafot* in the outer, and the discussion of the *Gemara* following each Mishnah.

In the manuscripts, the complete text of the Mishnah is given at the beginning of the chapter, and traces of this have been retained even in the printed texts; see, e.g. the beginning of tractate *Sanhedrin*. As a result one sometimes has a mistaken idea of the relative size of some of the tractates. Thus the fact that the *tosafot* of *Bava Batra* are more extensive than those of *Berakhot*, coupled with the fact that from folio 29 to the end the commentary, is by Rashi's grandson Samuel ben Meir, who was much more prolix than his grandfather, has had the result that *Berakhot* has only 64 folios compared to the 176 of *Bava Batra* though in fact the talmudic text of the former has 36 pages and *Bava Batra* 40. The first edition of the Talmud was followed by the edition of M.A. Giustiniani, also of Venice, in 1546–51. From then on the Talmud was printed in all major Jewish communities, either complete or in single tractates. Most famous among them are the editions of Lublin (1559–76 and 1617–39); Basle (1578–81); Cracow (1602–05 and 1616–20); the Amsterdam editions (Benveniste, 1644–48; 2nd edition, 1714–17); Frankfort on the Oder (1697–99); and Sulzbach (1756–63) known as the "Sulzbach Red" because of the front page printing of each title in red. Many of these editions contain numerous misprints, which were further confounded by the ruthless mutilations of the censors. Often Jewish printers exercised self-censorship. The best known among more modern editions is the "Vilna *Shas*," printed in Vilna by the brothers and the widow of the printer Romm, containing numerous additional commentaries and glosses. About a century ago, using the Munich manuscript and many other sources, Raphael N. Rabbinovicz, in his monumental work *Dikdukei Soferim*, undertook to bring out a critical edition of the Talmud. At his death, the work encompassed about three and a half of the six orders of the Talmud.

Zera'im, the first order of the Mishnah, including commentaries by Obadiah Bertinoto and the *Tosefot Yom Tov*, printed at the Romm press, Vilna, 1861. J.N.U.L., Jerusalem.

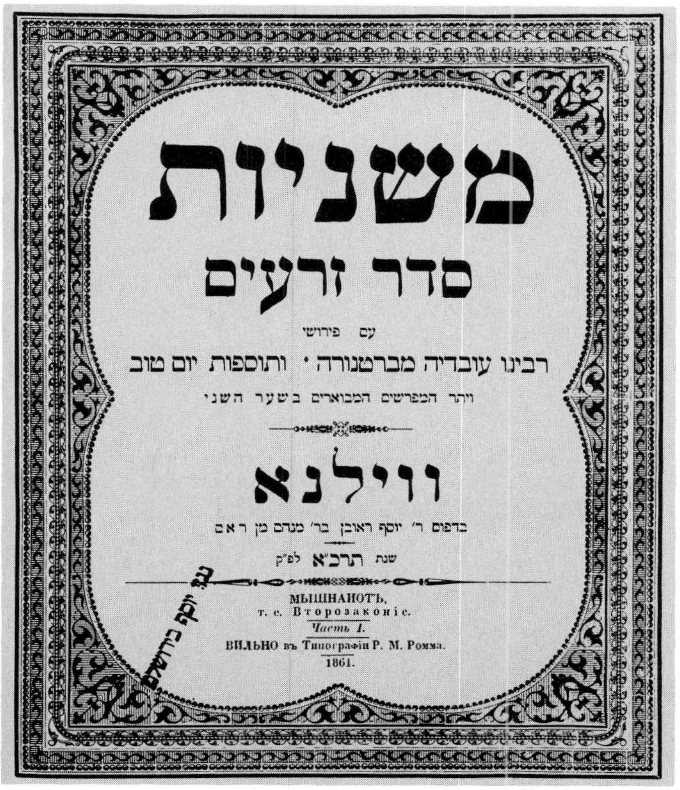
משניות
סדר זרעים
עם פירושי
רבינו עובדיה מברטנורה · ותוספות יום טוב
ויתר המפרשים המבוארים בשער השני
ווילנא
בדפוס ר' יוסף ראובן בר' מנחם מן ראם
שנת תרכ"א לפ"ק
МЫШНАЮТЪ,
т. е. Второзаконiе.
Часть I.
ВИЛЬНО въ Типографiи Р. М. Ромма.
1861.

PRAYER BOOKS

With the advent of printing, prayer books for different customs, both *mahzorim* for the whole year as well as *siddurim* in small format for use of the individual were printed. Among the incunabula there are already many prayer books. Prayer books of the Roman rite were published first (*Mahzor Roma*, Soncino-Casalmaggiore 1485/86; *Siddur Katan* called "Sidorello," 1486), then those of the Spanish rite (*Seder Tefillot*, 1490). Printed Spanish and Portuguese books have come down only in fragments. In the 16th century, German and Polish prayer books were published (*mahzorim*, beginning with 1521, 1522, and *siddurim*, about 1508), and those of the Romaniot custom (*mahzorim*, from 1510, *siddurim*, later still). Prayer books for the communities of southern France were not printed until the 18th century (*Mahzor* Avignon 1765–66, Carpentras 1739–62), while the *Tikhlal* of the Yemenite Jews was published only at the end of the 19th century (Jerusalem, 1894–98). Certain categories of prayers such as *selihot* and *kinot* for the Ninth of Av were printed long ago in special editions (e.g. *selihot* according to the German custom, Soncino 1496; *kinot* for the Ninth of Av according to the Polish custom, Cracow 1584), although in the main they were also incorporated in the *maḥzorim*.

TYPES OF PRAYER BOOKS. In the course of time the following types of prayer books became established among Ashkenazi Jews: (1) *Ha-Maḥzor ha-Gadol* in folio (also called *Kol Bo*) containing, according to the ancient custom, all the prayers of the year – weekday, Sabbath, festivals, and special days; (2) the so-called *Maḥzor,* which included only the festival prayers, usually a separate volume for each festival; (3) the small *siddur,* containing only the regular prayers; (4) *Ha-Siddur ha-Shalem,* completed by the addition of the *yozerot* for the special Sabbaths, the *hoshanot, seliḥot* for fast days, *ma'arivim* for the nights of the festivals, and supplemented at times by the Book of Psalms and *ma'amarot.* The Sephardi Jews, on the other hand, arrived at the following subdivision: (1) *Tefillat ha-Ḥodesh,* comprising the prayers for weekdays, Sabbath, the New Moon, Ḥanukkah, and Purim; (2) *Mo'adim,* consisting of the prayers for the three pilgrim festivals; (3) *Rosh Ha-Shanah,* for the New Year; (4) *Kippur* for the Day of Atonement; (5) *Ta'aniyyot,* which also included the Ninth of Av and its *kinot.* Only the Jews of Italy and Yemen maintained the original form of the *Maḥzor ha-Shanah,* which contained all the prayers in cyclical order; small *siddurim* were, however, also published by them.

TEXTUAL EDITIONS. As to the text of the regular prayers, the *siddur* of the Sephardi Jews was edited in the 16th century in accordance with the "intentions" *(kavvanot)* of Isaac Luria; as a result hardly any pre-Lurianic prayer books are extant. In many editions they made the divine names conform with the Lurianic "intentions" by a different pointing or by interlacing the ineffable name with various forms of the word *Adonai.* The text of the Ashkenazi *siddur* occupied several scholars, particularly in the 17th to 19th centuries, who published the prayer book in new editions or wrote books in which they justified sustainment or amendment of the text: Naḥman Lieballer (Dyhrenfurth, 1690); Azriel and his son, Elijah of Vilna (*Derekh Si'aḥ ha-Sadeh,* Frankfort on the Main, 1704); Solomon Zalman Katz Hanau (*Kunteres Sha'arei Tefillah* and the ed. *Beit Tefillah,* Jesnitz, 1725); Jacob Emden (Yavez; *Lu'aḥ Eresh,* an appendix to his prayer book, Altona, 1769); Mordecai Duesseldorf (*Kunteres Hassagot al Siddur Sha'arei Tefillah,* published after his death, at Prague in 1784); Isaac Satanow (*Va-Ye'etar Yiẓḥak,* Berlin 1785, who polemicizes with all his predecessors); Judah Leib Ben Ze'ev (*Tikkunei ha-Tefillah,* published after his death with the edition *Tefillah Zakkah,* Vienna, 1816); Wolf Heidenheim (*Siddur Safah Berurah* with notes at several points, Roedelheim, 1806). In the course of time, Heidenheim's text was accepted as a sort of standard text. All disputes about the text, however, turn on such grammatical niceties as the insertion of a *dagesh* or *meteg* and matters of pointing, and only very rarely on establishing the text. In the case of Heidenheim, particularly, and those following him, it should be pointed out that they preferred, to too great an extent, the language of the Bible to "the language of the scholars."

CRITICAL EDITIONS. Critical treatment of the

Page from a *maḥzor* showing the Rosh Ha-Shanah prayer *Ha-Melekh,* printed by Joseph Bak in Weckelsdorf, 1680. This was the only Hebrew work printed in that city. J.N.U.L., Jerusalem.

הלכות יסודי התורה
הלכות דעות
הלכות תלמוד תורה
הלכות עז וחקות הגוים
הלכות תשובה
ספר שני והוא ספר אהבה
הלכות קרית שמע
פרק ראשון
פרק עשירי
נגמר ספר ראשון

Colophon page of Volume I, Books 1–7 of Maimonides' *Mishneh Torah,* printed in Rome, 1475. J.N.U.L., Jerusalem.

prayer book begins with the activity of E.L. Landshuth who contributed to the *Siddur Hegyon Lev* (published by Z.H. Edelmann, 1845) the commentary *Mekor Berakhah,* in which he consistently gathered the sources of the prayers and tried to establish the date of their compilation and composition. This method was continued by W. Jawitz (*Mekor ha-Berakhot,* 1910), A. Berliner (*Randbemerkungen zum taeglichen Gebetbuch,* 2 vols., 1909–12), and S. Elbogen (*Der juedische Gottesdienst,* 1913, 1931).

THE MISHNEH TORAH

The major halakhic code of Maimonides, the *Yad ha-Ḥazakah,* which is also called the *Mishneh Torah,* was printed at least four times during the incunabula period (see also above Chapter 4). Apparently all the printings were complete editions. At that time only Maimonides' text was printed; the glosses of Abraham ben David (the Rabad) and what have become the standard commentaries were added gradually, starting from the sixth edition printed by exiles from Spain in Constantinople in 1509. In that edition a considerable part of the Rabad's glosses were included as well as the *Hagahot Maimuniyot,* the *Magid Mishneh* of Don Vidal of Tolosa and the *Migdal Oz* of Shem Tov ibn Gaon. The text generally followed that of the first edition (Rome, before 1480).

During the Golden Age of Hebrew printing in Venice in the first half of the 16th century, the *Mishneh Torah* was printed three times in full editions. The first of these printings, by Bomberg in 1524, differed considerably from a textual point of view from the earlier editions because a great number of manuscripts and marginal glosses were used in its preparation. In 1550 another edition was printed by Bragadini and the following year Giustiniani issued his edition in competition with Bragadini's. Giustiniani's edition was banned by rabbinical authorities because he had stolen the manuscript of a commentary meant for Bragadini. For the tragic outcome of this episode see Chapter 5, page 98.

A new edition of the *Mishneh Torah* was printed in Venice in 1574 by Parenzo. The commentary *Kesef Mishneh* by Joseph Caro, the author of the *Shulḥan Arukh,* was printed in this edition which was very advanced with regard to the exactness of the text of the other commentaries. Because of its importance for the development of *halakhah,* the Parenzo edition served as the model for most subsequent editions. The actual text is an amalgam of the Constantinople edition (1509) and the Venice edition (1524) and for the first time the laws within each chapter are numbered.

In 1702 Immanuel Athias in Amsterdam printed another complete edition of the *Yad* in which the important commentary of Abraham di Boton, *Leḥem Mishneh,* appeared for the first time. The commentary had been printed in Venice in 1609, as a separate book. This edition also contained the source references for the *Magid Mishneh* and the *Kesef Mishneh* as well as parallel sources in the *Tur* and the *Sefer Mitzvot Gadol (Semag).* Later a complete edition was printed in Jessnitz in 1739 in which the commentary *Mishneh le-Melekh* by Judah Rosanes (printed as a separate book in Constantinople, 1731) was included. Full editions were printed in Fuerth in 1765 and in Berdichev in 1808 as well as in many other places.

By 1970, approximately 65 separate complete editions of the *Mishneh Torah* had been printed. In those of the last 50 years dozens of commentaries and novellae on the work have been included, usually at the end of the book. Prime among the modern enlarged edition is that of Shulsinger, which was printed in New York in 1947. This edition contains some 60 commentaries and has become the model for subsequent editions. It also contains photographs of Maimonides' own manuscript, fragments of which were found in the Cairo *Genizah*. In addition to complete editions, hundreds of partial editions have been printed with various commentaries. These were usually printed by the authors of the commentaries.

THE ZOHAR AND KABBALAH

The *Zohar* was printed amid a fierce controversy between those who opposed its publication, among whom were some important kabbalists, and its supporters. The first two editions of the *Zohar* were published by competing printers in the neighboring cities of Mantua (1558–60) and Cremona (1559–60). The *Tikkunei ha-Zohar* was also published separately in Mantua (1558). The editors of these two editions used different manuscripts – hence the differences in the order and in detailed readings. Immanuel of Benevento who established the Mantua text used ten manuscripts, from which he arranged his edition, and chose the text which he considered to be the best. Among the correctors at Cremona was the apostate grandson of the grammarian Elijah Levita, Vittorio Eliano. They used six manuscripts. The Mantua *Zohar* was printed in three volumes in Rashi script, while the Cremona *Zohar* was in one large volume in square script. Both of them contain a large number of printing errors. According to size, the kabbalists called these two editions *Zohar Gadol* ("Large *Zohar*") and *Zohar Katan* ("Small *Zohar*"). The *Zohar Gadol* was printed on two more occasions in this form, in Lublin in 1623, and in Sulzbach in 1684. The Polish and German kabbalists up to about 1715 generally used the *Zohar Gadol*. All other editions follow the Mantua format. Altogether, the *Zohar* has been printed more than 65 times and the *Tikkunei Zohar* nearly 80 times. Most of the editions come from Poland and Russia, but there are also printings from Constantinople, Salonika, Smyrna, Leghorn, Jerusalem, and Djerba. In later editions they added the variant readings of the Cremona text and corrected many printing errors. They also added variants and readings from the manuscript of the Safed kabbalists, indications of biblical sources, and introductions. The *Zohar* was printed twice in Leghorn with an (incorrectly) vocalized text. Those sections in the Safed manuscripts which were not found in the Mantua edition were, except from the *Midrash ha-Ne'lam* to Ruth, printed together in a separate volume in Salonika in 1597, which was called *Zohar Ḥadash* in the later editions. The best of these are Venice, 1658, and Munkacs, 1911. All the sections of the *Zohar* were included in the complete edition of Yehudah Ashlag, Jerusalem, 1945–58, in 22 volumes, with a Hebrew translation and textual variants from the earlier editions. The *Tikkunei ha-Zohar* began to appear in 1960, and by 1970 was not completed. A critical edition based on early manuscripts does not yet exist.

Title page of *Tikkunei ha-Zohar*, Mantua, 1558. Cecil Roth Collection.

The printing of several classical works contributed a great deal to the dissemination of the Kabbalah, particularly in the middle of the 16th century. At first no opposition was roused – neither when Recanati's book was produced in Venice (1523) nor when several other books came out in Salonika and Constantinople – although these works did not receive the *haskamah* ("approval") of the rabbinic authorities. However, when the printing of the *Zohar* itself and the *Ma'arekhet ha-Elohut* (1558) was contemplated, the plan gave rise to bitter arguments among the Italian rabbis; a few of the leading kabbalists violently opposed it, saying that they were afraid that these things would fall into the hands of men who were both ignorant and unprepared and so be liable to lead people into error. The burning of the Talmud in Italy on the order of Pope Julius III (1553) played a part in this controversy, for there were those who feared that the widespread publication of kabbalistic works would in itself tend to stimulate missionary activity. Some kabbalists who at first were opposed to the idea later became the chief protagonists of the printing of the *Zohar,* e.g. Isaac de Lattes, the author of a decision in favor of the printing of the *Zohar,* which appears at the beginning of the Mantua edition.

Perspective diagram of the world of ten *Sefirot,* the ten spheres or emanations through which the Divine manifests itself. From Moses Cordovero, *Pardes Rimmonim,* Cracow, 1592. J.N.U.L., Jerusalem.

At length, the protagonists prevailed, and the publication of other works of Kabbalah in Italy, Germany, Poland, and Turkey met with no further opposition.

THE HAGGADAH

The earliest known edition of the *Haggadah* to be printed separately was produced in Spain at Guadalajara about 1482, on 12 pages in double column. Only a single copy is known to exist, and it may well be that other, perhaps earlier, editions have disappeared. The bibliography of the Passover *haggadot* published by A. Yaari in 1960 includes 2,717 entries, but taking into account later supplements (about 1,000 bibliographical units), omissions and later editions, there can be no doubt that the total to the present date is at least 5,000. In the text of the

First page of the earliest known *Haggadah,* produced in Guadalajara, Spain, in 1482 by Solomon ben Moses Alkabez. The only known copy of this incunabulum is at the Jewish National and University Library, Jerusalem.

הגדות של פסח

כשבאין מבית הכנסת שוטפין
כוסות וממלאין אתם יין מזוג
ונותנין כוס לפני כל אחד
בהסבה ואפילו עני המתפרנס
מן הצדקה חייב לשתות ארבע
כוסות:
ושמים הקערה בשלחן ומברך
הגדול שבהם בחכמה ואומר:
סברי מרנן ברוך אתה יהוה
אלהינו מלך העולם בורא פרי
הגפן באי אמה אשר בחר בנו
מכל עם ורוממנו מכל לשון
וקדשנו במצותיו ותתן לנו יהוה
אלהינו באהבה מועדים
לשמחה חגים וזמנים לששון
את יום חג המצות הזה את יום
טוב מקרא קדש הזה זמן
חירותינו באהבה מקרא קדש
זכר ליציאת מצרים כי בנו
בחרת ואותנו קדשת מכל
העמים ומועדי קדשך בשמחה
ובששון הנחלתנו ברוך אתה
יהוה מקדש ישראל והזמנים:
ברוך אתה יהוה אלהינו
מלך העולם שהחיינו וקימנו
והגיענו לזמן הזה:

ואם חל להיות בשבת אומר
ויכלו השמים והארץ
וכל צבאם ויכל. אלהים ביום
השביעי מלאכתו אשר עשה
וישבת ביום השביעי מכל
מלאכתו אשר עשה ויברך
אלהים את יום השביעי ויקדש
אתו כי בו שבת מכל מלאכתו
אשר ברא אלהים לעשות:
סברי מרנן ברוך אתה
יהוה אלהינו מלך העולם בורא
פרי הגפן: ברוך אתה
יהוה אלהינו מלך העולם
אשר בחר בנו מכל עם
ורוממנו מכל לשון וקדשנו
במצותיו ותתן לנו יהוה אלהינו
באהבה שבתות למנוחה
ומועדים לשמחה חגים וזמנים
לששון את יום המנוח הזה
את יום חג המצות הזה את
יום טוב מקרא קדש הזה
זמן חירותנו באהבה מקרא
קדש זכר ליציאת מצרים כי
בנו בחרת ואותנו קדשת מכל
העמים ושבת ומועדי קדשך
בשמחה ובששון הנחלתנו
ברוך אתה יהוה מקדש
השבת וישראל והזמנים:
ואומר שהחיינו

ואם חל להיות במוצאי שבת
יתחיל ואומר בורא
פרי הגפן וקדוש ואומר ברוך
אתה יהוה אלהינו מלך העולם
בורא מאורי האש: ברוך אתה

Fragment of an incunabulum *Haggaddah,* printed by Soncino at Soncino, c. 1485. A. Freiman, *Thesarus Typographiae Hebraicae Saeculi,* Paris, 1924–31.

Page from the *Prague Haggadah,* 1526, printed at the Kohen press and partly illustrated by Hayyim Shahor. J.N.U.L., Jerusalem.

Haggadah included in the prayer book according to the Italian rite (Casalmaggiore, 1486), there is a conventional representation of the *mazzah,* as in some of the earliest *Haggadah* manuscripts, and these may be considered the earliest known illustrations to the printed *Haggadah.* The crudely executed but by no means ignorant illustrations in the Latin *Ritus et celebratio Phase* (Frankfort, 1512) by the Christian Hebraist Thomas Murner, drawn by his brother Beatus, may have been inspired by a Jewish model. In the extremely rare *Seder Zemirot u-Virkat ha-Mazon* (Prague, 1514) there are figure woodcuts on the same subjects which appear later in illustrated *haggadot,* and may derive from some lost edition. Of the earliest known illustrated edition, hypothetically attributed to Constantinople about 1515, only fragments remain. From the worn state of some of the blocks it may have been a reprint. From these fragments it is obvious that the whole work must have been lavishly illustrated.

PRAGUE EDITION (1526). The continuous record of the illustrated printed *Haggadah* begins with the Prague edition of 1526. This magnificent work, with its profuse marginal cuts and decorations and its superb borders, is among the finest productions of the 16th-century press. The beauty of the work lies above all in the disposition of the type and the exquisite balance of the pages. Its most remarkable feature is three pages with engraved borders in monumental gothic style. The printers and publishers were Gershom Solomon Kohen and his brother Gronem (Geronim). The artistic work was apparently executed partly by Ḥayyim Shaḥor, Gershom Kohen's collaborator, who sometimes signed his initials, and partly by a gentile assistant. Some of the decorative features were derived from non-Jewish works, including the Nuremburg chronicle of 1484. In recent years the Prague *Haggadah* has been reproduced repeatedly in facsimile. The cuts and illustrations in the publication were long imitated, deteriorating progressively as the years went by. The Prague edition of 1556 retained some of the original elements but this was not the case with the one published in 1590 or with other commonplace editions that continued to appear in Prague and elsewhere down to the mid-18th century. An interesting new edition, apparently by Ḥayyim Shaḥor, appeared in Augsburg in 1534. This, however, had little influence and only one complete copy is preserved.

MANTUA EDITION (1560, 1568). The next important step in the record of the illustrated *Haggadah* was the Mantua edition of 1560, published by the *shammash* (sexton), Isaac ben Samuel. This repro-

Plate 42. Silver *maḥzor* binding, Galicia, early 19th century. One panel depicts the Binding of Isaac; the other, Jacob's dream of the angels ascending and descending the heavenly ladder. Israel Museum, Jerusalem.

Plate 43. The bindery of "Lifeline for the Old," Jerusalem. Photo: Werner Braun.

Plate 44. Reading room in the Jewish National and University Library, Jerusalem. Photo: Werner Braun.

Plate 45. Open stalls at the Hebrew Book Week, Jerusalem, 1974. Photo: Werner Braun.

duced the text of the Prague edition page for page and letter for letter in facsimile, but introduced new illustrations and marginal decorations which had already been used in non-Jewish publications and were in conformity with Italian taste. The format was repeated with remarkable success in another edition published in Mantua in 1568 by a non-Jewish firm which concealed its identity under the name Filipponi. The marginal decorations were specially recut for this production, which rivals the Prague edition of 1526.

VENICE EDITIONS. The Mantua editions served as precise models for a group of illustrated *haggadot* in smaller format produced in rapid succession at the turn of the century (1599, 1601, 1603, and 1604) in Venice, which had become the great center of Jewish publishing. These converted the hybrid but impressive Mantua editions into a cohesive but unimpressive unity, reproducing every accidental decoration and copying every accidental marginal detail. The major illustrations at the foot of the pages were expanded into an entirely fresh series of 17 engravings, some of them appearing more than once. These illustrated the *seder* service, the subject matter, and the story of the Exodus. Thus, this is the first *Haggadah* which is consistently and systematically illustrated.

In 1609 the veteran printer Israel ha-Zifroni of Guastalla planned an edition with completely new illustrations. Printed for him by Giovanni da Gara, it was set in bold type, each page within an engraved architectural border. The illustrations were placed at the top or foot of almost every page in the early part of the volume, and more sparsely toward the end. There was one important innovation in this edition: in a series of small panels on an introductory page, the various stages in the Passover celebration are illustrated with men and women dressed in contemporary fashion; a later page similarly illustrates the ten plagues. These features were henceforth to become usual in illustrated *haggadot.*

The illustrations of the first part of the *seder* service (before the meal) are almost wholly devoted to the

Colophon page from the *Mantua Haggadah,* 1560, which reproduced the text of the *Prague Haggadah,* using new decorations. J.N.U.L., Jerusalem.

The Ten Plagues depicted in the *Venice Haggadah,* 16th century. Cecil Roth Collection.

Cover and title page of a German army *Haggadah* used during World War I. Pictured on the cover are Franz-Joseph of Austria (right) and Wilhelm II of Germany, Bruenn, 1915. B.M. Ansbacher Collection, Jerusalem.

Title page of the *Haggadah* issued for U.S. soldiers by the National Jewish Welfare Board during World War II. B.M. Ansbacher Collection, Jerusalem.

Exodus, while those in the second part (after the meal) deal with the biblical story in general and with the messianic deliverance. In 1629, a further edition based on ha-Zifroni's with a similar format was published in Venice by the Bragadini press. This continued to be reproduced, without any basic change but with increasingly worn types and indistinct blocks, until late in the 18th century. The illustrations continued to be copied in *haggadot* printed in the Mediterranean area, especially in Leghorn, almost to the present day. Thus the pattern of the traditional illustrated *Haggadah* was established.

AMSTERDAM EDITIONS. In 1695 there appeared in Amsterdam a new edition of the illustrated *Haggadah* which followed closely, in its general layout as well as in detail, the example of the now accepted Venetian prototype. The illustrations were, however, much improved by being engraved on copper. The artist was Abraham ben Jacob, a former Protestant preacher who had converted to Judaism. He chose many of the same incidental scenes as had appeared in the Venice *haggadot,* but he drew them afresh, basing his work on the biblical pictures in the *Icones Biblicae* by Matthew Merian the Elder; he probably used the second edition of the work which had appeared in Amsterdam in approximately 1655–62. Abraham ben Jacob also used miscellaneous scenes taken from other works by Merian. Thus the four sons of the *Haggadah* text (depicted together for the first time in one illustration) are miscellaneous figures brought together from various publications of Merian, without any attempt at grouping. The "wise son" and the "son who could not ask," for example, come from an engraving of Hannibal sacrificing before the altar, while the scene of the sages celebrating at Bene-Berak is reproduced – with some alterations – from Merian's picture of the feast given by Joseph to his brethren. The first map of Ereẓ Israel known in a Jewish publication was added on a folding page at the end of the book. A further edition of the work was produced in Amsterdam in 1712, with minor differences, and the name of the artist was omitted from the title page.

As the Venice *Haggadah* of 1609/29 was widely imitated in southern Europe, so the Amsterdam editions had an enduring influence on the *haggadot* produced in the Ashkenazi world. The pictures were imitated, if not copied, time after time with increasing indistinctness in innumerable editions illustrated with woodcuts or steel engravings. Such editions appeared in Frankfort in 1710 and 1775, in Offenbach in 1721, and in Amsterdam in 1765 and 1781. Throughout the 19th century and down to the present day the illustrations, including the four sons and the Passover at Bene-Berak, continued to be reproduced in ever-decreasing quality in hundreds of cheap *haggadot* published on both sides of the Atlantic. The Amsterdam editions also inspired a number of illustrated *haggadot* by 18th century German Jewish manuscript artists, some of whom even improved on the original.

SOME LATER EDITIONS. A few independently conceived *haggadot* of the later period may be mentioned: the Trieste edition of 1864 with 58 original copper engravings of considerable artistic merit by K. Kirchmayer; the Prague edition of 1889 with illustrations by the Slovak artist Vyril Kulik; and the curious lithograph edition published in Poona in 1874 for the benefit of the Bene Israel community. In the 20th century, editions have appeared illustrated (or in some cases entirely executed) by artists of the caliber of Joseph Budko, Jakob Steinhardt, Arthur Szyk, Albert Rothenstein, and Ben Shahn, and, in Israel, by J. Zimberknopf and David Gilboa, the last being written in scroll form.

Page from a *Haggadah* issued for soldiers of the Haganah in 1948, with illustrations by A. Alweil. B.M. Ansbacher Collection, Jerusalem.

Emergency *Haggadah* of the Israel Defense Forces with abridged ritual and large print, for soldiers on front-line duty, 1967. B.M. Ansbacher Collection, Jerusalem.

11. libraries

In Italian communities almost every *talmud torah* possessed a library. The rules of the Verona *talmud torah* of 1650 require a special room to be set aside for the library. The present library of the Rome community, which has a fine collection of manuscripts and early printed books, is the direct successor of a medieval *talmud torah* library. The same is true for a number of other communities such as Ferrara, Reggio Emilia, Pisa, and Leghorn. These libraries were often enriched by the acquisition of private collections. The library of the Talmud Torah School of the Sephardi congregation of Amsterdam is mentioned by the bibliographer Shabbetai Bass in his *Siftei Yeshenim* (1680).

PUBLIC LIBRARIES

The 19th century saw the development of public libraries. These took on various forms: 1) communal libraries; 2) voluntary libraries; 3) libraries attached to rabbinical seminaries; 4) departments of Hebraica and Judaica in national, university, and municipal libraries.

COMMUNAL LIBRARIES. The first of the modern Jewish communal libraries was established at Mantua at the end of the 18th century, and was followed by others. In Germany many communities established

Waterlogged books drying after the fire in the library of the Jewish Theological Seminary in New York, April 19, 1966. Jewish Theological Seminary of America, New York.

The main reading room of the Strashun Library, Vilna, in the 1920s. Yad Vashem Archives, Jerusalem.

Senior Library at Mount Scopus Memorial College, Victoria, Australia. The individual study cubicles are an aid to the students' concentration. Allan Studios, Collingwood.

their own libraries, intended mainly for the use of teachers and young people. Berlin, Frankfort, Hamburg (reestablished after World War II), Munich, and Breslau possessed numerous libraries, as did the communities of Vienna, Prague, Warsaw, Vilna, and Zurich. The library at Zurich is still in existence. Synagogue libraries in the United States developed differently from those of European Jewish communities. Most U.S. synagogue and temple libraries are school libraries, designed to work closely with the synagogue religious schools. There are three large congregational libraries which serve the needs of the entire congregation and, by extension, the entire community: the Temple Library in Cleveland, Ohio; the Wilshire Boulevard Temple Library in Los Angeles, California; and the Temple Emanu-el Library in New York City, New York.

ORGANIZATIONAL LIBRARIES. A number of Jewish organizations have developed substantial libraries. Their holdings vary considerably according to the requirements of the particular organization. They include the American Jewish Archives in Cincinnati, Ohio; the American Jewish Committee Blaustein Library in New York City; the American Jewish Historical Society Library in Waltham, Massachusetts; the Biblioteka Żydowskiego Instytutu Historycznego in Warsaw; the Bibliothèque Centrale Juive in Geneva; the Bibliothèque de l'Alliance Israélite Universelle in Paris; the Centre de Documentation Juive Contemporaine in Paris; the Jewish Education Committee in New York City; the Jewish Public Library in Montreal; the Leo Baeck Institute Library in New York City; the Mosaiska Forsamlingens Bibliotek in Stockholm; the Mount Scopus War Memorial College Library in Melbourne (destroyed by fire in 1970); the Wiener Library in London; the YIVO Institute for Jewish Research Library with branches in Buenos Aires and New York; and the Zionist Archives and Library in New York City. Other voluntary bodies interested in cultural work established popular reading and lending libraries, such as Jewish trade unions, Zionist and Socialist societies, women's organizations, and youth movements, etc. Originating with the Haskalah movement, these were frequent in Eastern Europe whence they spread to wherever Jews emigrated in Europe and the Americas. The persecution of Jewish religion and culture as well as of Zionism in Soviet Russia led to the closure of most of these libraries, though some Yiddish ones continued to operate – at least until 1948.

RABBINICAL SEMINARIES. It was in Italy, too, that the first rabbinical seminary library was established, at the Collegio Rabbinico Italiano which was located first in Padua, and moved from there to

The Jewish Theological Seminary, Breslau, founded in 1854. This photograph was taken in 1904. Hebrew University, Jerusalem.

Rome, Florence, and again back to Rome. The Breslau Jewish Theological Seminary followed; its library attained considerable importance, incorporating among others the Saraval collection. The Berlin Rabbinical Seminary too had a fine library, and so had the Hochschule (Lehranstalt) fuer die Wissenschaft des Judentums, which received Abraham Geiger's collection. Then followed Jews' College, London, owning the Montefiore, Green, Loewy, Zunz, and Buechler collections; the Ecole Rabbinique de France in Paris; the Sephardi, Ashkenazi, and Eẓ Ḥayyim seminaries in Amsterdam; the Israelitisch-Theologische Lehranstalt in Vienna, and the Budapest rabbinical seminary. The Mocatta Library in London is housed at University College, London, and administered by the college in association with the Jewish Historical Society of England. It was destroyed in a German air raid in 1940, but was reconstructed on a modest scale. In the U.S. the library of the Jewish Theological Seminary has the most important collection of Hebraica and Judaica of both manuscripts and printed books outside Ereẓ Israel. In 1966 a disastrous fire – and the water used to put it out – destroyed a large section of it, which as far as possible was reconstituted. Among the collections it received were those of Sulzberger, Steinschneider, Halberstamm, and E. N. Adler. Other important libraries are attached to Hebrew Union College-Jewish Institute of Religion, Cincinnati and New York (Klau Library and E. Hirsch-G. Levi Library), Dropsie College, Philadelphia, and others. Jewish teachers' seminaries too, particularly in the United States, have developed their own libraries.

NAZI PERSECUTION. The persecution of European Jewry by Nazi Germany (1933–45) brought with it the wholesale confiscation of both public and private libraries. Some of the books were moved to the Institut zur Erforschung der Judenfrage in Frankfort on the Main. Toward the end of World War II, the looted books were brought by the Nazis to central storehouses in southern Germany and western Czechoslovakia. When recovered after the war, mainly by a body called "Jewish Cultural Reconstruction," they were returned wherever possible to the heirs of their owners. More than 1,000,000 volumes remained and were distributed to Jewish libraries and cultural educational organizations in Israel, America, and other parts of the Diaspora. However, the incunabula and manuscripts that belonged to these Jewish libraries vanished after World War II. It is assumed that these materials were hidden by the Nazis in unused mines.

JEWISH SECTIONS IN GENERAL LIBRARIES. The importance of the Hebraica and Judaica collections in

The A.L. Green Memorial Library at Jews' College, London. J.N.U.L., Jerusalem.

The fire at the Library Tower of the Jewish Theological Seminary of America, New York, in 1966. Jewish Theological Seminary of America, New York.

A lecturer and students reading ancient manuscripts from microfilms at the Dropsie University, Philadelphia.

the great national libraries for the preservation of Jewish literary and scholarly treasures can hardly be exaggerated. In antiquity the famous library of Alexandria contained the Septuagint and other Judeo-Hellenistic works. Medieval monastery libraries frequently contained Hebrew, particularly Bible, codices, records of persecutions, expulsions, book burnings and confiscations filled their shelves, as well as those of episcopal and princely palaces and of medieval universities. The interest in Hebrew studies produced by the age of Reformation and Humanism led many Christian scholars such as Johann Reuchlin and J.A. Widmanstad (1506–1557) to collect Hebrew manuscripts and books. Here again priority belongs to Italy, where until the 19th century the most important collections were to be found in Rome, in the Vatican Library, the Biblioteca Casanatense, Biblioteca Angelica, Biblioteca della Pia Casa dei Neofiti, Biblioteca Vittorio Emanuele (originally in the Collegio Romano) and the Biblioteca Nazionale (some very valuable mss.). The Biblioteca Palatina in Parma incorporates the famous Rossi and also the Foa collections. Mention should also be made of the Biblioteca Mediceo-Laurentiana at Florence, the University Library of Bologna, the Royal Library at Modena, the Biblioteca Marciana at Venice, and the Ambrosiana at Milan. The valuable manuscript collection at Turin was destroyed by fire in 1904. Italy lost its primacy in this field to England when the Bodleian Library acquired the great collections of D. Oppenheim and H. Michael and the British Museum, the Almanzi Collection of Hebrew manuscripts. These two libraries have since been systematically completed and expanded. The Cambridge University Library is famous for its Cairo *Genizah* treasures, the largest such collection in the world. Also at Cambridge is the W. H. Low Library of Hebraica in Trinity College. In France the Bibliothèque Nationale in Paris and the Strasbourg University Library have important Hebraica and Judaica collections. In Germany the state libraries in Berlin, Munich, and Hamburg, and the municipal libraries of Frankfort and Leipzig have Hebrew collections, as has the Academy Library of Leyden (rich in Karaitica) and the Amsterdam University Library which includes the Rosenthaliana; the Royal Library in Copenhagen with the Bibliotheca Judaica Simonseniana; the Austrian National Library at Vienna (before 1918, the Kaiserliche und Koenigliche

The Leo Baeck Institute, New York.

Hofbibliothek); the Hungarian National Library at Budapest (with the Kaufmann Collection); the Asiatic Museum (containing the Friedland and Chwolson collections, by Firkovich and Antonin) and the Saltykov-Shchedrin Library at Leningrad; the Lenin Library, and the Oriental Institute of the Academy of Sciences Library, both at Moscow.

In the U.S., the New York Public Library and the Boston Public Library possess particularly important Jewish departments, as does the Library of Congress in Washington, D.C. University libraries that have substantial Jewish collections include the following: Brandeis University, Brown University, Columbia University, Harvard University, New York University, Ohio State University, Princeton University, Rutgers University at New Brunswick, University of California at Berkeley, University of Michigan, University of Southern California, University of Texas, University of Wisconsin at Madison, Wayne State University at Detroit, and Yale University.

From 1968 an Association of Jewish Libraries was active in the U.S. – a merger of the Jewish Librarians Association and the Jewish Library Association consisting of two divisions: a synagogue, school, and center library division, and a research and special library division. It issues the *AJL Bulletin* as well as an annual volume of *Proceedings*.

IN ISRAEL

In 1867, Albert Cohen, the representative in Palestine of Baron Rothschild, established a small library in Jerusalem, which was administered by Dr. London, a physician in the Rothschild Hospital. Before the end of the century two more libraries were founded: the Abrabanel Library in 1884 which developed into the Jewish National and University Library; and the Sapir Public Library in Petaḥ Tikvah. Up to the establishment of the State of Israel, development was slow, being left to the private initiative of individuals or such bodies as the Histadrut, which in the 1920s, had a central library with tens of thousands of volumes, serving labor settlements. After the establishment of the State of Israel great advances were made. The expansion of the school network, of local government, the research needs of scientific institutions, the expansion of agriculture and industry, all these made necessary the establishment (or development) of public or special scientific libraries as well as university and school libraries.

THE JEWISH NATIONAL AND UNIVERSITY LIBRARY serves as the library of the Hebrew University in Jerusalem. The library dates from 1892, when B'nai B'rith founded a public library in Jerusalem to which in 1895 a Bialystok physician, Joseph Chasanowich, presented his collection of 8,800 books, mostly in Hebrew. Other gifts followed and by 1920, when the library was taken over by the Zionist Organization, the number of volumes had reached about 30,000. Under the direction of the philosopher Samuel Hugo Bergman, who was librarian from 1920 till 1935, the number of volumes increased to

The strikingly angular building of the Zalman Aranne Library at the Ben-Gurion University of the Negev, Beersheba.

300,000. Between 1936 and 1946, under Gotthold Weil, about 150,000 books were added. When the Hebrew University was opened on Mount Scopus in 1925, the library was transferred to it, and in 1930 it was installed in the Wolffsohn building.

In 1948, when communication with Mount Scopus was broken off as a result of the War of Independence, the library contained nearly half a million books. Curt Vormann, who had been appointed librarian only a few months earlier, had to build it up anew in western Jerusalem, where it was housed in the Terra Sancta building. With the help of friends and supporters in Israel and abroad, it acquired tens of thousands of books and was brought back into working condition. In the years following World War II, the university (later joined by the Ministry of Religious Affairs) salvaged hundreds of thousands of books in Europe, as well as hundreds of manuscripts (chiefly Hebraica and Judaica), the remnants of Jewish public and private libraries looted by the Nazis. Many of these were incorporated into the National Library; the rest were distributed among university, public, synagogue, and yeshivah libraries throughout the country.

Following an agreement with the Jordanian government in 1958 (through the mediation of the secretary-general of the U.N., Dag Hammarskjold), about 350,000 books from Mount Scopus were gradually transferred to the Israel-held sector of Jerusalem. In 1960 a library building was opened on the new campus at Givat Ram. At the beginning of 1968, the library possessed about 1,500,000 volumes, over a quarter of them Hebraica and Judaica, together with 6,100 Hebrew and 800 other manuscripts. In 1962, the Institute of Microfilms of Hebrew Manuscripts was transferred to the library from the Ministry of Education and Culture. From then until 1971 it had acquired 25,000 photocopies of Hebrew manuscripts from 18 countries, together with thousands of photographs of *genizah* fragments. Since 1924, the library has published a bibliographical quarterly, *Kirjath Sepher,* listing all current publications in Palestine and Israel and all Judaic publications appearing elsewhere. An Institute of Hebrew Bibliography in the library records all books published in Hebrew characters. Since 1956, a graduate library school has been functioning at the library.

The library possesses a number of special collections: the Salman Schocken collection of Hebrew incunabula; the Ignaz Goldziher collection of Orientalia (especially of Islamica and Arabica); the Harry Friedenwald collection on Jews in medicine; the Abraham Schwadron (Sharon) collection of Jewish autographs and portraits; the Immanuel Loew collection of Judaica and Hebraica (including his personal archives); and the A. S. Yahuda collection of Orientalia, Hebraica and Judaica. The library also has the personal archives of Aḥad Ha-Am, Martin Buber, Joseph Klausner, Stefan Zweig and S. J. Agnon.

OTHER UNIVERSITY LIBRARIES. The Technion in Haifa, the universities of Tel Aviv, Ramat Gan (i.e. Bar Ilan), Haifa, Beersheba, and the Weizmann Institute in Rehovot operate their own libraries. In most university libraries individual departments have built up their own specialized collections. The total number of books in all these institutions in 1970 was estimated at seven million. University libraries maintain contact with and assist and advise each other as

Periodical room at the Hebrew University library, c. 1930. The Matson Photo Service, Alhambra, California.

Traveling library of the Ḥabad movement. *Challenge,* London, 1970.

well as other libraries and serve a circle of readers far beyond their own staff and students.

PUBLIC (MUNICIPAL) LIBRARIES. In 1968, 733 Jewish locations in Israel were served by 441 public libraries with 611 service points, covering 97% of a population exceeding 2,300,000. Library service was available in 209 urban centers and 400 village settlements, the mobile libraries of WIZO serving both types at the same time. Kibbutzim have also built up libraries. Kibbutz Kefar Giladi (population c. 700) has a library with 35,000 volumes. There are seven district libraries, each with responsibility for no less than ten settlements. The number of volumes in these public libraries (1968) was 4,328,700, of which 42% was fiction, 41.3% nonfiction, and 16.7% children's books. Of all these 84.6% were in Hebrew, 6.5% in English, and 8.9% in other languages. The number of registered readers was 227,300, 42.7% of whom were under 13.

The public libraries department of the Ministry of Education and Culture supports the setting up of public libraries, in particular in development areas and settlements established since 1948. In conjunction with the Israel Library Association and the Graduate Library School of the Hebrew University, the Ministry has formed a Guidance Center for Public Libraries, which assists with basic and current catalogs, publishing *Yad la-Kore,* a quarterly for librarianship and bibliography, arranging training, refresher courses and seminars for librarians, centralized book buying etc.

One of the early bookplates of the Hebrew University Library. J.N.U.L., Jerusalem.

The central library of the Tel Aviv Univeristy, Ramat Aviv. Photo: Werner Braun, Jerusalem.

The U.S. Information Centers and those set up in Jerusalem, Tel Aviv and Haifa by the British Council, the (Italian) Dante Alighieri Society, and the Centres de Civilisation Française also serve as public libraries.

SPECIALIZED LIBRARIES. In 1970, 280 specialized libraries with 2,700,000 volumes operated in Israel, among them the Knesset Library, those of various ministries, public corporations, museum libraries (the Bezalel Library of the Israel Museum holds 30,000 volumes), hospital libraries for the use of doctors and nurses; trade associations, factories, and economic concerns too have their own specialized libraries. All these were organized by the Israel Society of Special Libraries and Information Centers of 1966. Of particular importance in this connection are libraries devoted to Judaic and rabbinic studies such as (1) the Jewish Theological Seminary-Schocken Library (55,000 volumes, 200 manuscripts, 20,000 photostats); (2) the Central Rabbinical Library, attached to Hechal Shelomo, which received important collections saved from the Holocaust as well as from other sources (50,000 volumes and many valuable manuscripts); the libraries of (3) the Mosad ha-Rav Kook (60,000 volumes and many manuscripts) and of (4) Yad ha-Rav Herzog (40,000 volumes; 10,000 microfilm copies of Talmud texts and commentaries, also from the *Genizah*); (5) the Yeshurun Synagogue Library, all of these in Jerusalem; and (6) the Rambam Library in Tel Aviv, and others.

appendices

TRANSLITERATION TABLE

The following table shows the system we have used in all cases except in a very few where there is an accepted English spelling.

Consonants:

א	not transliterated
בּ	b
ב	v
ג	g
ד	d
ה	h
ו	v; when it is not a vowel
ז	z
ח	ḥ; pronounced like the "ch" in Loch Lomond
ט	t
י	y; when it is not a vowel
כּ	k
כ	kh; pronounced like the hard German "ch" as in *Ach!*
ך	kh; this is the final form of כ , i.e., the way it is written at the end of a word
ל	l
מ	m
ם	m; final form of מ
נ	n
ן	n; final form of נ
ס	s
ע	not transliterated
פּ	p
פ	f
ף	f; final form of פ
צ	ẓ; pronounced "ts" as in tsetse fly
ץ	ẓ; final form of צ
ק	k
ר	r
שׁ	sh
שׂ	s
תּ	t
ת	t

Vowels:

*ָ *ַ *ֲ	a
*ֶ *ֵ *ֱ	e
*ִי *ִ	i
*ֵי	ei
*וֹ *ֹ	o
*ֻ *וּ	u

א and ע as pronounced by most Hebrew speakers have no sound but take the sound of the vowel. Occasionally, when they appear inside a word we use an apostrophe (') to indicate that the two vowels should be pronounced separately.

READING LIST

Amram, D.W., *The Makers of Hebrew Books in Italy*, Philadelphia, 1909.

Assaf, S., *Be-Oholei Ya'akov*, Jerusalem, 1943, pp. 1–26.

Benayahu, M., *Ha-Defus ha-Ivri be-Cremona*, Jerusalem, 1971.

——, *Haskamah u-Reshut bi-Defusei Venezyah*, Jerusalem, 1971.

Berliner, A., *Ketavim Nivharim*, Jerusalem, 1945–49, vol. II, pp. 145–161.

Bloch, J., *Early Hebrew Printing in Spain and Portugal*, New York, 1938.

——, *Venetian Printers of Hebrew Books*, New York, 1932.

Cahana, Y.Z., "*Ha-Defus be-Halakhah*," in: *Sinai*, 16 (1945), pp. 49–61, 139–59.

Carmilly-Weinberger, M., *Sefer ve-Sayif*, New York-Jerusalem, 1966.

Clair, C., *Christopher Plantin*, London, 1960.

Freimann, A., *A Gazetteer of Hebrew Printing*, New York, 1946.

——, *Thesaurus Typographiae Hebraicae Saeculi XV*, Berlin, 1924–31; 1971².

Friedberg, H.D., *Ha-Defus ha-Ivri bi-Krakov*, Cracow, 1900.

——, *Toledot ha-Defus ha-Ivri be-Arim she-be-Eiropah*, Antwerp, 1937.

——, *Toledot ha-Defus ha-Ivri be-Polanyah*, Tel Aviv, 1950.

——, *Toledot ha-Defus ha-Ivri bi-Medinot Italyah*, Tel Aviv, 1956.

Goodman, P., *American Jewish Bookplates*, New York, 1956.

Habermann, A.M., *Ha-Madpisim Benei Soncino*, Vienna, 1933.

——, *Ha-Sefer ha-Ivri be-Hitpattehuto*, Jerusalem, 1968.

——, *Toledot ha-Defus bi-Zefat*, Safed, 1962.

——, *Toledot ha-Sefer ha-Ivri*, Jerusalem, 1945.

Halevi, S., *Ha-Sefarim ha-Ivriyyim she-Nidpesu bi-Yrushalayim*, Jerusalem, 1963.

Homeyer, F., *Deutsche Juden als Bibliophilen und Antiquare*, Tuebingen, 1966.

Marx, A., *Studies in Jewish History and Booklore*, New York, 1944.

Marx, M., *Gershom Soncino's Wander-years in Italy*, Cincinnati, 1936.

——, "Gershom Soncino," in: *Sefer ha-Yovel . . . A. Marx*, New York, 1943, pp. i–x.

Popper, W., *The Censorship of Hebrew Books*, New York, 1899.

Prijs, S., *Die Basler hebraeischen Drucke*, Olten–Freiburg im Breisgau, 1964.

——, *Der Basler Talmuddruck, 1578–80*, Olten–Basel Lausanne, 1960.

Rabinowitz, R.N.N., *Ma'amar al Hadpasat ha-Talmud*, Jerusalem, 1952.

Rosenbach, A.S.W., *An American Jewish Bibliography*, Baltimore, 1926.

Shunami, S., *Bibliography of Jewish Bibliographies*, Jerusalem, 1969³.

Sonne, I., *Expurgation of Hebrew Books*, New York, 1943.

Sonnino, G., *Storia della tipografia ebraica in Livorno*, Torino, 1912.

Tauber, A., *Meḥkarim Bibliografiyyim*, Jerusalem, 1932.

Weinberg, M., *Die hebraeischen Druckereich in Sulzbach (l669–1851)*, Frankfort-on-Main, 1904.

Wengrov, C., *Haggadah and Woodcut*, New York, 1967.

Widmann, H., *Geschichte des Buchhandels vom Altenis bis zu Gegenwart*, Wiesbaden, 1952.

Yaari, A., *Bibliografyah shel Haggadot Pesaḥ*, Jerusalem, 1960.

——, *Diglei ha-Madpisim ha-Ivriyyim*, Jerusalem, 1943.

——, *Ha-Defus ha-Ivri be-Arẓot ha-Mizraḥ*, Jerusalem, 1937.

——, *Ha-Defus ha-Ivri be-Kushta*, Jerusalem, 1967.

——, *Meḥkerei Sefer*, Jerusalem, 1958.

Zilberg, G., *Ha-Ot ha-Mudpeset be-Yisrael*, Tel Aviv, 1961.

Zlotkin, M.M., *Shemot ha-Sefarim ha-Ivriyyim*, Neuchatel, 1950.

ALPHABETICAL INDEX TO TITLE PAGES